ELON COLLEGE

❧ ELON COLLEGE ❧

ITS HISTORY AND TRADITIONS

DURWARD T. STOKES

Elon College Alumni Association

Elon College, North Carolina

Then here's to the oak, the brave old oak,
Who stands in his pride alone!
And still flourish he, a hale green tree,
When a hundred years are gone!

H. F. CHORLEY
The Brave Old Oak

◄§ CONTENTS ৡ►

Except where otherwise specified, all photographs and illustrations are from the Elon College archives.

As the centennial of Elon College nears, alumni, students, faculty, officials, and friends share a keen sense of unity and dedication. At the same time, their interest quickens about the origins and evolution of the institution that is so close to their hearts—one that has risen from a small establishment, founded by the Christian denomination, into one of the major, independent liberal arts colleges in the region.

This history, which will serve as an appropriate means to launch the centennial celebration, not only traces the growth and traditions of Elon College, but also interweaves the story of the town of the same name, the surrounding area, and to some extent the Christian Church. Beyond that, this volume illuminates the nature and role of colleges in the pattern of American education, as well as their contributions to the advancement of their states and the nation.

Durward T. Stokes, the author of this work and coauthor of the *History of the Christian Church in the South*, is an alumnus and professor emeritus of history who was acquainted with every president of Elon and personally witnessed many years of its development. These qualifications have enabled him to render an eminently readable and accurate historical account.

As Chairman of the Board of Trustees, I heartily recommend this book to all Elonites and other readers.

THAD EURE
Secretary of State
State of North Carolina

~ ACKNOWLEDGMENTS ~

This book could not have been written without the encouragement, assistance, and cooperation of the president, administrative staff, and faculty of Elon College, as well as scores of its alumni, students, and friends. My deepest indebtedness is expressed to all of them, and it is regrettable that each of them cannot be named here.

President J. Fred Young not only conceived the idea of publishing this history, but also lent his unstinting and enthusiastic support to the project. Invaluable aid was also provided by the college library staff, under the supervision of Librarian Theodore E. Perkins and Associate Librarian Guy R. Lambert.

Thad Eure, North Carolina's Secretary of State, furnished highly useful data from governmental sources, and the files and personal recollections of Dean Emeritus A. L. Hook proved to be unique in their value. Dr. J. Earl Danieley reviewed the portion of the manuscript pertinent to his administration; Dr. Jo Watts Williams supplied significant details concerning the Smith presidency; and Dr. Robert C. Baxter, the college's Vice-President for Legal Affairs, read the entire manuscript and offered helpful suggestions.

Gratitude is also extended to Alumni Secretaries William B. Terrell and William R. Ginn; various municipal officials and citizens of the town of Elon College; and the Reverend James M. Waggoner and Melvin L. Shreves, whose aid made possible accurate coverage of athletic and sport activities.

For data supplied as well as assistance rendered, I am probably most indebted to the Reverend T. H. Mackintosh and his wife, the former Mary Graham Lawrence. For years they have combed newspapers, journals, and other periodicals for items concerning Elon College and have obtained additional data through correspondence and personal interviews. Their cataloged collection of facts relating to the institution is of inestimable worth to researchers and historians.

Mrs. Emma D. Lewis, Mrs. Shirley Crawford, and Mrs. Evelyn Campbell, of the college secretarial staff, provided highly efficient typing services.

The manuscript was edited by Robert G. Ferris, of Chapel Hill, who also prepared the index. And he and Richard Hendel, the designer, guided the book through the maze of publication.

Finally, and above all, a tribute is due to my wife, Enita Nicks Stokes, whose encouragement and support throughout the project was stimulating and heartwarming.

DURWARD T. STOKES

ELON COLLEGE

⊰ CHAPTER I ⊱

PREPARING THE SEEDBED

Again you shall plant vineyards
upon the mountains of Samaria;
the planters shall plant and
shall enjoy the fruit.
JEREMIAH 31:5

Elon College was founded by the Christian Church, a religious organization in the southern United States that originated as the result of a secession of Methodist ministers dissatisfied with their episcopal denomination in the late eighteenth century. The period between this religious schism and the opening of Elon's doors in 1890 lacked only two years of being a full century because the infant church consumed that much time in growing to maturity while overcoming various adversities. Before the Christian Church in the South could found a four-year, liberal arts college, theological differences needed to be resolved, economic stability attained, four years of strife endured, organizational plans evolved, and growth in membership achieved. By a herculean effort, the college was finally established on the basic principles of the parent denomination as a nonsectarian, coeducational school to foster learning as well as Christian morality among its students and to prepare ministerial aspirants for their lifework.

To clearly understand this event, it is necessary to examine the historical founding of the church and its early educational efforts that were the forerunners of the college. The Methodist Episcopal Church was founded in America during the last days of 1784, and Bishop Francis Asbury was its leading ecclesiastical authority. Most of its clergymen were itinerants, appointed annually to their stations or circuits by the bishop without regard to the personal preferences of the appointees. James O'Kelly, one of the leading preachers, considered this exercise of the prelate's power entirely too autocratic. His contention was that any minister given a post he considered incompatible should have the right to request reassignment to another, but Asbury refused to make this concession. As time passed, the argument became more heated, both sides gained adherents, and the subject became a primary issue in the Methodist Episcopal Church. The matter was finally settled in 1792, when, at a conference in Baltimore, a majority of the clergymen voted their approval of the bishop's policy. The crestfallen O'Kelly and his colleagues, feeling they could no longer officiate effectively as clergymen under the system, withdrew from the conference and later from the Methodist Church.[1]

Because subsequent negotiations failed to heal the breach, the secessionists met in 1794 at Old Lebanon Church, in Surry County, Virginia, and formed their own religious organization. They discarded the name "Republican Methodists," which had first been chosen, and decided that "Christian" would be a more appropriate one. They also agreed on several cardinal principles. Jesus Christ was considered to be the only head of their church. There would be no earthly hierarchy, or episcopate, because they would be governed by a majority vote of the members assembled in conferences. Their only creed was the Holy Bible, which could be interpreted by each member according to his own conscience. From such an inauspicious beginning, the church slowly began to grow in North Carolina and Virginia.

Ironically, the very flexibility of its simple policy concerning dogma prevented the new organization from rapidly becoming a large and widespread American religious denomination. Shortly after its founding, a proposal was received to merge with the Christian Church that had been organized by Abner Jones in New England, and a few years later a possibility arose of uniting with the followers of Barton W. Stone in Tennessee and Kentucky. Both these opportunities were thwarted by a failure to agree on the subject of baptism. The northern group, whose background was Baptist, insisted that immersion be the only form authorized. O'Kelly adamantly contended that the mode chosen by the convert, whether immersion or sprinkling, should be recognized as authentic, though he preferred the latter method. His refusal to abandon this position not only prevented a merger at the time, but divided the southern Christians into two groups. O'Kelly and his followers organized the North Carolina and Virginia Christian Conference, and others formed the Eastern Virginia Christian Conference. These two did not officially unite until 1854, when they mutually established the General Convention of the Christian Church. Until that time, membership in both conferences grew slowly and was largely confined to the states of Virginia and North Carolina.

After the convention began to function, friendly overtures were again received from northern Christians, who had relaxed their stand on immersion to some extent. At that time, the excellent prospects for a merger were smashed by the sharp division of North and South on the subject of slavery. The ensuing Civil War then interrupted further negotiations, and it was not until 1922, in a conference in Burlington, North Carolina, that the Christian Church in both sections of the United States and in Canada united into a single denomination. This did not include the church founded by Stone, which had become the Disciples of Christ, but it did embrace the congregations known as "Christian Churches."

This union was achieved without the sacrifice of O'Kelly's simple cardinal principles, to which the southerners had clung faithfully for more than a century. The Bible remained the only creed, and each member enjoyed the privilege of interpreting it for himself, which included choosing the mode of baptism desired. After a merger with the Congregational Churches in 1931, and with the Evangelical and Reformed Church in 1957 that formed the United Church of Christ, the guiding principles adopted at Old Lebanon in 1794 remained unchanged among the Christians in the South.[2]

During the long struggle, at first for survival and then for growth, the numerically small and financially weak church founded by O'Kelly enjoyed little opportunity to further education. In addition to these handicaps, the founders considered their primary aims to be diligent evangelism and the nurturing of Christian piety rather than the fostering of education. Most of the clergymen were self-taught, after having obtained the rudiments of learning during their childhood. Few, if any, enjoyed an opportunity to acquire a classical edu-

The campus during the 1950s as viewed from the south gate.
Photo by James P. McGaughey.

cation, but they were convinced that the Christian gospel could be preached effectively without one. However, they respected learning, and used whatever knowledge they possessed to its fullest extent. O'Kelly was a prolific publisher of essays, several of his colleagues wrote pamphlets, and one was the author of a lengthy book.[3] Nevertheless, they considered secular education a problem for the individual to solve rather than the responsibility of the church.

Happily for the progress of learning, the policy of the organization as a whole did not deter some of its clergymen and laity from becoming schoolteachers. These men conducted neighborhood schools in eastern North Carolina and Virginia, often using the congregation's meetinghouse for their classes. In the general area where Elon College was to be founded, Daniel Turrentine held classes in a small building adjacent to the New Providence Christian Church during the early years of the nineteenth century. This school was located at that time in rural Orange County, but the site is now in the city of Graham, the county seat of Alamance County. After the teacher's death in 1824, his son, John S. Turrentine, followed by others, continued the operation of the school for many years. Enrollment was usually at capacity level.[4]

In 1826, in another section of the state, a progressive step was taken that afforded an opportunity for schooling to those living at a distance too great for daily commuting to classes. The Reverend Daniel W. Kerr opened Wake Forest Pleasant Grove Academy for males near Raleigh, North Carolina. He was assisted in its operation by his wife, the former Rebecca P. Davis, "a fine scholar and a lady of culture."[5] Twelve years later, the couple moved their institution westward to a site in Orange County, twelve miles north of Hillsborough, where it was known for a short time as Mount Pleasant Academy. Its curriculum and accommodations were advertised as follows:

> 1st Class—English Grammar, Penmanship, Geography, with the use of Maps and Globes, History, Philosophy, Astronomy, Chemistry, Rhetoric, &c.
> 2nd Class—Latin, Greek and French Languages. The price of tuition will be five dollars per session for the first class, and ten dollars per session for the second class. A session will consist of five months. At the expiration of the first session there will be a public examination and a vacation of two weeks. The

subscriber will render every possible attention to the morals and habits of the students placed under his care.

Board can be had convenient to the academy at five dollars per month, and in good families.[6]

By 1839 the school had become Junto Academy, the name it would bear for the remainder of its existence.[7]

When Kerr opened his boarding school, he became the pioneer sponsor of institutional education among the Christians, though his undertaking was strictly a private enterprise. However, he felt in harmony with the doctrine of his church when he proudly claimed that the academy was "conducted upon the true principles of Christianity, without any sectarian influence or bias." This liberal attitude aroused opposition, for he complained that an attempt was made to "prostrate" his undertaking by "a strong and tremendous combination of sectarian bigots." His fellow Christians responded to his calls for support, and the school continued to prosper. In 1848 it was moved to Pittsboro, in Chatham County, North Carolina, and closed two years later, when its founder died.[8] The value of Junto Academy was multifold. Not only had it provided an opportunity for many individuals to improve their knowledge, but it had also set a standard for higher learning among the Christians that was influential in future educational efforts of their church.

Kerr's widow was left with insufficient financial resources "for the support of herself and that of an aged mother." Bereft of her husband, she was unable to continue the operation of an academy for male students. Subsequently she moved to Graham, where she was assisted by Mrs. E. C. Hardin in opening Mrs. Rebecca P. Kerr's Female Seminary. Classes began in the summer of 1851, and the school may have succeeded the Young Ladies' Seminary that was in operation at Graham earlier in the year under the direction of the Reverend William Nelson and his wife, who were assisted by a Miss Paisley, of Guilford. Regardless of this possibility, the Kerr Seminary was the first school for women in the state known to have been conducted by members of the Christian Church. In 1852 the Reverend Isaac N. Walter published a tribute to its progress and a plea for its patronage by the Christian membership. Because no further record of the institution has been found, presumably it was in existence for only a few years [9]

Before the middle of the nineteenth century, the official attitude of the Christian Church toward education began to change. New leadership had arisen that was not sympathetic with the old policy and was fully aware of the efforts other religious denominations were making to provide schools for their youth and training for their future ministers. The Christian organization had provided none of these benefits for its people. This was especially embarrassing because most of the membership lived in North Carolina and Virginia, states in which a number of church-related colleges were in operation, in addition to two of the outstanding universities in the South.

Recognition of this situation had produced action as early as 1841, when the North Carolina and Virginia Christian Conference created a committee "to devise and report a plan for educating pious young men for the ministry," and D. W. Kerr was appointed as agent "to correspond with such persons as would be disposed to give . . . their countenance and support." [10] Unfortunately, probably because of insufficient backing, this committee failed in its assignment, but the idea was not abandoned. In 1845 another committee was appointed to consider the matter.

At that time, the conference was engaged in launching *The Christian Sun*, a sorely needed church periodical. Several previous attempts to publish a denominational journal had been financial failures, which caused support of the new venture to take precedence over other projects. For that reason, and probably for others, the Committee on Education rendered a negative report:

> We recommend, after having maturely considered the subject, that Conference take no further action on the subject of education than merely to consent to the formation of an Educational Society, to be composed of those who may voluntarily aid in the promotion of the object under consideration, and that Conference limit its efforts to sustaining the Itinerancy and the Christian Sun. [11]

Acceptance of this recommendation meant that church support of a school was again postponed, but it was not destined to remain so for many years.

Although this proposal was adopted by the conference, some of its members were too dissatisfied to consider the matter permanently settled. Their hopes for a change in policy were revived at the 1849 conference. At that time, the *Sun* was virtually self-supporting, and less excuse existed for delaying an educational program. Action was spurred by a communication from a member congregation: "A Letter from Union Church was read, bringing before Conference the propriety of establishing a seminary of learning at the town of Graham. Referred to a select committee."[12] This request from an Alamance County church was probably inspired by the fact that both Mrs. Kerr's school for women and the Reverend John R. Holt's institution for male students were already in operation in the town of Graham.

Holt had initiated the enterprise in 1839 near his home in Orange County, and served as its principal. The curriculum was "designed principally to be preparatory to admittance into our University, or any similar institution in this country." Because of his success, the owner moved his school to Graham in 1849, where he could cater to a larger clientele. The town was on the route of the North Carolina Railroad, then under construction. This afforded a transportation advantage, and homes were more numerous in which students could obtain room and board than were available in a rural area. The institution prospered in its new locality to the extent that its facilities soon required enlargement. William H. Eley, who had been a fellow student of Holt's at the University of North Carolina, was made assistant principal. Later, Albert G. Anderson, who had taught a neighborhood school, was added to the staff. The successful functioning of the Kerr and Holt institutions had made Graham a center of learning in North Carolina for the Christian Church.[13]

The Union Church's overture was based upon this fact, and it produced the following results in the same session of the conference at which it was introduced:

> The subject of education was next presented from the committee to whom its consideration had been assigned. A Standing executive committee of ten were appointed to mature some plan by which may be erected within our limits an institution for the promotion of general education; and also to afford facilities to young men who expect to engage in the gospel ministry to prepare for that importan [*sic*] work.[14]

This was in reality a commission with the power to act, and it lost no time in doing so.

The decision was made that the most practical plan would be for the church to acquire Holt's school and operate it as the Graham Institute. To make this a truly denominational project, cooperation was readily obtained from the Eastern Virginia Christian Conference. On October 31, 1850, that body voted "to unite with our brethren of the North Carolina and Virginia Conference in the 'Graham Institute,'" and its proportionate number of trustees for the proposed school was appointed at the same session.[15] This spirit of generosity on the part of the Virginians would later become one of intense loyalty to Elon College, and would constitute invaluable support of that institution from its founding to the present.

Encouraged by this cooperation, the committee took the initiative and paid John Harden sixty-two dollars for one and one-half acres of land in Graham, which was deeded on April 2, 1850, to "Bennet Hazell, John R. Holt, Eli F. Watson, and William Tarpley," committeemen of the Christian Church, "for the purpose of erecting thereon a male academy."[16] In September of that year, the conference approved that step, and took further action to advance its new project:

> That the Committee on Education are authorized to employ a travelling agent to solicit donations, contributions, &c. For the completion of the Graham Institute and the promotion of Education generally amongst the Christian Church south. On motion, that a committee be appointed to prepare an address upon the subject of Education in behalf of the Graham Institute to be published in the columns of the Christian Sun.[17]

The conference then named its proportionate share of the trustees for the school to serve with those already named by the Eastern Virginia Christians.

The invitation to participate in the enterprise was also accepted by other members of the Southern Christian Association. That organization, formed in 1846 and succeeded by the General, or Southern, Christian Convention a decade later, was a confederation of all the conferences composing the southern Christian Church. Established as a result of editorial persuasion in the *Sun*, the association's purpose was "to correct and foster any object of general interest that may be set forward." The membership, in addition to the North Carolina and Virginia, and the Eastern Virginia organizations, included a North Carolina conference, in the eastern section of that state, and smaller conferences in Alabama, Georgia, Tennessee, and western Virginia. The inclusion of trustees from all these organizations made the association technically the founder of the school, which was thereby established as an enterprise of the entire denomination. This progressive step also marked a change in policy and the beginning of the official encouragement of secular education by the Christian Church.[18]

On July 16, 1851, the incorporation of Graham Institute was announced. E. F. Watson, John Trollinger, Chesley F. Faucette, Pleasant A. Holt, Alfred Apple, Joseph B. Hinton, T. Bolling, Henry B. Hayes, Thomas J. Kilby, William B. Wellons, H. L. Eppes, and Edward H. Herbert were appointed as trustees.[19] The school opened its doors early in 1852. Not surprisingly, John R. Holt was placed in charge as principal, and William H. Eley appointed as his assistant. Courses were offered in the Latin, Greek, and French languages; mathematics; navigation; geology; astronomy; "Mental, Moral and Natural Philosophy"; chemistry; rhetoric; logic; "and all the various departments of a liberal English education." Board was available with "pleasant families in the Village or country" at from six to seven dollars per month. Tuition for the "elementary branches" of English was ten dollars per session, and fifteen dollars for the other departments. In addition, "Gratuitous Instruction" would be given "young men preparing for the Ministry in any of the Protestant denominations of the day."

The trustees also announced the policy of the institution through the columns of the *Sun*:

> The disciplinary regulations will be sufficiently strict and rigorous, yet attempted with clemency and forbearance. And whilst every exertion will be made to inculcate and nourish in the minds of pupils, principles of morality and religion no denominational influence will be exercised over their religious sentiments and opinions. . . .
>
> Students over 15 years of age, before admission in the School are required to furnish satisfactory testimonial of good moral character and respectability.
>
> Whilst their connection with the Institute shall continue, they are expressly required to refrain from the use of ardent spirits; from frequenting places where liquor is vended; from

engaging in the play of cards or other games of chance or hazard; from attending horse-races, cock-fights, &c.; or from engaging in anything calculated to disturb the quietude and peace of the citizens. The infraction of any of these requisitions will subject the transgressor to immediate expulsion.[20]

The regulations were not unusually strict for the time, and the policy was typical of the denomination in that it stressed religious life without any emphasis on sectarianism.

In 1852 the Reverend I. N. Walter, one of the first promotional agents for the school, described its physical plant:

> The Institute is a plain substantial brick building, fifty by thirty feet, two stories high, containing four rooms, and finished in a plain, neat style, has a fine location, in a beautiful grove adjoining Graham a new and flourishing village, and shire town of Alamance County, and is regarded as one of the most healthy locations in the State, surrounded by a beautiful, and fertile country, and wealthy, intelligent citizens, and offers many inducements from these considerations to parents to send their sons to this place.[21]

The school was situated on present South Maple Street, then on the outskirts of Graham, and not on the site of Holt's academy, which apparently was across town on North Main Street. The building was evidently new, for it had been erected for the institute. However, as Walter indicated, the institution was only open to male students, and Mrs. Kerr's seminary remained the only one for women in the area among the Christians.[22]

Although the institute was opened with enthusiasm, its founders soon realized that maintaining the facility was a major financial undertaking for a relatively small religious denomination, especially one whose only unified agency lacked fiscal power. Then as now, the tuition received was insufficient to operate such an institution, which meant that this income needed to be supplemented by funds raised elsewhere. Because these had to come from voluntary contributions by the conferences or by individuals, they were an uncertain asset at best. In 1853 the North Carolina and Virginia Conference was pleased that $500 had been subscribed,[23] but additional assistance evidently did not materialize, which soon placed the institute in financial difficulties. Holt retired as principal about 1856, and moved to Chatham County, where he taught in various schools the remainder of his life. He was replaced by Job H. Swift; Edwin W. Beale served as his assistant.[24]

Conditions failed to improve under the new supervision, and the school was forced to suspend operations pending better arrangements for its support. However, the Christians were not defeated, and in 1857 the Eastern Virginia Conference, after being informed that Graham Institute had "nearly failed financially and denominationally," received a challenge from its Committee on Education:

> We are grieved at its adverse condition, but it is useless to sit clothed in sackcloth, and mourn over blighted hopes and past misfortunes. Rather let us arouse from our stupidity, awake from our lethargy, and bend ourselves to the task, and resolve to do something. Let us be determined to educate our sons at home. We have the means at our command to aid the Graham Institute from its embarrassments, or to get up a new school in our midst.[25]

The report concluded with a proposal that a committee be appointed to confer with the institute's trustees in an effort to solve the problem. This recommendation was passed, and the plan became effective when approved by the new General Convention of the Christian Church, the organization created in 1856 that combined the conferences under a central government.

The trustees and the committee jointly attacked the problem by placing the institute in the hands of a joint-stock company, organized "to conduct it as a denominational school." Agents were appointed to solicit the $4,000 needed to supplement the undertaking. Then, at the request of the Reverend W. B. Wellons, president of the stock company, the General Christian Convention took the school "under its fostering care" by appointing a Board of Visitors to supervise the entire operation.[26]

The next step was to discard the name "Institute." This was effected on January 21, 1859, when the North Carolina legislature issued a charter for Graham College to Alfred A. Iseley, John Faucette, Peter R. Harden, Bennett Hazel (Hazell; Hayzell), and Willis Sellars, incorporators.[27] It was then decided that the new institution would be coeducational, another progressive step.

The new program was placed under the supervision of William H. Doherty (Doughtery), a native of Ireland and an honor graduate of Royal Belfast College. Within a few years after his earlier arrival in the United States, he had become a minister of the northern Christian Church in Ohio. An experienced educator, he had served as Professor of Belles Lettres under President Horace Mann at Antioch College, Yellow Springs, Ohio.[28] The faculty of Graham College included his two daughters, the Misses I. E. (Belle; Isabel) and M. A. (Mary) Doherty, as well as C. R. King, and Mrs. Daniel Hardin, the latter of whom served both as matron and music teacher. The term was twenty weeks; departmental tuition was $10 for the Primary, $15 for the Secondary, $25 for the High School; $15 was assessed for music, and $10 each for French, German, and drawing. Special emphasis was given to a "Biblical class," conducted by the principal, which included Hebrew, Greek, church history, and "Sacred Rhetoric" for "pious Young Men, preparing for the Christian Ministry." This revised plan was put in operation when the school opened in March 1859, "under the most favorable auspices," as Graham College.[29]

The board of trustees included W. H. Doherty, Thomas J. Fowler, P. R. Harden, Bennett Hazell, John Faucette, William H. Faucette, Alfred Moring, W. B. Wellons, Thomas J. Kilby, Robert H. Holland, Edward C. Riddick, Meredith H. Watkins, Jubilee Smith, James Minnis, and John Walker. On May 27, 1859, in consideration of $142.50, John Harden deeded 5.7 acres to the board, including the land on which the building stood; thus the institution had ample room for expansion.[30]

The opening of the school was an occasion for general rejoicing. The Committee on Education proudly informed the Eastern Virginia Conference that it was pleased with the prosperous condition of the institution, which promised "great usefulness to the church of our love." The report continued in a happy vein:

> . . . and especially are we pleased to state that there is a Biblical department . . . offering superior advantages to young men studying for the ministry. And we are glad to know that five

young men—young men of piety and intelligence—young men in whose hearts our principles are deeply instiled [*sic*], and who promise much usefulness to the cause of Christian liberty, are availing themselves of these advantages.[31]

The report concluded with the observation that about seventy students were enrolled in the college under its corps of "efficient teachers."

No list of the student body of the college has been found, but it is known that both Daniel A. Long, who became a prominent minister and educator in the Christian Church, and his brother, William S. Long, who was to serve as the first president of Elon College, were among the group. Eli T. Iseley was another of the numerous students educated at the institution.

Unfortunately, the roseate prospects of the college were soon dimmed by a tragic circumstance. Doherty had been accepted into membership in the North Carolina and Virginia Conference, where he was given several responsible assignments. His sermons were considered excellent homilies by the Eastern Virginia Conference, and he was regarded as a ministerial leader in the church in addition to being a capable educator. He was evidently a brilliant man but suffered a weakness for alcohol. This affliction was intensified by the heated political arguments and radical governmental changes that took place at the beginning of the war following the formation of the Confederate States of America. Accused of "intemperance and falsehood," he was finally expelled from the conference in 1866, after a lengthy and thorough investigation of the charges. Happily, he later mastered his weakness and spent productive years as a minister and educator in the city of Washington, D.C., where he died in 1890 during his eightieth year.[32]

Because of these regrettable events, Doherty's connection with the college had been severed in 1861. Two men, whose names were recorded only as Brem and Bray, then took charge of the school until 1863, when wartime conditions forced a suspension of its operation. This was not evidence that the enterprise could not be successful under normal conditions, for almost every educational institution in the South was forced to close its doors until the war ended in 1865.

When the college closed, it was in debt. To satisfy a claim of

$175.50 held against it by B. F. Roney, on September 1, 1863, the property had to be sold. At the sheriff's sale, Henry J. B. Clark and Alexander Miller, trading as Clark and Miller, were the highest bidders and paid $4,500 for the entire property.[33] The $4,000 remaining after the liquidation of the debt was invested in Confederate bonds by the trustees for use in launching a new enterprise when hostilities ceased. Tragically, when peace was finally established, the securities were worthless, and nothing remained as a financial nucleus for a new beginning. The former academic building was used as a tobacco factory until 1869, when Clark, who had become the sole owner of the property, sold it for $1,000 to Mrs. Mary E. Harden, wife of J. W. Harden, of Graham.[34] Under these circumstances, Graham College became only a memory, and the educational efforts of the Christian Church in North Carolina came to a standstill.

Fortunately for the Christians, the discouraging failure in institutional operation did not deter some individuals in the church from devoting their efforts to providing educational benefits. Foremost among these were the Long brothers, William S. and Daniel A., born on October 22, 1839, and May 22, 1844, respectively, on an Alamance County farm near Graham. Their parents were Jacob Long, a successful farmer, and Jane Stuart Stockard Long, daughter of Colonel John Stockard and a woman of high intellectual capacity. From their mother, the sons inherited a keen appreciation of learning, along with the belief that it should be available to both men and women alike. This conviction was a prominent characteristic of both men throughout their careers, and played a significant role in forming the policy of Elon College when it was founded.[35]

When William was ready for college at the age of sixteen, his father deemed it unfair to give him the necessary funds because he felt unable to make an equal gift to each of his remaining six sons and one daughter. The problem was solved by a loan, which was later repaid, and the process repeated until all the Long children had received a college education.[36] In 1860, by which time the basic preparation for his lifework had been completed, the young Graham College graduate was licensed to preach by the North Carolina and Virginia Conference.[37] On June 25 the following year, he married Artelia Elizabeth Jane Faucette, daughter of John Faucette, the superior court clerk of Alamance County. The couple then moved to Halifax

County, Virginia, where the minister engaged in pastoral duties and the supervision of an academy.[38]

When the war ended, Long returned to his home county in North Carolina, where he opened Graham Female Seminary, which filled the need formerly supplied by Mrs. Kerr's school.[39] In addition to this occupation, he was appointed as Superintendent of Public Instruction for Alamance County. The choice of Long for this important post stemmed from an event that had occurred during his student days. In 1858 he assisted Professor W. H. Doherty in conducting "the first teacher's institute ever held in North Carolina," at the courthouse in Graham. Calvin H. Wiley, North Carolina Superintendent of the Common Schools, attended the meeting, where he was so impressed with the assistant that he requested him to compile data on the local schools. According to the *Raleigh News and Observer*, "Shortly afterwards, Mr. Long was appointed examiner of teachers, or superintendent of schools for Alamance, and from that time, with the exception of short intervals, he served as county examiner or superintendent under every State superintendent, except the present one, Dr. E. C. Brooks."[40] In 1872 Trinity College (now Duke University) recognized Long's efforts by conferring upon him the degree of Master of Arts; and in 1890 Union Christian College, of Merom, Indiana, awarded him a Doctor of Divinity.

The Graham Female Seminary was a successful enterprise from its beginning, but it failed to satisfy its founder's ambition to provide academic opportunities for both sexes. Graham had previously been selected as the educational center for the Christian denomination in North Carolina because of its central location and transportation advantages. The town was located on the North Carolina Railroad, the headquarters of which were only two miles westward at the growing town of Company Shops (now Burlington). In addition, the membership of the Christian Church was especially strong in the area. These advantages increased in significance after the war, and Long felt that he was in an ideal location to establish a larger institution if he could finance its operation. The logical place to seek financial support was the Christian Church.

Thus, Long made his appeal to the church constituency in 1870 by arranging for publication of the following proposition in the *Christian Annual.*

I propose, 1. To allow the denomination the use of my buildings in Graham for a school, and I agree to keep them in good order and suitable condition.

2. That the school be arranged to afford instruction to young men preparing for the ministry, and at the same time conduct a high school in which others may qualify themselves for teaching and other pursuits.

3. That the Conference employ one competent instructor and place him in the school with myself as joint principal.

4. That one-third of the tuition fees go toward the salary of the teacher the Conferences may employ. The remainder to myself as wages and for keeping up repairs to the premises.

5. That this arrangement continue five or ten years, or until a school can be established elsewhere.

6. That each Conference acceding to this proposition elect two directors, whose duty it will be to arrange a course of study, text-books, tuition, &c. and exercise a general oversight of the school.[41]

A short time before publication of this challenge, the Southern Christian Convention, formerly the General Convention, had announced its policy regarding higher education:

> The Convention therefore recommended that the Conferences immediately use such means as may be available for the purpose of establishing schools of fair grade, at which all our children and young men can be successfully prepared for a university. When all our Conferences shall have successfully established high schools at which young men may fully prepare for the various business pursuits of life, and for teaching satisfactorily in the primary schools, we may proceed to the erection of a College of high grade.[42]

Bearing this in mind, the North Carolina and Virginia Conference's Board of Education reported in 1870 that, because Long's proposal "will likely meet the present wants of our people, we recommend it for your adoption."[43]

This was agreeable to the conference, but action was deferred until the cooperation of the Eastern Virginia Conference could be solicited. That body, engrossed with the founding of its own Suffolk Collegiate Institute, in Suffolk, Virginia, declined to join in the sponsorship at the time. The result was that no financial support from the church could then be obtained.[44]

Although discouraged by this outcome, the young educator did not cease his efforts for educational expansion. Using his own resources to their fullest extent, on December 30, 1871, he purchased the former Graham College property for $2,500 from Mrs. Harden.[45] After the buildings were repaired and refurbished, he opened Graham High School in 1872. He was joined as coprincipal by his brother, D. A. Long, who had taught school in Rockingham County, Virginia, after having served in the Confederate Army. Patronage was immediately encouraging, for fifty-eight students were enrolled by the close of the first year's session.[46]

In 1874, partially to ease William's financial burden, Daniel purchased the property from his brother, and it was then incorporated as Graham High School. To accommodate the growing student body, Miss Jinnie Albright and William W. Staley, a Christian minister who was an alumnus of the school, were added to its faculty.[47] In addition to Staley, graduates who also became ministers of the church included Peter T. Klapp, Stephen I. Ellis, Malcolm L. Hurley, D. M. Williams, A. A. Iseley, and Jeremiah Holt. Another outstanding alumnus was David F. Jones, who went to Japan in 1887 as the first missionary to that country from the "Christian Church in the United States and Canada."[48]

Throughout this period of growth, the institution maintained high academic and moral standards. In 1878 Principal Long received testimonials to that effect from several leading educators in the state. Braxton Craven, of Trinity College (now Duke University), considered the school "one of the best in the country." The students "have evidently been well taught," was the opinion of President Kemp P. Battle, of the University of North Carolina. These commendations were echoed by W. N. Wingate, of Wake Forest College, who added, "What is of even more importance, they have always been studious and exemplary in their deportment."[49]

Encouraged by their success and ambitious to meet the increasing demand for higher education, in 1881 the Longs obtained an amendment to the school's charter that changed its name to Graham Normal College.[50] This event was formally announced at the closing exercises of the high school in May. Following the declamations by members of the Philologian Society, President Long reported:

> Tonight the "Graham High School" ceases to exist. This Institute will henceforth be known as "Graham Normal College." It will be the object of the Faculty to continue the classical and Mathematical course, for those who either desire to prepare themselves for any of the Colleges or Universities of the country, or to enter at once upon the duties of active business life. . . . We have adopted the course of study recommended by the State Board of Education and will introduce the books, which the State Board has recommended, at the commencement of the next session and continue the pupils in those studies recommended by the State Board of Education. In this way we hope to aid our state and county in furnishing teachers for our free schools. This is, so far as we know, the only Normal College in the state which will continue its exercises throughout the year.[51]

Blessing the launching of the new enterprise, the local newspaper commented, "Long life and usefulness to this old school under its new name."[52]

The physical plant of the college was described in detail in 1964 by Mrs. Walter P. Lawrence, who had been Annie Graham when she attended the school:

> The College was a two-story brick building on the south edge of Graham. Inside the structure, on each floor was a central hall with a classroom on each side of these halls—that is, two classrooms upstairs, two downstairs. The building faced east. Behind it, about fifty or seventy-five feet, was the home of Mr. and Mrs. J. N. H. Clendenin, where young women students roomed and boarded (Mrs. Clendenin was the sister of W. S. and D. A. Long). The Clendenin home was a two story frame dwelling which was connected to the College by a covered walkway. Behind the College to the north and a little farther away than the Clendenin residence was a row of single rooms. Here the male students roomed. They got their meals

at the Clendenin home. In addition to the boarding students—
a small group—there were several day students.

Miss Lena Beale, the teacher of music, lived in the Clendenin home, but the other faculty members lived in the town
of Graham. Reverend N. G. Newman, an instructor to the
school, shepherded the student body each Sunday on its
weekly trek from the College through Graham to Providence
Church on the north side of the village. Here by requirement
the students attended church service.[53]

When the college opened, Professor Alexander McIver was one of
the teachers. In 1884 the faculty was enlarged. In addition to the

*Dedication of state historical marker commemorating Graham
College on April 12, 1981. From left to right:* Dr. Clyde L. Fields,
superintendent of the Southern Conference of the United Church
of Christ; Dr. Robert B. McQueen; Joe A. Mobley, of the State
Department of Archives and History; M. L. Copeland, chairman of
the Graham Historic District Commission; the Reverend Donald
C. Nance; William I. Ward, Jr.; Elon President J. Fred Young; and
Graham's mayor, Myron A. Rhyne. *Photo by Ed Barlow.*

president, it included C. W. Smedes, B.A. (University of North Carolina); Captain J. L. Scott, B.A. (Davidson College); J. L. Foster, B.E. (Graham Normal College); and Mrs. James A. Graham, from Hillsborough. Henry J. Stockard, John U. Newman, and Silas A. Holleman were later added to the staff.[54]

The faculty and student body of the college were of high caliber throughout the institution's existence. Five became college presidents: D. A. Long of Antioch College (Yellow Springs, Ohio) and later of Union Christian College (Merom, Indiana); W. S. Long of

Mrs. Walter P. Lawrence, nee Annie Graham, graduate of Graham and Elon colleges and instructor at the latter. For a number of years before her death in 1969, two years after this picture was taken, she was Elon's oldest living alumna.

Elon College; H. J. Stockard of Peace Female Institute (now Peace College), in Raleigh; and Julius Foust of State Normal and Industrial School (now the University of North Carolina at Greensboro). Numerous others made creditable records in the professions and various business fields. Many student romances blossomed into happy marriages that produced influential families throughout North Carolina, Virginia, and other states. The accomplishments of the alumni were a tribute to the high standards maintained by the capable leadership of the school.[55]

In the successful operation of Graham Normal College, the original idea of William S. Long had evolved from a small, neighborhood academy into a creditable high school, and then to a growing junior college, but the ultimate goal of a four-year liberal arts college had not been reached. The institution envisioned was to be for both men and women because the educator considered coeducation "the Divine plan," for "it meets all the questions growing out of economy, morals, and manners, as no other system has done [and] will for this reason win universal adoption."[56] As time passed and the Graham school's affairs continued to run smoothly, Long began to consider means to accomplish this feat. Only time would tell whether or not he would be successful.

CHAPTER II

PLANTING THE SEED

Large streams from little fountains flow,
Tall oaks from little acorns grow.
DAVID EVERETT
Lines Written for a School Declamation

During the decade that followed rejection of Long's 1870 proposal
for a denominational school, the affairs of the Christian Church improved in several ways. By the time Reconstruction ended in 1877,
home rule had been restored to the former Confederate states, which
eased both political and economic turmoil to some extent among
the membership. In addition, the General Convention of the Christian Church, which later became the Southern Christian Convention, had functioned successfully as a clearinghouse for united denominational action, and had become a potential asset for advancing
such causes as education. Furthermore, the young men added to the
church's clergy had enjoyed better educational advantages than
many of the older ministers, and they enthusiastically advocated the
sponsorship of learning by the denomination. Their convictions
were supported by the success of Suffolk Collegiate Institute, established at Suffolk, Virginia, in 1871, which proved that the church
could maintain and operate a school, despite earlier failures to do so.

Another reason for a renewed emphasis on education within the
denomination was the fact that both the institute and Graham Normal College were only junior colleges, and graduates of either institution were forced to study elsewhere to complete a full liberal
arts education or to acquire the necessary training for a profession. A
four-year college was essential for this purpose, and neither the Long
brothers nor any church conference felt financially able to attempt

such an undertaking. However, numerous leaders among the Christians were convinced that a united denominational effort might successfully do so.

This possibility inspired action at the 1882 session of the Southern Christian Convention, when its Committee on Schools and Colleges made a definite recommendation:

> We are seriously impressed with the belief that it is the duty of the church to provide for the intellectual training and culture of all the young under our control. We also believe no less in the special qualifications and preparations of the men whom we license to preach the gospel, than we do in the divine call given them for this sacred position. Realizing, as we trust all do, that our future prosperity depends largely upon the intelligence of our people—our clergy and laity—and having considered the means within our reach for meeting the demands of the church in this vital matter, we do therefore recommend:
>
> 1. That this Convention proceed at once to establish a College at some suitable point within our borders, at which our boys and girls and our young men seeking to enter the ministry may be educated. Said College, with all its appurtenances, to be owned by the stockholders who may become such upon the subscription and payment,—or as hereafter provided,—of twenty-five dollars for each share of stock by each of them taken. Said stock may be taken by individuals, churches or other associations, and shall entitle the persons holding or legally representing the same to one vote for each share in all meetings of the stockholders.[1]

This proposal was followed by a detailed plan to finance the school. Stock was to be subscribed either by cash or by promissory notes, payable in two, five, or ten years, depending upon the amount, and bearing 6 percent interest. When payment was completed, the stockholder was entitled to 5 percent interest on the investment, "payable in tuition, and not otherwise," at the college. Special inducements were offered to stimulate cash payments:

> 4. These further inducements are offered to all who make cash payments: those who pay twenty-five dollars cash, will be

permitted to keep one student at the College one year, at ¾ rates of tuition per session and interest thereafter in tuition as above mentioned.

5. Those who pay fifty dollars in cash, will be permitted to keep one student at the College two years at ¾ rates of tuition per session and interest thereafter in tuition as above mentioned.

6. Those who pay one hundred dollars cash, will be permitted to keep one student at the College four years at half rates of tuition per session and interest as above.

7. Those who pay two hundred and fifty dollars cash, will be permitted to keep one student at the College ten years at half rates for tuition per session and interest thereafter as above.

8. Those who pay five hundred dollars in cash, will be permitted to keep one student at the College continually free from all tuitional charges. All these inducements not to include incidentals and other extras.[2]

The institution was to be governed by fifteen trustees, two-thirds of whom were required to be stockholders and members of the Christian Church. To expedite the plan, a General Agent was to be appointed by the convention "to secure subscription of stock, gifts and donations for the College."

All these recommendations were adopted by the convention, which specified that, when "$10,000 in cash and bonds" had been collected by "the General Soliciting Agent," trustees would be elected and the college incorporated.

D. A. Long was the agent appointed to raise the necessary funds, and the goal had nearly been reached when in 1883 he moved from Graham to Ohio, where he accepted the presidency of Antioch College, to which he had been elected. Thereafter, the campaign lagged, and, inasmuch as the sum required to found the school was never fully subscribed, the project was abandoned.[3] This may have been a blessing in disguise because the plan devised was similar to that used by the northern Christians to open Antioch College, which soon failed disastrously.[4] The unsuccessful effort also convinced many that the proposed college could only be established by financial support from the general funds of the entire church, supplemented by private donations, and by tuition charged to the students.

Wiser by this experience, the determined Christian leaders immediately began to revise their approach to the problem. In 1886 the
Southern Convention authorized its Committee on Schools and Colleges to "establish a Theological Department in one of the schools or
colleges now under the management of our people." The project was
to be financed with $400 the first year and $200 annually thereafter,
to be raised by quotas requested of the member conferences. Success
blessed this undertaking. Suffolk Collegiate Institute was selected,
and the Reverend W. W. Staley was elected to "the chair of Theology" that was to be established by the convention at that institution.[5]

The convention's Committee on Schools and Colleges was composed of W. S. Long, J. W. Harden, J. P. Barrett, and F. O. Moring, all
men of sound judgment and dedication. They interpreted the enthusiastic reception of the theological seminary proposal to indicate
that the time was ripe to reattempt the launching of a denominational college. They met in Graham during 1887 on March 28 and
again on May 23 to discuss "the propriety and importance" of the
matter. As the result of an agreement reached in their deliberations,
they leased the Graham Normal College for a period of three years
on terms "deemed very reasonable." A new collegiate institution
was then organized. The faculty consisted of W. S. Long, president
and professor of natural science and history; J. U. Newman, professor of ancient and modern languages; S. A. Holleman, professor
of mathematics; and H. J. Stockard, professor of English literature.
August 8 was announced as the opening date of the first session of
the college, which was to be "denominational" but not sectarian.
This news was welcomed by *The Alamance Gleaner*, a Graham
newspaper, which commented, "All should feel highly gratified at
having such an institution in their midst, and help sustain it."[6]

Long was a natural choice for the presidency of the school inasmuch as he was the most outstanding educator among the Christians in North Carolina at the time. His experience as an administrator and teacher for two decades was invaluable. In addition, he
had served for years on the education committees of his conference
and of the convention. These assets were supplemented by his skill
in planning an enterprise and by his determination to pursue it successfully, regardless of the personal effort and sacrifice required. His
election to the principal office of the new venture was a wise move
on the part of the committee.

The committee's initial step, though made with assurance, was but a temporary move pending its official confirmation by the convention. When and if that was obtained, a permanent location needed to be chosen for the college. Interest was soon aroused in several communities other than Graham to have the institution located in their area, and they all initiated steps to advance this aim. To facilitate the final decision, on July 3, 1888, the committee authorized Long "to visit various points" to determine the inducements and advantages they each offered. This assignment was promptly undertaken by the energetic official.[7]

Both the North Carolina and Virginia Conference and the Eastern Virginia Conference, in their 1887 sessions, had enthusiastically endorsed the action of the committee and requested its approval by the Southern Christian Convention.[8] That organization met quadrennially, and was not scheduled to convene again until 1890. However, the convention's president, W. W. Staley, wisely decided that a delay of three years in acting upon such an important matter was impractical, and convened a special session in September 1888.

The session, held at the New Providence Christian Church in Graham, was one of the most significant meetings in the long history of this governing body, and the decision made in the assembly constituted one of the most progressive steps ever taken by the Christian Church in the South. The principal item on the agenda was the report of the Committee on Schools and Colleges. It began with a review of the activities of the past year, which were already generally known, followed by a request for action:

> 1. We therefore ask the Convention to determine upon the place of permanent location, and to take such other steps as may be deemed proper in order to establish upon a permanent bases [sic] an Institution of high grade for the purpose of promoting education, morality and religion.
>
> 2. We recommend that this Convention elect fifteen Trustees to take charge of the enterprise, and that the entire control and management of the College, the property it may acquire, and its business affairs, shall be entrusted to and exercised by said Board of Trustees. For the guidance of said Trustees, and for the purpose of setting the work in order, we submit a Con-

President William S. Long.

stitution and By-Laws, subject to revision and modification as therein provided.[9]

In summary, the principal provisions of the "Constitution of Graham College" were that the institution would "be owned by the General Convention of the Christian Church"; management would be vested in fifteen trustees elected by the convention from the church membership; and, to obtain staggered terms for the board, "of those first elected, one-third were to hold office for two years, one-third for four years, and one-third for six years." The board's duties included electing "a Faculty, consisting of President, Professors and Tutors," fixing their salaries, and determining the price of tuition for the institution. In addition to his other duties, the president was to be "the general financial agent" and "General Superintendent" of the college.

The instrument contained numerous financial provisions:

> Section 1. *Of the Funds of the Institution.* All the funds and means shall be divided into two classes, to be designated and known as the Endowment Fund, and Building and Incidental Fund.
>
> Sec. 2. The Endowment Fund shall consist of the whole of all such gifts, grants, donations and bequests to the Institution as by the terms of the gifts, grants or bequests may be made or designated, as to or for the use of said Endowment Fund. The said Endowment Fund shall in no case be expended or diminished, except in case of forfeiture or actual loss; but shall be kept, retained and preserved as a permanent fund for the endowment of the Institution, and shall be put at interest and secured, as in the wisdom of the Board they may think best.
>
> Sec. 3. The Building and Incidental Fund shall consist of the whole of all donations given to secure the location of the College, all receipts for tuition in the Institution, all the interests arising from the Endowment Fund, the whole of all gifts, grants, donations and bequests made or to be made to the Institution to which, by the terms of the gifts, donations and bequests, no other direction is or may be given.
>
> Sec. 4. The Building and Incidental Fund is chargeable with any and all sums and amounts paid or to be paid for or on account of the College grounds, the buildings and improve-

ments made or to be made thereon for the Institution, all the apparatus and furniture for the use of the Institution, all the necessary books and stationery for the use of the officers and agents of the Institution, and for the salaries of the President, Professors and Tutors of the Institution, the compensation of all officers and agents of the Institution, and for fuel, lights, &c., for the use of the Institution.[10]

Faculty duties were also specified:

> Section 1. *Duties of the Faculty*. The Faculty of the Institu-
> tion shall, by its President, at each annual meeting of the
> Trustees, make a full report in writing, showing the state and
> condition of the Institution, and its operations during the fiscal
> year, noting by name the cases of peculiar merit; and also pre-
> senting, as far as can be prepared, a catalogue of the then cur-
> rent session of the Institution.[11]

The remainder of the constitution was more or less stereotyped in nature. It designated the duties of the vice-president, secretary, and treasurer; the time and place of meetings; as well as periodic reports required from and the functions of an executive committee. Nothing pertinent to the operation of a college seems to have been omitted from the document. When the report, including the constitution, was read to the convention, it was approved without a dissenting vote. (For the full text of the instrument, see Appendix A.)

The first trustees were then elected:

> 1. For Two Years.—E. A. Moffitt, Asheboro, N.C.; J. M.
> Smith, Milton, N.C.; J. H. Harden, Big Falls, N.C.; F. O. Mor-
> ing, Raleigh, N.C.; S. P. Read, Palmer Springs, Va.
> 2. For Four Years.—E. T. Pearce, News Ferry, Va.; Willis J.
> Lee, Norfolk, Va.; P. J. Kernodle, Suffolk, Va.; J. F. West, Wav-
> erly, Va.; E. E. Holland, Suffolk, Va.
> 3. For Six Years.—Rev. W. W. Staley, Suffolk, Va.; Rev. J. W.
> Wellons, Franklinton, N.C.; Rev. W. S. Long, Graham, N.C.;
> Dr. G. S. Watson, Union Ridge, N.C.; Rev. M. L. Hurley, Frank-
> lin, Va.[12]

Next on the agenda of the special convention, individuals from communities ambitious to be the home of the new college were invited to offer financial inducements. Men named Caldwell and Hagan offered 40 acres of land in the suburbs of Greensboro or $2,500 in cash. A Mr. Summers, representing Gibsonville, tendered $4,400 and 40 acres of land. James A. Turrentine, speaking for Burlington, proposed $5,260 in cash. Jacob A. Long, on behalf of Graham, proffered $2,760 for a location anywhere in the town or $250, upon the condition that the college remain where it was then located, in which case P. R. Harden would donate four acres of land "beside the present location."[13]

Because the proposals were so numerous, the convention astutely decided that a large assembly was not the best place to examine each offer fully, and appointed a Provisional Board to make the final decision. It was composed of W. S. Long, president; J. P. Barrett, secretary; F. O. Moring, treasurer; and J. H. Harden and G. S. Watson, members-at-large.[14]

From left to right: *Colonel Junius H. Harden, Dr. George S. Watson, Dr. William S. Long, and Dr. J. Pressley Barrett, who were members of the committee that selected the site for the college; and the Reverend James W. Wellons, an original trustee. This photo was taken about 1920 in front of* ~~West~~ East *Dormitory by Professor A. L. Hook.*

After J. P. Barrett had been elected as agent to further the financing of the project, the convention adjourned, committed to the establishment of a proposed four-year liberal arts college but having made no appropriation for its construction and support. Nevertheless, it was a progressive step, promptly championed by the *Sun*:

> This institution, if it ever was, is no longer the pet scheme of any individual—it is the enterprise of the General Convention of the Christian Church in the Southern States. . . . Now let no hand be lifted save in its behalf, and within a few years we may see our church blessed with an institution of which we may be justly proud, and which will educate our young people and make them a shining light in the Church and blessings to society.[15]

For some reason, Barrett did not accept the post of agent, which was then assigned to President Long. In assuming this additional responsibility, the 49-year-old educator concisely stated his aims: "I want to see a first class college equipped and endowed, doing work for the *Christian Church* and the world. When that is accomplished I shall be ready to close my life work. Until that is done, I shall devote all the energy I have to it, and work and pray for it."[16] He was as good as his word, and lost no time in beginning his endeavors.

The first step that needed to be taken was selection of a permanent site for the college. This was not a simple matter because inducements continued to be submitted in addition to those presented at the convention during its 1888 special session. J. H. Moring, representing Morrisville, North Carolina, offered 50 acres of land. W. H. Trolinger, spokesman for several landowners, proposed a tract of similar acreage at Mill Point, a freight loading station on the Richmond and Danville Railroad (now the Southern Railway), five miles west of Burlington, in the same state. "Who next?" inquired the pleased, but possibly surprised, President Long.[17]

Due consideration was given to all the communities bidding for the location, but one by one they were rejected in favor of the town of Graham. The Alamance County seat had long been the educational center of the Christians in North Carolina, and the church membership was especially strong in the area. In addition to the facilities that were essential, it also offered some that were desirable for the new enterprise. These included proximity to Graham Normal College, which the planners preferred should retain its separate identity as a preparatory school.

For all these reasons, the Provisional Board decided on October 26, 1888, that the college would be located in Graham on land lying between the residence of Captain E. S. Parker and Providence Church. This was on the east side of the present 600 and 700 blocks of North Main Street.

> The lot contains about 15 acres of land on an elevated spot, with an inclined plane in the rear, so giving fine natural drainage, and, all in all, making a beautiful location. This whole lot will be used for the College buildings and campus, while just across the road the Committee had secured a good tract of land to be used for residences, &c.[18]

Both the *Alamance Gleaner* and the *Christian Sun* triumphantly published this news for their readers, and the latter added a boost for the enterprise by stating, "The Christian Church is in a grand struggle—battle—against ignorance and idleness and the church expects every man to do his duty. Hurrah for the College."

Unfortunately, this decision was no sooner announced than complications were encountered. The Provisional Board was unable to acquire part of the real estate it sought. The reasons for this failure are now obscure, but they were sufficiently serious to cause the church officials to change their plans and seek another location. This news greatly disturbed Graham's representatives, J. A. Long and J. D. Kernodle, who requested and received a written explanation of the situation by the Provisional Board in the *Gleaner*:

> *To the Friends of Graham College, Graham, N.C.:*
> The disappointment in the Whitsett land has greatly confused our plans. We have opposing influences to contend with and yet we wish to do our duty by the Church we represent and also to Graham. If Graham can offer us the following inducements we will locate in Graham:
> 1. The title to the present College property at Graham.
> 2. The title to the Emanuel Ruffin land.
> 3. The title to the four acres offered by Mr. P. R. Harden.
> 4. Two thousand dollars in cash April 1, 1889.

5. A good road between the same points.

6. A good side walk between the same points.

7. A petition from the citizens—a majority of the leading men—to the legislature to make a change in the charter prohibiting the manufacture and sale of ardent spirits within the corporation of the town.[19]

In response to these terms, the Graham officials stated, "As to inducements 1, 2, 3 and 7, they were ready to be complied with literally at any time, 6 is nearly completed, 5 is being discussed by the business men in a business way, and 4 no doubt would have been literally complied with."[20]

The Provisional Board did not consider this statement a guarantee of eventual compliance with its terms, and was too impatient to delay the project longer. The difference of opinion between the contending parties provoked a spirited argument, which was fully publicized by the editors of both the *Alamance Gleaner* and the *Christian Sun*.[21] As a result, the harassed board decided the wisest course to follow was to choose a site that was not within the boundaries of any municipality. If this were done, no town would be favored over all others, and all would be equally disappointed. Furthermore, the college could be more easily planned and its officials could to some degree direct and control the community expected to grow up around it. Mill Point was the one location available that met all of these requirements, and on December 20, 1888, it was officially chosen as the site of the proposed college.[22]

The loss of the enterprise was a severe disappointment to Graham, especially after its expectations had been raised so high, but it accepted defeat graciously under the circumstances. W. S. Long hastened to calm the troubled waters by announcing:

> The public should remember that *it is not proposed to move* GRAHAM NORMAL COLLEGE TO MILL POINT, N.C., BUT GRAHAM COLLEGE, THE NEW ENTERPRISE OF THE CHRISTIAN CHURCH. Graham Normal College suspended operation in order to give place to Graham College. When the latter, which is a denominational school, goes to the new place at Mill Point, then the former will resume work under efficient management and will seek to sustain its well-known reputation as an undenominational school in the building now in Graham.[23]

This announcement soothed ruffled feelings, and it is a credit to the townspeople of Graham that they became, and have remained, loyal to the new college in every manner possible. This attitude is especially commendable in view of the tragedy of July 22, 1892, when the Graham Normal College, while undergoing extensive repairs, burned to the ground.[24] For reasons of his own, D. A. Long, the owner of the property, did not rebuild the school, and Graham lost both the old and the new institutions. The fire not only robbed the town of an asset, but also deprived the Christian Church of a preparatory school operated within its membership. This was a severe loss to the denomination's educational program.

The site selected by the Provisional Board consisted of two or three houses clustered around a small railroad freight station at the edge of a thickly wooded area. Located in Alamance County's Boone Station Township, named for Boon's Crossing, a juncture of two wagon roads a few miles to the southeast, Mill Point was established to handle freight hauled by wagons to and from the railroad and two cotton mills, approximately seven miles to the northwest. One was the factory founded by John Q. Gant at Altamahaw, and the other, owned by Captain James N. Williamson, at Ossipee. The latter industrialist built a house near the station but rented it, for he lived in Graham.[25] Westward along the railroad, Gibsonville was two miles away and Greensboro, fifteen; eastward, Burlington was five miles distant and Graham seven miles. In 1888 a post office was authorized for Mill Point, and Gant was appointed as postmaster.[26] Except for the arrival and departure of puffing trains and creaking wagons, the tiny community was a quiet place at which a college could be built with few, if any, distractions.

The grove in which construction was planned contained at least thirty-three varieties of trees. These included white, red, black, Spanish, pin, and post oaks; hickory; dogwood; two kinds of pine; cedar; holly; black and sweet gum; black jack; chinquapin; poplar; silver maple; elm; hackberry; wild grape; muscadine; persimmon; two kinds of haw; sarvis; sassafras; mulberry; walnut; willow; ironwood; ash; and locust. These were identified by J. P. Barrett, editor of the *Christian Sun*, who inspected the site in January 1889 and pronounced it, "altogether one of the finest locations, naturally, to be found in the South."[27] At the time of his visit, the Reverend A. F. Iseley was busy superintending twenty workmen in clearing the

grove for buildings. No tree was removed unless absolutely necessary so that the school might have a shaded campus. Eventually
some of the forest's giants spared would succumb to the ravages of
time, which sixty-eight years later would keep Iseley's great-grand- uncle
son, J. E. Danieley, then president of the college, busy planting new   Frank
trees. However, because of proper planning and later conservation,
the campus has always enjoyed an abundance of trees.

While this preliminary work was under way, for legal reasons the
choosing of a name for the college could no longer be postponed.
"What shall it be?" queried President Long of "Brethren South,
North, East, West."[28] The matter was soon decided, and the suggestion accepted was influenced by the fact that most of the trees left
standing were massive oaks. The name, "Elon," which is the He-
brew word for "oak," was adopted for the school, and it also became
the name of the town. Both J. U. Newman and P. J. Kernodle have
been given credit for the suggestion, and it may have been a joint
idea, but actually the individual responsible is unknown. At any
rate, the name was approved in 1889, and has never been changed.[29]

While the name was being proposed and accepted, the democratic
Long welcomed constructive advice with another question:

> What plan is best, and when the buildings are erected, how
> should they be heated and lighted? Suggestions along these
> lines will be helpful. We want modern buildings with modern
> improvements. We cannot be behind the age in which we live.
> We will be able to get enough with what we have to build good
> substantial houses. The wood to burn brick will be cut, and
> hauled, the grove trimed [sic] up, and every thing made ready
> for work in earnest at the opening of spring.[30]

The president then announced that bids were receivable for 500,000
brick. In the role of financial agent, he then traveled extensively in
North Carolina and Virginia seeking contributions with which to
pay for the structures.[31]

After the adoption of the official name, the legislature of North
Carolina chartered Elon College on March 11, 1889. The instrument
contained the usual provisions for incorporation. In addition, it
placed the institution "at all times under the control of the general
convention of the Christian Church," specified that $500,000 worth
of property held by the trustees would "forever be exempt from taxa-

tion," authorized all property held by the trustees for Graham College to be transferred to Elon College, and established the following restrictions:

> Section 10. That it shall not be lawful for any person or persons to set up any gaming table or any device whatever for playing at any game of chance or hazard, by whatever name called, or to gamble in any manner, or to keep a house of ill-fame, or to manufacture spirituous or intoxicating liquors or otherwise to sell or convey for a certain consideration to any person any intoxicating liquors, within one and a half miles of said College; any person who shall violate any of the provisions of this section shall be guilty of a misdemeanor.[32]

Fortified by this authority, the college officials were prepared to attend to their legal affairs. (See Appendix B for full text of the charter.)

Immediately following the incorporation, by execution of five deeds, the trustees obtained title to a tract of land at Mill Point. William H. and E. A. Trolinger were paid $212.50 for 48 acres; $5 to Alonzo and Isabella Gerringer for 1.59 acres; $5 to W. F. and Mollie C. Ireland for 8 acres; $34 to Joseph and Eliza James for 17.72 acres; and $5 to Edmund and Mary A. Ingle for 2 acres. Within the next few months, William P. and Harriet Huffines received $10 for 3 acres; David and Emeline Staley $5 for 2½ acres; and Sidney and Rosa Troxler $5 for 4 acres. Thus the college acquired a total of 86.81 acres at a cost of $281.50, or approximately $3.24 per acre. This was a bargain, which the sellers intended it to be, for land in the area was selling for $6 to $12 an acre at the time.[33]

When these transactions were completed, planning was accelerated. It was not confined to college buildings but included the community expected to grow up around the institution. Keeping this in view, the entire tract deeded to the trustees was surveyed and platted by S. A. Holleman, a member of the Graham College faculty.[34] Twenty-five acres on the north side of the railroad were reserved for the physical plant of the school. The remaining acreage was laid off in squares, four acres each in size, and transversed by streets eighty or one hundred feet in width. Eighteen lots west of the campus were offered for sale for business houses, and forty lots east and north of the campus for residences.

All the streets were designated as avenues and given commemorative names. Manning, Beale, and Wellons avenues were named for John N. Manning, E. W. Beale, and W. B. Wellons, respectively, all ministers of prominence in the Christian Church. Lee honored W. J. Lee, of Norfolk, Virginia, an original and esteemed trustee of the college; Holt was named in recognition of the influential Alamance County family of that name; and Williamson for Captain J. N. Williamson, who was credited with contributing "the largest cash donation to the enterprise," though he was not a member of the Christian Church. Trollinger (alternate spelling) was a tribute to William H. Trolinger for his advocacy of the Mill Point location.

Antioch was named for the Syrian city where the followers of Jesus Christ were first called Christians; and Haggard for the Rever-

Original plat of the town of Elon College.

end Rice Haggard, who is credited with first suggesting the use of the "Christian Church" name by O'Kelly's followers. Lebanon was inspired by Old Lebanon Church, in Surry County, Virginia, where the Christians had met in 1794 to organize their church; and O'Kelley (misspelled) honored the Reverend James O'Kelly, founder. Kerr was named in memory of D. W. Kerr, the pioneer educator; Summerbell honored the Summerbell family, of which Martyn and Joseph J. Summerbell were distinguished ministers and scholars among the northern Christians at the time; and Iseley recognized the assistance of the Reverend A. A. Iseley in building the college.[35]

Only East and West College avenues were given other than commemorative names. Both of these were designed to terminate at the institutional area, but actually they were joined by a road that bisected the campus until 1924, when construction of the present wall terminated its use. Wellons, Iseley, and Barrett avenues were never opened because the development of the town made them unnecessary for various reasons. In 1940 Kerr was closed between East College and East Haggard avenues, and Beale was closed in 1955. Other than these changes, the streets remain as they were originally designated.[36]

Once this plan was completed, Long solicited buyers for the lots. In an article in the *Sun*, he stressed the convenience of having four passenger trains that stopped daily, and noted that these were supplemented by a new depot, telegraph office, and post office. He pointed out other advantages:

> The temperature is mild—averages 50 degrees. The healthfulness of this section is unsurpassed in the South. No blizzards, no cyclones (such as often visit other sections) were ever known here. No yellow fever, no cholera, no epidemics of any kind, has ever visited this portion of country. Here complete religious and political freedom are enjoyed by all races, whether native-born or of foreign birth. The manufacture and sale of ardent spirits, gambling, &c. are by the charter, forever prohibited within one and a half miles of the College.[37]

The president also promised that a church would be organized for the community and that regular services would be held in the planned college chapel until a church building could be constructed. He concluded his article by stating that, though Elon College was the property of the Christian Church and would "forever remain such, yet its doors will ever be open to all who come seeking light and truth."

Long's invitation to buy real estate met with immediate response, and the community enjoyed a "residential building boom." In the early sales period, most of the purchasers paid approximately $100 per lot, which was highly profitable and aided the institution's meager building fund.[38] Houses were built by Captain J. N. Williamson, Walter L. Smith, W. Samuel Tate, Jerry Whitesell, the Reverend Henry Hines, and the Cable brothers, Boston and Peter. Others soon were under construction. Several families became residents of the community to enjoy proximity to the school so that they could lower the costs of educating their children. J. A. Long, brother of President Long and agent for Graham during the contest for the location of the college, was one of these. He built the house at 201 East Trollinger Avenue, which is still standing. An icehouse was later added to the premises, the only one ever built and used in the village. Walter L. Smith, the first station agent, opened a store, and other commercial enterprises soon began.[39]

As a result of this growth, on April 7, 1893, the community was incorporated as the town of Elon College. S. A. Holleman, professor of mathematics at the college and the man who had drawn the town plat, became the first mayor of the new municipality, and presided over the board of five commissioners entrusted with its government. These consisted of Peter Hughes, W. S. Tate, John E. Long, Dr. W. T. Herndon, and Thomas Stroud. The name of the post office was changed from Mill Point to correspond with that of the town, and James E. McAdams, who had succeeded Gant in the office at Mill Point, served as its first postmaster.[40]

While these events were transpiring, construction on the campus was being pushed as rapidly as possible. The bid for brick made by W. H. Trolinger and Peter Hughes had been accepted, and, after Hughes retired from the partnership, Trolinger fulfilled the contract. The brick were made "in the ~~southeast~~ west corner of the village south of the railroad." Numerous employees, including James Buchanan ("Buck") Gerringer and "Bud" May, were kept busy hauling them by wagon to the construction site. Thomas Bradshaw, of Graham, undertook the grading of the land, and John W. Long, the area's foremost mason, was the building contractor. William S. Long, Jr.

("Will"), the president's son, served as timekeeper, paymaster, and general assistant to his father.[41]

The name of the architect who designed the first building is unknown, but the structure was described in detail by the president:

> The main building, intended for the College purposes, society halls, museum, library, &c. is now (August 6th) going up. It is a splendid structure, 129 feet long and 57 feet wide, three stories high, with an octagon front 25 feet in diameter, running up 104 feet, and an observatory in the top. It is designed to put up later a dormitory on the west for girls, and one on the east for boys, making a handsome and valuable property.[42]

Within a few weeks after the walls of the main building were under way, work began on the East Dormitory, to be used to house women students. It was located on the east side of the main building, both of which faced south and stood in the approximate center of the campus.[43]

When construction began on the first two buildings, funds on hand were insufficient to insure their completion. Nevertheless, the spirit of generosity exhibited by supporters of the project was encouraging to the officials. The sum of $4,000 had been donated by the people in the Mill Point area to obtain the location of the college. J. P. Bland, of Pittsboro, made the first individual cash contribution and W. S. Long, the first subscription. The Berea Christian Church, in Nansemond County, Virginia, raised $636.05 by conducting the first public appeal for funds. W. J. Lee, a member of that congregation and a trustee of Elon College from its founding until his death, was responsible for $250 of the sum. Others were also generous, and the board began building, faithfully expecting that money would be obtained as needed.[44]

Amid general rejoicing, on May 7, 1889, the ground was broken for the foundation of the main building, and thirteen days later the first brick was laid by "Lizzie" (Elizabeth) Jane Long, the youngest daughter of the president.[45] After this beginning, sufficient progress was made by July 18 to place the cornerstone in the wall of the main building. A crowd estimated at between one and two thousand people assembled for the gala occasion. The ceremony was performed by the Masons of Bula (Beulah) Lodge, who marched to the site under the direction of Walter G. Adams, Master of the Lodge, and J. A. Turrentine, marshal for the day. According to "Will" Long, who witnessed the event, the niche left in the wall for the purpose had been constructed "so perfectly that the stone was pushed into place without a particle of change."[46]

In keeping with an ancient custom, a number of articles were deposited within the cornerstone. These included a Bible; copies of *The Principles and Government of the Christian Church*, the *Alamance Gleaner*, the *Burlington News*, the *Christian Sun*, and the charter of Elon College; names of the architect and builders of the college; contract for the construction work on the college; a "circular announcing the Craigville, Massachusetts, camp meeting"; a history of the Bula Lodge of Masons; a volume entitled *Facing the Truth*; a catalog of Graham College; and various coins.[47]

At the conclusion of the Masonic rites, the main address was delivered by John M. Moring, of Pittsboro, who substituted for Colonel Leonidas L. Polk, of Raleigh, who was prevented by illness from attending. The orator, former speaker of the state House of Representatives and an alumnus of Graham College, was accompanied by his daughter, Alberta, who later was to become a member of the Elon faculty.

Remarks were then made by President Long; the Reverend W. T. Herndon, a minister in the Christian denomination from Morrisville, North Carolina; the Reverend A. T. Hord, pastor of the Baptist Church, in Burlington; C. W. Hunt, editor of the *Burlington News*; J. P. Barrett, editor of the *Christian Sun*; and Dr. George W. Long, who practiced medicine in Graham. The entire assembly was then welcomed to an abundant meal, followed during the afternoon with ice cream, lemonade, milk shakes, melons, and other refreshments. Music was rendered throughout the day by the Glencoe Cornet Band, under the direction of Captain J. H. Holt, Jr. The occasion was one of "rare pleasure," and "grand" for the college, according to the *Sun*'s editor, who also observed, "The order was excellent, every body behaved admirably, even the dogs were not troublesome."[48]

Before the visitors dispersed, a collection was taken that totaled nearly three hundred dollars. One contribution that merited special notice was two silver dollars given by Miss Annie Morton, a young woman who supported herself on wages of forty cents per day. Her economic situation was comparable to many of the southern people at the time, and her generosity typified the financial sacrifices made by scores of people to build Elon.[49]

Although the spirit of generosity prevailed among the supporters of the college, construction consistently ran ahead of contributions. The extent to which this burden weighed on the president's shoulders and the measures he was forced to take to carry on the project were later related by his son, "Will":

> The work had to be rushed, but a reverse came. One day when the eleven-o'clock train arrived, which brought the mail from the bank in Durham where my father did his banking (Alamance County had no banks then), he received a letter from the bank stating that unless certain persons signed certain notes the bank could not allow any more money. It became necessary to do something at once. Father called me at 11:30 A.M. on an awful hot day and said, "Will, go get old Bob and the cart." (Old Bob was a famous old horse that my father rode thousands of miles to raise funds to erect Elon College. He was the most famous horse I ever knew.) I got old Bob and the cart and these instructions, "Go to see Dr. George Watson beyond Union Ridge, fourteen miles away, and have him sign this paper and tell him that if he does not sign it the work on Elon College will be stopped." I made the trip and found Dr. Watson just after dinner. He ordered old Bob fed and he told his wife to get me something for my dinner. He signed the paper and I returned as quickly as possible, in order to keep the workers from scattering and leaving the work unfinished. We pushed on until we came to another difficulty. My father sold his house and farm, two miles east of Graham, to his brother, Daniel Albright Long, in order to keep the farm in the family. He used this money to bridge that gap. The amount was $4,500.00.[50]

By such means and the diligent assistance of all concerned, the work continued without interruption. Long, himself, carried boards for the carpenters whenever he found time to do so. His wife aided immeasurably by using one of the three rooms in their cottage for cooking meals and a second for serving them to her family and the workmen. This was no small task for the frail woman, but it was accomplished cheerfully. The Longs' goal was the opening of the college, and anything that might interfere was eclipsed in the process. As Long stated, "No language can fully and adequately portray the powerful solicitude, the sacrifices, and mental agony of some of those who led in this movement," but who considered the completion of the institution a suitable reward.[51] This was not only a reference to himself and his family, but also to all those noble men and women who used their material and physical means to build Elon College.

Because construction was proceeding as rapidly as possible in the spring of 1890, the opening of the college was announced for autumn of that year. However, as the deadline approached, it became clear that progress had been estimated too optimistically. As a result, despite frantic efforts, the buildings were woefully incomplete on September 2 when the first men and women began arriving to enroll. S. M. Smith, a prospective student from Auburn, North Carolina, alighted at Elon from a late afternoon train and frankly described his introduction to what was to become his alma mater:

> I was sent to the "Elon College Hotel," run by Mrs. Walter
> Smith, wife of the depot agent. After supper the students who
> came in on that train met Dr. Newman at the station, and
> with a kerosene lantern he led us along a foot path up through
> the campus to the college building, which had not been com-
> pleted. I remember we climbed a ladder to get in the front
> door. Upstairs in the chapel we went through the routine of
> registering and getting acquainted with each other. The only
> lights in the chapel were tin kerosene lamps hanging on nails
> driven in the mortar between the bricks [the plaster coating
> had not been applied to the interior walls at the time]. The
> seating was split-bottom chairs, with an occasional ten or
> twelve foot rough board extending from one chair to another to
> increase the capacity as students arrived. The rostrum was
> built of rough timbers which had been used as scaffolding
> around the building.[52]

An even more serious disadvantage was that the dormitory was not ready for occupancy. This situation posed a problem far more difficult to solve, but, after considerable frenzied activity, lodgings were found for the women in private homes. Smith and a few other men arranged to stay at the hotel or elsewhere in the village, but most of them, unable to find local accommodations, "camped out" on the third floor of the College Building, as the main building was designated during the early years.[53]

Half a century later, Smith vividly recalled the beginning of his four-year residence:

> At the "Hotel" that first night, I was assigned a back room. I shall never forget my feelings the next morning. It was pouring rain. From my window I could see only woods with a small cottage in the distance. . . . It began to dawn on me that I was seventy-five miles from home, and about to become a student in college. *Home-sick*—yea, that's what it was. *Nostalgia*, they call it now-a-days, but it's all the same.[54]

In an effort to cheer the new arrivals amid such depressing conditions, young Long organized a string band, which included the depot agent, a merchant, and several carpenters, to serenade the females in the evenings. This musical gesture helped make homesickness and temporary conditions more bearable, while affording the musicians an outlet for their talents.[55]

Seventy-six students were enrolled when the college opened, and more arrived before September 24, when classes began. W. H. Albright (Elon '93), H. C. Simpson (Elon '96), and D. W. Cochrane (Elon '94), all claim the distinction of being the first student to matriculate. No positive proof is now possible, but Cochrane's name is the first in the college Registration Book. However, the college catalog for 1911–12 states that "the first student on the ground" was a merchant and that was Simpson's occupation at the time. The Elon Alumni Association acknowledged Albright's claim, which was based on his own memory, when it invited him to deliver the principal oration at the 1943 commencement, though illness prevented his acceptance.[56] Regardless of who was first, the students soon adjusted to their new environment, and conditions vastly improved within a short time. Despite the inauspicious beginning, both men and women soon exhibited affection and loyalty for the institution and many returned annually until the requirements for their graduation were fulfilled. One of these was Smith, who later received his diploma and served for a period on the faculty.[57]

Although the College Building was incomplete, the thirteen finished recitation rooms on its first floor were usable for the beginning of classes. The second floor contained space for a reading room, an office, five music rooms, and a chapel that measured seventy-one by sixty-five feet and could be made twenty-nine feet longer by opening folding doors at one end. On the third floor were rooms to be used for two society meeting halls, a library, a museum, and six dormitory accommodations. The tower on top of the building was intended to be used as an observatory.[58]

The halls were twelve feet wide and the stairways correspondingly broad. The rooms were either fourteen or sixteen feet high. They were lighted by large windows that were raised and lowered by weights. Transoms topped each interior door. The society halls and chapel were heated by stoves, the one for the latter room a gift from the Odell Hardware Company, of Greensboro. All the other rooms contained fireplaces in addition to separate flues, which could be used for stoves if desired. The building was cleverly designed to allow for future improvements because ample room was provided in

Main (Administration) Building, completed in 1890.
It was destroyed by fire in 1923.

the basement for furnaces should central heating ever be installed.[59]

Long and his colleagues planned wisely, built well with the means available, and were rewarded by an initial student body of appreciable size and caliber. The administration was handicapped with unfinished buildings and financial indebtedness, but it opened the school's doors on the scheduled date and expressed confidence in the future. Through the efforts of many people over a long period of time, on September 2, 1890, Elon College officially became a living institution and joined the list of four-year liberal arts colleges in the state.

CHAPTER III

THE SEEDLING

For there shall be a sowing of peace;
the vine shall yield its fruit, and
the ground shall give its increase,
and the heavens shall give their dew.
ZECHARIAH 8:12

The loss of Graham College by fire doomed the plan to use it as a preparatory school for Elon College, or any other collegiate institution. Because President Long and his colleagues considered the function of the destroyed school an essential part of their program, they solved the problem by adding a preparatory department to Elon, and appointed S. A. Holleman as principal. All applications for admission to the college were accepted, provided the applicants furnished suitable character references. Upon their arrival, they were examined to determine whether or not they should be placed in the college proper or in the "prep," or Academic Department. This plan worked well, for a vast difference existed between the qualifications and previous education of prospective students.

The Academic Department offered a two-year program. The first-year courses included arithmetic, grammar and composition, geography, elocution, Latin, and U.S. history. Those offered in the second year were algebra, grammar, arithmetic, Latin, bookkeeping, and commercial law. The last two were electives, but all of the others were required. In the early years of operation, the ages of students enrolled in this program ranged from one of nine years to those in their teens.[1]

At the conclusion of these studies, students were prepared for the college. They could choose between a Classical Course, which would earn them the degree of Bachelor of Arts, or the Philosophical

Course, which resulted in the degree of Bachelor of Philosophy. However, little difference existed in the studies required for the two different degrees. Both were designed for completion in four years and included courses in English, Latin, Greek, German, French, algebra, plane and analytical geometry, chemistry, physics, zoology, botany, and general history. Only a few requirements varied in the two plans. Students enrolled in this program during the early period ranged from those in their teens to one forty-three years of age. In addition, the postgraduate degree of Master of Arts was offered to "those who have pursued a prescribed course of study and stood an approved examination." The requirements were planned by the faculty for each individual applicant for the advanced degree.[2]

The college was always aware of the practical side of education. In addition to the numerous classical courses, its first curriculum offered a business course, which included bookkeeping, commercial law, penmanship, arithmetic, telegraphy, typewriting, and stenography.[3]

In addition to Holleman, who was working toward a B.A. degree while teaching, President Long was professor of biblical instruction as well as natural and social science. He held the M.A. and D.D. degrees. J. U. Newman, who had won a Ph.D. from the University of Chicago, was professor of Greek and higher mathematics. James O. Atkinson, who had earned an M.A. at Wake Forest College, was professor of Latin and "Moral Science." These three men were all ordained Christian ministers. Emmett L. Moffitt, M.A., was professor of English and modern languages, Miss Lena B. Beale taught music, and Miss Alberta Moring taught painting and drawing. In 1891 the Misses Maud Robbins and Lorena Long were added to the staff to give music lessons.

The following year, to handle the growing student body, more additions were made to the faculty. They included four adjunct professors: R. G. Kendrick, B.A., for Latin and German; Herbert Scholz, B.A., for English and political science; S. J. Durham, B.A., for English, political science, and German; and Miss M. Irene Johnson, B.A., for mathematics and French. Engaged for vocal and instrumental music were Misses Janie Price, of the Cincinnati Conservatory, Emma Harward, of the Boston Conservatory, and Chattie Cushman, who had studied at Leipzig. Miss Almira Johnson was added to the staff as matron, and Dr. George W. Kernodle as college physician.[4]

Professor S. A. Holleman, original faculty member.

Moffitt had graduated from Graham College, where Newman and Holleman had both been instructors, and Scholz and Miss Johnson were graduates of Elon College in 1891 and 1892, respectively. Several of these teachers were working toward higher academic degrees when they became affiliated with the college faculty. In 1892 both Atkinson and Moffitt obtained leave to pursue further studies at Harvard University, and earned graduate degrees from that institution. Courses of postgraduate studies were worked out for both Holleman and Scholz. When these were completed, at the University of North Carolina and elsewhere, Elon conferred the M.A. degree upon them.[5]

For an infant institution, the academic standing of Elon's faculty was at least average, and possibly better than that of similar colleges. Unlike today, graduate schools were few in the United States at the time, and the plan by which the college assisted its instructors to obtain higher scholastic rank was common practice.

On June 2, 1891, the two-day exercises of Elon College's first commencement began. This was not only a notable event throughout the Christian Church, but also one in which "naturally very considerable interest" was felt in Alamance County. This was especially true of Graham, whose citizens attended to such an extent that the local newspaper commented, "Everybody who could get a conveyance is gone from this place—the town turned out."[6]

Commencement programs of that day were not merely graduating exercises, but the culmination of the outstanding scholastic accomplishments of the entire student body for the year. It was also a time of social conviviality to the extent that the usually strict rules governing student conduct were relaxed in order to permit the men to escort the ladies to the various events.[7]

This manner of closing the college year was typical of educational institutions at the time and served as a pattern that, except for periodic modifications, was a format for similar occasions at Elon and elsewhere until well into the twentieth century. The *Christian Sun* printed the entire 1891 program.[8]

During the course of the commencement events, an exhibit arranged by the art teacher, Miss Moring, attracted complimentary attention from the numerous visitors. The pictures displayed were the work of the Misses Lena B. Beale, H. Rawls, M. Irene Johnson, Emma Williamson, Kate Clendenin, B. Moring, and Mesdames S. A.

Holleman and J. U. Newman.[9] This constituted the first public presentation of the Art Department, whose courses have remained an attraction in the curriculum to the present.

The first graduating class was composed of Nathaniel G. Newman, C. C. Peel, and Herbert Scholz. All three had averaged more than 95 in their studies and graduated *cum maxima laud*, and all three ultimately became ministers of the Christian Church. Scholz earned a graduate degree from Elon and served on its faculty for several years. Newman, a brother of Dr. J. U. Newman, also achieved a graduate degree, and eventually served as pastor of the college church for a number of years.[10]

Also during the 1891 ceremonies, the administration used the authority granted by its charter to confer two honorary degrees. The first was a Master of Arts to H. J. Stockard, who had been principal of the preparatory school at the former Graham College. The second was the Doctor of Divinity to the Reverend J. P. Watson, editor of *The Herald of Gospel Liberty*, who had enthusiastically publicized the founding of Elon in the official organ of the northern Christians.[11] These were expressions of respect for scholarly achievement and gratitude for support of the institution, and were the first of many similar degrees to be conferred by the college on those it

First commencement program, 1891.

wished to honor. The prerogative was used for the third time shortly after the commencement was concluded when Elon conferred the Doctor of Divinity degree upon the Reverend Charles J. Jones, who had preached the baccalaureate sermon for the initial occasion.[12]

The first commencement was a success from every viewpoint. The second, in June 1892, was similar to it except that only one student was awarded a diploma. Miss Irene Johnson was not only the first woman to receive a degree from the college, she was the only person in its history to constitute the entire graduating class. "The College and state ought to feel thankful for such a lady," was the tribute from the editor of the *Christian Sun* for her accomplishment.[13] Miss Johnson was immediately elected by the faculty to the position of assistant professor of mathematics on her alma mater's staff, and remained in that position until 1900, when she married John M. Cook, who was also an alumnus of the college.[14]

Succeeding classes reflected the growth of the institution, for ten diplomas were presented to the graduating class of 1893 and eight in 1894. These groups combined produced eight teachers, four ministers, four lawyers, one farmer, and one homemaker.[15] Of the teachers, Walton C. Wicker, S. A. Holleman, Walter P. Lawrence, and Miss Annie Graham later served on the Elon College faculty. The number of graduates continued to increase after the early years of the institution.

Because no deans or administrative officers were assigned at the time, the faculty as a whole, under the chairmanship of the college president, attended to most of the institution's numerous affairs, except for fundraising, construction of buildings, and a few minor administrative duties.

As a consequence, the group met often and dealt with matters ranging from the trivial to the important. The record of the meetings has been preserved since January 1893, at which time R. G. Kendrick, secretary of the faculty, was reimbursed thirty cents for a book he had purchased in which to record the proceedings. Actions included approval of hiring a man for ten dollars per month to build fires and sweep the rooms; planning a schedule for the ringing of the college bell; authorizing the secretary to purchase chalk and erasers for the classrooms; setting up a bulletin board; purchasing two stoves; agreeing to present Bibles to the graduates; and instructing the library curator to renew the subscriptions to *St. Nicholas, Cosmopolitan*, and *Century* magazines.[16]

The following year, the faculty recommendations of periodicals for the library included *Cosmopolitan, St. Nicholas, Harper's Weekly, Harper's Monthly, Arena, Forum, Homiletic Review, North Atlantic Review, London News, Ladies' Home Journal, New York Herald* (weekly), *Atlanta Constitution* (daily), *Chautauqua Independent, Sunday School Times, Youth's Companion, Literary Digest, Quarterly Journal of Economics*, and *The Nation*. The number and type of periodicals remained about the same for several years after this list was adopted.[17]

Other items on the agendas of the faculty meetings included the approval of February 22 as a holiday in honor of George Washington's birthday; granting of permission for one literary society to hold an oyster supper; and allowing another to sponsor a strawberries and cream party. The faculty also requested the trustees to confer degrees, both earned and honorary; formulated the course offerings; planned the schedule of approved activities; and compiled the college catalog.[18]

In addition to these multitudinous duties, the faculty handled all phases of the academic work and supervised conduct of the students. The rules of discipline were strict, unnecessarily so it seems, but were similar to those at other colleges of the day. The list of regulations was approved by the faculty and published by the administration.[19]

In addition to these rules, students were given dress guidelines in the catalog:

> For economy and to avoid unpleasant distinctions in dress, young ladies will be required to wear a black uniform. The trimmings and scarfs to be determined by the individual's taste. It is desired that the quality shall not be expensive, but heavy enough to hold the color and last through the winter. For commencements a mull or *wash* dress. Graduates will be allowed to dress as they prefer.
>
> Young men need plain and substantial, but not expensive clothing. As a general rule, the more money a student spends on dress the less time is given to study.

> The government of the students is entirely in the hands of
> the Faculty, the President of which is the regularly authorized
> representative.[20]

A considerable amount of the faculty's time was spent in enforcing discipline and guiding the academic work of the students. Punishment often consisted of giving demerits, an accumulation of which could lead to suspension or expulsion, but other penalties could also be applied at the discretion of the faculty, whose decisions were final. A petition from one student to substitute music for a geometry course was denied, but the request of another to drop general history was approved. Two students were given permission to add biology to their courses "provided an average daily grade of 90 be maintained on all studies," or else it would need to be dropped. Another student was required to copy the U.S. Constitution as punishment for impertinence to a professor.

The excuses of one male student for failure to attend prayers were considered invalid, and he was given 40 demerits for 20 absences. Another was penalized two demerits for failure to attend Sunday school. Five demerits each were given to several for cigarette smoking, and five for a male passing notes to a female. Two students were given 25 demerits each for going bird hunting without permission. Two demerits were given to a female for not wearing the uniform. Another student, "cited before the faculty for putting an unexploded cap in the stove during recitation creating a disturbance," was placed on probation.[21]

From these and many similar entries in the faculty proceedings, it is apparent that no students have ever received more individual attention from the faculty than was accorded to them in the early years of the college's operation.

Academic excellence was always the goal of the faculty, and its members strove in every manner possible to assist their students to attain it. Considerable emphasis was placed on public speaking and literary composition. Each member of the graduating class was required to make a speech or write an essay. In preparation for this work, essays or speeches were frequently required in the various courses. This led to the following faculty ruling: "A motion prevailed that if a student misspells 40% of his words in a particular essay, that he is required to study spelling for 4 weeks, and further

Professor James O. Atkinson.

that his spelling be not an excuse for dropping other work."[22] There is no record of how often this penalty was invoked, but its adoption shows that the faculty intended for graduates to be literate to the highest degree possible.

Within a short time after the college opened, the students followed the custom prevalent in most institutions of higher learning at the time by organizing literary societies. The Philologian and the Clio were for men, and the Psiphelian for the women. Their purpose was to meet weekly "for improvement in composition, oratory, reading and debate, and acquiring a knowledge of parliamentary law." Suitable rooms were assigned the societies in the College Building for their meetings on Friday evenings or Saturday mornings. Within a few years, each of these "halls" was decorated with wallpaper and furnished in an attractive manner. By 1894 the students had raised and spent $1,451.00 for this purpose, including $100 for a chandelier.[23]

The value to the students of participation in the activities of the societies was considered sufficient for the faculty to make the following ruling: "Any student above 2nd academic who is not an active member of one of the Literary Societies be required to write an essay of 1,000 words every two weeks, the subject to be given him by the Prof. of English."[24] This coercion was modified by the social side of the organizations. Frequently one or the other obtained permission to have an "ice cream supper" or a party of some kind, and the three societies became the center of social life at the college during its first three decades.

Some of the parties were not only for pleasure but also to raise funds for some particular project of the organization. The public was invited to attend these affairs, at which the guests paid for their refreshments. In 1892 one such occasion was publicized by a newspaper announcement: "A high pink tea and social reception will be given in Elon College chapel Saturday evening, May 20th. Doors open at 7:30 p.m. Ice cream, cake, Norfolk strawberries and Elon cream will be served by the pink tea girls in attractive style and flowing abundance."[25] These affairs were popular, and by such means the societies financed the furnishing of their meeting places and contributed to a number of college activities. Virtually every student belonged to one of the groups, among which strong, but friendly, rivalry existed until they were replaced by other organizations and officially disbanded in 1933.

In addition to the social life provided by the occasional society parties and the annual commencement, "get togethers" were held each month in the college chapel. President Long, ever the champion of coeducation, approved of the male and female students becoming acquainted with each other, but also held strict ideas about how their contacts should be regulated. The periodic affairs were his idea, and S. M. Smith recorded the manner in which they were conducted:

> Announcement was made by the president, Dr. Long, at chapel service one week before the eventful evening. This gave ample time for date-making, which was usually done while classes were changing periods. . . . These occasions were usually on Friday evening, as there were no college classes on Saturday. At the appointed hour, usually about eight o'clock, the old bell in the tower sounded a note of invitation, and the young ladies came over from the dormitory under the chaperonage of the matron or one of the music teachers. Young men came from homes in the village, and after a few preliminaries, the "walk-around" was on, Dr. Long and members of the faculty with their wives leading. Everybody who was fortunate enough to have a partner was required to walk—no sitting around. The route was practically in the shape of a circle. On some occasions couples were required to change partners, but this wasn't very satisfactory.
>
> There was no "receiving line," no punch bowl, no evening dress (decollete or tails), such wasn't in keeping with the spirit of the day. There was no program, or even music . . . except probably a slow march played by one of the music teachers at the beginning just to get things going.

Smith continued his description, but added an appraisal:

> These affairs came to be known later in colleges as "proms," meaning, of course, that the participants promenaded around the room, arm in arm. At Elon, however, they soon took on the name of "Cold Water Walk Arounds"—more or less in deri-

sion, I think. Out of these very occasions though, insipid as they were supposed to be at the time, grew courtships, and finally marriages that have honored the college and graced many communities, north, south, east and west.[26]

Such was the gaiety of campus life at the college in the 1890s, but there was no competing social entertainment, and the students anticipated the periodic socials eagerly and enjoyed them thoroughly. Smith was quite correct in his statement concerning happy marriages, for innumerable such unions were the result of courtships that began at the "proms."

Either late in 1890 or early the following year, a Young Men's Christian Association (YMCA) was organized on the campus by nineteen charter members. Within a few months, forty-five students were enrolled in the organization. Its activities included a Bible class on Sunday evenings, followed by a prayer service in the college chapel, conducted by one of the members. Several of the young men preached occasionally at different churches in the area. The students were impressed with the serious purpose of the association, which made the following report in October, 1892: "There are only one or two young men in College who have not united with us, and if prayer and solicitation will win them over, they will soon join our ranks for God and the right."[27]

Almost coincident with the publication of this statement, a Young Women's Christian Association (YWCA) was organized. Following the example of its male counterpart, the membership held gospel meetings every Sunday afternoon or Saturday evening. In 1893 "six Bible classes" of the two "Y's" were meeting one hour each week "for systematic Bible study." They also organized Sunday schools in the area, supplied teachers for such schools, and "established preaching points." By 1894 "every girl" and most of the men in the college had become active "Y" members, and both organizations continued throughout the years to be important phases of campus life.[28]

The Glee Club was another student activity that began soon after the college opened. The energetic members not only enjoyed their music, but were also interested in public performances. In February 1893 the club petitioned the faculty for permission "to have an entertainment" and charge admission. The proceeds obtained from the affair were to be used for the "further benefit of the Elon College Monthly." This request was granted, and the affair was doubtless a success.[29]

The object of the Glee Club's benevolence was the first publication undertaken by the students of the college. *The Elon College Monthly* was a joint enterprise of the three literary societies. In its first issue, dated June 1891, the purpose of the periodical was explained:

> We, the students of Elon College, have decided to put ourselves upon the plain of criticism. The idea has grown in our mind that we can publish a paper that will do to present to the public and herewith present the result of our first effort. . . . Where there is work, there is prosperity; where there is a mind, a working mind, there is progress.
>
> We beg that we may not be criticized too severely. We are young in the cause: we are "fresh." Bear with us patiently. If we go wrong, censure us, and we will thank you. If we do the best we can, bear gently with us. Give us an encouraging word and send in your name and your dollar.[30]

This simple statement marked the debut of the first medium for student expression at the college.

The *Monthly* usually contained twenty-five or more pages, seven by eleven inches in size. They were filled with articles and personal items written by students and included a few advertisements. During the approximately five years of the journal's publication, Professors E. L. Moffitt, R. G. Kendrick, Herbert Scholz, and Irene Johnson served terms as alumni editors. One student from each literary society formed the editorial staff. Serving one or more terms in that capacity were W. P. Lawrence, W. C. Wicker, J. W. Rawls, S. M. Smith, and W. D. Harward, from Phi; S. E. Everett, W. J. Graham, W. H. Albright, E. Moffitt, C. C. Ellis, J. E. Rawls, and P. P. Lee, from Cli; and Misses Irene Johnson, Annie Graham, Ella Johnson, and Irene Clements, from Psi. The business managers, also representing the three societies, included J. W. Rawls, S. M. Smith, and J. M. Cook, from Phi; W. J. Graham, J. H. Jones, and F. A. Holladay, from Cli; and Misses Annie Graham, Rowena Moffitt, and Florence Neff, from Psi.[31] Of these, Lawrence, Wicker, and Misses Graham and I. Johnson later became members of the teaching staff.

In 1894 a special issue was published by the female students. The editorial staff was composed of Misses Rowena Moffitt, Irene Clements, Emma Williamson, Ora Aldridge, Annie Gardner, and Jennie Herndon; Ella Johnson, Myrtle Daughtry, Ada Michael, Mollie Barrett, Florence Neff, and Ula Edwards were contributors.[32]

The contents of the various issues ranged from articles of general interest, such as "The Prisons of North Carolina," and "Should Women Be Allowed Suffrage," to others more pertinent to the college, such as "College Athletics" and "Reading Room Visitors." Editorials, YMCA Notes, Exchanges, and Personals were also a part of the format, and the latter featured alumni news.[33] Some of the contributions fomented administrative action, and all were at least generally informative to students and faculty. The *Monthly* served a useful purpose through 1896, after which its publication was discontinued for reasons unknown.

No athletic program existed at Elon during its opening years, though sessions of calisthenics were held regularly to maintain the health of the students. According to the catalog: "All are required to attend these exercises. They are not only exhilarating and healthful, developing and strengthening to all the bodily powers, but impart grace of motion and ease of carriage."[34] This program represented an acknowledgment of the value of physical exercise, but it did not go very far in supplying it.

A forthright summary of the situation was expressed by B. F. Long, Jr., in 1891 through the columns of the *Monthly*:

> I am sorry to say that the boys at Elon are not taking any exercise scarcely at all. . . .
>
> If the students would think how important it is for them to take exercise, they would, if they care anything for their health, no doubt do better.
>
> And now I appeal to the boys at Elon to try to see if they cannot do better in the future in this respect. The Faculty has kindly given us a ground and we can, by some work, make it one of the most beautiful in the State; and why not go to work and show our appreciation by putting it in condition for use?
>
> Why can't we have a foot ball team? We have as good material as any other college in the State—good active men, and a big center-rush. . . .

There is a pressing need now of a well equipped gymnasium at Elon. It would not cost a great deal and it would surely be a most benefitting thing to the students. Our health would be better, and we would be more capable of doing the work that lies before us. Let some friends of the institution who want to do something that will be of untold benefit to hundreds of boys and girls that will come here, equip a gymnasium, and thus add a most important feature to our college life.[35]

The writer's enthusiasm exerted an effect, though it was not until 1894 that the faculty granted permission for the "young men" to "arrange a room on the 3rd floor of the College Building for a gymnasium," on the condition that the lumber stored there be moved "to [a] place designated by the custodian." This was done, and the students "engaged the services of a local blacksmith to make a couple of swinging rings, and a shoe-maker covered them with leather." After this equipment was obtained, a "'skin-the-cat' pole was cut off the campus and securely fastened into the brick wall, a cannon-ball, secured from some place, was added, and the gymnasium was complete." Other equipment, of better design and construction, was later informally obtained and installed. When completed, the "gym" served its purpose adequately for a time, and constituted the nucleus from which an athletic program would be created at the college.[36]

At that time, Elon's first football team was also organized, to play intramural games. Years later, the team's captain, S. M. Smith (Elon '95), made the following comments about the new athletic organization:

The suits for the football team, as I recall, were made by some woman in the community. Every man on the team was supposed to wear long hair—about six inches at least. The game in those days was a sort of "knock-down-drag-out" affair, and it was necessary that the head be protected. Football harness such as the player of today wears had not been invented. The ball field was the southwest corner of the campus. I do not remember that we had any rules especially. The idea was to get the ball over the goal—just how we did it, didn't matter so much.[37]

In this manner, humorous as it seems today, football began as part of the athletic program of Elon College.

Both the Long administration and its successors attempted to keep the cost of attending the school as low as possible, but even so, the total expense represented a respectable financial outlay at the time. For the information of prospective students, an itemized list of anticipated expenses was published in the catalog.[38]

A dormitory for men on the campus was a primary need, and plans were made to give priority to such a project when finances permitted another building to be erected. Prospects for such expansion were dim in 1891, however, and for several years afterward, because the interior of the College Building contained unfinished sections and the proper equipment had not been added to the almost bare rooms in East Dormitory.

The incomplete condition of the buildings was publicized by a comment in the *Monthly*. In June 1891 under a column headed "Things That Make Me Tired," a contributor answered, "The scaffolding around the tower."[39] Referring to the same year, E. L. Moffitt later described the college:

> . . . letting my memory carry me back fifty years to this old grove, with its one building for administration, instruction and housing for male students, and it far from completed—walls not plastered, only a few split-bottom chairs for furnishings, no light but oil lamps, no heat but wood stoves, no water but the old college well, only five professors and two department teachers, and seventy-six students.[40]

This account by a contemporary did not paint a rosy picture, but it was doubtless accurate.

At the time of these frank comments, almost half of the total cost of the college, estimated at $16,000 in 1890,[41] remained unpaid. The trustees had borrowed money to make the first two buildings at least usable for the opening of the institution; they preferred to incur indebtedness rather than abandon the enterprise. To obtain the necessary loans, the board mortgaged the college property by executing deeds of trust to the following individuals: Clifford A. Norfleet, $400; D. A. Long, $4,000; W. H. Trolinger, $4,000; W. S. Long, $1,883.95; George Kernodle, $1,000; and John A. Mills, $1,258.62.[42] The total borrowed was $12,542.57, part of which was tendered in building materials and services and part in money, but the entire sum was spent on constructing and equipping the college buildings.

The Elon officials intended to retire this debt within a reasonably short time with contributions from the Christian Church and individuals, while barely paying current operating expenses with tuition received from the students. Unfortunately, plans for repayment were rudely interrupted by the disastrous Panic of 1893, which paralyzed the nation's economy. As a result, anticipated funds were not donated, which left the institution in a precarious financial condition as the interest mounted on debts it could not pay. The operation of the school continued by means of frugal management, but the situation was not an enviable one.

Because almost no clearing had been done on the "back," or north, campus, it was a thick grove of "oaks only two or three inches in diameter." The "front," or south, campus, the area between the buildings and the railroad, "had been cleared of large trees and undergrowth," but the brush which was cut down "had not been heaped and burned." During the first year of the college's operation, 1890, this unsightly rubbish was removed by the male students, according to N. G. Newman, who was one of their number:

> The final roundup of that [cleanup] was completed on one lovely Saturday morning in the spring of 1891 by the college boys, led and inspired by Prof. Atkinson. It was just in front of the East Dormitory, by this time completed and occupied by girls. These college lassies, with long dresses, long hair, and without rouge on their faces (can you believe it?) came out with the old fashioned cedar bucket and tin ladle and coyly and sweetly did the office of "water boy" to the great delectation of the thirsty toilers. A great occasion.[43]

This donation of physical endeavor for work the college could not afford to hire showed a pride in the institution on the part of the students that increased as time passed.

After this initial contribution, the students and faculty were unable to care for the extensive grounds to any further extent and they were neglected while construction was being fostered. This condition brought forth a criticism in 1893 from another unhappy contributor to the *Monthly*, who felt it would be "advisable—yes, a step in the right direction, to get our Campus in a little better dress before Commencement. Say, have those brick piles, etc., on the North side of the College [moved] for instance. A little grading on the walks would also help the appearance of things."[44] The harassed administration was fully aware of such defects and exceedingly anxious to correct them, but, when mortgages remained unpaid, no funds could be spared for campus beautification.

Under the circumstances, the students and faculty continued their efforts to improve their alma mater, especially during the 1892 spring term. The chapel, which was used more often by everyone at the college than any other room in the College Building, aroused their interest because of its condition. In Professor Atkinson's words, "There it stood. . . . with bleak, bare walls as unpolished and homely as they were mighty and repulsive." The effort to improve the room began with a meeting held in February at which faculty members were requested to pledge $10 each and students $5 each. In short order, $440 was pledged and the campaign began. Most of the students raised their contributions by soliciting their friends and parents. In March workmen were engaged in plastering the walls and ceiling. The project was soon completed, "making even a nicer appearance" than anticipated, and the students "were the principal medium through which the work was accomplished."[45]

This improvement helped stimulate the acquisition of better furnishings. In the summer of 1893, a pulpit for use in the chapel was presented to the college. The donor was Samuel L. Adams, a Durham lawyer, who later resided for several years in the town of Elon College. Inspired by this generosity, the administration strained its meager resources to order "opera chairs" for the room. Dr. Long predicted that, when they were installed, the chapel would be "a magnificent one indeed."[46]

Nothing further could be spent on the College Building at the time because East Dormitory demanded some attention. Plans were made to remodel it before the 1893 fall term began. Porches were to be added, blinds attached to the windows, the rooms carpeted, and grates installed so that coal could be used for heating. These improvements were intended to make the dormitory a "comfortable" and "desirable home for the girls," while also serving as a place for the boys rooming in the college "to take table board."[47] When this step was concluded, the institution could go no further until its indebtedness was liquidated, or at least reduced.

Meanwhile, that which had been accomplished required safeguarding, for disaster was always a possibility. In 1892 a blaze broke out in East Dormitory. "Lack of water made control of the fire difficult, but it was extinguished with damage confined to one room."[48] The danger to the college property from fire was emphasized in 1893 by the press:

> There came near to being a serious fire at Elon College one morning the latter part of last week. The fire was in one of the recitation rooms and was making some headway when discovered and was promptly put out. But for the closeness of the room, doubtless the elegant building would have been consumed. President Long on his usual round the night before found no fire in the room, hence the origin is unknown.[49]

Virtually no effective means of extinguishing a major conflagration were available at either the institution or in the town at the time, a handicap from which both suffered seriously for many years. The W. L. Smith and Company store went up in flames in 1891,[50] and other losses by fire in the town and college were to follow. The only real safety lay in fire prevention. The president was keenly aware of the need for this precaution, and he added his nightly tours of inspection to his multitudinous duties for that reason.

Except for eating and sleeping, the entire program of the school was carried out in the College Building. For this reason, the industrious faculty worked out a tight schedule, without which such a variety of activity, functioning simultaneously under one roof, would have created bedlam. The structure even served as the meeting place of the Elon College Christian Church, organized for the entire community immediately after the institution opened its doors, as President Long had promised. The loss of the building at the time would probably have ended the operation of the college, and every possible caution was taken to prevent such a calamity.

Despite all the obstacles and handicaps, by 1894 a total of 257 undergraduate students had matriculated at the college: 157 males and 100 females. Of these, 180 were from North Carolina, 76 from Virginia, and 1 from South Carolina. At the close of commencement that year, a total of 22 students had been graduated. These facts are a testimony to the success of the early years.[51]

The gigantic effort required to produce these admirable results had naturally taken its toll on the chief executive. As he said in a letter to the *Sun* in January 1894:

> On the 6th inst. I tendered my resignation as president of Elon to take effect at commencement next June, at which time the trustees hold their regular meeting. As some of the state papers have already referred to it, will you please insert this that the public may know my reasons for doing so, and understand the situation.
>
> In projecting this institution, soliciting funds, building, equipping, organizing, teaching, arranging affairs pertaining to the college within and without, the toil and care has been very exhausting. After five years of almost constant thought and unremitting attention to this enterprise I want relief that I may recuperate and enter some other field of usefulness.
>
> The college is firmly established in the heart of the people. It has a good patronage, and a strong and devoted faculty, of ten members. God will bless and prosper this work now and forever.
>
> > Very truly,
> > W. S. Long[52]

The resignation was regretfully accepted. It gave Long some respite, but it did not terminate his usefulness to the college. For several years, he continued to maintain his residence in the town. He served as adviser and financial agent for the institution for several years, and worked privately for its progress the remainder of his life. His contribution as the leader in founding and opening the college are acknowledged on its campus today by the handsome William S. Long Student Center, completed in 1966. Its lobby is ornamented by the former president's portrait, presented to Elon by his family at a Founders Day convocation two years after the facility was opened. On that occasion, the portrait was unveiled by Katherine Allene Williams and Talmadge P. Nelson, great, great granddaughter and great, great grandson of Long, respectively. In accepting the gift, J. Earl Danieley, then president of the institution, quoted a tribute from W. A. Harper, another former president of the college, who had praised the first executive as the "educational prophet of his native county and of his denomination."[53]

In addition to this commemoration, during the Danieley administration the trustees authorized the coveted title of "William S. Long Professor" to be awarded to some member of the faculty, which honored both the recipient and the memory of the founding president.

Dr. Long continued to reside in the town of Elon College for several years before selling the house he had built at 101 North O'Kelley Avenue (razed in 1978). He then moved to Graham and later to Chapel Hill. His first wife having died in 1903, he married Mrs. Mary Virginia Gaskins Ames. He continued to participate actively in the field of education until shortly before his death on August 3, 1924, in an automobile accident.[54]

CHAPTER IV

THE SAPLING

He is like a tree planted by streams of water,
that yields its fruit in its season,
and its leaf does not wither.
PSALMS 1:3

The increasing number of students and residents at the college during the first five years of its existence was accompanied by a proportionate commercial growth of the town. During the period, the mercantile establishments included the general stores of H. L. Hines;
Kernodle, Swain, and Kernodle; York, Edwards and Company; W. L.
Smith and Company; Herndon and Young; and C. A. Boone and Son,
which later became the store of T. G. Lowe and J. P. Mebane, trading
as Lowe and Mebane. Produce was handled by R. L. Ray before he
sold his business to Thomas E. Porter and Company. Several years
later, J. J. Lambeth's store succeeded the Porter enterprise. Shoes
were repaired by T. P. Whitesell, and Dr. George W. Kernodle opened
a small drugstore.

Three livery stables, operated by the Whitesell brothers, J. B. Gerringer, and Peter Hughes, respectively, were available for horsedrawn
transportation, which was often a necessity as well as a luxury of the
day. Mr. and Mrs. W. L. Smith were the proprietors of the Elon College Hotel, which offered "Meals at any Hour, Transient 25¢, Drum-
mers 50¢, Monthly Board from $10 to $15." The hotel was a valuable
asset to the community because it supplied the only accommodations for visitors who were not guests in private homes. The building is standing today at 113 West Trollinger Avenue and is the home
of Thomas L. Smith, the builder's son.[1]

The original railroad station, built for handling freight at Mill

Point, was on the north side of the tracks in the present 100 block of West Lebanon Avenue and contained no facilities for passenger traffic. The constantly increasing number of people using the trains was responsible for a news article in 1891 which announced that the Southern Railway planned to "enlarge the present depot at Elon College. On the opposite side of the tracks, the RR will erect a ticket office, telegraph office, and reception room."[2] This building, if it was constructed, was soon outgrown, for in 1894 the college faculty voted to request "a waiting room provided at the depot." No results were obtained from this action apparently, nor from a similar one the following year in which the present station was declared "inadequate." In 1897 the college and town administrations combined efforts to dispatch the chairman of the faculty to meet with the railroad commissioners at Raleigh "in the interest of a better depot." It was some time before this request bore fruit, but the mutual effort eventually succeeded.[3]

A spirit of cooperation usually prevailed between the college and the town, but occasionally they were not in harmony. By the authority of its corporate charter, the town's jurisdiction extended two miles from its municipal limits, within which area the sale of alcoholic beverages was prohibited by ordinance. The college charter specified that "no spiritous or intoxicating liquors" should be manufactured or sold within one and one-half miles of the campus, and in addition, the institution's regulations forbade the students to use intoxicants. In January 1899 a petition reportedly bearing two hundred signatures "from a good portion of the country" was sent to the state legislature requesting Elon College's town limits be reduced from three miles to one and one-half miles. Whether or not the municipal officials sanctioned this action cannot be determined because the records for the period no longer exist. However, the college authorities blamed the move on the "whiskey element," and adamantly objected to the change that could bring the legal sale of alcoholic beverages closer to the institution. "If any change be made we suggest that the corporate limits be extended to five miles," was the comment in the *Sun*.[4]

A counter petition was soon drafted, "signed by all the best men in the community," to be presented to the General Assembly "alongside the other." W. S. Long and E. L. Moffitt, editor of the *Sun*, were then dispatched to Raleigh by the Elon trustees to present their case to W. H. Carroll, Alamance County's legislative representative. As a result of this opposition, the objectionable bill was defeated in a legislative committee meeting. The outcome was unmistakable evidence that the college, though unable to control affairs outside its jurisdiction, could and would exert its influence to prevent any real or imaginary threat to its disciplinary standards.[5]

When Long resigned the presidency, the trustees elected the Reverend William Wesley Staley to the post. The minister, born in 1849, was a native of Alamance County, North Carolina, the son of John T. and Melissa Day Staley. Within a few years after his birth, Mrs. Staley was widowed, and the son labored industriously while a youth to help support her, even becoming a mail carrier at the age of fifteen for the Confederate government. The widow remarried, and her dutiful son later served as a benefactor to his half-brothers and sisters.[6]

Staley studied under the Long brothers at Graham High School before graduating from Trinity College (now Duke University) in 1874. That same year, he became a member of the Graham High School faculty and was also ordained into the ministry of the Christian Church. In 1877 and 1878 he pursued graduate studies at the University of Virginia. The next year, he married Martha F. Pearce, settled in Graham with his bride, and served for several years as Superintendent of Public Instruction for Alamance County.[7]

In 1882 Staley accepted a call to the pastorate of the Christian Church, in Suffolk, Virginia, one of the most prominent posts in the denomination. His success was immediate, and, within a few years, a new $40,000 church building was constructed and dedicated. When the Elon presidency was offered to him, he felt he could not conscientiously leave his growing congregation. In addition, it may also have been financially difficult to move his residence at the time because he had contributed a year's salary to the building of the new church.[8] Furthermore, Elon faculty salaries during the opening year averaged only $267.80, though the president undoubtedly received a larger sum.[9] Remuneration had increased by only a small degree in 1894, and Staley simply may not have possessed sufficient funds to relocate his family of a wife and three daughters. In addition to these factors, another, and perhaps the most influential of all, was that Staley liked Suffolk and Suffolk liked Staley, a mutual esteem that continued for the remainder of his life. The clergyman responded to

President William W. Staley.

the strong pressure exerted to retain him in his pastorate, but, at the same time, he was not indifferent to the welfare of his denominational college and was more than willing to serve it in any manner possible under the circumstances. After the trustees adamantly refused to select another candidate, he finally agreed to become a nonresident president, without salary or expense account, and his proposal was immediately accepted.[10]

To attend to his executive duties, Staley made frequent trips from Suffolk to Elon for supervisory and administrative purposes. Dr. J. U. Newman was elected chairman of the faculty and took charge of numerous routine matters formerly handled by the president. In September 1903 Newman became the Dean, when the title first came into use at the college. Earlier, in September 1895, the title of bursar had first been used, and a faculty member was designated to serve as the financial custodian of the institution.[11] Atkinson replaced Long as pastor of the college church. Under this plan, the faculty attended to a major part of the administration, which left the president free to wrestle with the serious financial condition of the institution.

Although a college president in absentia seemed an awkward arrangement in many ways, the decision of the trustees bore fruit. Staley proved to be the man needed at the time. Because of the prestige he enjoyed in Suffolk as pastor of the Christian Church and president of the denominational college, he directed his efforts toward obtaining assistance from one of the financial institutions in that city. His efforts were successful, for on July 21, 1895, the Farmers' Bank of Nansemond loaned the trustees of Elon College $20,000, secured by a deed of trust on the college property. Half the sum was "to pay present indebtedness," and half was to be used for needed improvements. Ten days later, the preexisting mortgages on the institution's property were paid, which placed Elon College for the first time since it opened in a position to forge ahead.[12]

After the debts of the college were paid, the classrooms were vastly improved by the installation of sorely needed furnishings and equipment. Highly welcome additions to the College Building were several stoves, purchased for use in its lofty rooms instead of the less satisfactory fireplaces. Both the students and faculty also appreciated the proper type of desks, chairs, and tables.

While these welcome changes were taking place, the Southern

Christian Convention in 1896 made a specific recommendation for major improvements:

> (a) That the trustees of Elon College be requested to remodel the girl's dormitory, enlarge the rooms, complete the front, add to the north end, making about 30 first-class bed-rooms, a study room for the girls, room for superintendent and matron, dining hall and kitchen. The building should be supplied with water, and constructed so as to have the sanitary arrangements complete. A modern structure throughout. (b) that the women of the Christian church be requested to furnish the girl's dormitory; . . . (c) That there be a study room for boys is [in] the main building of the college.[13]

These suggestions were acceptable to the college officials, and plans were immediately put in motion to carry them out. A major part of the work was completed within two years, when the convention found East Dormitory "in excellent condition for the young ladies of the institution."[14]

The Elon trustees, never indifferent to their responsibilities, realized that the improvements had only been made possible by means of the large mortgage remaining to be paid. To meet that obligation, the board decided in June 1897 to issue bonds in the total amount of $20,000 to run ten years and pay 6 percent interest. The Southern Christian Convention met the following year (by this time it convened biennially instead of quadrennially), and endorsed the plan.

Acknowledging the responsibility of the church as the sponsor of the college, the convention approved a systematic means of aiding it financially:

> 1. That the conferences composing this convention be requested to pay annually the sum of $1,600 until these bonds are paid; that the apportionment be as follows: E. Va. Conference, $600; N.C. and Va. Conference, $325; Eastern N.C. Conference, $275; Western N.C. Conference, $250; Va. Valley Conference, $75; and the Ga. and Ala. Conference, $75. This money to constitute a college fund to be used in paying principal and interest on these bonds. That each conference pay the several sums annually to the treasurer of the college, to be used in paying the present indebtedness.[15]

In addition to this apportionment, the ministers and laymen of the church were urged to cooperate in every manner possible "to increase the patronage of the institution."

It is significant that the convention's Committee on Schools and Colleges provided the approved suggestions for additional construction and the financial plan to aid the college. The chairman of this committee for several terms was W. S. Long, and in 1898 James O. Atkinson, E. L. Moffitt, W. C. Wicker, and P. H. Fleming were his fellow committeemen. All were members of the college faculty except Fleming, who was secretary of the board of trustees.[16] The institution was fortunate in having a group so aware of its needs serve as its liaison with the convention, from which support was essential.

Although the financial plan "met a favorable response on the part of all the conferences,"[17] the money forthcoming could be used only for debt liquidation and not for further improvements. The funds that had been borrowed, helpful as they were, had been insufficient to complete the building program. As a result, in 1899 the disappointed faculty requested President Staley "to suggest some plan to finish the first and second floor of the college."[18] Money was also needed for expansion because, by commencement of the following year, 563 students had matriculated at the college since it opened, and 58 graduated, of which 26 had entered the ministry. The college had rapidly outgrown its meager facilities, and could not expand without a larger and improved plant in which to operate.[19]

Acutely aware of this condition, Long's committee presented these statistics to the convention at its 1900 session, and accompanied them with a proposal for increased support:

> We urge that the Trustees be requested to provide for these urgent needs of the college, and that this Convention pledge its hearty co-operation:
>
> 1. (a) The completion of the college building. (b) The enlargement of the girls boarding hall. (c) The enlargement of the college library. (d) The establishment of a chair in theology.
>
> 2. We recommend that the conferences be urgently requested to send up the full apportionment for the payment of the college debt.
>
> 3. We recommend (1) A call for a twentieth century Free-will

offering for education, to be known as the Twentieth Century Fund of the Christian Church, South.

The amount of this fund was to be "a minimum of $20,000," to be raised by increasing the apportionment for Elon of each individual church 12½ times its former figure.[20] The proposal was adopted, and hope for the college's expansion revived.

The chair of theology included in the convention's authorization was not a new idea, and the events connected with the subject led to major benefits for Elon College. In 1886 the General Convention had voted to establish and give financial support for such a position at Suffolk Collegiate Institute, and elected W. W. Staley to fill it. Four years later, when the convention next met, because Staley had resigned from the assignment, the chair was transferred to the newly opened Elon College.[21] This was in effect an empty gesture, for no funds were supplied for its maintenance and support. The result was that a chair of theology never existed as a separate position on the college faculty. This did not reflect indifference on the part of the academic administration, but, because of the financial strain in founding the school, the matter had to be postponed. Long and his colleagues optimistically envisioned not only a chair but also a Department of Theology that would eventually become a seminary at Elon for the purpose of training ministers for the Christian Church, all of which were a part of future plans.

Hope for such an eventuality was raised in 1896 by the announcement of a gift from Francis Asbury Palmer, a wealthy banker and philanthropist of New York City. Interested in fostering ministerial training, he selected four institutions, of which Elon College was one, and offered to found and endow a Chair of Christian Ethics at each. The trust fund he proposed to set up would yield $2,000 annually to each institution for the support of the position. The donor named the Reverend T. M. McWhinney, of Ohio, nonresident professor to visit all four schools for lectures, and chose Dr. W. S. Long to be resident professor at Elon.[22]

While the negotiations made necessary by this philanthropy were in progress, Palmer's interest deepened in the college he was never to see. This moved him to bequeath $30,000 to it in his will. Then learning of the need for immediate financial improvement, in 1901 he offered to advance $20,000 of the bequest provided the college raised $12,000 within a specified length of time. After a strenuous effort, the challenge was met by the February 1, 1902, deadline, and the Southern Christian Convention gratefully received the gift for its college. The Twentieth Century Fund, which had accounted for $10,940.17 of the money donated to meet the challenge, was then dissolved as no longer necessary.[23]

The New York banker was pleased with the response to his benevolence, and then offered to advance the remaining $10,000 of the legacy, provided the denomination would raise $8,000. Efforts were being made to meet this challenge when he died on November 2, 1902. It was then learned that his faith in Elon was sufficient for him to leave instructions for the remaining bequest to be paid regardless. The struggling institution thus received the $10,000, and also raised the sum no longer necessary to meet the challenge conditions. Both

Student-faculty group about 1896. The last two men in the back row on the right are students L. L. Lassiter and C. H. Rowland; the seated man in the front row is Professor J. O. Atkinson; the others cannot be identified.

tokens of Palmer's generosity were the largest windfalls the infant institution had received up to that time.[24]

Preceding Palmer's generosity, the first gift made to the endowment fund was $1,000 from the Reverend O. J. Wait, of Fall River, Massachusetts, and the second was $25 from the Reverend J. J. Summerbell, editor of *The Herald of Gospel Liberty*. Both these men belonged to the Christian denomination in the North and, like Palmer, had never seen Elon College.[25] Other gifts were also made and appreciated. This enabled the Committee on Schools and Colleges to proudly inform the 1904 session of the convention, "It is a matter for thanksgiving to God that the college is, for the first time in its history, out of debt, with buildings completed, and the sum of $30,000.00 to the credit of the Endowment Fund, the income from which is $1,505.00 a year."[26]

The glad tidings were also announced to the public by the ever-sympathetic *Gleaner*:

> Rev. Dr. W. W. Staley, Prest. of Elon College, arrived here Monday night from Suffolk, Va. Tuesday morning he had a mortgage which was originally for $20,000 cancelled off record in the office of the Register of Deeds. He stated that the college is now clear of debt, which should be a matter of great joy to all friends of the institution. We learn from Dr. Staley that the erection of a new and commodious dormitory with all modern conveniences is under advisement. The school needs more dormitory room to enable it to accommodate its growing patronage.[27]

Attaining the enviable position of owning the college property free of encumbrances, plus a substantial endowment safely invested,[28] relieved the Elon board of trustees, but it did not end their financial problems. During the first decade of the college's existence, an attempt was made to pay the operating expenses with the tuition and fees received from students, while contributions and the Southern Christian Convention support was used for building construction. This plan, born of necessity, was speculative from the beginning and proved a dismal failure. The charges for board and room barely enabled the dormitory and dining hall to operate without a loss, but the tuition was insufficient to pay the personnel. From

1890 through 1902, only $39,959.31 was received from fees to apply against a total payroll of $49,372.85; the deficit was $9,413.54. This loss of almost $800 annually had to be paid with funds earmarked for construction, which further delayed the completion and expansion of the physical plant.[29]

This situation was not caused by an increase in faculty pay, which averaged $367.81 in 1890 and only $386.55 in 1902, but no salary was included for the president in the latter figure because he was serving without remuneration at the time. However, the total payroll more than doubled during the decade inasmuch as the staff was increased from six to twelve members because of the growing student body. The low pay did not appear to affect individual motivation, as attested by Staley when he informed the 1902 session of the convention that the "faithful and efficient" faculty "works for less salary than any other first-class church college."[30] Dealing with this situation was one of the next major tasks facing the trustees.

President Staley concluded that the answer to the problem was to increase the size of the student body. He was reluctant to raise tuition fees, for doing so might make attendance financially prohibitive for some prospective students. He reasoned that larger classes could be conducted without an immediate addition to the teaching staff, but more students could not be enrolled until housing could be provided for them. The answer was a new dormitory, but no funds were on hand with which to build one. The trustees agreed with the executive's proposal, but were opposed to going into debt again. Contributions for the purpose did not materialize to any encouraging extent at the time, and the matter was postponed from one board meeting to another without decisive action.[31]

The happy climax of the financial campaign, in 1904, had not been foreseen two years earlier, when meeting the Palmer challenge appeared only a remote possibility. During the laborious efforts to raise money, it became evident that sentiment was growing in the Christian Church opposing operation of the college with a nonresident president. The hardworking and poorly paid faculty rallied to their executive's defense by passing a resolution, which also requested some relief for its members:

> Whereas many and devious rumors are extant regarding the
> future presidency of Elon College, and feeling that such discus-

sions are not promotive of good, we the faculty in session desire

First, to express our appreciation of and confidence in Dr. W. W. Staleys [*sic*] administration as president.

Second, That for the best interest of the College, he be continued in said position.

Third, That the present Chairman of the Faculty be continued but that he be relieved of the work of Custodian of buildings and grounds.

Fourth, that the literary work of the College be continued in departments as at present, and that one person be added to the Faculty to meet the demands of the Ac. [Academic] Department.[32]

By 1905 the faculty had become less patient because the institution was then out of debt, but no improvements to the school or financial relief for the staff appeared forthcoming. For the most part, the instructors were young, enthusiastic, and ambitious for both the college and themselves. This was to be expected, for a number of them were alumni. However, they had homes to build and pay for, families to rear, and higher degrees to earn if possible. When the trustees continued to postpone action, they expressed their sentiments in a letter, which was a response to an inquiry from the president:

Moved that we say in reply to Dr. Staley that we wish neither to criticize nor condemn for neglected duty. That is not within our province but our purpose is rather to impart information as seen from the actual needs of the Institution.

1. There is a great need of having better methods in our boarding arrangements for young ladies, for more room, and better sanitary conditions.

2. There is a great need of having better methods in our boarding arrangements for young men where they can be kept under better discipline.

3. There is strong pressure brought to bear by the growing sentiment of the church that we must move forward and we the Faculty at the center of operations are fully convinced that unless we move forward that the College cannot hold its own.[33]

Immediately after taking this action, "Professor Lawrence was appointed to appear before the Board of Trustees & make known the needs of the Institution as seen from the standpoint of the Faculty."[34]

Upon receiving his staff's opinion, and influenced possibly by other considerations, Staley reasoned that his major tasks had been accomplished and that the time was ripe for a change in leadership. Accordingly, he resigned the presidency at the June 1905 commencement, and Professor Emmett Leonidas Moffitt was elected to the position.[35]

Staley's retirement was amicable, and Elon had every reason to be proud of his administration. He not only served eleven years as president without salary or expenses, but paid full tuition for his three daughters, Bessie ('98), Annie ('02), and Willie May ('04), to attend the college,[36] in addition to making personal donations to the institution. In his obituary, it was estimated that the value of his services and gifts was the equivalent of about $30,000.[37]

While the officials grappled with the problems of indebtedness and future expansion during the Staley administration, means were somehow found to make a number of improvements in existing facilities. Additional equipment was added to the science laboratories and classrooms. In 1894 the college museum was founded and housed in the College Building. B. F. Black, a student, was made curator of the "many donations of historic interest and curiosities," including a collection of minerals especially useful to the geology classes. The project aroused the interest of North Carolina Congressman W. W. Kitchin, whose influence was responsible for a gift from the Smithsonian Institution, of Washington, of five hundred natural history specimens for the collection. These included a large number of marine invertebrates and "a set of casts of prehistoric relics."[38]

Samuel L. Adams, a Durham lawyer who had become a resident of the town of Elon College, contributed a portrait of his ancestor, Richard Stanford, founder of an academy, who also was a member of the North Carolina delegation in the U.S. House of Representatives from 1796 until he died in 1816, while still in office. The donor also gave the museum original copies of Stanford's letters to his wife, his century-old traveling trunk, and pages from the "annuals of Congress with extracts of speech on removal of the National Capital, in which Edenton, N.C. is suggested." H. W. Scott, then mayor of Graham, presented a German Bible, printed in Berlin in 1778, and purchased at the sale of personal effects of Mrs. Catherine Albright. Although 115 years old, the book was "in a good state of preservation."[39] Under Black's dedicated curatorship, the collection of scientific and historic items grew rapidly in size and interest until the museum became one of the most interesting features of the college.

By 1895 it had become evident that the increasing number of men and women who had studied at Elon were interested in a continued relationship of some kind with their alma mater. This fact was responsible for a meeting on June 13 in the YMCA Hall that formed the Elon College Alumni Association. The organizers were N. G. Newman, Herbert Scholz, both of the class of 1891; Irene Johnson, 1892; Annie Graham and W. C. Wicker, 1893; S. A. Holleman, Rowena Moffitt, and W. P. Lawrence, 1894; and J. W. Harrell, Irene Clements, and S. M. Smith, 1895. The purpose of the organization was to maintain "as far as possible, the memory of College days among the Alumni, and to keep their interest united for the good of the College."[40]

W. P. Lawrence was elected as secretary, and he immediately informed the public through the columns of the *Sun* that the first project of the group was to add a thousand books to the library, especially in the field of English literature. Largely because of this effort, during the school year 1897–98, 190 volumes were added to the library, which increased the total collection to 1,401 books. In that same period, 1,110 books and 1,160 periodicals were borrowed by the students, a testimony to the usefulness of the facility.[41]

The association also sponsored reunions of former students at the annual commencements, and one of those attending was chosen to deliver the Alumni Address, or Oration, on the occasion. (For a list of Alumni Orators, 1896–1954, see Appendix C.) A banquet was also enjoyed, a custom that is still part of the college program, though now held on Alumni Day. By 1897 thirty-nine members were enrolled in the association, which became and continues to be a primary asset of Elon.[42] In many ways, the founding of this organization was the most significant event in the first decade of the institution's operation.

The policy of the college from its opening was to present guest speakers whenever possible, but, because of the expense involved,

Miss M. Irene Johnson (later Mrs. John M. Cook) was the first woman to graduate from Elon and the first female member of its faculty.

the program was usually limited to single addresses by persons nearby. However, in 1897, through the generosity of F. A. Palmer, the Reverend Frank S. Child, pastor of the First Congregational Church, of Fairfield, Connecticut, gave a series of lectures on history and literature during a week's visit to the campus. His "scholarship, eloquence, and spiritual power" were so pleasing that arrangements were made with the New York philanthropist to sponsor a similar series annually. Child was eventually made a nonresident member of the faculty and honored with the degrees of D.D. (sometime before 1900) and LL.D. (1911). This was the real beginning of special presentations by scholars from in and out of the state, a feature that was to grow in importance as the years rolled by.

During the Staley administration, the trustees also voted to award honorary D.D. degrees to Caleb A. Tillinghast, R. S. G. McNeille, Alva H. Morrill, and James O. Atkinson.[43]

During the early years of the college's operation, sometime before 1894, an Athletic Association had been formed. Headed by a staff member, its purpose was to enroll all male students as members for a small fee, and to encourage intramural sports as far as the limited facilities permitted. The membership dues, supplemented by occasional ice cream suppers and dramas for which admission was charged, supplied the meager funds for purchasing athletic equipment.[44] Plans for female participation in the program were held in abeyance until additional facilities could be procured.

Typical of the association's activities was the field day held on November 24, 1894, at which time a "large crowd" witnessed the different games and contests. These included a tennis match; a 100-yard dash; and broad, running, and standing high jumps. The culminating event was a football game, in which the newly organized intramural team participated. The players on the first team of the sport recorded at the college included B. F. Black, S. M. Smith, G. C. Wadford, C. C. Ellis, A. Brothers, J. E. Rawls, J. C. Holladay, F. A. Holladay, J. P. Lee, T. L. Moore, and W. H. Young. They were defeated in a contest against students who lived in the residences of President Long and Professor Holleman.[45]

Facilities for playing the game must have been crude because the college then apparently lacked a properly graded gridiron, and the playing field has not been identified. Neither has any additional record of the team's performance been found, but presumably it engaged in other contests inasmuch as A. R. Lawrence, athletic editor of the *Monthly*, predicted, "We cannot, and do not, expect to win many games, but we can win some."[46] Nevertheless, regardless of the results, in 1894 Elon College fielded an "official" football team.

Because of the increasing enthusiasm for sports, the confinement of Elon's athletic program to intramural games had not completely satisfied the student body during Long's administration, nor did it do so under his successor. Agitation was growing for participation in intercollegiate games, a problem Staley inherited and which he turned over to the trustees and his faculty for solution.

Interest was especially keen in baseball games played by teams of the educational institutions in the state against each other. Elon students were proud of their school and its athletic potential, real or

Some students and faculty in 1896. Only part of the group can be identified. The fourth, fifth, sixth, and seventh in the second row are Professor J. U. Newman, President W. W. Staley, and Professors W. P. Lawrence and S. A. Holleman, the ninth is C. H. Rowland; the fifth in the third row is L. L. Lassiter, the ninth is L. I. Cox, the tenth is J. E. Rawls; the third in the fourth row is C. E. Newman, the seventh is J. W. Harrell.

imagined. They were anxious to join in the competition, but the rules did not allow the men "to leave the College to engage in athletic contests." However, permission was obtained in 1899 to play a game at Elon with Bingham, a nearby preparatory school. The contest took place on a crude diamond near the campus in an area that had formerly been a cornfield. This was Elon's first baseball game with another school. The results were not impressive; the visitors won by a score of 25 to 5. Undaunted by this defeat, however, the Athletic Association petitioned the trustees for authority to participate in intercollegiate games, which meant playing away from the college, but the faculty declined to endorse the request. This left the decision in the hands of the board.[47]

When the matter was broached to the trustees, they authorized the faculty to use its judgment in the matter. Thus empowered to act, the staff took a tolerant view of the situation to some extent, and in 1900 approved an occasional game with another institution away from the campus, subject to the following stipulations:

> 1st. A failure to make a grade of 70 on any subject or being demerited by the faculty shall prevent any student playing on an inter-collegiate game.
>
> 2nd. Any student under 21 years of age must have written permission from parent or guardian to the Chairman before being allowed in an inter-collegiate game.
>
> 3rd. All parties must be bona fide students for two weeks previous to the inter-collegiate game that play in the match game.
>
> 4th. None but those who are placed on the match team are allowed to go to any contest if on school day and if on holiday rules for visiting away from the College apply.[48]

Permission was then granted to play at Guilford College on March 31, and the same team on April 14 at Elon College. The faculty approved all the players requested for Elon's first intercollegiate contest except one, who was "adjudged not eligible for being inattentive to class duty and smoking cigarettes." Although Elon was defeated in both games, by scores of 38 to 3 and 32 to 3, the students were jubilant over having won the concession to play against other college teams.[49]

Once the policy was established, other games were occasionally permitted, but the rules were strictly upheld. The members of the team for each contest were approved separately, and no student was allowed to play if he had not conformed with the regulations. This was not entirely satisfactory to the student body, but the faculty stood firm in enforcing its requirements. Among the teams played during this period were those from the Bingham School and nearby Whitsett Institute. A practice game with a Burlington team was also permitted. In 1905 the faculty approved a recommendation from the Athletic Association that provided for tuition to be offered to two men to train the baseball team and play on it. This is the first instance of approving paid athletic participation at the college and the beginning of the coaching system.[50]

After this departure from custom, the faculty took the precautionary measure of approving two rules recommended by its Athletic Committee: that persons so employed be professors of the Christian religion; and that student athletes should make grades of the average of 80 percent.[51] The second stipulation was the only one that seriously affected the players, and the college was on its way toward increasing participation in college baseball.

Football also aroused interest. In 1900 Miss Jennie T. Herndon, of the faculty, and a Mr. Eley, a student, requested approval of an ex-

Freshman class, 1901–2.

hibition game of that sport in Burlington, but the chairman of the faculty ruled it out of order "by action of the Trustees." However, T. R. Jones was allowed as an individual to play in the state contest that year.[52]

In 1904 A. L. Lincoln and Long Holleman presented a petition from the Elon Tennis Club requesting permission to accept the Bingham Tennis Club's invitation for a match. This was referred to the faculty Athletic Committee and probably approved.[53] Tennis

Women students resting beneath the Senior Oak after a game of tennis, in the early 1900s.

was popular at the college and the court, located about where the A. L. Hook Dormitory now stands, was in frequent use during good weather. Later, two additional courts were constructed in the northwestern corner of the campus near the present site of McEwen Dining Hall. The southwestern corner of the campus, now the library parking lot, was designated for playing baseball and other games. No suitable field for football existed at the institution. All the other facilities were used to the utmost as athletics continued to grow in

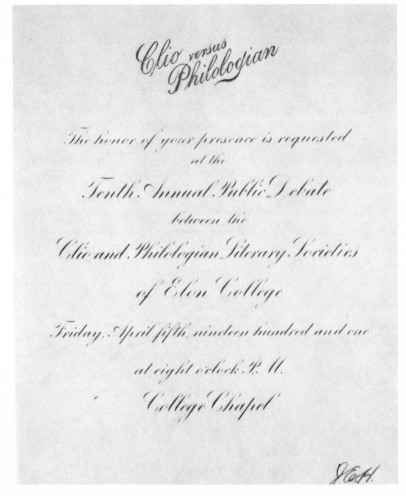

Invitation to the annual Clio-Philologian literary societies debate in 1901. These occasions were highlights of the college program.

popularity and students increased their participation, regardless of whether or not games were won or lost.

Enthusiastic as they were over sports, the students also demonstrated strong scholastic interests. In October 1900 the faculty granted permission for the student body to arrange an intercollegiate debate with Guilford College. Many similar contests were to follow with other institutions.[54]

Another major accomplishment during Staley's administration was the final completion of the College Building, in 1903. This long-awaited achievement was attributable primarily to individual campaigning. Miss Herndon, daughter of the Reverend W. T. Herndon, had pursued further studies after her graduation in 1896 and returned to teach elocution and physical education at the college. She personally raised $500 for the project, an effort that aroused the interest of others. Colonel Robert L. Holt, of Burlington, donated several hundred dollars, and additional contributions paid for the work necessary to finish the twelve-year-old structure. This improvement was a major asset to the institution because every foot of available space needed to be utilized for the expanding activities of the college.[55]

In 1894 the administration relaxed its rules concerning uniforms to the extent that seniors were permitted to wear a special type of cap to denote their rank. However, in 1901, a request for the male representatives of the societies to wear "full dress suits" at commencements was disapproved. This action was probably taken to spare some of the students from the extra expense of purchasing the outfits, which might have been a financial burden. Three years later, the senior class decided it would prefer to have Elon conform to the traditional customs in vogue at other colleges. To achieve this aim, DeRoy Fonville, representing the class of 1894, requested the faculty's permission to wear caps and gowns at commencement. The request was granted, the custom begun that year, and since that date the graduating seniors have worn academic regalia when they received their diplomas.[56]

Interest in scholarship was stimulated in 1901 when Mr. and Mrs. Samuel L. Adams offered to present a medal annually to the member of the graduating class who delivered the best oration. This was the first Elon College student award of which there is any record, and it was given in memory of Richard Stanford, whose portrait and relics had already been presented to the museum by the Adams family. The first winner of the Stanford Medal was A. Rudolph Eley, of Norfolk, Virginia. Inspired by this prize, in 1904 E. L. and E. Moffitt offered a medal annually in memory of their father, E. A. Moffitt, who had served many years as a trustee of the college. This award was to be given to the lady of the graduating class reading the best essay. The first winner of this distinction was Willie Staley, the president's daughter. Another award was the Long Medal, honoring the first president of the college, which was given to the "member of the graduating class making the highest grade in scholarship through entire college course." It was first awarded in 1905, and the winner was Mary Lou Pitt. These prizes were the forerunners of many to be given later, all of which challenged and rewarded the best efforts of the students.[57]

During the Staley administration, a number of changes occurred in the personnel of the faculty. In 1894 J. M. Bandy was professor of mathematics and supervisor of the Elon Teachers' Institute, a pro-

Room in the Main Building used exclusively by the Clio Literary Society in the early 1900s. Similar special rooms were reserved for the Psiphelian and Philologian literary societies.

gram designed to supplement the training of public school teachers.[58] The following year, W. P. Lawrence (Elon '94) became professor of English, and was a member of the faculty, except for two intervals, during the remainder of his life. Miss Annie Graham (Elon '93) served as instructor in the Preparatory Department for several years before and after she became the wife of Professor Lawrence. When she died in 1969 at the age of ninety-seven, Mrs. Lawrence had been for several years the oldest living alumna of the college and was probably the last surviving member of Dr. Staley's staff.[59]

In 1894 E. L. Moffitt retired from the faculty to become editor of the *Christian Sun*.[60] Two years later, W. C. Wicker (Elon '93) became professor of natural science and head of the Preparatory Department. He also served on the faculty at various other times throughout his life.[61] In 1898 Miss Julia Long was employed as instructor in music, Miss Jennie T. Herndon (Elon '96) taught physical education, and Miss Belle Gaines became the college matron.[62] The next year, Miss Florence Wilson joined the staff as music teacher; Miss Elise Ramsay served as her assistant. Miss Alberta Moring, who had become Mrs. J. M. Roberts, continued to teach art until 1901, when she was succeeded by Miss Ella Boone.[63]

Miss Irene Johnson retired from teaching in 1900 when she be-

Group of coeds, about 1900.

came Mrs. John M. Cook. That same year, S. M. Smith (Elon '95) became professor of chemistry and biology, and P. J. Kernodle joined the staff to teach physics and astronomy, but also served as principal of the Commercial Department.[64] Howard B. Holmes became professor of English and German in 1901, and served in that capacity until his sudden death in August 1904, the first Elon faculty member to die. Out of respect for the memory of their departed colleague, the

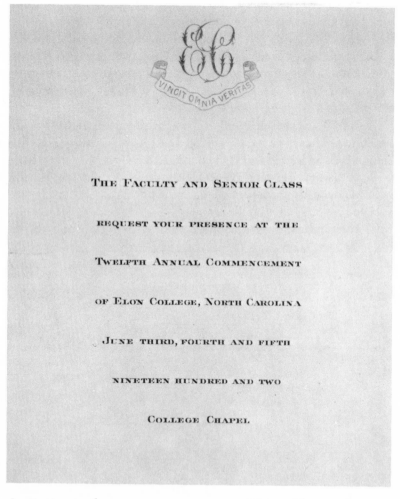

THE FACULTY AND SENIOR CLASS

REQUEST YOUR PRESENCE AT THE

TWELFTH ANNUAL COMMENCEMENT

OF ELON COLLEGE, NORTH CAROLINA

JUNE THIRD, FOURTH AND FIFTH

NINETEEN HUNDRED AND TWO

COLLEGE CHAPEL

Invitation to the 1902 commencement. The emblem is the only evidence found of the use of a college seal before the adoption of an official one in 1908.

faculty passed resolutions in his memory and moved "that the Charter of the College be draped thirty days in token of our deep sense of mourning." Holmes was replaced on the faculty by W. P. Lawrence, who had been engaged in other pursuits for approximately two years.[65]

In 1903 the new People's Bank, in Burlington, persuaded mathematics professor S. A. Holleman to become its cashier, for him the beginning of a successful commercial career. In the same year, Jetson J. Lincoln (Elon '04) became principal of the Academic Department. The following year, Andrew R. Ramey was hired as adjunct professor of Latin.[66] The veterans Newman and Atkinson remained on the faculty during the entire Staley administration. During this period, Dr. Newman served as chairman of the faculty except for the year beginning June 11, 1897, and ending June 10, 1898, when Professor Atkinson occupied the position.[67]

Relieved of the presidency, Dr. Staley devoted full time to the church at Suffolk, which he served the remainder of his life. He was one of the most widely known citizens of the Virginia city, distinguished by his courtly bearing and the high silk hat he always wore. He was so esteemed by all who knew him that he was respectfully dubbed the "Bishop of Suffolk." The minister continued to serve the interests of Elon College in any manner possible and frequently visited the institution on whose behalf he had labored so mightily. His service as the second president of the college was acknowledged when a new dormitory, constructed in 1968, was named Staley Hall in his honor.

CHAPTER V

THE GROWING TRUNK

The monarch oak, the patriarch of the trees,
Shoots rising up, and spreads by slow degrees.
JOHN DRYDEN
Palamon and Arcite

North Carolina-born Emmett Leonidas Moffitt was thirty-seven
years of age when he was installed as the third president of Elon. He
was educated at Graham Normal College, Trinity College (now
Duke University), and Harvard University. He served on the Elon
faculty as professor of English from 1890 until 1894. He then resigned to edit the *Christian Sun* until 1900, after which he became
secretary-treasurer of the Asheboro Wheelbarrow Company. He was
also the son of a veteran member of the institution's board of trustees. This background made Moffitt thoroughly familiar with the operation of the college, and his business ability made him confident
its needs could be supplied.[1]

Armed with this assurance, the president soon aroused his trustees to action. Taking advantage of the college's financial credit,
which had been stabilized under his predecessor, he persuaded the
board to borrow $20,000 in July 1905 from the Farmers' Bank of
Nansemond "for the purpose of building a new Dormitory, or adding
to the old Dormitory, or both, the proper equipment of the same or
for other necessary improvements."[2] Construction began immediately on West Dormitory, to house women and to include a dining
hall to serve the entire college. Upon its completion, East Dormitory
would then become a residence hall for men. In optimistic anticipation of this expansion, applications for residence in the new dormitory were taken in April 1905; corner rooms in West were to cost
$2.50 extra per term, and men who were to take their meals in the

dining hall were to be granted preference over others for the rooms in East.[3]

Within a few months after work began on the new building, it became apparent that the funds on hand were insufficient for the planned improvements. The president decided that if more money needed to be borrowed, the loan should be made large enough both to complete the dormitories and modernize the entire plant. Convinced that this plan was wise, the board arranged a new loan with the Farmers' Bank of Nansemond in the amount of $35,000. The money was to be used for discharging the indebtedness of the college "and to fully complete the new Dormitory, erect a lighting plant, water plant, heating plant, and make such further repairs, improvements and additions to the College property as are essentially necessary."[4] When the outstanding obligations were retired, which included repayment of the $20,000 already owed to the Farmers' Bank, the trustees announced that $15,000 was available for improvements in light, water, and heat. Shortly thereafter, the campus became a veritable beehive of activity.[5]

The major project was construction of the three-story West Dormitory, which harmonized architecturally with the College Building and East Dormitory and was aligned with them. The front entrances to each were on their southern sides. The main part of West measured 158 feet across its front and was 45 feet deep. The ell, usually referred to as the Annex, was 40 feet by 80 feet in size. The walls were of brick laid in running, or stretcher, bond, a type of masonry then in general use. The building was planned along thoroughly modern lines for the time. The east and west wings and the Annex were each separated from the central section by fire walls, were topped with brick parapets extending several feet above the roof, and were equipped with automatic metal fire doors. (These precautionary architectural features were to save the main body of the building from destruction in 1942 when the Annex burned.)[6]

West was ornamented by wide porches extending across the front of its central section on all three floors. In addition to the front entrance, doorways were located in the ends of both the east and west wings. A modern touch was a freight elevator in the eastern end of the Annex. The main part of the structure contained dormitory rooms for a hundred women students. The second floor of the Annex was used as a dining hall for the entire student body, and provided

President Emmett L. Moffitt.

space for a kitchen, pantries, storage rooms, refrigerator room, and quarters for custodial personnel. Men entered the dining hall by a wooden outdoor stairway.[7] The first floor, sometimes called the basement, was assigned to the males for a gymnasium. This finally provided them a place for an indoor basketball court, though passing the ball was somewhat impeded by the thick columns that supported the upper story. Nevertheless, it was better than anything previously available, and was enthusiastically enjoyed by the athletes.[8]

As West neared completion, porches were also added to the front of the three stories of East Dormitory, and other improvements were made to convert the building into a suitable residence hall for men. Modern bathrooms, connected to the new sewerage system, were then installed on each floor of both dormitories. After this accomplishment, the entire college was supplied with steam heat, running hot and cold water, and electric lights. One of the most conspicuous improvements was illumination of the campus, which was still a fairly thick grove in some places, by ten arc lights. The electric power was shared with the community. On January 1, 1907, the electric lights were turned on for the first time at the college, in the town, and at the Christian Orphanage. According to the meter, 440 lights were served, which was barely half the plant's capacity.[9]

The powerhouse for the operation of these utilities was a brick building erected on the west side of the Haggard Avenue entrance to the campus, near where the steel water tank stood until recent years. The first floor of the structure housed the intricate machinery that operated the central heating, lighting, and water systems. The second floor was kept empty for the installation of a steam laundry, if ever desired. This possibility was never realized, and the space was used for living quarters by six students who helped pay their college expenses by stoking the boiler and performing other chores connected with the operation.[10]

Because the old college well soon proved inadequate for the increased demands, in 1910 a new well more than 100 feet deep that yielded 100 gallons of water per minute was bored near the pumping station. The entire system was enlarged and a capacious water tank erected on the roof of West Dormitory for storage. Upon completion, these improvements provided sufficient water for the college and the town, "if desired." The town "desired" the benefit, and its citizens shortly thereafter enjoyed running water.[11] The event was triumphantly heralded by the *Weekly*: "We now have clear, pure water. On October 27, T. M. Cable, engineer and electrician at the central power station, turned steam on the new pump installed in the deep well. The pump works perfectly, and there is no trouble now in keeping the big tank on West Dormitory full."[12]

The tank referred to was similar to a huge barrel. Built of wooden staves, bound together with metal bands and topped with a conical cover, it was erected on a wooden trestle above the dormitory roof. Holding 10,000 gallons and elevated 40 feet above the ground, the tank supplied sufficient pressure for the entire water system. Within a few weeks after it was filled, the final details of the new project were completed, and the college buildings were plentifully supplied with water, which was especially welcomed in the dormitories.[13]

When President Moffitt's program was completed in 1910, the college joyfully passed from the era of kerosene lamps, wells, and fireplaces to that of electric lights, running water, and steam radiators. The modernization had notably enhanced the value of the institution's property. In 1904 it had been appraised for insurance purposes at $19,000 for the College (Main) Building, $1,000 for furniture,

College chapel in the early 1900s.

$3,000 for the dormitory, and $1,000 for dormitory furniture, totaling $24,000.[14] Four years later, the figures were $20,000 for the College Building and its equipment, $4,000 for East Dormitory, $13,000
for West Dormitory, and $3,800 for the Power House, making a total
of $40,800. In 1912 the value increased to $46,800.[15] A major part of
the improvements had been made possible by the use of borrowed
money, and the next most pressing task confronting the administration was repayment of the loans.

To concentrate on debt retirement, it was absolutely essential that
the college be operated without any substantial deficit. This required strict economy and careful management. For these reasons
and the desire to supply the students with plentiful wholesome food,
the institution cultivated its own orchard, planted vegetable gardens, and maintained its own dairy and herd of swine. Seven or eight
cows and two mules were stabled in a barn located just west of the
present Gymnasium, and the pigpen was on the site where the Powell Building now stands. An addition to the barn contained the
"churns, separator, and other necessary equipment for an up-to-date
dairy," which were installed in 1907. A small farm was operated on
the road to Burlington, managed by a black man named Sam Haith.
Smaller tracts were also cultivated elsewhere. From all of these
sources, the college obtained most of its vegetables and feed for its
stock. This effort to be self-supporting was successful to the extent
that in 1908 and for years thereafter the dining hall operation showed
a profit, a result not easy to achieve.

Most of the faculty members who had families to support followed
suit. Because money was scarce but land was plentiful, most residents maintained their own kitchen gardens, and kept cows, chick-
ens, and pigs for their own use. Dr. J. U. Newman pastured his cattle
for years in the present 300 block of East College Avenue. On one
occasion, Professor Lawrence treated his colleagues at a faculty
meeting with apples from his orchard on East Haggard Avenue. Such
measures cut living costs and aided subsistence.[16]

Beginning with the opening of Elon, the graduate degree program
had been a successful academic feature. To further this program,
President Moffitt announced in 1905 that the college was "now in
position to allow its graduates to take an M.A. degree by correspondence . . . and many are now taking this work." The requirements
consisted of fifteen academic hours of study "in not more than three

departments, and in one, if so desired." A maximum of three years was allowed for completion of the program. Graduate students, whether for study in residence or by correspondence, were required to register annually, as were the undergraduates, but only paid tuition for the first year of study. This amounted to five dollars per quarter and five dollars for a diploma.[17]

When a candidate applied for an M.A. degree program by correspondence, the procedure was the same as for one who was in residence. An example is the application of Edward French (Elon '05), which was referred by the faculty chairman to Professors Wicker, Newman, Kernodle, Ramey, and Harper for handling. They agreed on the courses the student should study, the textbooks he should use, the types of papers he should prepare, and the examination schedule he should follow. The faculty accepted the proposal of the committee, and authorized the secretary to notify the applicant of the requirements. Upon the completion of this program, the staff would request the trustees to confer the degree upon the student. Because of unforeseen cirumstances, French was forced to delay begin-

Clio Literary Society, about 1906.

ning the course, but eventually did so and was awarded the degree at
the 1911 commencement.[18]

Several higher degrees were acquired by the correspondence method, though most awarded during this period were earned by students
in residence. The latter included, in 1906, Jetson J. Lincoln; in 1907,
Anna I. Helfenstein and D. R. Fonville; in 1908, John W. Harrell and
Ned F. Brannock; in 1909, Virgil C. Pritchette and John T. Kernodle;
and in 1911, Asa L. Lincoln and Nathaniel G. Newman.[19] Graduate
study attracted numerous enthusiastic participants, and continued
to be a part of the academic program until the era of World War I.

In October 1905 W. T. Walters (Elon '03) wrote to the *Sun* that "the
college's great need now is a magazine" that would be of interest to
students, faculty, and alumni.[20] Two years passed before this suggestion stimulated any action. The Publications Committee of the faculty then recommended publishing *The Elonian*, a monthly periodical of ten issues annually. The project was proposed as a joint
enterprise of the three literary societies and the Alumni Associa-

Student body in May 1906 on the steps of the Main Building.

tion.[21] Representing a committee of the association, Professor Harper solicited the cooperation of the societies with the following proposal: "It is estimated that the magazine will cost about $500.00 for ten issues. Now if you could get $200 worth of advertisements, if each Alumnus would take the magazine, and if each member of each society would do likewise, you could just about raise the money."[22] The societies were promised any profit made; in case of a loss, one-fourth of it would be borne by each of the organizations and the Alumni Association.

After the literary groups acquiesced, J. T. Kernodle, Annie Spencer, Ruth Stevick, J. W. Barney, C. C. Howell, C. W. Johnson, Herbert M. Scholz, and Effie Iseley were appointed as editors; and J. A. Vaughan as business manager. The first issue appeared in November 1907. The 49 pages of the publication, 5½ by 7½ inches in size, contained essays, fiction, and college news.[23]

The project proved to be a burden in several ways, which prompted the three societies to inform the faculty in October 1908 that they were unwilling to continue sharing responsibility for the enterprise. Publication of the periodical was therefore suspended, and a college weekly proposed to succeed it.[24]

Judging from past experience, it was apparent that successful publication depended upon enthusiastic faculty participation and a certain amount of financial stability. To attain these requirements and provide the institution with a periodical, on February 15, 1910, *The Elon College Weekly* was launched as a stock company. The shares were soon subscribed, which provided capital. The elected officials included a number of faculty members. Officers of the company were Dr. E. L. Moffitt, president; A. L. Lincoln, secretary; and Professor T. C. Amick, treasurer. The staff was composed of Professor W. P. Lawrence, managing editor; J. W. Barney, A. C. Hall, and Miss Affie Griffin, associate editors; Professor W. C. Wicker, circulation manager; and Professor Amick, business manager.[25] Forty issues per year were planned for the four-page journal, which was ten by fifteen inches in size. The stockholders anticipated that subscription rates of fifty cents per annum for cash, or seventy-five cents for time payment, plus revenue from the advertising would defray operational costs. When the first issue was released, the college and town had a newspaper.[26]

The advent of the new journal was announced in the *State Dis-*

The Elon College Weekly.

EDUCATION AND LITERATURE.

Vol. 1.   Elon College, N. C., February 2, 1900.   No. 20.

THE CHARACTER OF GONERIL.

A Lesson from the Characters Here in Portrayed.

ACCUMULATING AND GIVING.

"If There Were no Great Fortunes There could be no Great Benefactions."

Purpose in Hamlet.

Front page of the college's first newspaper.

patch as a reestablishment of a weekly begun "about ten years ago," which ran about three years before publication ceased. On June 12, 1899, the Elon faculty had "moved that such members of the Faculty as will voluntarily do so undertake the publication of a weekly journal for next year." The motion passed, and Professor Atkinson was elected as editor and Professor Lawrence as business manager. At a staff meeting on the 16th, the decision was made to name the paper *The Elon College Weekly*, whose subscription price was fifty cents per year.[27] No further mention of the project has been found, but the journal evidently existed for a brief period.

Another step was taken in the maturing of Elon in 1908 when the trustees adopted an official seal for the institution, which has ever since remained the official emblem of the college. The creator was Professor Wicker, who relied upon his knowledge of Masonic symbolism in designing the emblem. Probably its first appearance was on the cover of the college catalog issued in 1911, when the design was described in detail:

> Around the rim of the seal are the words "Elon College, North Carolina," also the words "Numen Lumen," the former meaning spiritual light and vigor, and the latter, intellectual light and intellectual resources, stand in the rim of the seal as the motto of the college. Within the seal are two pillars representing strength and power. The Holy Bible is also represented and this indicates that upon which the institution is built. Above the Bible are represented some books which stand for knowledge and culture. The candlestick with the flaming torch represents the light the college spreads abroad over the earth. Above all is the All Seeing eye that has for more than twenty years kept watch over the college, its faculty, its student body, the homes represented in the College, and those who are interested in the progress and advancement of the College. The date of the founding of the college, 1889, is also included in the seal.

In far more mundane terms, the *Weekly* commented, "We feel that the seal shows in a general way that for which Elon College stands, spiritual and intellectual development, progress in all the sciences and arts, strength of manhood and womanhood, light for the benighted and ignorant, and all guided by the all seeing eye of the Omnipotent."[28]

While the improvements to the physical plant were under way, the friends of the college continued to show their interest in its academic program. Dr. Robert M. Morrow, a Burlington dentist, established the R. M. Morrow Thesis Medal in memory of his deceased son, R. M. Morrow, Jr. The award was to be presented to the senior writing the best thesis in any department. First awarded at the 1906 commencement, the winner was A. W. Andes, whose manuscript was entitled "Education, Crime, and Economy." The following year, Dr. J. J. Summerbell, of Dayton, Ohio, offered a prize of seventy-five dollars for the best essay written by an Elon student on the Tenth Commandment. In 1909 General Julian S. Carr, a Durham industrialist who had long been a benefactor of the college, endowed the Reverend J. W. Wellons Scholarship Medal, in honor of that venerable Christian minister, to be awarded to the student achieving the highest scholastic record for the year. W. F. Warren was the first recipient, qualifying with a 97.5 percent average. Also at the 1910 graduating exercises, two medals were awarded to J. W. Barney, who later became a member of the college faculty; and the Stanford Medal was presented to Leon Edgar Smith, destined to become the fifth president of his alma mater. All these prizes, given in recognition of scholastic achievement, served as an impetus to the student body, and many were won by men and women who later became instructors, trustees, or benefactors of the college.[29]

A unique event occurred during this period: the college family acquired a patriarch. The Reverend James W. Wellons, then in his eighties, was obliged to retire from the active ministry because of his age. He had been born in Sussex County, Virginia, on January 1, 1826, a brother of the distinguished Christian clergyman William B. Wellons. From his youth he had served his denomination zealously in many capacities. He was an original member of the college board of trustees and an enthusiastic supporter of the institution. Busy with the affairs of his church, he had never married nor established a home of his own, and, when retirement became inevitable, he had no place in which to live.

Because of his long years of faithful service to the denomination, the Christian Church arranged for the clergyman to reside at the college. The only comfortable place for him was in the new West Dormitory, in the section that was barred to all males except on rare occasions. Making an exception to the rules, the administration equipped a room for him near the front entrance to the building, without anticipating that Wellons would occupy it for more than two decades. The services of "Uncle Pinkie" Comer, a black man, were obtained to care for the old minister's needs, and the first and only male ever to room in West Dormitory moved into his quarters.

Known respectfully far and wide as "Uncle" Wellons, the newcomer was happy in his new home, and soon became as much of a fixture at Elon as the old college well or the Senior Oak. He was a tall, bearded man of large frame, who usually wore a long frock coat and supported himself with a walking stick in each hand as he strolled about the campus accompanied by his shaggy black dog. By no means completely incapacitated, Wellons assisted Dr. Atkinson in editing the *Christian Sun*, preached frequently at the college church or in other pulpits in the area, and even cultivated a garden near the present home of the college president. Invited to faculty meetings, he occasionally attended, and continued to serve as a trustee of the institution until the day of his death.

Wellons was usually requested to ask the blessing in the dining

Psiphelian Literary Society, about 1910.

hall before the meal began, a custom not particularly popular with the hungry students who stood watching the food grow cold during his lengthy prayers. Frequently during the meal, the paternal clergyman advised the diners on good table manners in a stentorian tone that filled the room. Some of his comments were possibly intended to be humorous, such as the admonition to refrain from eating beans with a knife, but all were heard, whether or not they were heeded. Despite the occasional impatience of the students with his habits, the old man was a fixture of the institution for many years, respectfully treated, and known to all as the patriarch of the college.

Finally, increasing infirmities forced "Uncle" Wellons to leave his beloved Elon and spend the last four years of his life at the Masonic Home, in Greensboro, where he could obtain special medical care. Nevertheless, he returned to the college on his hundredth birthday and stood to preach a sermon to the college congregation, again a lengthy discourse. When he died on June 10, 1927, his funeral was held in Whitley Auditorium, the meeting place of the college church, and he was buried in the town's Magnolia Cemetery. There never has been, and probably never will be, another person associated with Elon College in the same capacity as this patriarch.[30]

Student activities continued to be concentrated primarily in the three literary societies because practically every student belonged to one of them, and all were engaged in worthwhile projects. In 1906 the Clio organization completed the outstanding feat of placing desks and other equipment valued at $900 in the classrooms, a highly practical contribution to the college.[31]

Although the Psiphelians, the only women's society, faced no competition, intense rivalry arose between the two men's groups. This was especially evident in the annual debate between the Philologians and the Clios, an event that became the annual highlight of student activities. Because the enthusiastic support of their champion speakers in 1906 exceeded proper bounds, the debates were banned for a year because of "rowdy audiences." The penitent students then pledged that "conduct would be exemplary in the future," and the contests were resumed the following year.[32]

Meanwhile, the Ministerial Association and the "Y's" had continued their programs, and by 1911 a college band had been organized. R. A. Campbell was the director, assisted by W. N. Huff. According to the Weekly, in March the band consisted of the largest number of musicians since its beginning, and promised "some lively and patriotic tunes at our ball games and other gatherings during the coming spring."[33]

One of the most vexing faculty problems during the Moffitt administration began when the renovated East Dormitory was opened as a residence hall for men. The college students were young, energetic, and mischievous, as they still are, and sometimes went too far with their pranks. On several occasions, men were disciplined for throwing water out of upper windows onto people passing below, or for having a quarrel that ended in a fistfight, sometimes almost a "free for all."[34] The faculty's solution to this dilemma was to place the maintenance of discipline in the hands of the students themselves.

This was accomplished in September 1909, when Dr. Moffitt appointed Professors Lawrence and Amick to organize the East Dormitory Self-Governing Club, and draft a constitution and bylaws for its operation. The rules were soon completed; they specified that the officers were to be a president, vice-president, secretary, and treasurer, elected annually. From twelve names of dormitory residents submitted by the students, the faculty would choose six to constitute the executive board. The students were requested to report infractions of the regulations to the president, and the board would then deal with the matter.

A fine of twenty-five cents was imposed for making unnecessary noise; loafing in another student's room during study hours; behaving indecently; and throwing trash, the contents of slop jars, paper, or water from the windows of the building. A minimum fine of twenty-five cents and a maximum fine of a dollar could be inflicted for using indecent language. For continuous misbehavior or more serious offenses, the student could be required to vacate the dormitory. Cases this severe were reported to the faculty, which usually backed the student board in its decisions. The net finances accumulated by fines were to be used for the benefit of the organization as determined by the club members assembled in a business session.

The first president was C. C. Fonville and Sipe Fleming was secretary. The original board members were W. H. McPherson, R. A. Campbell, W. H. Fleming, R. L. Walker, W. P. Warren, and F. S. Drake. This system constituted the first form of student government established at Elon College.[35] The men's behavior did not sud-

denly become angelic, but it vastly improved and afforded some relief to the heavily burdened faculty.

Hazing was never a severe problem, but occasionally the boyish
pranks got out of hand and attracted faculty intervention. The case
that demanded the most official attention in the period could well
be termed "The Great Apple Hunt of 1909." In September a number
of upperclassmen persuaded two new students to accompany them
on a quest for some apples. Because the expedition was planned for
the middle of the night, it is assumed that the fruit was to be obtained by raiding some farmer's orchard. The plan devised was as follows: as soon as the men arrived at their destination, one or more
students hidden nearby would fire a gun to indicate that the land-
owner was about to apprehend the trespassers. Somewhat hesitat-
ingly, the gullible youths walked with the group a distance of some
two and one-half miles from the college. Upon their arrival, the
arrangements worked as scheduled. At the sound of the gun, the
frightened boys returned to the dormitory with all possible speed, to
the merriment of the planners of the prank.

The faculty learned about the affair, as faculties have a way of doing, and considered the matter too serious to disregard. Several
meetings were held at which all suspects were questioned, but the
evidence given was so confusing that the exact amount of individual
guilt could not be determined. The case was finally settled by seven
students signing a statement in which they promised to refrain from
hazing in the future, and this concluded the "great apple hunt." The
result was that hazing immediately became subdued if not eradi-
cated entirely for a lengthy period.[36]

The popular Child lectures were continued during the Moffitt
years. Also, in 1911, the Francis Asbury Palmer Board enabled its
president, Dr. Martyn Summerbell, to make the first of several visits
to Elon. His three initial lectures on the rise of Protestantism in
Switzerland and France, given to interested audiences, were a notable addition to the academic program.[37]

The granting of honorary degrees continued during the period, all
of which were awarded to clergymen of the Christian Church. The
D.D. degree was conferred on Warren H. Denison, of Huntington,
Indiana, in 1908, and on P. W. McReynolds, of Defiance, Ohio, in
1909. In the latter year, the LL.D. degree was awarded to Drs. Martyn Summerbell and Joseph J. Summerbell. In 1910 James F. McCul-

loch, of Greensboro, who was also the editor of *Our Church Record*, and A. W. Lightbourne, pastor of the People's Christian Church, of Dover, Delaware, were the recipients of the D.D. degree. In 1911 former President Staley and Frank S. Child were honored with the LL.D. degree.[38]

A special feature of the 1909 commencement was the presentation to the college of a life-size portrait of W. S. Long by admirers of the first president. It was hung on the Chapel walls, where those of other former presidents would be placed later.[39]

Shortly after its organization, the Alumni Association had begun an endowment to finance a student scholarship. In 1910, by which time $650 had been raised in cash and pledges, the association granted the Alumni Junior Scholarship of $50 to J. S. Truitt for "literary tuition." The organization also subscribed to two shares of stock in the *Weekly* publishing company.[40]

Throughout President Moffitt's incumbency, the Athletic Association continued to improve its program, especially in baseball. The faculty was not opposed to athletics, but apprehensive, with good reason, that enthusiasm for sports might overshadow the effort to acquire an education, which was the primary reason for students attending college. Therefore, the approval of the staff for athletic expansion was won slowly, but it was eventually obtained.

A measure of success was achieved in June 1906, when the board of trustees voted to allow intercollegiate games under strong faculty supervision in all sports except football. The rules accompanying this permission required a faculty member to accompany the team whenever away from Elon, and rules of conduct applied to the players for all games, whether at the college or away. Each player needed to maintain a grade average of 80 percent, be charged with less than ten demerits, and could not be paid to play. The association was not to acquire any debts. Furthermore, the trustees said, steps would be taken leading eventually to Elon's membership in the Southern Intercollegiate Association.[41]

This welcomed ruling gave Elon permission to compete with other teams it wished to play against, but it did nothing to improve the expertise of the team members. The college had been conspicuously defeated in the earlier games played and had no desire to remain the loser indefinitely. A coach was needed, and in 1906 J. A. Vaughan, manager of the team, informed the faculty he knew a qualified man who would come to Elon as a student for forty dollars a month, plus board and tuition. This information was referred to the Athletic Committee, which took no action on the proposal but did rule that "all men on the ball team [were] to practice from 2:45 to 4:45 P.M. daily when the weather is suitable, unless prevented by illness."[42]

In May 1907 the Athletic Association requested faculty endorsement of a petition requesting the trustees "to provide an Athletic Coach and Baseball Park for the next scholastic year." The faculty unanimously approved the request, "provided the Trustees feel able to bear the expenses."[43]

The official reaction to the petition was favorable. By the purchase of an additional lot, the administration was able to set aside four acres between East College and Haggard avenues for an athletic park. The facility was ready for use no later than 1910 because the following year a grandstand was erected, whose seating capacity was 200 people. It was constructed in such a manner that a second section could be, and later was, added. Also a bandstand was built to seat the twenty "wind jammers" and "fram frammers" of the college band so that the games could be enlivened with their music. The park, used until the 1920s, was reserved for the use of the college baseball team, and other students who wished to play continued to use the diamond in the southwestern corner of the campus. Four tennis courts were constructed on the western edge of the park.[44]

Furthermore, in the spring of 1908 arrangements were made for M. B. Murrow to coach and play on the baseball team. His qualifications and status of previous employment are unknown, but he was the first person referred to in the faculty records as an athletic coach at Elon College.[45]

Aided by a coach and a proper field, the team's improvement seemed assured. This enabled Manager W. C. Pritchette to obtain approval for a schedule of twenty-five games, seventeen away from Elon, for the 1908 season. Only ten of these are known to have been played, but Elon won 60 percent of them, which increased enthusiasm for the team on the part of the student body and administration.[46]

Unfortunately, the desire to win was strong, but the number of skilled players was limited. Subsequently, and with faculty approval, three men were added to the team in 1909 who were not students and were thus classed as professional players. The Collegiate Athletic Association, which Elon had not then joined, would not permit its member schools to play a team that was not composed entirely of bona fide students. This required a scheduled game with Trinity College to be canceled and confined Elon's opponents to institutions that were not members of the association.[47]

This situation was not entirely satisfactory because the Elonites wished to qualify for games with all schools, not merely a few. In May 1909 the faculty Athletic Committee took the first step in a plan designed to solve the problem:

> ... to put out a baseball team able to meet other colleges will require at least 8 men who are not already here. Therefore it is hereby moved and carried that the Faculty approve employing a coach this spring provided a suitable one can be secured at approved price and that a base-ball team in training for the season of 1911 be put out, with such players as can be secured from the present student body as may be arranged on the understanding that these games be considered as practice games.[48]

Under this plan, the college could eventually become a member of the Collegiate Athletic Association and play games against its member teams.

While the plan was being formulated in 1909, Murrow was succeeded by W. H. ("Reddi") Rowe, who was employed to coach all sports. He was replaced the following year by L. L. Hobbes (Hobbs), Jr.[49] In March the *Weekly* lauded the new coach's efforts:

> The baseball club played a practice game on the home grounds Monday afternoon, the 7th, with the team from Whitsett. The effort to make athletics purely a sport rather than professionalism has some show here. The game was pluckily played throughout, and the score was 9 to 3 in favor of Elon. ... Mr. Hobbs, the base-ball coach, is working up considerable interest in this great American game.[50]

That year, out of fourteen games played, Elon won seven and tied two—the best season's record for baseball up to that time. A part of this success is attributable to an outstanding new pitcher, Bunn Hearn, a native of Chapel Hill.[51]

At the conclusion of the 1910 season, Hearn signed a contract to play professionally in the National League. Under these circumstances, he abandoned plans to remain at Elon to graduate, but agreed to coach the team until time to join the St. Louis club for spring practice in 1911. He became the first athletic coach at the institution to be accorded faculty status and also the first alumnus known to have risen from the Elon team to the ranks of big-league baseball. After he embarked on the new phase of his career, the pitcher kept in touch with his alma mater as much as possible and later married one of his fellow students, Ethel Crews Barrett, of the class of 1914.[52]

While Hearn was coaching the team, the writers in the *Weekly* exerted their strongest literary efforts to arouse student enthusiasm: "Coach Hearne [Hearn] continues to give his squad plenty to do. . . . It is about time for the student body to get up a little "pep" too. Don't expect nine men to do it all. They can play the game but they can't win unless they have the hearty cooperation both in money, sympathy, yells and enthusiastic support of every man in the college. Let's get behind them and put out a winning team. This means you!"[53]

In the spring of 1911, Henry M. Hedgepeth, a Fayetteville native, arrived on the campus to enroll as a student, pitch for the baseball team, and serve as coach after Hearn's departure. "Light Horse Harry" was a 200-pound "giant southpaw" with experience, and he was reputed to be "a first class slab artist." He proved to be an excellent player, and, a short time later, became the second Elon student to qualify for baseball on the national level.[54] However, the team as a whole was weak. The problem remained the same: a professional coach training a sufficient number of basically qualified athletes was necessary if the college was to rise to greater heights in collegiate baseball. This was the situation at the end of the 1911 season, when the Moffitt administration ended.[55]

In October 1909, while "Reddi" Rowe was coach, the trustees agreed with a faculty recommendation "that Football games be allowed under the rules and qualifications for base ball and that for the first year only such games be allowed as will not require the team to be absent from the hill over night." Students under the age of twenty-one years who wished to play were required to obtain written permission from their parents or guardians.[56]

Almost immediately afterward, a practice game was played with

Greensboro High School. Then, on October 23, the team played Bingham Military Academy, at Burlington. This was the first college football game officially noted in the faculty records. The Elonites were the victors, which many considered a good omen.[57]

At this point in the growth of the new sport, the college faculty's indignation was aroused by a published account of the October 23d game with Bingham that was "uncomplimentary" to the Elon players. The writer, who acknowledged authorship, was given the ultimatum of "apologizing to the satisfaction of [the] Athletic Committee of Elon College before 9 o'clock A.M. Saturday, November 6," or permission would not be given to play a game scheduled that day at Mebane with Bingham. Evidently the demand was ignored; consequently, the game was not officially sanctioned.[58] Whether or not the matter was clearly understood by Coach Rowe and the players cannot now be determined, but the team went to Mebane to play regardless.[59] The faculty did not overlook this violation of its authority, and immediately ruled that no more football games would be played away from the campus until deliberations over the matter were concluded, though a game at home on November 13 was permitted.[60]

1909 football team, posing by the Senior Oak.

On November 19 the faculty ruled that "in view of the insubordination and disobedience of the football team in going to Mebane contrary to instruction of the Faculty, that no more football be allowed this football season." Although doubtless unpopular, this announcement should have ended the matter. However, six days later, on Thanksgiving Day, the coach took the team to Burlington, where it played Durham High School (YMCA). Although the Elonites won the game, they had violated the rules of the college, according to its officials.

The explanation given for the action was that the game was played on a holiday, and each player participated as an individual on his own responsibility. The outraged faculty refused to consider such an excuse, and promptly dismissed the coach "on the grounds that he has failed to work in harmony with the Faculty, and has led students to disregard its authority." Each student who participated was given 40 demerits; and, if juniors or seniors, deprived of all special privileges. This ended the matter, and it also ended football at the college for a decade. The officials were willing for the athletic program to be expanded, but it had to be done according to their rules or not at all.[61]

Tennis had been played at Elon since its founding, and continued to be enjoyed during the Moffitt years. One reason for its popularity was that it could be played for individual pleasure and did not need to be a group enterprise, as explained in the March 1911 *Weekly*: "Manager Lincoln has this phase of our life well under way and the greatest difficulty at present seems to be a lack of courts. Can't we have a few more, somehow? This is a sport that can be indulged in by both branches of a co-ed school and as long as this is true it will have its friends."[62]

Shortly after this article appeared, the college took a wider interest in tennis:

> At a meeting of the joint athletic committee last week it was moved and carried that we co-operate with the University of North Carolina, Wake Forest, A. and M., Davidson, and Guilford colleges in organizing the Inter-Collegiate Tennis Club of North Carolina.
>
> The Club had its first meeting at Chapel Hill, April 20, 21. Already we can see interest in tennis becoming stronger. Two

or three courts are full of play every afternoon that weather will permit and on the "Varsity court" the team is doing hard practice of from three to five sets every afternoon.[63]

The tennis court used by the women was in the northwestern corner of the campus on the site of the present parking lot for McEwen Dining Hall. The varsity court, located on the southern edge of the campus approximately opposite the present A. L. Hook home, was the best of several at the college available to the men and was used for the intercollegiate matches. The existing records of the college team's performance during this period are fragmentary, but they are sufficient to establish the proficiency of the players. Although these matches lacked the glamour of baseball games, the sport continued to attract student participation and enhance the growth of athletic talent.[64]

During the expansion of the athletic program, the basketball players were the thwarted group. No proper court existed on which to practice, much less one on which visiting teams could be invited to play. Because of this handicap, and inspired by the enthusiasm for the sport, the YMCA began a movement in 1910 to raise funds with which to erect a gymnasium large enough to accommodate basket-

Women tennis players in front of West Dormitory, about 1910.

ball. By September of that year, $250 had been subscribed and additional contributions were made later. This was a relatively small beginning for such a large undertaking, but the student organization persistently advocated the project throughout the Moffitt administration. Meanwhile, both men and women played on the makeshift court in the West Dormitory though at different times.[65]

In May 1911 the "Rules Governing Intercollegiate Athletics" were printed in the college catalog for the first time, to "remove all chance of misunderstanding" on the part of the athletes. In summary, only registered students taking a full work load, averaging 80 percent in grades, and having less than 10 demerits would be allowed to play in any intercollegiate game, and no player would be allowed to participate in these contests who received financial aid, directly or indirectly, by reason of his playing on the team.

In addition, the following new provision was instituted by the administration: "The Athletic initial "E" shall be awarded at the close of the athletic season in the spring of each year to those students who have played in 80% of the intercollegiate games of the year in any one sport, such as tennis, basketball, and baseball, and no other student shall be entitled to wear the initial letter."[66] This action constituted another "first," and was the beginning of a custom still practiced by the institution.

A short time before this announcement was made, the goals of the institution's athletic program were published in the *Weekly*:

> We want college ball by college men, men who when off with the team will represent the college as well as the athletic association; men who have a regular course and who can discuss the workings of the college and its various departments in an intelligent and interesting way; men who go to college for business and not merely to play ball. Of course we are aware that every institution has at least some of the latter class, but we, to say the least, would not encourage such. We want pure athletics by straight-forward, clever fellows and are proud to say that the team representing Elon College this season is by far the nearest approach to what our ideas of what a college team ought to be that we have ever had, and we believe that a little more attention to points above mentioned will make Elon a worthy adversary of any college team.[67]

The catalog compiled in 1911 also contained another new phase of the institution's program, this one in the academic field. It was announced in the *Weekly*:

> For the first time in the history of the college, the matter of giving scholarships has found a place in the catalogue. The Board of Trustees will give one scholarship to one high school graduate from each high school of which an Elon College graduate is principal. The scholarship covers the literary tuition of each scholarship student in any of the literary courses of the college. We trust that at least one graduate from each of these high schools will take advantage of this opportunity that the Board of Trustees has offered.[68]

This generous bid for students was accompanied in the spring of 1911 by the establishment of the Inter-Scholastic Declaimers' Contest for students at high schools whose principals were Elon graduates to "encourage literary society work" and to "give practice in the field of public speaking." The winner was to be presented with a gold medal by the college faculty. The affair was held on April 14. Officiating as judges were the Reverend S. L. Morgan, pastor of the Burlington Baptist Church; Professor G. C. Singletary, superintendent of the Burlington city schools; and Dr. Atkinson of the Elon faculty. Fourteen students from various North Carolina high schools participated.

During the afternoon, the eight leading speakers were selected. This group included a future governor of the state, W. Kerr Scott, from Hawfields High School, who spoke on "America's Need of Christian Young Men." The final competition between the eight was held in the evening, at which time Richard K. Redwine, of Churchland High School, in Davidson County, North Carolina, was declared the winner for his declamation "The Mothers of Men."[69] This project attracted considerable interest and represented another "first" in the expanding activities of the college.

During the Moffitt administration, events occurred occasionally that disrupted the usually placid life of the community. In March 1900 a yard fire one Sunday was reported somewhat humorously by the *Weekly*, which apparently blamed the blaze on sparks flying from a railroad engine's smokestack: "A great fire broke out here Sunday 21st sweeping over vast acres of one man's lawn, and the question arises as to whether the owner of the premises will sue the Southern Railroad for damages or the town fine the former for desecrating the Sabbath."[70] The railroad freight depot, on the north side of the tracks half a block west of Williamson Avenue, served as a storage house for cotton until the baled lint could be hauled by wagons to the Ossipee Mills. In January 1907 a fire destroyed the storage platform and ruined two hundred bales of cotton. The blaze could not be extinguished, but was kept from spreading to other nearby buildings. After the conflagration, the insurance adjuster hired local boys to pick over the damaged bales for possible salvage. Staley Wicker, son of Professor Wicker, was one of those employed.[71]

On December 13 in the same year, the two-story frame Club House No. 2, located next to the old post office, was destroyed by fire. It was a cooperative enterprise under private management in which fifteen students "clubbed" together to obtain board and room for low cost. The Christmas musical recital was in progress at the college when the alarm sounded, "causing all the men to exit from the audience," but no means were available to save the building and its contents.[72]

In 1908 an evening passenger train was wrecked on the tracks "a few hundred yards east of the station." Spreading rails were the apparent cause. The engine turned over on its side; and the tender did the same on the opposite side of the tracks. No one was seriously hurt, though the fireman and engineer experienced "narrow escapes." The latter was taken into the nearby home of Dr. George S. Watson for first aid. The citizens of the town "threw open their homes to the unfortunate passengers" until a relief train arrived for them several hours later. This unusual event caused a local sensation, and it was fortunate that the accident was not a calamity.[73]

In 1905 the Christian Church began plans to establish an orphanage on the south side of the railroad tracks at the town of Elon College. A large acreage was procured for this purpose. Within three years, the main building, barn, and other outbuildings were completed and the Christian Orphanage, today the Elon Home for Children, was in operation to care for homeless youth. This project was a step in the overall plan of the church to make the town a center for its denominational activities.[74]

Despite its limited equipment for fire protection, the municipality progressed commercially. In 1909 the State Highway Commission and the Alamance County commissioners authorized the 5.6 miles of road leading from Burlington via Elon College to Gibsonville to be macadamized. This improved traffic artery into the town was the forerunner of its hard-surfaced streets.[75]

The official records of the town of Elon College from its incorporation until 1913 have been lost, but from other sources it is known that in 1893 the mayor was John M. Cook, a student at the college; the commissioners were S. A. Holleman, J. W. McAdams, W. Huffines, S. Crawford, and the Reverend C. A. Boone; and Seymour Williams was chief of police.[76] The office of mayor was filled in 1896 by L. I. Cox, another Elon student, and in 1905 by P. J. Kernodle, a member of the college faculty.[77] In 1911 W. P. Lawrence, of the faculty, was serving as mayor. A citizens convention was held on April 25 to nominate officials to be voted on May 2 for the next administrative term of office. The nominees, elected without opposition, were W. P. Lawrence, mayor; W. T. Noah, J. C. McAdams, J. Fletcher Somers, O. B. Barnes, and T. C. Amick, aldermen; and R. J. Kernodle, chief of police. In June Noah was elected as mayor for three months while Lawrence was on leave for a summer teaching mission in Ohio. Of the seven officials elected, two were members of the college faculty, evidence of a cooperative spirit between the municipality and the institution.

While in session, somewhat after the fashion of the New England town meetings, the convention considered other matters of civic interest:

> The question as to the increase in the rate of taxes from 20 cts., to not exceeding 30 cts. on the one hundred dollars, and from 60 cts. to not exceeding 90 cts. on the poll, for the purpose of lighting the streets of the town was discussed, and the sentiment expressed was almost unanimous in favor of the lights.
>
> Dogs running at large in the town came in for a round of denunciation so that the new Board of Aldermen . . . are likely to find strong sentiment in favor of a strict dog law.[78]

On December 18, 1909, the Elon Bank and Trust Company was chartered. The authorized capital was $20,000, $5,000 of which was paid in. The institution opened its doors for business on January 1, 1910. Its officers were O. B. Barnes, president; J. Fletcher Somers, cashier; and W. P. Lawrence, L. I. Cox, J. C. McAdams, H. C. Pollard, J. B. Gerringer, G. S. Watson, and O. B. Barnes, directors. By the end of the year, the bank had erected its own building at the corner of South Williamson and West Lebanon avenues. "The new handsomely equipped banking house" contained a time-lock steel safe, a fireproof vault, "and the latest and best design and pattern in fixtures." [79]

At the annual meeting of stockholders in January 1911, the cashier reported that accounts numbered more than 150 and that the corporation had realized 4.4 percent. The following officers were then elected: O. B. Barnes, president; H. C. Pollard, vice-president; and J. Fletcher Somers, secretary-cashier. Barnes was one of the owners of the Elon Milling Company, a flour mill near the edge of the town; Pollard was an office supervisor at the Ossipee Mills; and Somers was manager of the mercantile department of the Elon Supply Company, a retail grocery and drugstore. In addition to these officers, E. L. Moffitt, J. B. Gerringer, G. S. Watson, J. J. Lambeth, T. C. Amick, J. L. Foster, J. A. Whitesell, J. W. Ingle, J. W. Patton, M. A. Atkinson, D. W. Brown, and W. P. Lawrence were elected as directors. Of this group of officials, two were members of the college faculty and another was president of the institution. [80]

Another civic development of the period was the organization of the Elon Lodge No. 549, of the Ancient Free and Accepted Masons. Granted a dispensation by the Grand Lodge of North Carolina on September 7, 1906, the fraternal order was chartered on September 7 of the following year. The first officers were W. C. Wicker, master; J. W. Ingle, senior warden; and J. W. Patton, junior warden. Details of the activities of the lodge are not available, but in 1911 W. A. Harper was worshipful master. Later, both Patton and Wicker became Masonic lecturers, and served their order in that capacity for many years. [81]

Some of the residents of the town were attracted to the municipality because they found it to be a pleasant place in which to reside. Among these were Jesse Winborne, and his wife, the former Tranquilla Helen Jones. After retiring from business in eastern North Carolina, Winborne built the house still standing at 129 East Trollinger Avenue, and lived there with his wife in his old age. When he died in 1907, his will named Professors Staley, Lawrence, and Atkinson as executors of his estate, then appraised at $15,000. The income from the property was to be paid to Mrs. Winborne during her life-time, after which several bequests were to be honored. Two-thirds of the residue were then to be given to Elon College and one-third to the Christian Orphanage. This was the first known legacy willed to the college by a resident of the town. Final settlement was not effected until 1923, when Elon received approximately $4,855.28 from the bequest in addition to $500 that had been received at an earlier date.[82]

Other patrons of the institution remembered the college in their wills also. In 1909 Captain P. H. Lee, of Holland, Virginia, left the school $1,000, though the money was not received immediately. Other bequests were also made from time to time.[83]

In 1909 numerous faculty activities and changes were announced:

> Prof. P. J. Kernodle, for ten years in the Math. chair, resigns to enter the publishing business in Richmond, Va. Prof. N. F. Brannock goes to Johns Hopkins University for a year's gradu-ate work and will return next year as Prof. of Mathematical Sciences. Prof. V. C. Pritchette goes to the University of Va. for graduate work. Miss Elise Ramsay retires from the faculty after nine years of successful work in the music department. She is succeeded by Miss Linda Barnes, who goes to the New England Conservatory for the summer as do Misses Wilson and Pitt also of the music department. Miss Allen of the Department of Expression will not return. Miss Bryan, of the Art Department, studies in Washington during her vacation. Prof. T. C. Amick of West Maryland College was elected principal of the prepara-tory department.[84]

The following year, W. A. Harper was made the dean, and Dr. E. E. Randolph, John T. Cobb, and Miss Mary Lou Pitt took employment elsewhere. Sylvester G. Rollings (Elon '08) was appointed to teach history and sociology, W. F. Warren was hired as an instructor, and Miss Ethel Clements was employed to teach "Expression" and phys-ical education. No record exists of other changes in the staff during the Moffitt administration.[85]

In 1898 the Southern Christian Convention had authorized raising an annual quota by its member conferences of funds to be used in support of Elon College. One of Moffitt's first acts as president was to assign a faculty member to each of these units to insure meeting the quota by a personal canvass. The plan was evidently successful because it was continued each year thereafter.[86]

While the college was being modernized, the president was busy with plans to pay for the improvements that had been made. His plan to launch a $50,000 fundraising campaign for that purpose was approved by the trustees at commencement in 1909, and later endorsed by the Southern Christian Convention. C. R. West, of Newport News, Virginia, started the drive by donating $500,[87] but other contributions were somewhat slow in coming in. However, in February 1910 Moffitt was able to announce triumphantly:

> Under the plan as fixed upon, we were not able to make any general canvass until at least ten men should be found who would agree to give one thousand dollars each. . . . Before the first of last January I succeeded in finding these ten friends: Bros. J. E. West, C. A. Shoop, W. H. Jones, Jr., G. W. Truitt, K. B. Johnson, W. J. Lee, Julian S. Carr, J. Beale Johnson, Arch B. Farmer, and Mrs. K. B. Johnson.[88]

From this start, also aided by the support of the *Sun*, the drive slowly but surely gained momentum toward the attainment of its final goal.

Elon band, about 1910. The leader, R. A. Campbell (Elon '11), is standing on the extreme right; Professor W. C. Wicker is next to him.

During Moffitt's last year in office, he was plagued with poor health and was critically ill at one time. He was not physically robust, but "a small man with a rather pointed chin and a brisk business-like manner."[89] The intense financial campaigning, added to his other presidential duties, were too much for his impaired health. Much as he desired to complete the drive for money, he was forced to resign in June 1911, when the trustees met. The board regretfully respected his wishes, then elected Dean Harper as his successor.[90]

Early in his presidency, Moffitt's competence had been recognized when Union Christian College, in Indiana, "the most prominent college of the Christian Church in the middle West," conferred the LL.D. degree upon him.[91] A tribute in the Sun also acknowledged his ability in a summary of his administration:

> For six eventful years, Dr. Moffitt has guided the affairs of the institution with a safe and steady hand. Under his administration the College has increased its plant by two new buildings and modern equipment, and has increased its usefulness and influence by a larger patronage and a growing constituency. He retires from the honored position, which he has filled so well, with the esteem and confidence of the people he ever sought to serve.[92]

Moffitt sold his home at 105 East Trollinger Avenue and returned to commercial pursuits in his native Asheboro. His three children later graduated from the college: S. Rhodes in 1922, Margaret (Mrs. Frederick William Van Buskirk) in 1928, and Emmett L., Jr., in 1933.[93]

In his later years, the former president returned to live in the town of Elon College near the institution he had fostered with all of his energy since leaving its presidency. On March 28, 1941, in his seventy-second year, he attended an Elon alumni meeting at the Alamance Hotel, in Burlington. As guest speaker for the occasion, he delivered a rousing address on the past accomplishments and future potential of the college. Upon its conclusion, he resumed his seat and immediately expired. His last mortal act was performed on behalf of the institution he had modernized, for which his memory is honored on its campus today by Moffitt Hall, built in 1968 for use as a dormitory.[94]

CHAPTER VI

THE SPREADING BRANCHES

The girt woak tree that's in the dell!
There's noo tree I do love so well.
WILLIAM BARNES
The Girt Woak Tree

William Allen Harper was born in Berkeley, Virginia, on April 17, 1880, the son of Joseph and Mary Melissa McCloud Harper. He graduated from Elon in 1899 with a grade-point average of 97.4 percent, the highest attained by a student since the opening of the institution.[1] After receiving his diploma, he took charge of an academy at Chance, North Carolina, for the summer, then became principal of Oakhurst Academy in the fall. On November 21 he married college classmate Estelle Walker, of the Union Ridge community in Alamance County, North Carolina. Already showing capability as an administrator, during the next three years Harper served as assistant principal of the city graded schools of Franklin, Virginia, and as superintendent of the city graded schools of Smithfield, North Carolina.[2]

In 1903 Harper was elected to the chair of Latin at his alma mater, but arranged for a leave of absence to work on a graduate degree at Yale University.[3] After earning his M.A. degree in 1905, the professor began his duties as an Elon faculty member, teaching Latin and religious education. In 1908 he was elected as Dean of the College, and served in that capacity until he became the fourth president, the first alumnus of the institution to fill the position.[4]

The new executive was young for a college president at the time; he was only thirty-one years of age when he took office. However, this proved to be an asset rather than a handicap. Filled with ambition for the institution, he immediately plunged into his duties with

President William A. Harper.

all the vigor and enthusiasm of a young man. He also enjoyed the advantage of becoming the head of an expanding institution rather than one faced with the problem of immediate survival, which had plagued some of his predecessors.

The total enrollment for the fall term in 1911 was 267, the largest since the opening of the college.[5] This alone increased the need for a larger plant, which was augmented by the demands of the expanding athletic program. The women requested a gymnasium for their exclusive use, and the men desired one in which they could play visiting teams before spectators. All the academic departments needed more equipment for their courses, and other facilities were necessary if expansion was to continue.

The $50,000 fund instituted by former President Moffitt successfully grew until it was fully subscribed by 1912,[6] which assured the payment of the mortgage on the college and gave the administration funds with which to work. Additional financial aid was also anticipated from other sources, which encouraged the trustees to authorize another building program.

First, the three existing tennis courts for men and two for women were put in "excellent condition." Female basketball enthusiasts were placated by the construction of an outdoor court.[7] Next, East Dormitory was overhauled. The ceilings and walls were tinted a "light drab"; the door and wainscoting were "grained in oak"; and steam heat, showers, and tub baths were installed. This made the building more attractive and comfortable than it had ever been since it was constructed. Fire escapes were added to the dormitory and to the Administration Building (Old Main), and $1,268.13 were spent building a three-story porch, 10 feet wide and 140 feet long on the northern side of West Dormitory. Also in the latter building, where it seemed space could always be found, an infirmary was equipped on the third floor through the generosity of Dr. J. E. Lincoln, of Lacey Springs, Virginia, and Mrs. S. W. Lincoln, of Broadway, in the same state. Several years later, it was reported that the facility had not been used, but it was a valued asset in case it should be needed.[8]

These improvements were completed by the end of the 1912 spring term, when further plans were revealed:

> The greatest event of commencement, however, was the announcement by the Corporation's secretary that the Board

of Trustees had decided to fit up the gymnasium room of the West Dormitory for the young ladies and to erect a modern gymnasium in addition the equal of any in the State for young men and that these improvements would be ready for the next fall term, if possible. The Building Committee for these improvements is the president, Dr. W. W. Staley, and Kemp B. Johnson. Plans from architects will be received and the contract let as soon as possible. This addition to Elon's equipment will place it on a par with that of any college in the South.[9]

The first phase of this welcome project, completed on schedule, at a cost of $1,437.08, was described in the *Weekly*:

The changes at West Dormitory are extensive and add greatly to the appearance and convenience of the building. The gymnasium has been converted into a handsome dining room by raising the floor on a level with that of the main building, plastering the walls, and ceiling the overhead. The large columns have been removed and the floor above is now supported by four heavy truss rods. All the other rooms in the lower story of the north extension has [sic] been nicely furnished, two being thrown into one large kitchen with butler's pantry between that and the new dining room. The old dining room on the second floor becomes the young ladies' gymnasium. With these extensive improvements to this commodious and well-appointed building, equipped with steam heat, baths, toilets, and electric lights, young ladies will have a most comfortable home during their college career at Elon.[10]

The second part of the project had also begun in June 1912, when the trustees approved the expenditure of $12,000 to erect North Dormitory, which would contain living quarters and an adequate men's gymnasium. The president was enthused over the decision, and predicted the new facility would attract twenty-five extra students annually for two years. Construction, which began immediately, had made sufficient progress by the opening of the fall term in September that the prediction was made that the building would be completed and equipped for occupancy by the end of the calendar year.[11]

While this project was underway, the "Physical, Chemical, and

Expression class, about 1912. From left to right, front row: *Violet
E. Frazier, Kallilee Brothers, Mary L. Williams, and Annie L.
Wicker Johnston.* Second row: *S. S. Myrick, Ethel Barrett Hearn*
(front), *Sallie Foster* (rear), *Hugh P. Cline, and Nellie S. Fleming.*

Biological Laboratories, together with the Library," were improved. In the latter, a wall was removed to provide a new reading room and the old one used for additional stack space "with adjustable shelving around the walls." The old bookcases were removed and "a gallery built on all sides of the room." The gallery was reached by a stairway. Shelving extended from the floor to the 16-foot-high ceiling. This practically doubled the capacity of the library.[12]

The Music Department, in which 87 students were enrolled in 1912, received the next attention, as announced in the press: "The College has recently installed new Mason pianos throughout, two car loads of them, so that every piano in the Music Conservatory, whether used for practice or instruction, is absolutely new." The thirteen new instruments were obtained at a cost of $1,500 by trading in the ten pianos that had served the college for many years. This additional equipment immeasurably facilitated the musical program of the college.[13]

The impetus given the department at this time may have been partially generated by the influence of the president's wife, who had studied music extensively after graduating from Elon. Mrs. Harper later served as president of both the North Carolina Federation of Music Clubs and the South Atlantic District of Music Clubs. She also founded and edited the *North Carolina State Music Bulletin*, and was the first from the state to become a life member of the National Federation of Music Clubs. Her interest in the field constituted an inspiration as well as a challenge to the college music teachers throughout her husband's administration.[14]

More than $3,000 was also spent for a steel, 50,000-gallon capacity water tank, which was mounted near the Power House on a steel tower 70 feet high. This vital utilitarian structure did not enhance the aesthetic appearance of the campus, but it became a landmark until it was removed in 1978. Despite the precautionary measures to prevent such actions, for years some students contrived to paint the senior class numerals in large figures on the side of the tank. Those of the previous year were painted over in the process. After several decades, this hazardous practice was abandoned as the students found other outlets for their energies. The old tank on the top of West Dormitory remained as an auxiliary, but not a necessity. Eventually it became dilapidated and was removed. Meantime, the increased waterpower enabled the college to provide more efficient service and to extend sewer lines to the Christian Orphanage property, a major advantage to that charitable institution.[15]

Another problem was created by the increasing number of students, which by 1912 overtaxed the facilities of both the college and the town to supply them with room and board. To meet this situation, the Young Men's Cooperative Hall was built at a cost of $1,400. It was located on the north side of Haggard Avenue at the present entrance to the gymnasium parking lot. The one-story frame cottage served as a boarding place for a maximum of 50 males and was popularly known as the Young Men's Club. Although the building contained residential quarters for the stewardess and her family, in addition to kitchen and pantries, most of the interior space was used as a large dining room. The building was rented by the college to a student organization, which operated it on a cooperative basis. In September 1912 the Young Men's Club was organized for that purpose in Dr. Harper's office. A constitution and bylaws were adopted and the following officers elected: W. T. Lewis, president; A.C. Bergeron, vice-president; L. W. Fogleman, secretary; F. W. Ford, manager-treasurer; C. B. Riddle, bookkeeper; and Mrs. A. L. Battle, the stewardess. The organization, which opened for business with thirty members, had soon enrolled all the diners its facilities could accommodate. The project, operated at cost, enabled the members to obtain board at a much cheaper rate than elsewhere.

This plan was suggested by the private dining clubs for men already in existence at Elon. The first of these had been organized in 1900 by the Walters brothers, W. T. (Elon '03) and Charles Manley (Elon '04). The latter was elected manager of the enterprise, and he was responsible for collecting the board money from the members, buying provisions, hiring a cook, and generally supervising the club. A house in the town was rented for the use of the diners. Board was obtained at cost, which included the manager's salary of one dollar per week.[16] The success of the enterprise led to the formation of others and eventually to the college using the plan on a much larger scale.

Upon the completion of the dining arrangement for men, the president busied himself with a plan to supply more economical accommodations for women. The Harpers had purchased the large house built by the Moring family at 301 East College Avenue. Because their only child, Walker A. Harper, had died in infancy, the presidential family enjoyed a surplus of room. By adding another room and bathroom, plus installing water and heat, a major part of the dwelling was converted into Young Ladies' Hall. Under the capable management of Mrs. Sadie V. Jones, the fifteen residents performed the work necessary for maintenance, and obtained their board at cost. This considerably reduced their living expenses. When Dr. Harper later moved into a home he built farther east in the same block, the hall was able to increase the number of female residents.[17]

Encouraged by the success of his experiment, Harper persuaded the trustees to erect a building on the campus to be used for a similar purpose. In 1913 the Young Ladies' Cooperative Hall, sometimes called the New West Dormitory but usually known as Ladies' Hall, was completed. It was located on the site of the present Sloan Dormitory. The main part of the brick building was two stories in height. A one-story annex was situated at its rear, and a basement ran under the entire structure. Architecturally, the edifice was similar to the larger West Dormitory, which it paralleled, and was ornamented by a two-story porch across its front. Plans and specifications were drawn by Burwell Riddick, of Suffolk, Virginia, as a gift to the college. Completed at a cost of $6,000, the building contained dormitory, dining, and laundry facilities for sixty-four female students.[18]

The occupants of the new hall performed most of the work necessary for its operation. Under the supervision of a matron, they made the beds, cleaned, did the laundry, served the meals, washed dishes, and assisted with the cooking. By these means, living expenses for the school year were pared to $60, which compared with $75 to $125 paid by students who lived elsewhere. This was an economic boon at the time.[19]

These projects did not interfere with the construction of the new gymnasium-dormitory building which, somewhat surprisingly, was completed on schedule and ready for occupancy on January 1, 1913. The oblong brick structure, whose main entrance was on its western end, was built parallel to Haggard Avenue and located approximately where the Caroline E. Powell Building now stands. The gymnasium-dormitory rose three stories in height over a full, partially underground basement, in which showers, toilets, lockers, and similar fixtures were provided in addition to a large floor space. The gymnasium on the first floor was three stories in height; from a balcony on three sides of the two upper stories doors opened into dormitory rooms on the sides. These accommodated 100 men. The balconies were wide enough so that the track team could use them for indoor practice.

The gym floor, "laid in Michigan hard maple," measured 60 feet by 100 feet. A basketball court at the center was 45 by 80 feet in size. Adequate room was left on two sides for spectators. Completely equipped with gymnastic apparatus, the facility compared favorably with any college gymnasium in the state at the time. The building was opened amid much rejoicing by faculty and students, and on January 27, 1913, the first basketball game with a visiting team was played on its court. This contest was followed by many others; and, at the conclusion of the 1913–14 season, President Harper jubilantly informed the trustees of the winning of the North Carolina state basketball championship, "no mean distinction for the first year of the gymnasium."[20]

The space available in the basement was partially utilized for new chemical and physical laboratories. These were equipped "after the Johns Hopkins style." Heating and lighting were supplied by a "new Tirrill Gasolene Gas Plant."[21] The remaining floor space was used for the new Domestic Science Department, and contained the kitchen for this function. A small vault in the building was used to store college records.[22]

The new domestic science course proved to be so popular that the department outgrew its quarters the first year, and was moved to the ground floor of Ladies' Hall. This was a practical move because an academic unit exclusively for women was much better housed in a building designed for females rather than in one primarily for men. It also enabled the department to give a certain amount of college credit to the women who were gaining practical experience in domestic science through their part in the maintenance of Ladies' Hall.[23]

As is often the case, the estimated cost of $12,000 for the North Dormitory was insufficient; the completed structure cost $26,000. This deficit placed the trustees in a financially embarrassing position that they had sought to avoid, but their problem was solved by aid that came as a surprise. At commencement in 1913, the Alumni Association acknowledged that providing a scholarship for a member of the junior class was all that it had done "of a permanent character" for its alma mater and indicated it was then "in a position to undertake a permanent work for the College." Through a committee composed of the Reverend W. T. Walters, D. R. Fonville, and Alonza T. Banks, the association made the trustees an offer to pay the entire cost of North within a ten-year period. The only condition of this magnanimous proposal was that the name of the structure be changed to the "Alumni Building." The relieved board unanimously accepted the offer and its terms.[24] This action constituted the first major move of Elon alumni to aid the college, a practice that has continued to the present. Because the building contained the gymnasium, the donation also revealed the enthusiasm of the association for college athletics, which has never abated.

Regardless of the interest generated, raising the necessary funds was an ambitious undertaking, though by 1912 some 198 people had received Elon degrees and hundreds of others had studied to some extent at the institution.[25] Nevertheless, participation in the project was limited to "only graduates of the college and those who had been students in it." A captain was appointed for each class to canvass the members for subscriptions; and an "Old Guard" committee, composed of the Reverend B. F. Black, Miss Annie Watson, A. T. West, and the college president, who was also a member of the association, solicited nongraduates for contributions.[26] Everyone went to work with a will. The drive, which was ultimately successful, was acclaimed by Dr. Harper as "the dawning of a new day of prophetic greatness for the College."[27]

The next move in the facilities program of 1912–13 was to improve the College Dairy by "concreting the floor and installing modern stanchions for each of the herd of cattle."[28] At the same time, the trustees considered it advisable to remove the herd of swine penned near the campus to a more remote location. An agreement was made to place it on Dr. Atkinson's farm and to feed it with the waste from the dining halls. This move was not intended to cost any money, but the hogs died of a disease contracted during the transfer and caused a considerable financial loss.[29] A new herd was then placed in the old location, an unwise move in view of the growth of the town. As a result, on July 21, 1913, municipal authorities declared the college hog pen a nuisance and ordered its removal. Arrangements were then made to keep the animals elsewhere, and eventually the dairy was also moved to another location.[30]

Last of all, the campus received attention. The ten arc lights, so prized when first installed, were replaced with thirty large Mazda electric lamps, which provided far better light. Fences were erected around the coal pile and the barnyard. Even the old college well house was not neglected, and was replaced by a "beautiful summer house for the young ladies." This concluded the first Harper building and expansion program. It placed the college in a better position to care for the physical needs of its students than at any time previously. It also left the administration free to concentrate on expanding the curriculum and further improving the academic program.[31]

From the opening of the college, its presidents had been keenly interested in preparing teachers for the public schools. Efforts to provide such training were gradually expanded until a four-year Teachers' Course became part of the curriculum. Students completing the first and second years of this course were granted a teacher's certificate, upon application. Those finishing three years won the degree of Licentiate of Instruction (L.I.). Students who completed the entire four years of the program received the degree of Bachelor of Pedagogy. In the catalog for 1914–15, this degree was discarded and the graduate received either a Bachelor of Arts or a Bachelor of Philosophy degree, depending upon the elective courses studied. The administration had been rewarded in 1913 for its emphasis on this offering when the state of Virginia announced its acceptance of an Elon College diploma "as a basis for the certification of teachers in that commonwealth."[32]

In addition, as soon as it became possible, the institution began holding Teachers' Institutes. Lasting from one or two weeks, these sufficed to fill the minimum requirements for the state at the time for those who could not attend college four years and also offered refresher study for certified teachers. The program had been emphasized consistently, and by the time Harper took office, the offering had been expanded to a "Special Normal Term" of two months in residence "for teachers or those preparing to teach."[33] The course won the approval of numerous county superintendents of education, and, more significantly, of J. Y. Joyner, the state Superintendent of Public Instruction. He wrote:

> . . . believing that teachers will derive great benefit from the successful completion of this course under the instruction of the faculty of the College, carried on in the favorable environment of College life, I shall gladly recommend to county superintendents the acceptance of properly signed certificate of continuous attendance and of the successful completion of this work by public school teachers as a substitute for attendance on the biennial teachers' institutes required by law, as provided in section 4168 of the public school law.[34]

This official endorsement encouraged the administration to emphasize the program.

The course prepared prospective teachers for state certification, enabled teachers to renew their certificates as required by the state, gave them an opportunity to specialize in their chosen fields, and also prepared a student for entrance into the college as a candidate for a degree. The regular Normal Course included instruction in arithmetic, school law, English grammar, geography, history of the United States, agriculture, drawing, agricultural chemistry, reading, phonetics, spelling, physiology, hygiene, history of North Carolina, pedagogy, and civil government. For those wishing advanced studies, rhetoric, English literature, physics, astronomy, German, French, Greek, Latin, pedagogy, algebra, geometry, and history were offered.

While in residence, Normal students were privileged to enjoy all the facilities of the college, including membership in the societies, if desired. Eighteen students were enrolled in the course in 1913, an encouraging number for a small school. Both the Normal Course and the Teachers' Course continued to expand successfully. In the college catalog for 1915–16, these courses, previously listed under "Special Departments," were grouped together as "The School of Education." Thus, they achieved a comparable academic level with the major offerings of the institution. Eventually the school became the Department of Education, one of Elon's largest scholastic divisions, which prepares many graduates annually for teacher certification.[35]

In addition to teacher training and the liberal arts courses usually offered by colleges at the time, Elon also maintained special departments of art, music, expression, physical culture, domestic science, and commercial, as well as providing instrumental instruction through the college band. Occasionally unusual courses were added to the curriculum. These included penmanship, first advocated by the faculty in 1911, and taught by Professor Hilvard Elior Jorgenson in 1915; and piano tuning, taught in 1914 by A. C. Bergeron.[36] This latter addition may have been inspired by the acquisition of a concert grand piano for the Auditorium, "where the recitals of the Music Department are always given." The instrument was a Kimball, attributable to the salesmanship of J. P. McNally, a representative of that company, who moved to Elon and resided for several years in a house where the president's home now stands. (He was the father of C. P. McNally, Elon '20.)[37]

The piano, which was obtained at the greatly reduced cost of $500, f.o.b. Chicago, was described as "an exact reproduction of the concert grand used in her recent American engagement by Miss Myrtle Elvyn," who had also performed on the same type of instrument before the royal family of Germany. McNally was also responsible in 1920 for arranging a price reduction from $5,900 to $4,000 for a

Art class in the early years of the college.

Kimball pipe organ that the college purchased for the Auditorium. The instrument, which featured decorative show pipes, was operated electrically. It contrasted markedly with the small, hand-pumped organ, whose pipes were concealed, which had been in use since the beginning of the institution. The Music Department was justly proud of the significant additions to its equipment.[38]

The curriculum was broadened and strengthened by every available means possible. One change was the adoption of a set of standard requirements for graduate students to replace the preparation of individual lists. It was also specified that such studies would need to be pursued during actual residence at the college in the future. These actions placed the program on a more systematic basis than it had been previously.[39]

All the improvements made in facilities and courses collectively were highly rewarded. In January 1916 Professor Lawrence represented the institution in Chicago on the "auspicious occasion" when the Association of American Colleges admitted Elon to full membership as a standard college.[40]

This achievement almost coincided with a visit to the school by Dr. S. P. Capen, of the National Board of Education, who was engaged to investigate and classify colleges for the North Carolina Department of Education. The results of this visit were reported by President Harper to the trustees:

> He expressed himself as well pleased with our aims and sincerity. He pronounced our equipment good and gave us credit for fifty advanced courses, rating only fourteen as introductory. He suggested strengthening our entrance requirement in English, the specifying of certain branches of Natural Science for entry to particular courses, and the improvement of our library facilities. Our Natural Science department he thought in particular needed strengthening. He pronounced our scientific laboratories ample for all purposes.[41]

Capen also summarized his conclusions regarding Elon in a terse statement: "Well organized. Well administered. Honest. Devoted and capable faculty, paid starvation wages, but loyal. Fine, earnest student body. General impression excellent."[42] As a result of the investigation, the institution was rated as a Class A College, a happy outcome for all concerned.

As Capen commented, faculty salaries were undoubtedly low, but they had at least improved since the early years of the college. In 1913 the president's annual pay was $1,500; full professors, $900; athletic coach, $400 and board; top female professors, $800; and all other female instructors, either $300 or $400 and board. All except the chief executive were relieved of the onerous work of canvassing the field for prospective students and funds during the summer months.

This was a welcome change because the faculty, as it had done since the opening of Elon, not only taught a full load of classes but also attended to many of the duties that today are performed by administrative officials. This was evident in the duties assigned in 1912: J. U. Newman, Dean; Thomas C. Amick, Secretary of the Faculty; W. C. Wicker, Registrar; W. P. Lawrence, Curator of the Library; N. F. Brannock, Curator of Buildings and Grounds and Recorder; R. A. Campbell, Bursar; and A. L. Hook, Curator of the Museum. In addition, Lawrence, Wicker, Brannock, and Campbell were designated as advisers to the senior, junior, sophomore, and freshman classes, respectively, and Amick as adviser for the preparatory classes and special students. In 1914 the president's pay was raised to $1,800 and the department heads to $1,200. This still was not high remuneration, but the loyal faculty accepted it gratefully and continued its efforts to improve the college.[43]

During the early years of the Harper administration, the series of annual lectures given at the college by Drs. Martyn Summerbell and Frank S. Child were continued. Both these men were considered nonresident members of the faculty and so listed in the college catalogs. Summerbell was president and Child secretary of the board that directed the Francis Asbury Palmer Fund, which paid them for their services to Elon. From time to time, other gifts were received from this fund, of which the college is still a beneficiary.

In addition to these presentations, for several years a lecture course was conducted by Dr. W. S. Sargent, of Providence, Rhode Island, secretary of education of the American Christian Convention, with which the Southern Christian Convention maintained a fraternal relationship. Many of the faculty had always been called upon to present public lectures during the year, and in the catalog of 1915–16 a list of the speakers and a range of their topics was published for the first time. The lengthy and impressive list contained subjects that required a considerable amount of preparation on the part of the lecturers. Supplementing this program, the custom was continued for the Music and Expression departments to give recitals during the year and the Art Department an exhibit at commencement. The public was invited to attend all the programs because the faculty consistently voted that "there be no paid public entertainments or exercises" at Elon College.[44]

Dr. Harper adopted the custom of delivering the monthly pay checks at faculty meetings. The idea may not have been original with him, and, whether the practice was to encourage attendance at the meetings, or for convenience, or both, is uncertain. At any rate, it was the cause of an occasional jocular entry in the usually prosaic minutes of the meetings. In 1913 Secretary Amick wrote, "The faculty met at 9 o'clock P.M., with all present except Dr. Atkinson who was doubtless absent because he had not heard that there were any loaves and fishes for distribution." In the same year, another humorous entry was made: "The faculty met in regular session with all present except Dr. Atkinson and Prof. Lawrence whose voices were heard, but their spirits were engaged in another room on other business, since there were no loaves and fishes to be distributed this evening." Two years later, another entry read, "Drafts were distributed by the President for the last month's salary, for which the Faculty returned thanks."[45]

On another occasion, Dr. Ned F. Brannock apparently requested the aid of a student in making preparations for his course in astronomy. In response, a motion was passed and recorded, "Mr. Luther Riddick is allowed to move among the stars, and follow Prof. Brannock in his flight from zone to zone that Prof. Brannock in his weary journey may not have to sail alone." The secretary again departed from his usual routine entries when two letters, apparently from parents who were critical of the disciplinary policy of the college, were read to the faculty. "These epistles had a smack of all the learning and philosophy of every age from Socrates to the present," he wrote. The entry then continued, "The letters are commended to the kindly consideration of the faculty that they may more fully learn the principles and philosophy for school instruction and school government." However, these sort of items were rare exceptions in the usually formal recording of the faculty proceedings.[46]

Although Harper's expansion of the curriculum was commendable, he was no more successful than his presidential predecessors in establishing a Department of Theology. The funds with which to pay three additional faculty members to devote their full time to the ministerial students had simply never been available. However, the president revealed his concern for the matter in 1914 when he informed the Southern Christian Convention, "We have talked Theological Department for many years and it is now time we were taking definite steps toward its institution." The project, formerly assigned to the venerable J. W. Wellons, had failed because no appreciable sum had been raised. "The time was not ripe," explained Harper, "and it is not now ripe for the canvassing of the field for funds for this purpose." However, he did consider it timely to recommend and win approval of the convention for designation of a Christian Education Day, when free will offerings would be taken in each church for the project.[47]

Four years later, sufficient money had been contributed through this channel to pay for one professor of theology.[48] The appointment was never made, however, because World War I interfered with many plans at the time, and a Department of Theology was never established at Elon College.

Regardless of this failure, the institution made progressive strides as a church-related school. In 1915 an Elon student wrote a tribute to this achievement:

> Among the distinctly religious colleges in this part of the country that appeal to the people at large because of the stress laid on its highly moral atmosphere and religious spirit is Elon College. Between one-third and one-half of its total registration comes from other denominations. Here we find between thirty and forty students from the Methodist Episcopal church, nearly the same number from the Methodist Protestant church; and then between fifteen and twenty come from the Baptist church. Practically all the protestant denominations in the South are represented in its student body.[49]

The Methodist Protestants, whose severance from the Methodist Episcopal Church had been on basically the same grounds as that of the O'Kelly group that became the Christian Church, operated no denominational college of their own in North Carolina at the time and patronized Elon extensively until their own institution could be provided. The student commented on this fact in his statement:

> Those who especially concern us as Methodist Protestants are the Methodist Protestant students at Elon College. Of the forty or more Methodist Protestant students in the College, nine are preparing for the ministry in the Methodist Protestant Church, and one young lady is preparing to be a foreign missionary whenever she is ready for the work and the Board can make use of her services.[50]

This happy relationship continued until 1922, when the Methodist Protestant Church founded High Point College to serve the growing needs of its denomination. Elon President Harper was cordially invited to be present when the cornerstone was laid as a courteous acknowledgment of past cordial relations.[51]

While the efforts to finance theological studies were in progress, "Uncle" Wellons suggested that, until the desired department could be obtained, "more practical work" be added to the courses then being taught at the college.[52] This proposal met with administrative approval, and in 1915 an Extra-Bible Curriculum was added to the college offerings. It consisted of six courses, each of which met for an hour each week. They were required of all students though they carried no degree credit, nor was any tuition charged for them. However, the catalog stipulated, "no student who fails to pass in these courses during the period of residence here can receive a degree, certificate, or diploma."[53] The teaching load for this program was proportioned among the faculty, without acquiring new personnel. Both the administration and the church were pleased with this addition to the curriculum, and, since it originated, all students are required to complete a specified number of courses in religion in order to graduate.

Another forward step was taken in the spiritual life of the community in 1914, when Dr. J. O. Atkinson was elected as pastor of the College Church. Its services, held in the college chapel, had formerly been conducted by faculty members taking turns and by an occasional visiting minister, but no official pastor had served the needs of the congregation of students and townspeople. Welcoming the new assignment, Dr. Harper commented, "The election of a college pastor for all his time by the local church with the co-operation of the student body—a most happy circumstance, destined to mean much for the future internal development of the College, conditioned of course on getting the right man—which we have fortunately done."[54] The response to this change was immediate, and ever since the church has always provided the services of a regular pastor.

Both the Sunday school of the College Church and the Christian Endeavor Society were regularly attended by the students. The Ministerial Association (also called the Ministerial Band), the YMCA, and the YWCA continued to be active, and even the athletes were required to attend church services whenever the teams were away from Elon over the weekend. All these organizations, in addition to the church, placed as much emphasis on religious life for the students as existed in any liberal arts college of the day.[55]

The occasional injection of a humorous entry in the faculty minutes is better understood in view of the tedious hours spent by the secretary and his colleagues on student discipline and other matters that would be handled by a dean's office today. The teachers were scholars, and sought relief from their many routine duties by seeking an opportunity to associate with each other on their own intellectual level. This led to the formation of the Cosmopolitan Club in 1910, composed of "the members of the faculty and others desiring to enter into cultural literary work." Dr. J. U. Newman was president and Professor A. Liggett Lincoln the secretary-treasurer.[56]

The organization held its first fortnightly meeting in the Lawrence home. The program consisted of a paper by Professor Harper: "Roman Literary Life during the Silver Age as Revealed in Pliny's Letters," which was read and discussed. For the second meeting, Professor Brannock was scheduled to present a study entitled "The Beginnings of Chemistry."[57] The club remained a valued part of the Elon community life until it became inactive in 1914 for reasons unknown. The general use of the automobile by that time supplied convenient transportation to cultural events in nearby municipalities, which made an organization supported entirely by its own membership less attractive and essential. Efforts to revive the Cosmopolitan were unsuccessful.[58]

Another college enterprise, which was an asset to the community as well, encountered difficulties in 1914. Two years earlier, when R. A. Campbell was the editor and C. B. Riddle business manager, the *Weekly* had boasted of 2,415 subscribers,[59] but had not prospered financially, according to an item in the *Sun*:

> *The Elon College Weekly* appeared this week for the first time since the holidays and is become a monthly. The subscription list and support accorded the paper in other ways did not justify its further publication as a weekly. During its four years of history it has lost over $400. It is trusted that the friends will come to the rescue and redeem the situation for it henceforth.[60]

Unfortunately, the monthly issuance failed to solve the financial problem, and publication soon ceased. The college and the town were then dependent upon the newspapers in the area, particularly the "Elon Letter" column in the *Sun*, for news coverage until 1920, when another college paper was founded.

At about the same time the *Weekly* ceased to exist, a different type of publication was born at the college. In 1907 the faculty had recommended that the senior class undertake publication of a college yearbook of not less than 150 pages, named the *Cli-psi-phi*. No action was taken by the students until the project was revived in 1912, when A. L. Hook and C. T. Rand requested permission for the seniors to issue a college annual. The name originally proposed was changed to the more euphonious *Phipsicli*, which still honored the three literary societies from which it was derived. The proposal was approved on the condition that the book's contents be approved by the faculty.[61]

During the editorship of Rand, when Hook served as business manager, the first issue of the yearbook was issued in 1913. It was an immediate success and, except for the war years of 1918–19 and the depression year 1930, has been published annually at the college to the present. The liberal use of photographic material, accompanied by various articles, made the annual of inestimable historic and sentimental value to the college and its alumni as time passed, a function the publication still accomplishes.[62]

In 1898 the Southern Christian Convention had moved the office of the *Christian Sun* from Raleigh to Elon College. This was a convenience to Dr. Atkinson, who edited the periodical from 1900 to 1916.[63] For more than a decade after the move, the editorial work took place in the college town, but the printing was done either in

Greensboro or Burlington. However, because the church required other printing, in 1912 the convention voted to build its own plant at Elon College. A lot was secured on West Trollinger Avenue, next to the bank, and a brick two-story building erected for the Christian Publishing House. The first floor contained offices and the rooms to house the modern press and the Merganthaler typesetting machine. The second floor contained a large room for meetings in addition to several dormitory rooms for male students. The $12,000 structure was completed and equipped early in 1913, ready for occupancy.[64]

This was but another step in the denomination's plan to concentrate its activities at Elon. It was also a boon to the college administration, as announced by President Harper: "It has long been a necessity and is become a convenience before undreamed of. It does all the College printing and supplies besides dormitory space for twenty-four young men, in rooms lighted by electricity and equipped with both steam heat and sewer facilities."[65] C. W. Montgomery came to Elon from Troy, Ohio, to superintend the operation, and the printing presses were soon busy with the work of both the college and the church, though outside commissions were also sought.

The enterprise was operated by the Southern Christian Publishing Company, and, though its directors were elected from nominees supplied by the Southern Convention, it was strictly a private enterprise dependent upon making a financial profit for its existence. In the beginning, some commercial firms provided patronage. The Modern Progress Publishing Company of Burlington's *Modern Progress*, a journal "of today and tomorrow," was printed by the company. However, these contracts were too few to keep the presses operating at capacity, and commercial orders were sought elsewhere than in the college town. The suggestion was made by some Christian Church leaders in 1915 that more business might be obtained if the company moved to Burlington. This the directors declined to do, but they opened an office there in an effort to obtain more job printing orders.[66] The *Sun* then dismissed the matter with the comment: "Burlington friends are bringing influence to bear to have the Publishing House moved to that city. Why not Burlington people move to Elon? All Elon needs to be a city is more people. It is already a mighty good place to live."[67] And it was a good place to live, though not necessarily a good place for commercial profit.

In November 1913, after only ten months of service, ill health forced Montgomery to resign. He was succeeded by Edwin D. Fowler, of Burlington, who made a valiant but unsuccessful effort to operate the business profitably. Finally, in 1916, after the company reported a net operational loss of $5,000, the convention leased the *Sun* to Carl B. Riddle, a 1916 graduate of Elon. Two years later, the office of the journal was moved to Burlington, and the Southern Christian Publishing Company went out of business. The building it had occupied was then designated as South Dormitory and used by the college as a residence hall for men until fire destroyed it in 1956.[68]

Riddle had engaged in numerous activities during his student days at Elon. He served as bookkeeper of the Young Men's Club, business manager of the *Weekly*, and secretary to President Harper. By correspondence, he collected statements from sixty-two persons relating to the manner in which they had worked for their education. He edited and assembled these in *College Men Without Money*, which was issued in 1914 by the Thomas Y. Crowell Company, of New York. As far as has been determined, this was the first book by an Elon undergraduate that was ever published.[69]

The volume included the accounts of Viola E. Frazier; J. F. Morgan; Charles H. Rowland; Charles M. Walters, who graduated from Elon; Mary E. West, who attended the institution; and W. P. Lawrence, who became a member of the faculty after his graduation. Two other contributors, H. E. Jorgenson and W. W. Staley, were educated elsewhere, but the former became a member of the Elon faculty and the latter served as the second president of the college.

The book was acclaimed as an inspiration to many students who were having financial difficulty in attending college. It was also in keeping with the efforts of the Elon administration to assist students financially to attend the institution, as stated in the catalog: "Elon has always encouraged its students to help themselves, not only in the preparation of lessons for the class-room, but also in paying their necessary expenses. And while the village is small, and practically devoid of industrial establishments, yet the number of students who pay their own way by work at off-hours has always been reasonably large and has steadily increased."[70] The number continued to increase, as did the means by which the college could assist students, until student aid eventually became a significant part of the institution's operation.

Although Riddle, who became an ordained minister of the Christian Church, was unsuccessful in publishing the *Sun*, he was wedded to journalism and followed that profession the remainder of his life.[71]

The college had always encouraged a spirit of democracy among its students, particularly evident in the regulation requiring similarity in the wardrobes of female students. However, the rules gradually became less rigid as time passed, though the administration still stressed uniformity and "sensible" dress. In 1911 the requirement that the ladies wear uniforms was abolished, and the new regulations printed in the catalog of that year:

> No uniform is required, but simplicity in dress, both for young men and young women, is required. Decollete dresses will not be permitted. On all public and evening occasions, except at Commencement, white simple dresses shall be worn. Parents and guardians are earnestly requested not to let their daughters spend too much on dress, and the right is reserved to refuse to allow a dress to be worn that in the opinion of the Faculty is too expensive or too elaborately made. Dress hats may be worn on Sunday morning, but shall not be worn on any other public occasion at the College nor to recitations. When possible all clothing should be made at home.[72]

A few months later, the faculty made another change by approving the recommendation of its Committee on Uniforms that "the young ladies be allowed to wear gingham dresses after April 1, 1912."[73]

These changes did not mean that all the old policy had been completely abandoned. In 1913, when fashion favored the "hobble" skirt, a garment in which the wearer could only walk by taking short and mincing steps, many women slit their skirts so they could take longer strides in walking. Through Miss Bessie Urquhart, the Dean of Women, the Elon girls requested permission to wear this type of garment. They defended their petition on the grounds that female members of the faculty did so. The faculty ceased being liberal at this point, and requested the female instructors to conform to the same regulations that governed the students. The ruling was then passed "that no slit, curved, or divided skirts, or any skirts that had any divided effect by having pieces of material of another color set and sewed in should be worn by the young ladies of the college, and that Miss Urquhart should be empowered to carry out this regulation." Despite this rebuff, the coeds no longer needed to wear the drab uniforms, which they considered a definite improvement in the rules.[74]

Decorum was also maintained in other ways, according to the convictions of the highest authority. "The Board of Trustees have prohibited young men from wearing track team suits on the campus or grounds of the college," it was announced at a faculty meeting. "Also young ladies are not allowed to attend any games in the gymnasium where these suits are worn by any of the young men in the game," concluded the ruling.[75] This regulation was still in effect three years later when the Executive Board of the trustees permitted the track team to practice on a four-acre lot east of the campus, but "no ladies of the college" were to be present at these events.

All problems were not solved by these rulings, however. In 1913 Athletic Director Doak and R. N. Miller, director of the gymnasium, addressed an inquiry to the trustees: "Will the regulation basket ball suit, which leaves about four inches of the lower limb bare at the knee, between the pants and the top of the stockings, and which also leaves the arm bare from the shoulder, be allowed?" The athletic officials explained that if this privilege was not permitted, "our men will be absolutely handicapped in inter-collegiate contests if not allowed to wear the regulation suit." Permission was then granted to wear the uniform requested, but not by a unanimous vote. One trustee voted, "Yes as to Jerseys; no as to trousers and stockings," while another approved only when the suits were worn indoors.[76]

Entirely aside from the matter of decorum, the design of the athletic uniforms had earlier forced a final decision in the choice of official colors for the institution. The college colors were apparently first mentioned in 1894, when an item in the *Sun* noted that forty students from eastern Virginia passed through Raleigh in a special railroad coach en route to Elon. "The car was decorated with the college colors, pink, white, and blue." Possibly, the reporter mistook garnet for pink, for in 1907 the faculty moved that the colors of the three literary societies, garnet, white, and blue, be combined to constitute the official colors of the college. This combination was not popular with the athletes when the teams began playing in intercollegiate contests. Their opponents wore two-color uniforms that designated their schools, and the Elon men desired the same arrangement for their alma mater. Partially for this reason, in 1909 Professors Harper and Edgar E. Randolph were appointed as a faculty committee to deliberate the matter. Their conclusion was to leave the decision up to the president and female instructors of the institution. Although it was not recorded, this group apparently made a final choice because a college Bulletin, in May 1911, contained the notice that it was "bound and printed on the covers in the College Colors, Maroon and Old Gold."[77] This combination has been pleasing to all connected with the institution since that date, and widespread use of the colors has been made in numerous ways since their selection.

Elon College has always been proud of its wooded campus, often boastfully described in the catalog as "one of the most beautiful in the South," and efforts have been made to keep the grove attractive.[78] When the custom began for each graduating class to present their alma mater with a parting gift, the offering was often directed toward beautification of the grounds. The senior class of 1900 planted a Norway maple tree, and the class of 1914 donated sixty silver maple trees to fill in bare spots on the campus.[79]

When the original clearing of underbrush and thinning of trees took place in the grove, the work had been supervised by "Will" Long, the president's son. One young white oak tree, called a "hunchbacked," grew from the ground in a curve the height of a man before its trunk straightened out. Young Long convinced his father, after some argument, that the peculiar tree was an object of beauty that should be spared, and "the old veteran of the forest primeval" became a major Elon landmark. It eventually became known as the Senior Oak because of its age, and is still standing in front of West Dormitory. The tradition arose and lasted for many years that every student at the college be photographed at some time or other beside the oak, and it is still a favorite spot for taking snapshots.[80]

Under the leadership of its president, A. L. Hook, the senior class of 1913 decided to depart from the tree-planting custom, and obtained permission instead to plant ivy around the old tree. This was accomplished in a ceremony of "dignity, solemnity, and significance" on November 29, 1912, though the weather was cold and snow lay on the ground. Led by the members of the junior class, the seniors marched in procession to the scene, where Hook described their purpose in leaving a living memento in Elon's soil. "Tis the universal desire of man to have his deeds follow him in the recollection of his successors amid the busy scenes of life," he declared, "and in obedience to this innate desire we plant this ivy here, emblematic of our hopes in immortality and the freshness and vigor of our devotion to the College."[81]

After this prelude, the program continued, "Each man of the class planted his sprig of the historic green around the giant of more than a century of winters, and as he did so one of the fair sex of the class, emblematic of coeducational idea of the College, rendered a pleasing little speech appropriate to ivy and the oak." Following the planting, A. T. Banks delivered a scholarly oration, after which a benediction by President Harper concluded the ceremony.[82] The members of the class of 1913 were evidently far more proficient in other ways than as gardeners, for the ivy died within a year, though the spirit with which it was planted lived and has never ceased to exist among Elon alumni.[83]

Scholarship on the part of many students was excellent. Competi-

Clio Literary Society, about 1910. On the extreme left in the front row is Professor J. J. Lincoln, and next to him is President E. L. Moffitt.

tion was keen for the prizes awarded each year, which included a new one in 1913. The president of the college offered a gold medal to the winner of the North Carolina Inter-Collegiate Peace Association's local contest. In 1914 this award was won by W. J. B. Truitt, who then took first place in the state contest.[84]

The college catalogs of the period explained the need for student regulations in a condensed statement:

> The government is mild and parental, yet firm and decided. The effort is constantly being made to cultivate and elevate Christian character, governed by a firm principle, a high sense of duty and propriety, and an earnest love of right.
>
> The rules of the school are few, the ideal principles of honor and self-respect being largely relied on to maintain discipline and produce best results in demeanor, scholarship and character.
>
> When a student registers he signs an agreement to obey the rules, and disobedience is considered sufficient ground for asking him to withdraw from the institution.[85]

Elon's student body adhered to this standard and behaved well on the whole. But, with a group so large, disciplinary measures were sometimes necessary by the faculty. Some of these were almost trivial, such as the regulation prohibiting "snow balling on the campus."[86] Another case, more involved, was that of the Potato Pie Club. In 1912 a group of seven or eight male students, including S. S. Myrick, Ben Joe Earp, Alonzo L. Hook, and Walter C. Hook, formed this organization. All members wore identical red neckties and sat at the same table in the dining hall. As they arrived for a meal, each student stood stiffly behind his chair until all were present and took their seats in unison. It is now obscure as to whether or not the name was inspired by a fondness or a distaste for potato pie. Whichever it was, the name had some connection, complimentary or otherwise, with the fare served in the dining hall.

The club naturally aroused curiosity, and Myrick decided to make a public explanation of its purpose during one of the meals. Permission to do so was refused by Mrs. Sallie E. Holland, the matron, but the eager student made his speech regardless. The incident was reported to the faculty. The wary club members, sensing trouble ahead, promptly disbanded the organization. When questioned, they truthfully denied belonging to such a club, for it did not exist at the time. Not hoodwinked by this maneuver but in a lenient mood, the faculty forbade any future revival of the club, gave Myrick five demerits, required him to apologize to the matron, and ruled "that all announcements of any public nature whatsoever should be made by the proper delegated authorities from the college rostrum." The short-lived Potato Pie Club became only a memory.[87]

Another much more serious incident occurred in 1911 in East Dormitory. While a group of men were congregated in a room one night, someone suggested, partly in fun and partly in a serious vein, that one of their number needed a bath. This brought a spirited retort from the designated student that aroused tempers. One word led to another and a scuffle took place. It culminated in the subject of the suggestion being dropped in a bathtub of water. He later charged the seven students involved with hazing, a forbidden practice the pranksters had not intended to commit. After a lengthy investigation, the faculty ruled that the affair did constitute hazing and expelled the perpetrators from the college.

The culprits then sent a signed plea for mercy to the faculty in which they promised never to behave in such a manner again. Receiving no encouragement from this effort, they then began to pack their belongings in preparation for leaving the college. At that point, a petition signed by 102 students, including the victim of the affair, was sent to the faculty requesting that the sentence be reversed and promising to refrain from and discourage "hazing or quasi-hazing" in the future. This move was effective, for at a hurriedly called meeting the faculty reinstated the seven shortly before the arrival of the morning train on which they had planned to depart.

The wisdom of this leniency bore fruit because not only did hazing subside, but also later four of those involved became successful business men and good citizens, two became prominent ministers of the Christian Church, and one was elected to the faculty of Elon upon his graduation, to serve it with honor and distinction the remainder of his life. The forgiving victim also became a minister of the gospel and enjoyed a fruitful career in that honored profession.[88] An unusual feature of this amusing incident is that Walter B. Fuller, the victim, was also chief of police of the town at the time.

The problems accompanying an increasing student body finally demanded a more practical administrative organization. This led to the ruling in 1913 that all matters of discipline and major decisions on courses of study be referred to the Dean of the College for handling except those that affected the students in general. Self-governing clubs, similar to that of East Dormitory, were organized for the Alumni Building and South Dormitory (the Publishing House).[89] In 1916 Dean Lawrence informed the student body that permission had been granted to elect a student senate to assist with disciplinary matters. The student assembly then voted to place this responsibility on the senior class, which was granted recommendatory original jurisdiction over discipline, including absences of the men from town; faculty concurrence was necessary to impose sentences.[90]

These changes relieved the busy faculty considerably, though gen-

Group of ministerial students at Elon in 1913. From left to right, front row: *R. F. Brown, J. T. Apple, Ben Joe Earp, J. W. Short, J. F. Morgan, A. T. Banks, and W. D. Ray.* Second row: *J. B. Hurley, O. D. Poythress, E. T. Cotten, C. W. Rountree, and W. T. Lewis.* Third row: *L. W. Fogleman, D. T. Surratt, D. F. Parsons, and C. B. Riddle.* Fourth row: *W. C. Hook, F. C. Lester, and E. S. Rainey.* Fifth row: *J. V. Knight, W. B. Fuller, A. K. Rippey, and S. S. Myrick.* Sixth row: *H. S. Smith, F. H. Anderson, H. M. Neese, and W. H. Neese.* Last row: *B. M. Williams, W. L. Monroe, and T. J. Green.*

eral matters still came to its attention for decisions. Finally, also in 1916, approval was given for the male students to carry the suitcases of the young ladies to the depot "under limited conditions." The town authorities were also requested to prohibit moving picture theaters "since a company cannot afford to give a good reel for the amount it would receive." Male members of the student body who owned automobiles were given permission to act as chauffeurs for the ladies provided a chaperon sat with the driver on the front seat "enroute to and from Burlington and other places of interest."[91]

The advent of the automobile was also responsible for another ruling. Before 1913 the only mention of campus traffic was a reprimand given to a young man for showing off on horseback in the driveway. However, when a student drove a car over the walks, action was deemed necessary. The result was the posting of placards that read: "No Riding or Driving on the Walk" and "Private Driveway. No Traffic." These were the first official traffic regulations for the campus.[92]

In 1911 Robert S. Doak was added to the faculty, assigned an English, a Latin, and two mathematics courses to teach, and also given "full charge of the work in athletics." He is usually regarded as Elon's first professional coach, though he was unable to devote his full time to sports. He was a product of Guilford College, where his athletic prowess had been outstanding. Under his supervision, all branches of sports at Elon improved; for example, the men's basketball team won the state championship in 1913 and 1914. Doak also directed the women's basketball team, but it was not allowed to play match games.[93] Under his guidance, several stars emerged, but their individual records were not always indicative of the caliber of the teams on which they played.[94]

In 1916 Elon College joined with the University of North Carolina and State Agricultural and Mechanical (A & M), Wake Forest, Trinity, and Guilford colleges in a set of revised athletic rules that were primarily intended to protect college sports from professionalism. In summary, it was specified that no student should play in intercollegiate contests until he had been a student a full year at the school he represented, and could then play only four years. It was required that he be an amateur, a professional "being defined as one who has played in a league under national protection." In addition, the player needed to pass 80 percent of the work required for his class the previous year and make a passing grade during the current year. It was also agreed that not more than eighteen baseball games or twelve basketball games would be played in one season. Any further regulations were left to the individual member institutions.[95]

This agreement ended the possibility of a good player enrolling in a college and immediately playing on one of its teams. Quite often, such an individual left school at the end of the season because his only purpose in attending was to engage in athletics. Situations of this kind, which had arisen both at Elon and at other colleges in the past, were to be prevented in the future by the clarification in the agreement of who was a bona fide student entitled to play on a school's team. It was one of Doak's outstanding achievements that he sponsored the approval of these regulations by the college Athletic Association and faculty.

In addition to the rules of the intercollegiate agreement, Elon also specified that "no student who receives financial aid, directly or indirectly, by reasons of his playing on the team or by reason of any

1914–15 basketball team. From left to right, front row: *"Mug" Massey, Tom Harwood, "Mollie" Morgan, and George Moorefield.* Second row: *Janis Bradford, "Hutch" Hutchins, Ayler Holland, and Bruce McCauley.* Last row: *Coach R. S. Doak, Russell ("Shine") Bradford, and C. C. ("Jack") Johnson.*

athletic service rendered the College shall be allowed in any inter-collegiate game, nor shall a game be played with any other College which violates, in that particular, this rule."[96] The regulations also prohibited any student from representing the college in any athletic contest "who had not conducted himself in an exemplary manner throughout the entire College year, the Faculty judging in each instance." The Athletic Association was also forbidden to make any debts it was not prepared to pay. The adoption of these regulations placed Elon athletics on a high level of amateur sportsmanship.

Doak was successful at Elon, but he also yearned to coach football, a sport the college adamantly refused to approve. This was one of the reasons he accepted an offer in 1916 to coach at Trinity College (present Duke University). He was succeeded at Elon by C. C. ("Jack") Johnson, who had graduated in 1914. His title was "Director of Athletics," and he taught no courses. He thus became the first coach who could devote full time to the sports program.[97]

The new coach also served on the faculty committee that enlarged the system of athletic awards in 1915. In addition to the coveted "E," which had long been awarded those who played in 75 percent of the intercollegiate games in any one sport, the monogram "E-C" was awarded to those who played in two or more regularly scheduled games in any one sport. For those who had already won the "E," a star was allowed to be added to it for each additional year of participation in any one sport.[98] These new recognitions of athletic prowess stimulated student interest in sports.

While the college was growing, so was the town, which even claimed to be "on the boom." In 1912 the Reverend James L. Foster planned to build two houses equipped with modern conveniences for rent "to prospective citizens." Five residences had just been completed, and three others were under construction. A correspondent wrote the *Gleaner* about the demand for these dwellings and many others because "The Graded School building, the Publishing House, the Gymnasium, and the new Men's Dormitory are bringing here a large influx of population."[99] A year later, an auction sale of 75 lots was advertised, to be conducted by the Central Loan and Trust Company of Burlington.[100] In 1913 the citizens voted approval for borrowing money to build concrete sidewalks, the owners of the abutting property to pay half the cost.[101]

From this point on, if it had not become clear earlier, it became conclusive that the town's future was for residential purposes, and not as an industrial or commercial center. The Elon Milling Company went out of business; W. T. Noah closed his hosiery mill and woodworking plant;[102] and eventually the church's printing venture was to be transferred to Burlington. The local bank was a major convenience to the townspeople, but it never engaged in large financial transactions that would cause it to expand into a large commercial institution. These gradual changes were not those that some of the early residents had envisioned. Nevertheless, it became quite evident that Elon was destined to be primarily a college town.

During this period, men associated with the college continued to share in the town's government. In 1913 the officials elected were W. P. Lawrence, mayor; W. C. Michael, J. U. Newman, D. W. Brown, H. D. Lambeth, and C. A. Hughes, commissioners; and Walter B. Fuller, chief of police. Lawrence and Newman were members of the college faculty, and Fuller was a ministerial student at the institution. The chief was a muscular specimen of a man who possessed boundless energy. In addition to his police work, he operated a laundry and delivered mail. This left him little time to study, which is one reason he remained at the college for almost ten years without graduating, during which time he was reelected to the position of police chief several times. His career was interrupted by military service during World War I, after which he became an ordained Christian minister in Virginia. On one occasion, he went home for Christmas and left the police work in the hands of another ministerial student, O. D. Poythress. Placing such responsibility in the hands of these men was a compliment from the townspeople to the students, though there was evidently very little demand for their services.[103]

While these changes were taking place in the town, administrative adjustments were also being made by the college. In 1909, by an amendment to its charter, the number of trustees was increased from fifteen to eighteen, to provide a wider representation. Another change in 1913 specified that a quorum of the board should consist of eight members. This amendment also included a provision to protect both commercial interests and unwise students. It read:

Section 2. That if any merchant, druggist, liveryman, agent or vendor of merchandise or commodity of any kind whatsoever shall sell the same on credit to any minor member of the student body of said College, while a student of the College, without the consent in writing of the President or Dean of said College, or of the parent or guardian or person standing in loco parentis of said student, such sales and contracts of sale without written consent, are hereby declared void and uncollectible. The provisions of this section shall not apply in case of board, room rent and medical attention, nor medicines furnished upon prescription of a physician or surgeon practicing according to the laws of North Carolina.[104]

This precautionary provision was doubtless inspired by one or more unpleasant situations that had arisen in the past, and the wisdom of its addition to the charter in order to prevent similar future problems is unquestioned.

In 1915 another amendment raised the number of trustees to twenty-five, though eight continued to be a quorum. Two years later, the charter was again amended to raise the amount of property the college could own free of taxes from $500,000 to $5,000,000. This change was obviously requested of the legislature in a spirit of extreme optimism, but it eventually proved to be a wise precaution for the future.[105]

In 1913 President Harper "conservatively estimated" the college plant to be worth $300,000, and the indebtedness was not pressing.[106] He then concentrated on a suggestion included in the Capen report that the college endowment be increased to at least $200,000 as soon as possible in order to place the institution in a sound financial position.[107] The campaign began the following year when the executive addressed the Southern Christian Convention:

> The paid-in and invested endowment of the College now amounts to $32,350.00. Besides this the College receives each year about $300 from the American Christian Convention, from $1,500 to $1,800 from the Southern Christian Convention, and from $2,500 to $3,500 from the Francis Asbury Palmer Fund. There is no greater need at this time than provisions for larger endowment for our growing College.[108]

This appeal exerted some effect, and contributions were gradually made. The trustees were sufficiently encouraged by the response in

1916 to borrow $75,000 from the Farmers' Bank of Nansemond, Suffolk, Virginia, to be repaid with donations anticipated in the future. Of this sum, $35,000 was used to retire a debt made ten years earlier at the same bank.[109]

A substantial part, if not all, of the sum desired might have been collected within a reasonable length of time had not the economy of the country been abruptly changed in 1917, when the United States entered World War I. That event ended Harper's halcyon days because many plans needed to be changed, suspended, or canceled. The executive did not know it then, but the problems he would face in the future would be gigantic when compared with those of the early years of his administration. However, these lay ahead of the days when Elon College began to contemplate its course of action in a world at war.

CHAPTER VII

THE STALWART TREE

The tall oak, towering to the skies,
The fury of the wind defies,
From age to age, in virtue strong,
Inured to stand, and suffer wrong.
JAMES MONTGOMERY
The Oak

When the United States declared war against Germany on April 6, 1917, the day was hailed as "memorable" at Elon College. On that very day, three of its "sturdy sons" volunteered in the service of their country: W. F. ("Happy") Odom, William M. Horner, and Elvin Tuck.

They were followed by large numbers accepted for the first Officers' Training Camp, and by still others for other departments of the service, until before Commencement in May it looked as if no male students would be left. Happy beat the hearts of those who love Elon when they consider the response of her sons to the opportunity to serve the cause of humanity.[1]

Reacting to the national emergency, the college varied the usual graduating procedure. For the first time in the institution's history, "men were graduated from her platform in Khaki, and for the first time also men in distant training camps were graduated in absentia."[2]

The faculty also ruled that credit would be given for any course interrupted by male or female students drafted for or enlisting in the armed forces, "the grades to be determined by the daily average." At the same time, the opinion was expressed that "the highest duty that a college man today owes his country is to seek some craft that will help produce foods for humanity rather than enlist in the

United States army."[3] This advice did not prevent the continued depletion of the ranks of the student body throughout the remainder of the year as more students were either drafted into the army or volunteered for military service.

The senior class of 1918 shrank from 46 to 30 members, but the college continued its program even though seriously handicapped. The alumni were also affected by the war. Within a year after America entered the conflict, 349 men and women of Elon's students and alumni were enrolled in the American Expeditionary Force or in other branches of the government's military service. Several men were commissioned as chaplains, including S. C. Harrell (Elon '09), Joseph C. Stuart (Elon '12), and B. F. Black and H. Shelton Smith (both Elon '17) in the army; and H. E. Rountree (Elon '06) and William W. Elder (Elon '10) in the navy.[4] All the participants in the war were lauded for their patriotism by President Harper: "While our hearts bleed that their going is necessary, we can only rejoice that Elon men and women in the hour of national danger have not forgotten the noble altruism that their Alma Mater has ever sought to inculcate in her sons and daughters."[5]

Before the conflict ended, the total number of Elonites in service rose to 601, of which 15 were casualties. The first one to make the supreme sacrifice was Charles N. Whitelock, of the class of 1918, who died at Camp Grant, Illinois, on October 1, 1917. He was the son of Judge O. W. Whitelock, of Huntington, Indiana, who was a trustee and director of the Christian Publishing Company, of Dayton, Ohio, and the father-in-law of Elon's Professor Ramey. The other casualties from the student body were Sergeant W. F. Odom, one of the first-day volunteers, and Sergeant H. H. Barber, both of the regular army, and Captain John Carl Miller, of the Aviation Corps. Miller's plane was shot down, and he was severely wounded, but ironically neither he nor the two sergeants died until after hostilities ceased. The remaining eleven casualties, whose names are now unknown, were alumni of the college. By order of the board of trustees, degrees were awarded posthumously to the four who were undergraduates.[6]

When the *Phipsicli* resumed publication in 1920, the issue was dedicated to the memory of the fifteen dead, who were paid this tribute:

And now that the war is over, the victory achieved, and the work of world-rebuilding to be undertaken, We who are left to do this work rejoice that we live in an hour like this and that we can labor in a cause like this. But we shall never forget the shed blood of the fifteen brothers of ours who died in France that this privilege might be ours. We miss their comradeship, the comradeship of noble hearts, in the tasks that challenge us on every hand. But their spirit of sacrifice is our rich inheritance and our hearts' devotion goes out to them in grateful acknowledgment of the debt we owe them, a debt we cannot discharge save in loving memory of their heroic deeds and of their sacrificial self-dedication to death on our behalf.[7]

This was an appropriate gesture after the war was over, but many events had transpired before victory could be celebrated.

Coincident with the opening of the fall term in 1917, President Harper went to Washington to confer with the secretary of war, the adjutant general, and other high governmental officials in an effort to obtain a military instructor for the college. Thwarted by the rejection of his request, he returned home, determined to make the best use of the institution's facilities possible to aid the war effort. Elon's faculty were also affected by the war, and those who left for military service included H. E. Jorgenson, Fred F. Myrick, and W. J. Cotten.[8] The administration was fortunate in finding suitable replacements for the vacancies, and the staff was sympathetic with the president's patriotic ambition.

The usual college program was then supplemented in a manner described by Harper:

The first year of the war found us giving military training at our own expense, drilling in our own uniforms and with wooden guns, since real rifles could not be procured at any price. Many of our boys volunteered during the year and were easily able to secure at once non-commissioned officers' rank because of the thoroughness of our military drill and instruction.[9]

The trustees also showed their appreciation of agriculture to the war effort by offering "to credit any Elon former student or new student of next year's student body who shall work on a farm this summer with three hours toward graduation."[10] These efforts demonstrated the willingness of the college to cooperate with the government's program, even if it caused some inconvenience to both the faculty and the administration.

In addition to participation in the training program, the student body revealed its sentiments regarding the national emergency in other ways. On October 31, 1917, the male undergraduates adopted a "College Man's War Creed," in which they pledged to use their "opportunities fully" to improve their minds in order to more effectually serve their country "and the cause of human freedom later, whether in private life or with the colors." They pledged personal economy and the prevention of property destruction so that the war might be prosecuted more effectively as well as the fullest possible support of the Red Cross, the Student War-Friendship Fund, and the Liberty Loan bond drives. In addition, they promised:

> That we will keep hate out of our souls so as to be able to recommend and endorse sane measures for the making of a lasting peace guaranteeing international good-fellowhip as well as cessation of fighting when time for reconstruction has arrived.
>
> That when our country calls, at whatever cost to ourselves or our cherished plans, she shall receive our unstinted service.[11]

The coeds followed suit on March 29, 1918, with the "College Woman's War Creed." Their aim was stated in the preamble: "Since this is a war of the masses and not of the classes; since it is a war of the race, and not of sex; since we who remain at home have our part in its winning, by rigid economy, stern elimination of waste, and every possible effort to 'keep the home fires burning,' we the women students of Elon College do hereby adopt this as our War Creed."[12] The women then pledged to improve their minds; practice self-denial to achieve economy in dress; and to taboo candies, soft drinks, "social eats," and the "innocent enjoyments of life that mean so much to a woman" to aid in the conservation of food and materials. They also agreed to support the loan drives, the "Y's," and the Red Cross. In conclusion, they also promised they would "pray that hate for our enemies may not canker our hearts, while interceding earnestly that God in His wisdom may speedily crown our arms with victory" and that "in this new hour of woman's freedom, we will endeavor to prove our right to it by serving nobly every call our nation may lay upon us, and gladly." [13] These creeds portray the patriotism of the Elonites at home during the war and were a fitting accompaniment to the large service flag, whose number of blue and gold stars was mounting, that Thomas Walter Bickett, North Carolina's governor, unfurled at the 1918 commencement. [14]

Immediately after this ceremony was concluded, Dr. Harper informed his trustees that a letter received on May 8, from Newton D. Baker, the secretary of war, announced a plan for colleges in which at least a hundred male students 18 years of age or over were enrolled. During the coming school year at institutions that qualified, "the government would furnish instruction and equipment so far as possible, leaving the students free to elect the work or not as they might prefer." [15] This opened the door for a governmentally directed military training program at Elon. The board promptly approved this proposition, and the administration began plans to have a unit of the Students' Army Training Corps, popularly known as the SATC, in operation at the college when the 1918 fall term began.

During the summer, the first preparation was made by selecting Professors Hook and Amick, of the faculty, and the student biology assistant, T. E. Powell, of the staff, to attend a school for military instructors at Plattsburg, New York. Fifteen students were selected to accompany them to be trained as assistants to them and the regular army instructors the government would send to teach the newly designed courses. [16] An accident prevented Hook from attending; Amick was forced to return because his weight proved to be a physical handicap; Powell completed the course. Upon the return of this group, Lieutenant Robert L. Wilson arrived at the college from Camp Beauregard, Louisiana, to serve as commanding officer and organize the unit. Associated with him were Lieutenants N. J. Fitzgerald, John J. Harrington, D. G. Fishbeck, and A. T. Johnson. [17]

In addition to daily military drilling, SATC personnel were required to concentrate their studies on courses in public hygiene, statistics, world politics, war issues, events of the war, surveying, topography, mapmaking, French, and military law and practice. If they could spare the time, they could take any other courses in the college curriculum. This program did not attract all Elon students because many did not understand it very well, and some even left school because of their opposition to the change. However, 112 men from the college and other institutions enlisted for the training, and the applications of 53 others were pending when the project ended.[18]

The opening of the fall term was postponed from September 11 until September 19 so that arrangements would be completed for inducting the men into the SATC on October 1, 1918. An elaborate ceremony was planned, including an opening by the band playing the national anthem, followed by the raising of the flag, administering the oath of alllegiance to the inductees, and the invocation by Dr. N. G. Newman. The order of the day was to include messages from President Woodrow Wilson, Acting Secretary of War Benedict C. Crowell, and the Chief of Staff, General Peyton C. March. Dr. Harper was then to introduce A. Wayland Cooke, the Greensboro postmaster, who would deliver a rousing oration. These events did take place, but it was not until October 5 that the ceremony could be held. The postponement was necessitated by the outbreak of Spanish influenza at the institution. The president said, "We did not know what it was, until we were all sick."[19] Although the military ceremonies were delayed only four days, the disease that interfered with them did not depart so quickly.

Within a matter of days, almost of hours, the college was in the grip of an emergency that threatened far more destruction to the community than the war overseas. There was no time to send the

SATC unit at Elon College during World War I.

students home, and, besides, the epidemic was rapidly spreading over the entire nation. This left the college no choice but to care for its own. Elon was the earliest of the North Carolina colleges to open that year, which was the reason the flu broke out there first. This circumstance was also the reason that medical attention was more readily available than it was a short time later, which undoubtedly prevented numerous casualties. However, because most of the student body was bedfast, professional assistance could not meet the demand, and the major part of the nursing was borne by the students who were not victims of the disease.[20]

Immediately, the gymnasium was filled with cots for the stricken men. Those who kept on their feet nursed the ill for two hours, rested four hours, then resumed the taxing schedule around the clock. M. J. W. White (Elon '22), who later became a medical missionary, rendered especially valuable assistance in caring for the men,[21] and others assisted him diligently.

In the women's dormitories (West and Ladies'), the no-longer unused infirmary soon overflowed, but beds were sufficient in the buildings for the patients. The coeds who resisted the disease cared for the sick. Eight of the women performed the nursing necessary in West Dormitory. Mrs. L. D. Martin (nee Annie L. Raper, Elon '19), who was one of the number, recalled that sometimes they had little or no sleep for twenty-four hours while caring for their suffering classmates.[22]

The Harpers shared in the emergency measures by taking seven of the most serious cases into their home, which was as many as could be cared for there, and the services of a professional nurse were obtained for these patients. Despite every effort, however, on October 11 one of the afflicted named Modesto Lopez, a student from Cuba, succumbed to the disease. He was originally from Spain, but because the Spanish consul was unable to arrange for disposal of the body, he was buried in the town's Magnolia Cemetery. Another individual who died at the president's home was Clarence A. Sechriest, a sophomore and brother of E. E. Sechriest, who was in service overseas at the time.[23] Miss Annie Floyd died at the Young Men's Club, where she made her home with her sister, Mrs. Thyra Swint, the matron of the club. Possibly, the scourge took the lives of one or two other victims, but these three are the only ones known today who died of the more than 300 cases of the flu at Elon.

Roby E. Taylor, an SATC trainee at the time, recalls that in response to an emergency plea, probably from military officials, three or four Roman Catholic nuns arrived to assist with the nursing. As a student aide, he remembers them praying by the bedside of Lopez before he passed away. They also waited on the men confined to beds in the gymnasium, which included Taylor himself when he became a victim of the disease. He has always warmly cherished the memory of those unselfish women, whose care led to his recovery. Dr. J. V. Dick, of Gibsonville, performed the seemingly impossible task of giving medical attention to those stricken, though little medical treatment was known for the disease at the time. However, the sick were cared for, and the physician and those who unselfishly assisted him as nurses are among the unsung heroes of the worst physical threat to the Elon College community before or since.[24]

No human beings could have endured the grueling pace these people were forced to keep for very long. Fortunately, within a relatively short time, the epidemic at the college began to subside, though its ravages continued elsewhere for weeks. Although the faculty was not spared, none of them died. Classes were never officially suspended at the college, though frequently one was automatically canceled when no one was able to attend. As the situation improved, the instructors and students regained their health, and within about two weeks after the epidemic began, the college schedule was beginning to operate smoothly again.

Meanwhile, the Elon campus had begun to take on a military appearance, though later than originally planned. The sight of men in uniform carrying rifles, all supplied by the government, became commonplace in the otherwise quiet grove. SATC students arose at five o'clock in the morning to engage in calisthenics before breakfast. They then drilled from eight until ten o'clock, after which they marched to their classes. The procedure was the same in the afternoon, and two hours were spent in the study hall each evening except on Sundays. At all times the men were subject to military discipline under the officers in charge of the unit.[25]

Unfortunately, the drill sergeant gave his commands in a loud voice accompanied by a flow of profanity, as he had been accustomed to do in an army camp. One of the enlisted men observed, "The use of such language on the campus of a Christian institution was not conducive to the best relations between the civil and military leaders at Elon."[26] Under these circumstances, doubts began to arise as to whether or not military training at the college was such a good thing after all. It was, therefore, quite a relief to the embarrassed administration when Lieutenant Wilson was reassigned on October 27 and left Lieutenant Fitzgerald in command.

The next change redeemed the program, as described by President Harper:

> On November 8, Captain Franklyn T. Lord arrived and with him that beautiful spirit of co-operation between the College and military authorities which the War Department had designed as the proper characteristic of the S.A.T.C. Captain Lord made military training popular, until even the Elon girls enrolled for the sport, substituting a modified form of drill for their regular work in physical culture.
>
> It may be safely said, if he had been the organizer of the unit, it would have been larger and certainly more respected by the students not in it. He diligently inquired as to the College regulations and traditions and rigorously enforced the one, while he graciously respected the other. Elon counts herself fortunate to have had this Christian gentleman represent our nation on the campus.[27]

Thus, an understanding commander popularized and justified the military program.

As the program became better understood, a number of male students, too young to enlist, and most of the ministerial students, volunteered for the training. They furnished their own uniforms and paid their own general expenses. The girls welcomed the opportunity to participate in some activity formerly restricted to men, and volunteered also. The result was a flowery compliment from the president: "It is good to see them drilling and clad in a uniform of their own selection, of blue skirts with white middy blouses and blue ties, but thoroughly democratic. The soldierettes are Captain Lord's peculiar pets, and well they may be, Amazons for endurance every one of them and Joans of Arc for grace and lovliness [sic]."[28] From this time until the program was concluded, the military training was the highlight of campus activities.

On November 11, 1918, the war ended, but the SATC program

continued until the government ordered it disbanded. The students hoped that this would soon be forthcoming, and began to refer humorously to the program as the "Stick Around Till Christmas" training. Discipline did not relax, however, for the unit was still a military one commanded by army officers.[29]

During its brief existence, the unit gave two public exhibition drills. On December 5 the men hiked to Burlington and back for a performance in that city. The following day, they were transported to Greensboro in a coach supplied by the courtesy of the Southern Railway, and performed in front of the post office. In the evening, they were given a gala banquet at the Guilford Hotel. Toasts were given by Drs. N. G. Newman, W. P. Lawrence, T. C. Amick, J. U. Newman and J. V. Dick; Professor H. Babcock; Lieutenant Fitzgerald; President Harper; North Carolina's Assistant Attorney General Clyde R. Hoey; A. Wayland Cooke, the Greensboro postmaster; and Garland Henderson, a local lawyer. A loving cup was then presented to Captain Lord and gold fountain pens to the members of his staff.[30]

On December 11 the men were honored by a reception given by

SATC unit in 1918 in front of the Main Building.

the class of 1919 in West Dormitory. During the event, the unit was officially disbanded:

> Promptly at 9 o'clock the company bugler sounded assembly and the men in khaki left the sides of the young ladies with whom they were busily engaged in a social way and filed into the dining hall of the West Dormitory which had been especially prepared for the occasion, and in the presence of several hundred of their ardent admirers, as each man's name was called he filed through the ranks, saluted the Commanding Officer, received his certificate of honorable discharge, saluted again, and with true military dignity returned to his place in the ranks. It was a simple, yet dignified ceremony and an impressive scene which terminated the service of the Elon S.A.T.C. men.[31]

The following day, the men departed for their homes, and on the 21st, the officers concluded their work and left the college. Bidding them farewell, the administration promised that "Elon's blessing and benediction accompany them wherever they may go."[32]

According to President Harper, the general impression of the students and the faculty was "that the college had made no mistake in assuming the responsibilities involved in placing a preliminary training camp for officers on its campus." It was also concluded that military training was possible without being made universal "and without degenerating into militarism." Nevertheless, the program had been expensive for the institution. In changing the curriculum, some students who refused to adjust to it left school, though this was offset to some extent by the return of some of the SATC men as regular students. Dormitory changes and the provision of additional dining hall space had also been costly. Although the government supplied uniforms, guns, and instructors, the expense to the college caused a deficit of $14,046.05 for the 1918 fall term. A portion of this sum was canceled through a compromise, which reduced the loss to $4,896.86.[33]

Because of the war, many cultural events at the college were discontinued, some never to be revived in the same manner, and this weakened the general program. The treasured *Phipsicli* suspended publication for the years 1918 and 1919, though it resumed in 1920. For the second time in one school year, the curriculum needed to be revised and teaching assignments readjusted to conform to it, which was a burden on both faculty and administration. Collectively, these changes set back the college's operation, but fortunately they were temporary, and reported to the trustees as instances of the sacrifices necessitated by the war. The president commented philosophically, "and perhaps we should not complain" because the war was won.[34]

Another result of the war was that the college needed to deal with a different type of student afterward. The contrast was marked between youth fresh out of southern high schools, many away from home for the first time when they arrived at college, and men and women who had participated in military duty during a war, either in their own country or in Europe. Those who returned to the campus to complete their education were older, more mature, more independent. Many of them were of voting age, a circumstance rare at the institution before the conflict. Several were married and accompanied by their wives, who also enrolled as students, a situation almost unheard of a few years previously.

The former methods of student discipline were no longer practical for these changed conditions, and the administration unhesitatingly accepted this fact. A new plan was adopted during the 1919 fall term. The *Sun* reported, "There has been a form of self-government in operation there [Elon College] in the men's dormitories for the past several years, but it was the form without the substance, and in this day of world-wide democracy the college authorities are prepared to meet the young men with the real article with the opening of the winter term on January seventh."[35]

The occasion for this comment was a section in the new 1918–19 catalog containing a "Constitution for Student Self-Government for Men in Elon College." Prefaced by a statement that a modified form of self-government had existed at the institution for many years, the announcement was made that the new authorization granted by the faculty would place full governmental responsibility on the male students. This operation was to be carried out by an organization outlined in the document's preamble:

> Beginning with the winter term of 1919, in accordance with an agreement with the Faculty, the government of the men of the student body of Elon College shall be vested in the hands of a Student Senate, which shall consist of a President of the

student body, elected from the men of the Senior Class by the men of all classes, and three representatives from the Senior Class, three from the Junior Class, two from the Sophomore Class, and one from the Freshman Class, the elections to take place by ballot by the men students of these respective classes, each class voting for its own representative only.

The officers of the Senate shall be a President who shall also be the president of the student body and ex officio a member of the Senate and President of the same; a Vice-President, a Secretary, and a Treasurer, and such other officers as the Student Senate may determine upon.[36]

The bylaws empowered the Student Senate to "try all cases of misdemeanor or misconduct from any source, pass judgment thereon, make rules and regulations," and appoint boards in each male dormitory to be responsible for the conduct in their own building. "Fines and tasks of work were to replace the demerit system, and the decision of the Senate was final in all cases except expulsion or suspension." Few regulations were specified. One was the prohibition of smoking on the campus. Another stated that any man convicted of cheating "on any papers" on which he had signed a pledge that the work was his own was to be expelled. As far as has been determined, this was the first formal statement concerning the operation of the Honor System at Elon.[37]

All officers were bound by an oath of office, and provisions were made for the impeachment of officers if ever necessary and for amending the constitution. The granting of this authority was one of the most forward steps taken by the faculty in many years relative to its relations with the male students. It was also a mutual advantage, for it allowed the men to exercise the authority for which they had qualified, and it freed the staff to a larger extent for concentration on an expanding academic program.

The operation of this plan was immediately successful, and it was soon noticed that there was a "growing sentiment for student self-government among the ladies."[38] This was quite true, for the women were not to be denied their rights. As a result, in 1919, the faculty granted a constitution for the "Elon College Woman's Association for Self-Government." The organization was given the following authority:

Section 1. The Association shall have the power to deal with all those matters concerning the conduct of its members in their college life which do not fall under the jurisdiction of the authorities of the College, or of the matrons of the halls of residence.

Section 2. The Association shall have the power of inflicting penalties to enforce its decisions, to the extent of recommending the expulsion of or suspension of a student to the College authorities after consultation with the Dean of Women.[39]

Details of administration were also specified:

Section 1. The Executive powers of the Association shall be vested in an Executive Board, composed of the President and the following class representatives, two Seniors, two Juniors, one Sophomore, and one Freshman. The President shall be chosen from the Senior Class by the Association. The Class Representatives shall be chosen by their respective classes.

Section 2. The officers of the Executive Board shall consist of the President, elected by the Association, and the Vice-President and Secretary-Treasurer, elected by the Executive Board from their number.[40]

In each of the residence halls for women, a proctor was to be elected by the students to be responsible to the Executive Board. The legislative power was vested in the entire association. A quorum was to consist of half of its members. In addition, provisions were made for impeachments and amending the constitution.

The instrument contained more regulations in its bylaws than those required of the men, but they were more liberal than the rules for women had formerly been. They included permission to go on chaperoned hiking parties by signing out in the "Hike Book," wearing evening dresses on occasions declared formal by the board, and shopping in the village or going out of town at certain times without a chaperon. Seniors were also permitted to enter the stack room at the library.[41]

The granting of this constitution represented a new phase of liberation for the coeds at Elon College, for they obtained concessions undreamed of prior to the war. They lost no time in taking advantage of their new status and organized the Student Council, as the board soon became known. The first president elected was Miss Toshio Sato (Elon '20), a popular student from Japan who was studying at the college so that she could return to her native land as a missionary.[42]

Student government in the full meaning of the term became an established system at the college when the constitutions for men

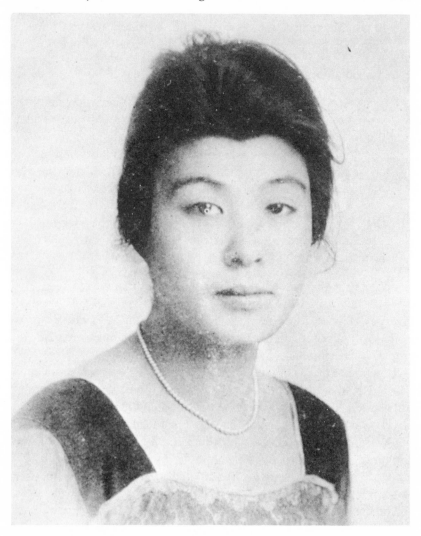

Toshio Sato, of Japan, member of the class of 1920 and the first Japanese graduate of Elon.

and women became effective. Over the years, modifications have occurred, numerous amendments to the bylaws have been made, and the first two plans have been merged into one system for both sexes, but the basic principle of student democracy granted in the original instruments has remained virtually the same.

Another factor that contributed to the success of student government was the decision in 1921 to close the Preparatory Department.[43] Elon College had offered a program ranging from elementary education to a college degree for thirty-one years. During this period, the students at the school ranged in age from those who were virtually children to others in their upper teens, or occasionally even older. However, the growth of the modern high school in the public school systems took care of preparation for college entrance, and Elon no longer needed to do so. This change eliminated the very young from the college and meant that the average student in attendance was older and more mature than formerly, and therefore better understood the responsibilities of self-government.

Fortunately, the administration anticipated the maturity of postwar students and was prepared for a more independent attitude on the part of the undergraduates. On November 1, 1920, the faculty received the following communication:

> The student body assembled in the College Auditorium today and decided not to attend classes tomorrow on account of the importance of the occasion of the National Elections. They appointed me as a committee of one to notify you of this fact.
>
> Respectfully submitted,
> R. S. Rainey[44]

Such a defiance of authority would have been almost unthinkable before the war. However, Ralph S. Rainey was a veteran of overseas service; had studied at the University of Montpellier, in France, under government auspices while awaiting transportation back to the states; and both he and his wife were enrolled as students at the college. Frequently dubbed as "Socrates" on the campus because of his maturity, he unhesitatingly served as the representative of the students.[45]

A few years earlier, in the prewar days, the faculty would hardly have replied in such a mildly compromising manner:

> The Faculty by taking note of this action of the student body in Chapel today wishes to say that the matter of granting holidays is largely a prerogative of the Board of Trustees beyond the holidays designated in the catalogue. The Faculty, therefore, being employees of the Board of Trustees will attend classes, Nov. 2nd as usual. Any student desiring to go ahead with his or her work is invited to do so. Those who will be absent will have such absences charged to the fifteen per cent limit; except such students as have to miss recitations in order to exercise their franchise as citizens.[46]

No record of attendance at classes on election day is available, but it was very likely fragmentary. This case represents an example of the new independence of the students, and it did not mean that they could do as they pleased from then on or were no longer subject to the rules of the college, but it was the first occasion on which they flouted the authority of the faculty en masse.

A prime example of the unyielding attitude of the administration to regulations it considered of basic importance was on the subject of dancing. In 1912 the trustees were requested to permit this form of entertainment at the college, to which they emphatically replied that "no dancing even as a form of exercise" would be allowed.[47]

The matter rested until 1921, when the male students decided they would rather dance with each other than not at all. They may have also hoped that, if this concession could be won, it might be a step toward permission to dance with the coeds, but this is pure speculation. Seeking to circumvent the rules, L. M. Cannon, president of the Student Senate, sent the following communication to the faculty:

> The Student Senate has voted by a two-thirds majority to submit, with the consent of the Faculty, to the Student Body the following amendment to our constitution to be accepted or rejected as they see fit.
>
> AMENDMENT. "Dancing between the sexes in any form shall be strictly prohibited."
>
> The object of this amendment is to prohibit DANCING in the commonly accepted sense of the word, but not what is termed "stag dancing."

We will be glad to have a report from the Faculty on this as soon as possible.[48]

The reply denied the request, but provided an explanation:

> In the matter of the Senate's recent action to permit "stag dancing" in the college, we beg to say, that we find it necessary to withold our approval, for the reason that such action is not in accord with the spirit and policy of the college and runs contrary to a specific ruling of the Board of Trustees.
>
> We would say further, that the policy of the institution is based on certain definite convictions, one of which is that the social dance, to which the stag dance is accessory, is a moral menace, as shown by the tragic facts of history, and especially in our own day. The recent vice investigation commission in New York and Chicago have published the statement that 75% of the red-light women in these cities declared their downfall due to the social dance. Another conviction is that Christian men in a Christian institution should move on the highest plane of moral action, which involves the sacrifice of personal rights or pleasure, for the sake of the weaker brother who may be caused to stumble by the example of the strongest. This principle as set forth by the greatest Christian leader of history is, "If meat makes my brother to stumble I will eat no flesh while the world standeth." Such self-denial for the good of others reacts with ennobling power in the lives of those who practice it, and we commend it as the ideal worthy to obtain among Christian men in a Christian college.
>
> Feeling that you would appreciate our position, and assuring you that in this as in all other matters, we desire only your own highest welfare and that of the college, we remain, Elon College Faculty.[49]

After copying this reply in the faculty minutes, Secretary Hook added a note, "The Senate accepted the above as satisfactory." At least it settled the matter for years until dancing between men and women was permitted at the college, but no more requests were made for "stag dancing."

In 1919 the Elon trustees provided another example that they supported the moral code in which they believed. The board learned that two faculty members had committed the indiscretion of playing cards in one of the offices at the college. This incident might have received only a reprimand had it been in the privacy of a faculty home, but the authorities could not overlook the fact that it occurred on the campus, where it was strictly against the rules. The indignant board expressed its disapproval of such conduct by stating it "would be gratified to receive the resignations of these two teachers to become effective at once, and the President is authorized to notify them of this action."[50] The order was doubtless obeyed immediately, regardless of the inconvenience to the college's program. This incident was also concrete evidence that both faculty and students were expected to conform to identical rules as far as moral discipline was concerned.

Although some new concessions for the students accompanied the authorization for self-government, the principal change was that the student organizations would try most of the cases involving breaches of discipline rather than the faculty. The basic rules had not changed, and included the prohibition of dancing, "card playing with cards commonly known as 'set back,'" gambling in any form, drinking alcoholic beverages, cursing, cheating, plagiarism, hazing, and the "moral sin." Minor regulations decreed against keeping animals, firearms, or mechanical musical instruments in the buildings. Men and women were still required to use separate entrances to the library, separate stairs in all buildings, and separate sides for their seats in chapel. All were required to attend the chapel programs, Sunday school, and church services. After a year of operating without it, the demerit system was reinstated in order that the deans could keep up with violations because 50 demerits automatically removed a student from college. Furthermore, all failing to pass 60 percent of their work in a semester were required to retire from college for a semester. Although some liberalizations had been made just after the war, many of the former restrictions remained in force for a decade or more afterward.[51]

The attitude of the college authorities should be viewed and judged in the light of the period, and not of the present. Regulations at the school were no more strict than at most southern church-related institutions until several years after World War I ended. The concessions made to the students were liberal for the day, but every effort was exercised to protect the moral welfare of all connected with the institution as its authorities interpreted their duty. The trustees, administration, and faculty can only be commended for striving to do so, and the willingness of most of the students to abide by their decisions was exemplary.

Elon's enrollment rose to a peak of more than 400 during the SATC period, and steps were taken to keep the cultural life of the school on a level with this number. In 1918 two new literary societies were organized, the Apollo for men and the Thalia for women. Because the size of the student body receded to approximately 350 after the war, the Apollo was disbanded. Also, the name of the women's organization was changed to the Psychaleon. The increased membership in all the societies had made them more impersonal and far less fraternal than they had been when they were smaller. For these reasons, their members were gradually losing their former sense of comradeship and enjoyment of the social association with each other.[52]

As a result of this, interest was aroused in organizations of purely a social nature, and various reasons were found to form a club of some kind for that purpose. County clubs were formed for personnel from Rockingham, Randolph, Guilford, Vance and Warren combined, Chatham, and Orange, all North Carolina counties. Regional groups included the Carolina Mountaineers; Yankees; and the Eastern Virginia, Central Virginia, and Valley of Virginia groups. Masonic members formed their own organization.

Overseas Men (veterans) was another. Less serious were the Loafers and DYC clubs. The principal purpose of almost all was to hold a banquet once each semester, and be photographed as a group for the *Phipsicli*. These activities were particularly enjoyable to the students who belonged to more than one of the clubs. They were strictly regulated by the administration, however, for at a faculty meeting in February 1921 it was noted, "Since the D.Y.C. Club did not furnish a satisfactory itemized account of its banquet expenses, this club cannot have another banquet this spring."[53]

These organizations supplied pleasant associations, but did not satisfy the desire of some students for a more formal type of club to which members were elected. They had not failed to notice the existence of Greek letter fraternities and sororities at other colleges, and began a movement to initiate somewhat similar organizations at their school.

The trustees viewed these requests of the students with leniency in 1920, and passed a set of standards for "not more than four clubs for each sex" on the campus. In essence, the regulations specified that the constitutions, memberships, and activities of all groups were subject to faculty approval, and all meetings were open to the public, "with no secret features whatsoever." Membership in each was limited to 25, and no student could belong to more than one club. Financial limits were $10 for membership pins, $2.50 for initiation fees, and $5.00 for annual dues. The club whose members attained the highest performance in scholarship and college honors annually was to receive a "suitable souvenir" for the attainment.[54]

Several clubs were in the process of organization when these regulations were published in the 1921–22 catalog, and a number of former clubs disbanded because the students became more interested in the proposed new ones. After the matter was deliberated by Dean Lawrence, permission was given by the faculty to use Greek letter names, which the students wished to do. Sigma Phi Beta was the first organized for men, followed immediately by Kappa Psi Nu and later, by Iota Tau Kappa. Beta Omicron Beta and Delta Upsilon Kappa, soon followed by Tau Zeta Phi, were organized for women. Usually the clubs held their meetings in the "Y" halls of the college, and each was allowed to hold one inexpensive social function during a semester. The students soon began to refer to the new organizations as fraternities and sororities, as the faculty had feared they might do if Greek letter names were used, but officially they were "social clubs," regardless of their names.[55]

In most cases, the arrangements provided by the faculty were satisfactory to the clubs, but one encountered some trouble. A member of Sigma Phi Beta rented a room at the Ward Hotel, in Burlington, and held a dance for those who purchased tickets. In view of the administration's strict views on dancing, the student was questioned about the affair. He blandly stated he had organized the entertainment to raise money for himself, which he said he needed. The faculty refused to accept this explanation in its entirety because the members of his club were the principal participants in the affair. The assumption was that the arrangement was primarily a subterfuge to hold a club dance. Because it took place off the campus, little could be done to the individual responsible, but the faculty used its authority to disband the Sigma Phi Beta Club for a year. After the period of suspension, it became active again, but it held no more dances in Burlington.[56] This was an unusual case, for in general the plan for the social clubs functioned very well.

In 1921 the YMCA, the YWCA, Christian Endeavor Society, Student Volunteer Band, College Sunday School, and the Ministerial Association founded the Religious Activities Organization in Elon College. Its purpose was "closer co-operation among the various religious organizations ministering to the spiritual life of the student body and desiring to correlate and coordinate them in such a way as to avoid needless duplication of effort, while at the same time designing to conserve and promote the best interest of each organization as of each student."[57] The aims of the organization were to "construct a program of Christian themes for the year," hold socials, and work "with the Department of Religious Education of the College," assisting in supervised programs for the Boy Scouts, Camp Fire Girls, black people, and the Christian Orphanage, in addition to

South campus in 1920. West Dormitory is on the left, the Main Building in the center, East Dormitory on the right, and the original athletic playing field in the foreground. Photo by Professor A. L. Hook.

"such other work as may from time to time be instituted."[58] This was a worthy move for religious emphasis, and it was successful.

There were also musical organizations for the students at the college: the band, orchestra, and, beginning in 1916, the Music Lovers' Club and the Choral Society of a hundred members. Under the direction of Professor Edwin M. Betts, the latter presented some fine public performances.

Realizing the value of communication, on June 14, 1917, President Harper began issuing *The Elon College News Bulletin*, a four-page leaflet distributed free. It contained items of interest concerning the college activities and was similar in function to the leaflets published today under the names of *Interaction* and *The Communicator*. It was suspended in 1922 because of a paper shortage.[59]

The next important step of the period in the field of publications was the founding of *The Maroon and Gold*, a weekly college newspaper that succeeded the defunct *Weekly*. On December 1, 1919, "the Faculty gave its hearty approval to the proposed college paper but does not stand for any indebtedness." Professor Myrick was then elected as incognito supervising editor.[60] The officers and directors of the paper were elected by the junior class "though it was not restricted to its own membership in making selections." The first editor was Percy E. Lindley. His principal assistants were L. M. and C. M. Cannon, and H. W. Johnson. The four-page newspaper was launched and published regularly until May 22, 1969, when it was suspended because of lack of interest.[61]

Another useful college publication, which originated in 1922, was a pocket-size handbook containing "indispensable information for students" and the basic integral governmental regulations of the college. It was conceived and edited by Dean A. L. Hook. A copy was given to each student upon registration. The cover of the small manual was maroon, and the lettering was in gold. It had been planned to name it *The Maroon Book*. The printer was given somewhat vague instructions in this regard, but understood the name was derived from the color of the cover. Unfamiliar with the college colors or the word "maroon," he interpreted the color as red, and printed *The Red Book* on the cover. Once this was done, the title was retained for each annual edition afterward.[62]

In December 1919 the faculty announced that two new courses would be offered the following year, a Bachelor of Science in engineering, and a Bachelor of Science in commerce.[63] The following year, because of the advent of the "wireless," as radio was first called, the versatile Dr. Hook and a group of his students constructed a crystal receiving set on the fourth floor of the tower of the Main Building. The chamber had never been finished, and they had to lay a floor and perform other carpentry to accomplish their purpose. Despite these obstacles, they succeeded in completing the set in time to hear the first broadcast from KDKA, the Pittsburgh station. This was the first college wireless station in North Carolina because the one at State College, in Raleigh, though begun first was not completed until later. The receiving facility was used until the building was destroyed three years later.[64]

In keeping with its concentration on preparing teachers, and in compliance with new state requirements, in 1922 the college made arrangements to supplement the program by using the combined graded and high schools of the town of Elon College for a practice and demonstration school. The project was placed under the supervision of Dr. W. C. Wicker, head of the college Department of Education; and Professor C. Humphreys served as principal. This system enabled the students preparing to teach "to receive practical training in the profession," and at the same time, the school children would be "benefitted by the institution of supervised instruction." Since this beginning, practice teaching has been a part of the college's educational program.[65]

In March 1922 the faculty received a petition signed by 99 students requesting that the quarter system replace the semester periods. The students contended they would then be able to concentrate on two or three courses daily instead of on alternate days and that failures could be made up more conveniently. It was also claimed that the system was proving successful at other institutions. After an investigation, President Harper reported that the plan had not met with favor at small institutions of learning, and men of authority did not recommend it. The request was then denied, which ended the matter at the time.[66]

Another event during the period was of special significance to the college. When the American Christian Convention met in 1914 at Springfield, Ohio, its affiliated organization, the Southern Christian Convention, was honored by a special place on the program designated as "Elon Celebration." Dr. A. B. Kendall, pastor of the Burlington Christian Church and recipient of an honorary degree from Elon, composed "Praises, Elon, Unto Thee," to be sung to the tune of "America" for the occasion. This was perhaps the first tribute to the college in song. The following year, Dr. Amick composed the lyrics of "Dear Elon," which was sung to the tune of the familiar song "Juanita." Several years later, a student, Sion M. Lynam (Elon '24), composed "Underneath Maroon and Gold," to be sung to the tune of "The Orange and the Black." Others contributed compositions, all of which were enjoyed, though none was adopted as the official college song.[67]

In 1921 Mark Z. Rhodes, a veteran of a military band that had served overseas during the war, came to Elon as a student and director of the college band. A talented musician, he wrote "Here's to Dear Old Elon," set to the tune of the trio from F. E. Bigelow's stirring march "Our Director:"

> So here's to dear old Elon,
> Faithful and bold,
> Here's to her banners of maroon and gold;
> Here's to men and women
> Who've come and gone
> Singing the victor's song of old Elon.[68]

This composition, immediately popular with the students and alumni, became and has remained the official alma mater of Elon College.

Although the song became dear to those connected with the institution, its meaning was not widely known by others. Occasionally at football games a visiting band played the Bigelow march and wondered why the Elon supporters rose to their feet in the middle of the rendition when the trio began. But the Elonites knew what they were doing, and still rise when the tune of their school song is played.

One of the concessions enthusiastically greeted by the student body and the alumni was the announcement in June 1919 that football would again be permitted at the college. Faculty opposition had dimmed with the passing of a decade, and changes in the method of playing the game had made it "no longer so brutal."[69] This decision was one of the factors that influenced the administration to provide a more suitable athletic field. It was anticipated correctly that the new sport would attract additional crowds of spectators, many arriving in automobiles, for which parking space was already insufficient at the Haggard Avenue location. Another problem was the proximity of the field to residences where the noise made during the games was sometimes annoying.

To solve the problem, a large field on the south side of the railroad tracks, west of Williamson Street, approximately half a mile from the town, was laid out. It was equipped with a running track, baseball diamond, football gridiron, and a grandstand. This facility brought the total of land in use for the athletic program to thirty-four acres, a large area for that purpose in a college the size of Elon at the time.[70]

The new location was appropriately named Comer Field, honoring "Uncle Pinkie" Comer, the black man who waited on "Uncle" Wellons and also looked after the athletic grounds. When first used, at games the college band and the ladies filled the original grandstand. The male spectators stood behind ropes at the side of the playing area. This was especially convenient when football was played, for the male onlookers could move up and down the field with the team, as long as they remained behind the roped-off area. Their view was better than in a 50-yard-line seat in the grandstand.[71] Accommodations at Comer were later greatly expanded.

The readmission of football to the college sports program was also responsible for a change in coaches. "Jack" Johnson was efficient in baseball, basketball, and track, but lacked training in football because it had not been played during his student days at Elon. He was happily settled at the institution, for he married Oma Utley (Elon '15), who served several years as college librarian at the time, but he was unwilling to undertake an assignment for which he was not prepared. He, therefore, resigned as Director of Athletics and continued his career elsewhere.[72] His successor was Frank B. Corboy, a proficient football coach from the University of Pittsburgh.

In 1919, during his last year as athletic director, Johnson had faced the formidable task of training a football team at a college where the game had not been played for ten years, and then only for a brief period. Although inexperienced with the sport, he attacked the problem with determination and Elon played three games that year. The first was won, which, though a good omen, did not prevent the loss of the two remaining. The last defeat, by Guilford, was the hardest to bear because keen rivalry had arisen between the two schools during the days when one of the Doak brothers was coaching at each institution.[73]

When Corboy arrived, he at least had the nucleus of a squad with which to work in football. As a result, from 1920 through the two following seasons, Elon was the victor in approximately half the games played. Keenest interest arose over the 0-0 tie with Guilford in 1921 and the overwhelming defeat of the archrival by a score of 20-0 the following year.[74]

The latter game was played on November 11, Armistice Day, in Greensboro. Because the date was celebrated as a public holiday at the time, the students were all free to attend, and most of them did so. Jubilantly returning to Elon in the small hours of the morning, they set fire to "the ancient municipal calaboose" as the culmination of their victory celebration. It was rumored that the act was inspired by a promise the students made to themselves that, if they won the game on Armistice Day, they would wipe out every institution that inhibited the freedom of citizens. Firing the old "slammer" was how they kept their vow, and the campus newspaper judged that "the city jail—as it is called in dignified circles—seemed glad to go up in flames in honor of such an important event in student life."[75] Once the building was demolished, the town authorities decided to use the county jail in Graham when they needed such a facility rather than to build a new one, and the municipality has functioned quite peaceably since under that arrangement. It is a compliment to law and order in the town that the jail, built around 1900, had been used so seldom that it had never been deemed necessary to arrange for heat in the building.

In 1921 newspapers referred to the college football team as "the Elon Eleven." The following year, it was called "the Maroon and Gold Machine," then "the Bear Cats," but, in the famous game with Guilford, it was described as the "Christians," in its fight against the "Quakers." This was the origin of the name for Elon's athletic teams, which became the "Fighting Christians," as they are still known.[76]

In addition to the progress of the college in football under Corboy, it maintained its proficiency in baseball, basketball, and track. Several individuals emerged as star performers during the period. These included E. S. ("Johnny") Johnson (Elon '22); L. J. ("Hap") Perry (Elon '23); Gordon A. Kirkland; and R. C. ("Bob") Browne, a brother of Pretto Browne (Elon '18), who married J. L. Crumpton (Elon '17), an Elon trustee and donor of the Crumpton Conference Center to the college in 1974.[77]

In addition to the various events taking place at the college, some interesting ones also occasionally occurred in the life of the town. In 1921 the Elon chapter of the Junior Order of United American Mechanics (Jr. O.U.A.M.), was host to several lodges from the area at a picnic on July 4. The event was held on the college campus and was attended by the lodge members, students, and townspeople. After the meal, a number of contests were held, which the newspaper described as follows:

> A wheelbarrow race which was won by Moses Caddell. Sack race won by York Brannock. Shoe race, in which shoes were discarded and then put back on during the race. York Brannock won the race for the boys, and G. E. Barker for the men. . . . The girls staged a 100 foot race, Mary Brannock being proclaimed the winner. The 100 yard dash contest went to Mark McAdams. The three legged race, after being tied three times, was decided in favor of Dan Newman and Fred Caddell. Following the races, the following were awarded prizes: Miss Elnor Doris Brown for being the prettiest girl; R. B. Hensley for being the ugliest man; W. E. Loy for having the largest family present; G. T. Wagoner for being the tallest man present, and Rev. J. D. Andrew for having the largest girth. Marvin Franklin was the lucky contestant in the pole climbing contest, receiving a watch for successfully climbing a 20 foot pole which had been thoroughly greased. The last contest was the bicycle race which was won by Jenkins Pritchett.[78]

It was an interesting and entertaining day for all.

Infrequently, a sensation rocked the usually placid life of the town. In 1918 a man walked into the Elon bank and arranged to open an account with $200 for his sister, a student at the college he said. He presented a check for $600, and the gullible bank clerk gave him $400 in change. The man then disappeared, the check turned out to be worthless, and no sister was found at the college.[79]

More sensational was the attempted robbery of the bank on the night of April 19, 1920. The intruders penetrated the outer door of the vault, but the inner door of the safe defied their efforts to force it open. Finally departing without the anticipated loot, they left only damaged fixtures behind. They were never apprehended.[80]

During World War I and in the years immediately following, the growing town conducted an increasing number of transactions with the college concerning utilities for the municipality. In 1917 the commissioners granted the college a franchise to operate an electric light and power system in the town. Another franchise was also granted to the Piedmont Power and Electric Company, of Burlington, to route its power lines through the town on condition it furnished the college plant with current to be used by the community. This

1917–18 basketball team. From left to right, front row: *E. S. ("Johnny") Johnson, Bill Stevens, E. A. ("Cutie") Tuck, Lyn W. Preston, and Marvin Gray.* Second row: *Coach C. C. ("Jack") Johnson, Dr. Jimmy Martin, Ben Cozart, and graduate manager A. L. Hook.*

arrangement continued until 1923, when both the college administration and the municipal authorities agreed to transfer the franchise to the Piedmont Company for its future operation.[81]

Each citizen who was connected with the college water supply was charged for the service by means of a meter installed on his line. This was financially satisfactory, but occasional leaks in the pipelines, low pressure during the summer months, and other inconveniences were responsible for the town's decision in 1924 to dig its own well and operate its own system.[82]

It is fortunate these changes were made because the growth of the community at the time indicated that one system of utilities was inadequate for both the town and the institution.

The Christian Church had every reason to be proud of its investment in Elon College because of the dividends it had paid up to this period. These were summarized for the Southern Christian Convention in 1920 by Dr. Harper:[83]

> In 1889, the year Elon was chartered, we had seventy-two ministers, two of whom were college graduates. We now have 100 ministers and 61 of them are college graduates. In 1889 we had 17 licentiates, none of whom were college men. Now we have 22 licentiates, and one-half of them are college men.
>
> The distribution of the 368 full graduates is indication, too, as to the faithfulness with which our college has lived up to her high profession of Christian service.
>
> | | |
> |---|---:|
> | In the Field of Religion . . . . . . | 66 |
> | In the Field of Education . . . . . | 127 |
> | In Other Professions . . . . . . | 40 |
> | In the Various Occupations . . . . . | 55 |
> | Christian Wives and Mothers . . . . | 68 |
> | In Universities for Further Preparation . . . | 12 |
> | Total | 368 |

This report was pleasing to the convention and one of which the college could be justly proud.

A unique honor came to Elon in 1921 when the people of Alamance County chose W. P. Lawrence, head of the English Department and Dean of the College, to represent them in the lower house of the state General Assembly. This was the first and only time a

Professor Walter P. Lawrence, Representative from Alamance County in the North Carolina General Assembly of 1921, while on leave of absence from the college. He is seated at his desk in the House of Representatives Chamber of the State Capitol, Raleigh.

faculty member of the college was elected to the legislative body, though others later campaigned ineffectively for the office and a member of the administrative staff won the distinction. Dr. Lawrence had been an active member of the Democratic party for years, having served as chairman at party conventions and also as an Alamance County commissioner. He demonstrated special interest in education and good roads. His career as a legislator was successful, but his primary love was Elon College, and he did not run for reelection to the office at the conclusion of his term.[84]

In the spring of 1920, the college faculty addressed a memorial to the board of trustees that called attention to the general rise in the cost of living that had begun during World War I and continued afterward. The document emphasized that the college staff had received no increased remuneration and needed it to meet the changed economic conditions. The board responded by raising full professors to $1,900 per year, plus $100 additional pay for each ten years of service. An increase of $300 was granted to the heads of academic departments with families, and $200 to those who were not full professors. The president and the athletic director were each raised to $2,500 per year.[85]

This was a welcome relief to the petitioners, but also an increased sum to be included in the annual budget of the institution, for 51 staff members needed to be paid. Assistance for this purpose was received the following year when the General Education Board of New York City sent E. C. Sage, its field secretary, to investigate conditions at the school. As a result of his visit, a grant of $5,000 annually for two years was made for the purpose of meeting the increase in professors' salaries.[86]

Meanwhile, the work of the faculty had been further streamlined by the creation of the President's Cabinet, a few professors chosen to meet frequently with Harper and function somewhat as a faculty executive committee. In 1922 authority was granted to the Dean of Women to form her own cabinet, consisting of the female instructors.[87] After these changes were made, the full faculty was only required to meet monthly or for called sessions, which enhanced the efficiency of the administration.

A regretted faculty change occurred on May 3, 1922, when nonresident Professor F. S. Child died at his home in Connecticut. He had lectured annually for more than two decades at the college, where "his last public service was the sermon preached at Elon on the third Sunday in April." The visits of the eminent clergyman had been made possible through the generosity of the Palmer Fund, which also sponsored the annual visits to the institution of nonresident Professor Martyn Summerbell. In addition, this fund, which had been given a broad range of powers when it was established by the New York banker, had sent the college cash gifts between 1908 and 1922 totaling at least $25,500, a deeply appreciated financial aid from a trust that still renders valuable aid to Elon College.[88]

As soon as the war ended, the Elon administration renewed its interrupted efforts to complete the Standardization Fund that had been authorized by the Southern Christian Convention in 1918. The original goal of $150,000 to be added to the college endowment fund was increased to $250,000. In 1920 the Christians also launched the Men and Millions Forward Movement, which would allocate

Garden party at President Harper's home during the 1920s. The lady seated in the high-backed wicker chair at the left is Mrs. Harper. The second man on the left is Dr. Harper, and the third is Dr. J. U. Newman.

$381,600 for the Standardization Fund if the drive were successful. The economic depression of the early 1920s slowed the progress of this drive, but it gained momentum as time passed, though its final goal was never reached.[89]

In 1920 the college plant and holdings were inventoried as follows:[90]

Total value of plant and equipment . .	$506,600.00
Total productive endowment . . .	237,614.05
Total of unproductive endowment, including	
unpaid subscriptions	303,251.91
Total of funds subject to annuity . . .	3,000.00
Total of other assets	37,500.00
Total assets	. $1,087,965.96
Less active liabilities	77,500.00
Net assets	. $1,010,465.96

This was a comfortable situation, and expectations were good that it would increase and benefit the college.

In 1922 William F. Corwith, of Brooklyn, New York, whose sister, Elizabeth P. Corwith, had married Professor Martyn Summerbell, gave $35,000 to found a Professorship in Christian Education, in memory of his wife. Later, Corwith served a term as an Elon trustee. At about the same time, the family of J. W. Carlton, of Richmond, Virginia, consisting of Pleasant J., H. A., and Luther C., and their sister, Mrs. Thomas S. Parrott (nee Nannie Carlton, Elon, '04), donated $25,000 to found a Professorship in Bible, in memory of their mother. Pleasant J. Carlton, an Elon alumnus, also later served his alma mater as a trustee.[91]

Among other benefits to the college program was the Alumni Scholarship Fund of $100, the fund created by Dr. Amick and to which he added annually, that provided loans at interest to deserving students. Dr. E. H. Bowling, of Durham, North Carolina, established a fund from which students, preferably those planning to become ministers, could borrow $60 annually, to be repaid with interest. The choice of beneficiaries was left in the hands of the college president. Ministerial students could also borrow from the income of a $5,000 fund contributed by I. W. Pritchard, of Chapel Hill, North Carolina. The Masonic Fund of $1,000, contributed by the Grand Lodge of

North Carolina, was available for loans to seniors, and all students were eligible to apply for aid from the Knights Templar Educational Loan Fund. Smaller gifts for student aid were $283.35 from Joseph A. Foster, of Semora, North Carolina, $50 from Miss Mamie Tate, and $100 bequeathed by the Reverend S. B. Klapp. The $1,000 bequest of Captain Patrick Henry Lee, of Holland, Virginia, was for general use, as were also the earlier gifts of the Reverends O. J. Wait and J. J. Summerbell.[92]

The Southern Christian Convention made plans to contribute $4,500 annually to the college. The Francis Asbury Palmer Fund, not to be confused with the endowment money contributed by the New York philanthropist, had not only been paying practically all the expenses of the Child and Summerbell lectures, but also gave the college gifts of money at regular intervals. In 1922 and for some years previously, these contributions had amounted to $4,000 per year. These were added to the permanent endowment of the institution. Such income, supplemented by other personal gifts, elevated the financial status of Elon College.[93]

During the early years of the Harper presidency, the honorary D.D. degree was conferred upon E. A. Watkins, Nathaniel G. Newman, George C. Enders, James W. Wellons, I. W. Johnson, J. W. Harrell, A. B. Kendall, and Charles H. Rowland; and the Litt.D. degree upon Edward Myers. In 1914 the LL.D. was voted for Judge Benjamin F. Long, a member of the Alamance Long family, and the Litt.D. for A. G. Caris, president of Defiance College, Defiance, Ohio. The following year, Fairfax Harrison, of Washington, D.C., president of the

Elon College railroad station about 1922.

Southern Railway Company, and W. S. Long, the first president of the college, were honored with the LL.D. In 1916 the faculty approved D.D. degrees for W. T. Walters, of Winchester, Virginia, R. M. Andrews, of Greensboro, and McD. D. Howsare, Eton, Ohio, but it is uncertain because of lost records whether or not they were ever conferred. However, in 1919 the D.D. was conferred upon Leon E. Smith (Elon '10).[94] The same degree was voted for George O. Lankford (Elon '07) and W. M. Jay, and the LL.D. was awarded to Charles S. MacFarland. Quite possibly other names belong with these, but no records are available at the present time for verification.

In 1922 the college administration was enthused by the decision of the American Christian Convention to hold its annual meeting jointly with the Southern Christian Convention in the First Christian Church, of Burlington. When the historic convention assembled, the Christian Church in the North, the South, the West, and in Canada united into one denomination. This unification strengthened the status of the church, in addition to increasing the interest of the Christians from other parts of the country in the southern institutions of the denomination. One session of the convention was held at Elon, during which the college royally entertained its guests.

Scene in the parking lot when the Reverend J. W. ("Uncle") Wellons preached on his 100th birthday in Whitley Auditorium on January 1, 1926. At the rear left is the North Dormitory, or Alumni Building; and, on the right, the Duke Science Building.

The delegates who were alumni of the institution thoroughly enjoyed "showing off" their alma mater to those who had never previously seen the school. This publicity encouraged the administration to expect more support from the denomination in the future, a prospect happily anticipated.[95]

Before the convention adjourned, it combined the boards of education, Sunday school, and Christian Endeavor of the church and created the office of Secretary of Christian Education to supervise the new agency. W. A. Harper was unanimously elected to this office, in addition to his other duties, and represented a tribute to his successful administration of Elon College.[96]

After this event, the college authorities relaxed somewhat and with good reason. The school had a full quota of students, including several from Cuba and one from Japan.[97] The increasing number of loyal alumni were filling positions of responsibility and even distinction in many parts of the land. On the campus, the buildings were in reasonably good repair, utilities were functioning properly, the college curriculum had been expanded, the athletic program was successful, and the pay of the competent faculty increased. Financially, the indebtedness was not enormous, and the campaign to increase the endowment was moving slowly forward. There were many reasons to be complacent, and to contemplate the future with optimism. So much for the plans of men, for in the beginning of 1923, Elonites were stunned when they awoke early one morning to discover their college on fire.

CHAPTER VIII

THE TREE AND THE TEMPEST

A sturdy oak, which nature forms
To brave a hundred winter's storms,
While round its head the whirlwinds blow,
Remains with root infix'd below.

HOOLE

At approximately 6:30 on the cold winter morning of January 18, 1923, William B. Terrell (Elon '25), after dressing in his quarters on the second floor of the Power House, where several students resided, went downstairs to look out a window of the building over the dark campus. His attention was immediately attracted by a light in one of the offices of the Main (Administration) Building. It was customary to turn on the electric current there each morning at 6:00 A.M., after it had been cut off late during the previous evening. Terrell naturally supposed that someone had negligently left a switch turned on the night before and that the light had automatically come on again when the power was restored. However, as he continued to gaze at the building, he realized the light flickered, indicating it was caused by a fire and not by an electric light bulb.

Terrell sprinted the hundred yards or so to the front door of Main. He intended to ascend to the second floor and ring the college bell to give the alarm, but when he entered the doorway he found the smoke was too dense for him to do so. Frustrated in this endeavor, he then began yelling "Fire!" as loud as he could while racing back to the Power House to telephone the Gibsonville and Burlington fire departments for aid. By the time he had made the call, students and administrators, in various stages of dress, were pouring forth from all the college buildings.[1]

The community was soon rudely awakened by the excitement.

One student frantically banged on the Lawrence front door while yelling, "Dr. Lawrence, the college is on fire!" The fire hose were soon attached to the hydrants by willing hands, but the water obtained was virtually useless because the Main Building was ablaze all over. The firemen summoned from the neighboring municipalities arrived in record time, but their hoses would not fit the college hydrants and would have done little, if any, good had they done so, for the institution's water supply was soon drained to a mere trickle.[2]

However, the chemical truck from the Burlington Fire Department proved to be invaluable. A strong north wind was blowing the flying sparks away from the nearer East Dormitory straight toward the Alumni Building, which obviously would soon be ignited. Students and firemen then climbed onto the roof of the structure and ripped up the tin roofing on the southern corner so that the chemical hose could be inserted in the opening and extinguish the blaze, which by then had started in the wooden eaves. This saved the building. The frantic efforts of others prevented nearby houses and

Remains of the Main (Administration) Building after it burned in January 1923.

buildings from catching fire. The one most in danger was the Young Men's Club, directly across the street from the Alumni Building. It was operated at the time by R. S. Rainey and his wife. Rainey promptly climbed to the roof of the cottage, where he brushed off falling sparks with a broom and wet the exposed area with water passed up in buckets by helpers from below. This crude but effective firefighting saved the building.[3]

By such cooperative efforts, all the buildings at Elon were saved except Main, which was hopeless from the start. At great risk, students dashed into that blazing structure and brought out a few typewriters, nothing more. As the fire consumed the upper floors, the large iron safes of the literary societies crashed downward into the center of the holocaust, where the president's safe had already fallen from his office. Finally, the old college bell, making its last clank, plummeted down from the tower to join them. By mid-morning, only the thick smoking walls remained of the structure that had housed offices; classrooms; the museum; the society halls; the "Y" meeting rooms; the library; and the chapel, with its new pipe organ, where more than 400 graduates had received their diplomas. In addition, the blaze consumed valuable college records that could not be replaced.[4] At least 90 percent of the administrative machinery of the institution lay in ashes. And, had it not been for the heroic efforts of the students, faculty, and townspeople, aided by the Burlington and Gibsonville fire departments, the entire college and a part of the town might have suffered a similar fate.

At the time, it appearing likely that all the college buildings would catch fire, the women busily removed personal possessions and furnishings from the West Dormitory and Ladies' Hall. When the Alumni Building began to blaze, the men who were not occupied with fighting the fire, did the same thing. When order was restored, the campus was strewed with these salvaged belongings, which were returned to their proper places with considerable labor. In the excitement, some trunks were brought outdoors by one person, but two were required to carry each back to the owner's room. Such occurrences are not uncommon under severe emotional stress, but seem humorous afterwards.[5]

The cause of the fire was never determined. One theory was that a gas jet had been accidentally left open in one of the laboratories and that this caused the building to be filled with gas during the night.

When the current was turned on the next morning, a spark from electrical machinery in the building caused a spontaneous combustion that resulted in a flash fire. Dr. A. L. Hook was inclined to consider this possibility plausible. Shortly after half past six that fateful morning, he looked out a window of his home beside the campus and saw Main blazing on all four floors. He did not think that the fire, which was only a glimmer a short time previously, could have spread so fast otherwise. Another, more familiar, theory was that defective wiring was responsible. The wooden floors in the building's interior were cleaned periodically with oil, which was highly flammable, and would have enabled a fire to spread rapidly. Nevertheless, no specific reason for the conflagration was ever determined, but this did not change the painful fact that Main and much of the college plant was gone. The remaining problem was what the next step would be.[6]

Fortunately, no life was lost nor was anyone seriously injured. Had the situation been less serious, the appearance of many Elonites would have been ludicrous, for they were grimy from their fire-fighting efforts, and hours elapsed before the college water power could rebuild the pressure sufficient for bathing. President Harper reacted

The 1923 loss of the Administration Building as reported by the college newspaper.

to the emergency with admirable calm. Before the blaze had entirely subsided, he summoned the faculty to a meeting in his home at ten o'clock that morning. He then directed an assistant to send telegrams to the trustees informing them of the tragedy and requesting their presence at the college on January 24 for a special meeting. The Alumni Secretary used the same means to notify the institution's alumni and friends of the calamity.[7]

It was providential that before the catastrophe the minutes of the faculty meetings and most of the sessions of the trustees, along with a few other valuable records, had been stored in the Alumni Building vault, which saved them. The contents of the four safes in the burned building were entirely destroyed by the intense heat. The brisk wind carried fragments of letters and books over an area two miles from the campus. Almost all the alumni and current student records were burned, a severe loss. Steps were immediately taken to replace all that was possible. Printed forms were distributed to the students on which they were requested to list the courses they had completed with the approximate grade for each. A further effort was made through the college newspaper: "Elon College catalogs are needed in replacing destroyed records. If you have a catalog (of any date) please mail it to Pres. W. A. Harper."[8] Response to these efforts and requests were gratifying and enabled many college records to be completely or partially restored.

Dr. N. G. Newman, pastor of the College Church, met with the faculty when it convened at ten o'clock, and opened the meeting with a prayer. Dr. Lawrence then made a motion that carried for the institution "to continue the work of the session." A mass meeting for students and the public in general was then called for eleven o'clock in the gymnasium.[9]

The announcement of the meeting spread rapidly. At the appointed hour, a large crowd of students, faculty, townspeople, alumni, and friends gathered in the Alumni Building. Numerous brief talks were made in which "a wonderful spirit was displayed," but no mention was made of suspending the work of the college. Several leading faculty members and students spoke. The president read several encouraging telegrams, the first of many to arrive, and the general consensus was that a bigger, better institution would somehow rise from the ruins of the old. The assembly then lustily sang "Here's to Dear Old Elon," and dispersed to begin the task of adjusting plans to continue the operation of the college under the new emergency conditions.[10]

The faculty reconvened at noon in the Harper home. It was announced that the use of the Masonic and Junior Order lodge halls, as well as other places, had been tendered for classroom purposes. The Publishing House could also be used in addition to the laboratories in the Alumni Building, which could serve dual purposes. Using all the available space, the faculty worked out a schedule "for all of the classes." It was also decided to hold "brief chapel exercises" in the dining hall.

Church services were scheduled to be held in the town's graded school building. Attendance by students was optional, but attention was called "to the fact that the trustees expect them to attend religious services." Opportunity was also given the students to hold voluntary Bible study classes in place of Sunday school. A room beside the bursar's office was designated for the return of library books and for general library purposes. The Power House whistle was to be used for the "signals" formerly given by the ringing of the college bell.[11]

Drs. Wicker, Amick, and Lawrence were appointed as a committee "to see about taking down the walls" of the burned building. The faculty was then dismissed with a prayer by Dr. Newman, so that the group could attend another general meeting at four o'clock in the gymnasium. At this assembly, plans and the new schedule were announced, and more newly arrived messages of sympathy were read. The faculty then convened again at five o'clock to postpone the evangelistic services planned for the following week. The members were also informed that the senior class had met and appointed a committee to cooperate with the administration in every way possible. The meeting then adjourned, ending the formal working period of a very long, busy day for the faculty and everyone else at the college.[12]

Many of the newspapers in the state employed their best editorial efforts to rally support for the stricken institution. The editor of the *Burlington Daily News* wrote:

> For about 30 years Elon College has been sending forth
> young men and young women into the world equipped for service. Today she stands wounded and bleeding and mutely ap-

peals for help. Her cry will be answered. We believe that the news will go forth to the world that she will arise forth, out of her ashes, equipped for greater opportunities and work and with a plant that will stand as a monument to what love and confidence can do when the cry for help comes.[13]

The following comment appeared in the *Greensboro Daily News*:

> The destruction by fire of the Administration Building at Elon College further cripples the already seriously handicapped system of higher education in North Carolina. It is not merely a loss to the college and denomination that owns it—it is a loss to the whole State, in that it reduces the facilities available for educating the young people of North Carolina at a time when the facilities are already taxed beyond their normal capacity.[14]

The *Raleigh News and Observer* quoted State Superintendent of Education Eugen C. Brooks in its editorial:

> The greatest loss, however, is not in the amount of property consumed by the fire, but in its handicap to continue the same service for the State that it has rendered for more than a generation. . . . North Carolina just to the same degree as Elon are made to suffer. . . . Patriotic citizens throughout the State will be given an opportunity to come to the assistance of this fine institution in its hour of distress and it should not call upon them in vain.[15]

A letter was published in the *Burlington Daily News* from North Carolina's governor, Cameron Morrison, to Walter E. Sharpe in which he announced he was issuing an appeal to the citizens to rebuild "that noble institution which is one of the beacon lights in education" in the state. Vows of support such as these were encouraging to the trustees as they prepared to assemble for the decision that it was their responsibility to make: to rebuild or cease operations.

Affairs at the school proceeded as smoothly as possible under the makeshift arrangements. The tall brick walls, left standing but weakened after the fire, constituted a hazard to campus traffic should they fall. This condition demanded immediate attention. Under Dr. Amick's supervision, a group of male students pulled them down, a dangerous undertaking in which providentially no one was injured.[16] Little could be done at the time to remove the debris because the bitter January weather prevented further activity. Ice was on the ground and freezing rain fell heavily on the 24th when the trustees arrived for their meeting.[17]

They convened in the president's temporary office in East Dormitory, the first occasion known when that building was used for such a distinguished purpose. En route from the railway station to the meeting place, the board members were deeply touched as they walked past the rubble that remained of the large structure they had last gazed upon with pride. One of the men remarked that he had "rarely seen a building more completely destroyed by fire." It must have been a particularly emotional experience for former president W. S. Long to view the wreckage of the building he had made such a heroic effort to construct. This did not deter him from opening the meeting with prayer and joining his colleagues enthusiastically in their plans for rebuilding.[18]

Despite the inclement weather, the occasion was "the largest meeting of the Board of Trustees it has ever been our privilege to attend," commented the editor of the *Christian Sun*. The principal action taken was also described in the journal:

> We first gave ourselves to what the situation calls for, and after some discussion, it was decided that the mere replacing of the building which had been destroyed would not answer the present need at all. It was therefore decided that we must now undertake to provide a building plan for the institution for the next hundred years. To do this the Board decided to plan for the erection of at least four new buildings, which with the college church which had already been planned, will make really five new buildings, viz.: The Administration Building, a Science Hall, Library Building and an Art Building. Of course to do all this will require a great effort, but the Trustees were in the right mood for undertaking great things for the college. The first will be to build the Administration Building, and then as fast as funds are available the other buildings will follow.[19]

To carry out this elaborate plan, it was proposed to raise $300,000 for buildings and equipment, and a similar sum for the endowment.

This was an ambitious undertaking, but "the Trustees seem confident that it can be done," observed the *Sun*'s editor.[20] Their enthusiasm is better understood in view of announcements that the citizens of Alamance County held a mass meeting in Burlington's Municipal Theatre on January 28 at which they agreed to undertake raising $100,000 of the needed money. The drive was started by a $5,000 contribution from Colonel Robert L. Holt, a county industrialist and former benefactor of Elon.[21] Besides this project, the wealthy Duke brothers, J. B. and Benjamin N., of New York, pledged $5,000 each. The faculty and college community proposed to attempt the raising of $20,000. The aged W. W. Staley offered $1,000, even if it meant postponing the placement of a tombstone on his wife's grave. A similar sum was promised by Mrs. Horace Philips, of South Carolina, daughter of the late W. H. Jones, former cashier of the Farmers' Bank of Nansemond, which had accommodated the college so often. A small, but unusually significant, gift was $50 sent by Charles R. Brown, dean of the Yale Divinity School, who only knew of Elon through students from there who later attended Yale. He did not actually see the college until the 1950s, when he made several visits to conduct the annual Religious Emphasis Week.

Various trustees pledged personal financial aid, including the cheering promise of $50,000 from Colonel J. M. Darden, of Suffolk, Virginia. In addition to these concrete gestures of aid, another factor was important, reported the *Sun*:

> One thing was especially encouraging, viz.: Every one about the college seems so full of hope and so determined to do his or her part to make it all mean a bigger and greater Elon. We did not hear one discouraging thought expressed. Out of the ashes of the building and the depression naturally arising from such a loss, we heard not one despairing thought expressed— every one seemed to be straining his vision to see what he could discover in the way of the best things for Elon College and her future usefulness.[22]

It is no wonder the trustees were inspired to approve an impressive rebuilding plan that posed an unprecedented challenge to the college's supporters and friends.

Herbert B. Hunter, of Burlington, North Carolina, the architect chosen for the purpose, soon produced a plan for the five proposed buildings. The Administration Building, whose three stories would be surmounted by a bell tower topped with a slender spike, was to be located approximately on the site of the building destroyed by the fire. Its length was 216 feet and its width 68 feet. A hall bisecting the length of the structure contained a rotunda on its first floor, from which a doorway gave access on the south side through a columned portico to an oval driveway that extended to the edge of the campus. A similar doorway and portico on the north side opened onto a parking lot, from which a double driveway led to the street. This arrangement would eliminate the old driveway because motor traffic would be restricted to these new entrances, of which the one on the south was considered the front. Cement sidewalks extended from both ends of the building to the campus boundaries.

The building was to be similar to the crossbar in a large letter "H." It was to be flanked at right angles on each end by two smaller brick three-story buildings, whose converging ends would connect with each other and the main building by ornamental brick colonnades. The other ends of each were to be ornamented with two-story porticoes similar to those of the Administration Building. The four flanking structures were each to be 120 feet long and 64 feet wide.

On the east side of the "H," the Science Building was to be located on the front, and the Christian Education Building would be directly behind it. These two were balanced on the west side by the Auditorium in front and the Library behind it. Enclosing the entire campus would be a brick wall, pierced by wrought-iron gateways opening onto the pedestrian walks and the driveways. The drawing of the five structures, designed in harmonious American colonial style of architecture and distinctive because of its colonnades, was attractive and impressive. Its release added considerably to the enthusiasm being generated for the rebuilding program.[23]

Several years before the fire, John King, of Suffolk, had presented the college with a campus plan, accompanied by $100 for its future execution, but it did not locate future buildings. It was also burned with the other records and therefore was of no value as a guide to Hunter, whose plans were based entirely upon his own ideas.[24]

It was anticipated that local funds would be raised to pay for the Administration Building, which was named the Alamance Building for that reason. Colonel Darden's gift covered the Auditorium, and President Harper thus began seeking sponsors for the three remaining units. The Carlton family, donors of the Carlton Fund, generously promised $50,000 for the Library. The Duke brothers, J. B. and Benjamin N., agreed to give $50,000 for the Artelia Roney Duke Science Building, a memorial to their mother, whose grave was located in Alamance County. One of the brothers was skeptical that this sum was sufficient to complete the structure, but was assured that it was the amount estimated by the architect and did not pursue the matter further.[25]

On a visit to Whittier, California, a short time after the fire, Dr. Harper conferred with trustee Michael Orban, Jr., of that city, who decided to donate $50,000 for the Christian Education Building. It was to be named for his father-in-law, the Reverend Isaac Mooney. This gift, and the others promised, completed the basic financing for the five buildings, and it was optimistically anticipated that funds for the equipment and grounds would be forthcoming. Contribu-

Ground-breaking for the Alamance Building in 1923. From left to right: three unidentified persons, Mrs. W. A. Harper, president W. A. Harper, Dr. J. W. Wellons, unidentified, construction foreman Stout, architect H. H. Hunter, Dr. T. C. Amick, C. D. Johnston, D. R. Fonville, Dr. R. M. Morrow, and Dr. W. P. Lawrence.

tions were being received regularly, including $25,000 from trustee W. F. Corwith, given for general use. In appreciation of his generosity, the 1923 *Phipsicli* was dedicated to him. Prompted by the assurance of financial support, the decision was made by the trustees and administration to begin construction of the five buildings simultaneously, and a contract for the purpose was made with the Joe W. Stout Company, of Greensboro.[26]

On May 23, 1923, the cornerstone of the Whitley Auditorium Building was laid by the Elon Lodge No. 549, Ancient Free and Accepted Masons, in conjunction with the Grand Lodge of North Carolina. Reverend J. W. Patton supervised the impressive ceremony. The building, which was not only to serve as the college auditorium but also to house the Music Department, was given by Colonel Darden in memory of his father-in-law, the Reverend Leonard Hume

Laying the cornerstone of Whitley Auditorium in 1923. The man in the center, who is standing and wearing a hat, is the Reverend J. W. Patton, who presided over the Masonic ceremonies. The bearded gentleman in front of the speaker is the Reverend J. W. Wellons. In the speaker's rear, the man seated in the second chair from the left is President W. A. Harper. The college well is to the right of the platform.

Whitley. A brief account of the clergyman's life was read by his son, George F. Whitley (Elon '02), after which Darden was given a rousing ovation by the audience. Dr. Atkinson then delivered an oration suitable to the occasion, which President Harper considered "a good day in Elon's history."[27]

At the commencement in May 1923, the cornerstone of the Alamance Building was laid in the presence of a crowd that included the incumbent Harper and all the former presidents of Elon College. A prominent county lawyer, Edward S. Parker, Jr., delivered the oration, and enthusiasm was high after his scholarly address. On behalf of those who contributed toward the cost of the building, W. E. Sharpe, of Burlington, presented it to the college, and it was accepted by former president E. L. Moffitt. Sharpe was chairman of the local drive to raise funds, in recognition of which the 1925 *Phipsicli* was dedicated to him. The commodious new structure in the center of the campus contained the executive offices of the institution, classrooms, the literary society halls, many of the special departments of the college, and an ample vault for the storage of records. The building was immediately put to advantageous use.[28]

Arrangements for the commencement that year posed several problems. It was first suggested that the baccalaureate sermon be dispensed with because there was no suitable place for it to be delivered at the college, but this seemed an intolerable departure from tradition. The matter was solved by an invitation from the First

Cornerstone ceremonies for the Alamance Building in 1923. The speaker was the Reverend Thomas Opie, of Burlington.

Christian Church, in Burlington, to hold the ceremony there. Transportation was arranged, and a large crowd heard the venerable Reverend Francis E. Clark, founder of the Christian Endeavor Society, preach to the seniors.[29]

For the first time, the graduating exercises that year were held beneath the campus oaks. A platform for the officials was erected slightly southwest of the present front entrance to Whitley Auditorium. The few chairs and folding seats available, supplemented by planks laid across the trunks of felled trees, were placed on the grass for the audience. In the absence of North Carolina's governor, Cameron Morrison, who had been invited but was unable to attend, Elon trustee J. E. West, at the time lieuetenant governor of Virginia, introduced the principal speaker, Governor E. Lee Trinkle, of the same state. Thus, the two highest political officials of the Old Dominion were prominent participants in Elon's first and only outdoor commencement. The balmy May weather also contributed to the success of the graduation program. The crude arrangements were ac-

1923 commencement, the only one ever held outdoors. The speaker is Governor E. Lee Trinkle, of Virginia.

cepted in good spirit, for everyone was happy that the college was to be rebuilt.[30]

The event also included another special feature. Several years previously, the Reverend James L. Foster, a former superintendent of the Christian Orphanage, had promised a present to the first boy or girl from the institution to graduate from Elon College. The winner was Thomas H. Andrews, of the class of '23, who was presented a hundred dollars in gold by Dr. Staley, on behalf of Foster who was unable to be present. This generous gesture inspired a comment from the Sun's editor: "We trust that the purity and beauty of the gold may ever furnish this young man a high ideal for his life and work. Set your mark high, young man, and then, by God's help, reach it." This advice was heeded, for the prize winner went on to graduate school and then became a highway engineer.[31]

As soon as the commencement was concluded, the campus became an even more noisy place. An increasing number of hammers, saws, machinery, and trucks made a variety of sounds as construction progressed. The bricks left whole after the fire were cleaned for reuse, and the broken ones were crushed and packed together to

Parked cars and construction underway at the 1923 commencement.

form a foundation for the Alamance Building and its adjacent parking lot. A considerable amount of the brick cleaning was performed by the local Boy Scouts. This was the only practical use of anything left by the conflagration; the new Elon was literally rising from the ruins of the old. Walls began to mount for the five new structures at the same time, a sight never before witnessed at the college. In 1925, by which time most of the construction had been completed, Charles D. Johnston, superintendent of the orphanage, and a crew of his boys seeded the entire campus in grass as a gift to the college.[32]

When Dr. Harper left for California, the foundation of the Science Building was already being laid under the supervision of Dr. Hook. After the president conferred with the Orban family, he made the decision to use that site for the Christian Education Building and place the Science Building in its rear, where it now stands. Hook was notified of the new plan, and halted construction pending completion of the new specifications. Afterward, the professor, whose primary aca-

Breaking ground for the Duke Science Building in 1923. The little girl holding the shovel is Sarah Virginia Hook; seated is J. W. Wellons; and the second and third men to his left, respectively, are Dr. J. P. Barrett and President Harper.

demic interest was science, often humorously observed that the Mooney Building was successfully used only because it was built on a foundation originally designed for a science building.[33]

The rebuilding progress, phenomenal for Elon, was the basis for the introduction of President Harper's report in 1924 to the Southern Christian Convention:

> Elon College is enjoying the crisis of her heroic career. Born in poverty, nurtured in sacrifice, threatened with destruction by a disastrous fire, hedged about with standardization tests she must meet or lose her prestige, Elon faces the future battered but undismayed. No college ever arose more triumphant from ashes than our Elon. And while the problems that confront her have sent many an institution tottering to her demise, Elon has all the vigor of youth and resiliency in her spirit.[34]

The remainder of the report did not cause so much jubilation among the audience.

Regrettably, not only were the walls of new buildings rising, but costs were unexpectedly escalating at the same time, according to the report. The revised estimates for the program were $425,000 for the five buildings, $75,000 for furniture, $52,000 for a campus fence and improvement of the grounds. The total was $552,000. Of this amount, $261,486.97 had been received in cash and $148,750.00 borrowed from banks against subscriptions. Faithful supporters had promised $80,000, "leaving a net balance of $61,763.03 yet to be provided." The president continued, "Before the fire, Elon had an indebtedness incurred over a term of years for buildings and occasional annual deficits in the sum of $114,750.00. When the rebuilding program is completed, Elon will be in debt perhaps $300,000, all of which will be covered by subscriptions except the original indebtedness, and we hope even that."[35] According to this statement, the completion of the program would leave the college with a new debt of $300,000—the original estimate of the entire cost of rebuilding.

The president softened this disappointing news by reminding his hearers that the college would be worth $1,359,005.95 when its debts were paid, a happy situation that evidently he fully expected. He concluded by bluntly announcing that "Elon must have at least a million dollars of endowment to be the college our hearts desire her to be. She must have $500,000 endowment immediately to meet the North Carolina State requirement. We must also join the Southern Association of Colleges and Secondary Schools as soon as we can qualify financially."[36] This figure was prompted by the fact that the Southern Association would not admit a school to membership unless its endowment totaled at least $300,000 and its indebtedness was properly secured. Recognition by this organization was highly desirable, for the standards for educational institutions were rising universally, and Harper intended for Elon's rating to be first-class, if possible.

In order to proceed with its building program, the college authorities could not wait for funds to be collected over a period of time, but needed to possess the cash with which to pay the contractors. To obtain it, on July 1, 1923, $300,000 was borrowed from the Farmers' Bank of Nansemond, secured by a mortgage on all the college real estate, buildings, equipment, and its endowment fund. This enabled construction to continue without interruption, but, within two years, rising costs made more funds necessary.

On September 1, 1926, a loan of $350,000 was obtained from the Virginia Trust Company, of Richmond, which financed the transaction by the sale of bonds bearing 6 percent interest. To guarantee payment, all the college property was mortgaged to the bank. In addition, all securities owned by Elon, including endowment investments, were placed with the bank in escrow. Any income from them was to be applied on the interest payments, and the surplus, if any, used to reduce the principal. To make this a first mortgage, the indebtedness to the Suffolk bank was paid, including $75,000 borrowed from that institution in 1916. Then the Farmers' Bank of Nansemond, influenced by the personal interest of its officials in Elon, loaned the institution $150,000, secured by a second mortgage on the college property.[37] Meanwhile, the Harper administration had continued its efforts to obtain aid from the Christian Church in retiring these loans because it preferred to be in debt to the denomination rather than commercial institutions.

On September 12, 1923, under the sponsorship of the Southern Christian Convention, Bethlehem College had opened its doors in Wadley, Alabama. The new school was founded to provide education opportunities in an area where the distance involved prevented many of its youth from attending Elon. The new school needed money for its completion, and the college in North Carolina needed funds for its rebuilding program. To expedite both, the convention approved the following recommendation at its 1924 session: "That the Convention issue its bonds . . . to cover the indebtedness and financial requirements of Elon and Bethlehem Colleges, providing over a term of years for the retirement of the interest and principal of the same, thus placing the schools on a safe financial basis. This would require $500,000—$400,000 for Elon and $100,000 for Bethlehem."[38] This authorization made the Elon administration feel financially secure about the costs of its rebuilding, which had already exceeded the original estimates.

When the convention met in 1926, the details had been completed and were accepted by the adoption of a resolution:

> *Resolved*, That the Board of Trustees of Elon College, N.C., do hereby authorize and empower its president to guarantee, in

College trustees in the mid-1920s. From the left, the fourth man is Charles D. Johnston; the eighth, ex-President E. L. Moffitt; the tenth, President W. A. Harper; the twelfth, ex-President W. W. Staley; the thirteenth, J. O. Atkinson; the fourteenth, P. H. Fleming; and the sixteenth, D. R. Fonville.

the name of said board, and on its behalf, the payment of certain bonds and the interest coupons thereto attached, said bonds not exceeding in the aggregate the sum of four hundred thousand dollars, issued, or to be issued by the Southern Christian Convention.[39]

The college was given a precise method of procedure for eventually liquidating the bonds:

The Board of Trustees of Elon College were requested to collect pledges due on Standardization and Emergency Fund subscriptions for the benefit of the interest and principal payments of the $400,000 of the bonds which will be turned over to them under the said Southern Christian Convention resolution. They are also to use their officers, as directed by the Convention, to raise during the term of years the bonds are to run, any additional amount needed to care for their part of the principal and interest.[40]

The bonds represented no cash for the college, but were listed among its current assets on its financial statement. This increased the institution's credit apart from its bonded obligations and was an agreeable arrangement to all concerned.

The apparent assurance of financial security relieved the college administration of much pressure, and was primarily responsible in December 1926 for the admission of the institution to membership in the Association of Colleges and Secondary Schools of the Southern States, an achievement long desired. The jubilant Harper reported this honor in 1928 to the convention with justifiable pride:

Now the graduates of Elon College are admitted without question to the graduate departments of universities anywhere in the world, and they are also granted certificates to teach on terms equal to the best in every state in the Union and also in foreign countries. The Convention is to be congratulated upon its wisdom in thus providing for Elon. Our next duty is to retire these bonds and relieve the Convention of its obligation.[41]

This announcement possibly smoothed the path for a final accounting of Elon's construction expenditures:

Inasmuch as certain items involved in the rebuilding program had to be adjusted since the Durham Convention, we think it well to detail at this time the cost of the rebuilding program, showing the origin of this indebtedness. The facts are as follows:[42]

Cost		Paid
$130,251.76	Alamance . . .	. $ 50,217.00
83,534.36	Whitley . . .	. 50,000.00
81,311.32	Duke	. 80,000.00
85,000.00	Carlton . . .	. 85,000.00
102,601.27	Mooney . . .	. 100,000.00
44,008.34	Outside service system . . .	. —
10,560.00	Porticoes . . .	. —
52,000.00	Entrance, grounds, walls . . .	. —
44,283.96	General expense items . . .	. —
130,714.38	Furniture and equipment . . .	. —
15,000.00	Library equipment .	. 15,000.00
18,147.32	Books for library . .	. —
24,700.03	Refinancing costs .	. —
	Raised for general purposes, cash and gifts . .	. 129,905.65
$822,112.74		$510,122.74
	Balance due on rebuilding program . . .	. $311,990.00

When these improvements were completed, the Elon College plant was valued at $1,202,051.04, in contrast with a value of $506,600.00 in 1920, and of $389,510 after the fire and before rebuilding began.[43]

This accounting concluded with the statement that the interest on Elon's financial obligations to the convention amounted to $36,750 annually. This sum had been raised previously by receiving a share in the convention's benevolent program, by the payment of pledges, and by gifts from individuals. The college planned to resort to the same method to raise the money in the future, separate and apart from its operating budget, which amounted to $149,000 for the year 1928–29.[44] This was a staggering load for the college to carry, but the Harper administration optimistically anticipated that the money would be forthcoming to enable it to fulfill its obligations without any interruption in the institution's operation. The president acknowledged that this was an ambitious goal to set under the circumstances, but the initial success of fundraising and the promise of further donations in the future by affluent supporters had stimulated the optimism of the executive and his trustees about their undertaking. For that reason, the die had been cast, and the walls continued to rise.

When the three-story Mooney Building was completed, it contained classrooms, offices, conference rooms, a small auditorium, and meeting rooms for the "Y's" as well as the social clubs. It also contained the only passenger elevator on the campus. Accommodating only one person at a time, it was installed primarily for the benefit of the aged "Uncle" Wellons. On October 3, 1926, impressive dedication ceremonies were held, attended by Michael Orban, his wife, and daughter (Mrs. G. S. Melville). The building was presented to the college by Dr. W. S. Alexander, pastor of the College Church, a personal friend of the donor, and accepted on behalf of the board of trustees by Dr. Staley.

The principal speaker for the occasion was Dr. Walter S. Ahearn, dean of the School of Social Service and Religion at Boston University, who had assisted in planning the building. According to the *Sun*:

> In his address he stated that the first course in religious education to be given at a college for credit toward an academic degree was only sixteen years ago, but that now 120 colleges in the United States were giving religious instruction in their curriculums, but that it had remained for Elon College to erect a building devoted exclusively to this purpose in connection with their college.[45]

The 101-year-old Wellons then pronounced the benediction, and educational activity began in "the first building wholly devoted to Christian education on any college campus in the world."[46]

On April 27, 1927, the Duke Science Building was dedicated in the presence of Mrs. Benjamin N. Duke, representing the family of the donors. The three-story structure, containing laboratories, class-rooms, and offices, was presented to the college by Alex H. Sands, Jr., private secretary to Mr. Duke, and accepted on behalf of the trustees by Dr. J. E. Rawls. An interesting personal note was also injected into the program:

> Mr. D. R. Fonville, an alumnus of the college and trustee, brought a word of appreciation for Mrs. Artelia Roney Duke, mother of the Duke brothers, in whose memory the Science Building is dedicated. . . . The Roneys and the Fonvilles have lived side by side in Alamance County since colonial days, and Mr. Fonville interpreted Mrs. Duke most fittingly. Mrs. Duke, on her mother's side, was a Trollinger, and she and the late W. H. Trollinger, who gave the Elon College campus, were first cousins.[47]

Governor Angus W. McLean, prevented from attending by illness, sent his prepared address, which was read by Dr. A. T. Allen, State Superintendent of Public Instruction, followed by the dedicatory speech delivered by Dr. Robert L. Flowers, of Duke University.

After the ceremony, the numerous visiting dignitaries were enter-tained at a luncheon. The Duke Science Building was then ready for the scholastic work it has housed since the gala occasion. In appre-ciation of this beneficial facility, the 1928 *Phipsicli* was dedicated to Benjamin N. Duke, and his wife, Sarah Pearson (Angier) Duke.[48] During the 1950s Doris Duke, daughter of J. B. Duke, made a contri-bution for the upkeep of this building, and Mrs. Mary Duke Biddle Trent Semans is now an Elon trustee.

The Carlton Library Building was ready for occupancy by the op-ening of the 1925 fall term. The facility was described in detail by C. M. Cannon, business manager of the college:

> This building is 120 x 64 feet, three stories high, of modern fire-proof construction, and is well stocked with valuable books. Special attention has been paid in collecting books to furnish the very best parallel and research matter for all the college courses. The stack-room inside the building where the books are kept, is built in the form of a vault, so that no acci-

dent could destroy it. The Southern Christian Convention, recognizing the double safety provision of this book-vault, has made it the depository for their permanent records.

The stack-room itself is five-stack stories high. Steel shelving, and marble floors and stairways are to be used in this vault-room. The total capacity of the library building is 225,000 volumes.

On the first floor are the reading-rooms, as well as offices, cataloguing and charging-rooms. The building is so arranged that the reading-rooms, reference shelves, and stack are convenient for the students, and they may secure the information desired in the minimum amount of time. The second and third floors contain stock and supply rooms, professors' studies, and seminar rooms. . . . Each department of the college has its seminar room with special reference works on the courses of that department.

Library experts have pronounced it one of the best libraries in the country, and the Christian Church and Elon are under lasting obligation to its donors.[49]

No part of the rebuilding program was of more value to the academic program of the college than the new Library. As soon as it was completed, it was utilized to its fullest extent and the lengthy task begun of acquiring more books to fill its capacious shelves. Gratitude for this gift was expressed by the dedication of the 1929 *Phipsicli* to trustee Pleasant J. Carlton.

The opening of the new facility was the occasion for changing the former policy for library management. Since the opening of the college, a faculty member had been designated as curator of the library, to head a committee of colleagues in supervising the operation. A nonprofessional librarian was then appointed and given a corps of student assistants. At the time of the fire, Miss Minnie Edge was the librarian, and Dr. Walton C. Wicker was the curator.

Because of the enlarged opportunities available when the Carlton Building was occupied, the board of trustees accepted the recommendation of its Administrative Committee and employed a professionally trained librarian, as the administration announced in the summer of 1923:

Miss Louise Savage, Randolph-Macon and University of Virginia, becomes Head Librarian and Dean of Women. She will also teach one class in Mathematics. Miss Savage comes to her executive work aflame with the idea of service after six years of similar responsibility in the Fort Loudoun Seminary, Winchester, Virginia. She is thoroughly committed to Southern ideals and a devout lover of young people.[50]

Miss Savage served in this capacity until 1930, when she was replaced by Miss Hallie I. Shearer, an experienced librarian who held a professional degree from the State Library College, at Albany, New York. Her expertise was considered fortunate for Elon because the Carnegie Corporation had made the college a beneficiary in its new loan fund, which made $2,000 available annually for the purchase of new books. In March 1931 the librarian reported that the library contained 16,756 books, 650 of which had been purchased with Carnegie funds. After serving a year, Miss Shearer was succeeded by Mrs. Oma U. Johnson, the widow of former Coach C. C. Johnson. She held the position, except for two brief intervals, until 1959.[51]

Calamity usually arouses sympathetic responses. For example, after the 1923 fire, the use of Burlington's Municipal Theatre was courteously extended to the institution, which no longer had available any place on the campus to give presentations before a large audience. This enabled the college program to be continued during the process of rebuilding.

This arrangement was especially valuable for the Concert Series program. On January 16, 1916, the Music Lovers' Club had been organized at Elon; Miss Mabel Harris, of the college music faculty, was president, and Miss Mary Ann Baker served as secretary-treasurer. It immediately became an active organization, one of its members serving as an official of the North Carolina Federation of Music Clubs, to which the Elon group belonged. Its membership was open to the faculty, music majors, and members of the college community.[52]

In 1921 the club arranged a concert and lecture course consisting of five numbers for the year, to be financed by the sale of season tickets. The college rule prohibiting "paid entertainments or exercises of any kind in the College or on the campus" was broadened to authorize the program and set a precedent for the future with the following exceptions: "A limited number of exercises may be held, subject to the President's approval, each year, at which a free-will offering may be received. A Lyceum Course may be arranged for the year by the President, as may also a Lecture Course in any one of the special departments, for both of which season tickets will be sold."[53]

The series was arranged by Professors Edwin M. Betts and Gilman Floyd Alexander, both of the college Music Department. The first season, a decided success, brought to Elon a distinguished group of instrumentalists, vocalists, and lecturers whose performances were appreciated by capacity audiences. This was the real beginning of the annual college lyceum program of the present.[54]

The following season, by the time of the fire, some of the performers had yet to appear and no building was available for them except the theater in Burlington.[55] This posed a transportation problem because the only means of arriving at the concerts at the proper time was by automobiles, which were far less numerous than they later became and few were owned by students. Responding to this dilemma, the people of Burlington, Graham, and Gibsonville voluntarily used their autos to transport the students to the neighboring municipality for the performance. This cooperative act on the part of the citizens inspired a comment from the editor of the *Gleaner*: "There is not the shadow of a doubt that the unfortunate fire has served to tie the communities about the college into a closer fellowship than ever for the college and has made the college feel its dependence upon the community."[56] This realization of mutual interests continued to increase, and is one of the richest assets of the college and its surrounding area.

When construction was completed, a more attractive picture than the complex of new buildings presented would have been difficult to imagine. The protective brick wall eliminated the numerous footpaths that had formerly crisscrossed the campus. This made formal landscaping possible, which increased the beauty of the scene. Elon was far better equipped to serve its student body and the general public than ever before in its history, and no time was lost in fully nurturing this potential.

It was with a feeling of justified pride that the new Whitley Building was first used for the 1924 commencement. The main floor and the rear and side balconies could seat several hundred people. The stage, equipped with maroon draw-curtains under a matching valance emblazoned with a large gold "E," was ample for all the college exercises and performances. A projection booth over the rear balcony made moving pictures possible. Behind the stage were the offices and studios of the Music Department. One room contained a two-manual Estey reed practice organ. However, the most universally interesting feature of the building was the four-manual Skinner pipe organ in the auditorium, on which the dedicatory recital was played on September 5, 1924.

The capacity audience included more people prominent in musical circles than any previous performance had attracted at the college. The presidents of both the North Carolina Federation of Music Clubs, and the Southern States Federation, were present, as well as representatives of other musical organizations, in addition to organists and teachers. All seats and every foot of standing room were filled, and those unable to gain entrance to the auditorium stood outside or sat in cars to hear the music through the open windows of the building.

The program began with a brief greeting from President Harper, in

Home of President Harper about 1925.

which he explained that the college had originally planned to install a smaller, less expensive organ, but Colonel Robert L. Holt had insisted that the institution possess the best one suited to its needs. This led to the acquisition of "the largest Skinner organ in any Southern college." Harper then introduced the visiting artist, Louis Potter, organist of Calvary Baptist Church, in Washington, D.C., who had played for so many chief executives of the United States he was known as "the organist to the Presidents." C. Asbury Gridley, of Greensboro, southern representative of the Skinner Organ Company, assisted in the program.[57]

Potter played fourteen numbers, some of which demonstrated the special features of the organ. He interspersed interesting short talks on the construction and capabilities of the instrument. The audience was enthusiastic in its praise of both the performance and the organ. The event was a highlight in the musical history of the college, and the institution was praised by one distinguished visitor for bringing to the state an instrument that raised the "standard of music in North Carolina."[58]

Music had been an important part of the college academic program from the opening of the institution, but the advantage of new equipment and facilities far surpassing those previously available stimulated further emphasis. In 1924 Betts resigned as head of the Music Department to attend the University of Virginia, where he pursued graduate studies in botany. This was an unusual change of interests, but one in which he was eminently successful. His wife, nee Mary Hall Stryker (Elon '24), also continued her studies and became a scholar of prominence in her own right.[59]

Beginning with the 1925 fall term, C. James Velie, former dean of music at Palmer College, succeeded Betts. A prodigy from his youth, the musician had been trained under private teachers, and had never completed his formal education. For this reason, he also enrolled at the college as a student, graduating with the class of 1928 while also a member of the faculty. Appreciative of the opportunities for performances at the college, Velie not only encouraged the concert series, but also concentrated on fostering local talent. This effort reached its first climax on December 13, when "a large portion of George Frederick Handel's 'Messiah'" was presented by the Choral Society and other personnel under his direction. Two of the soloists were Miss Florence Fisher, of the college music faculty, and Mrs. Velie,

Ministers and denominational leaders of the Christian Church attending a conference at Elon about 1925. From left to right, front row: *Pattie Lee Coghill, two unidentified persons, and Dr. W. T. Walters.* Second row: *Mrs. J. L. Foster, unidentified, Mrs. J. W. Patton, Mrs. W. T. Walters, Dr. Warren H. Denison, unidentified, Mrs. Harris, and the Reverend Stanley C. Harrell.* Third row: *Josephine Farmer, Essie Mae Cotten, Dr. Simon Bennett, Dr. J. O. Atkinson, Dr. J. W. Lightbourne, Dr. Roy Helfenstein, Dr. W. W. Staley, the Reverend S. L. Lynam, Dr. I. W. Johnson, and unidentified.* Last row: *the Reverend E. H. Rainey, Dr. W. M. Jay, and Herman Eldredge.*

O'Kelly Monument, in the Quadrangle.

nee Zenith Hurst and a sister of the Reverend Alfred Hurst, a minister of the Christian Church. The performance was received with such acclaim it became an Elon tradition. A major part of the famous oratorio has been presented at the college each December ever since.[60]

Because no academic summer school was conducted during this period, the school plant was free during the vacation months for denominational activities and special programs. In 1915 the Christian Church had begun a week-long "School of Methods," called a "Chautauqua" because of the general use of that term at the time.[61] Its programs were held at Virginia Beach, Virginia. In 1922, in the interest of obtaining a more central location, the annual event was transferred to Elon. Attendance increased from 43 adults and 50 children at the first session in the new location to 120 adults and 75 children the following year. The faculty of the Chautauqua included Miss Lucy M. Eldredge (Elon '21), who had become field secretary of the church Board of Education; her father, Hermon Eldredge, editor of the church's Sunday school literature; and the Reverend James H. Lightbourne, the church's Regional Director of Christian Education. In addition, numerous other ministers and educators supplemented the project. After a successful decade, the program was continued under the name of a "Summer Conference," instead of a "Chautauqua." The college was also used frequently for various other denominational meetings, and it continued to be emphatically a church-related institution.[62]

The pride of the Christian denomination in its college was again evident in 1926 when the Southern Christian Convention approved the placing of a monument on the campus as a tribute to the Reverend James O'Kelly, founder of the church. The 16,000-pound "Egyptian-style memorial" was eleven feet high and composed of the best Winnsboro granite. Two slender columns rising from a massive stone base were joined at the top by an ornamental granite slab. The open center contained a small stone urn. The trustees designated the grass plot directly in front of the Alamance Building as the site for the memorial. It was unveiled on October 9, 1929, the 103d anniversary of O'Kelly's death, by his great, great, great granddaughter, Dorothy Ann Harward.[63]

This was the only monument on the campus, and it added beauty and distinction to its surroundings. The attention of visitors to the institution was immediately attracted to the memorial, which soon surpassed the Senior Oak as a popular place to pose for photographs. Many years after it was completed, the ornamental urn disappeared, probably as part of a student prank. It was later replaced by a metal cross, too securely fastened in the granite for removal.[64]

Elon College was not only expanding its physical plant, but also its educational program, the primary reason for its existence. In 1928 President Harper proudly reported to the Southern Christian Convention that a total of 743 students, 420 men and 323 women, had been graduated in the 38 commencements of the institution. He said, "Of this number, 29 have passed to their reward." The following employment statistics were then given concerning the lifework "of those that remain":[65]

	Men	Women
Education	. 145	194
Ministry and missionary	. 107	3
Business	. 87	18
Homemakers	—	74
Public service	. 28	11
Law	. 18	—
Medicine	. 17	1
Engineers	. 12	—
Fine arts	—	2
Totals	414	303

Both the convention and the college were proud of this record, especially of the large percentage of graduates engaged in education and the ministry.

During and after the rebuilding, the college alumni continued to be active. In February 1928 the Alumni Association began to issue its first publication, *The Elon Alumni Voice*, a quarterly journal of approximately 60 pages. The front cover contained a quotation from Virgil, "Forsan Et Haec Olim Meminisse Juvabit" ("Perhaps it will be pleasant to remember these things"). The cover featured a drawing depicting Old Main burning, at the bottom, and the new building complex arising from the flames, at the top. Flanking these on one side was the Old Well, and the Senior Oak on the other. The staff was composed of John Willis Barney (Elon '10), editor-in-chief; and

H. Babcock (Elon '18), Lucy M. Eldredge (Elon '21), H. S. Hardcastle (Elon '18), and L. B. Ezell (Elon '21), associate editors.[66]

The foreword was written by W. H. Boone (Elon '94), president of the Alumni Association. Printed on glossy paper and well illustrated, the periodical's contents consisted of contributions by alumni. Typical articles were "Alumni and College Finance," by Stanley C. Harrell (Elon '09); "Elon's Athletes," by E. S. Johnson (Elon '22); "The Spirit of Chemistry," by C. P. McNally; "Participation of Alumni in the Government of Colleges," by W. A. Harper (Elon '99); "The Call of the Pulpiteer," by P. E. Lindley (Elon '20); "Jokesmith," by R. S. Rainey (Elon '22); and brief notes concerning current activities among the alumni. The *Voice* fostered unity in the association, but, unfortunately, after the February 1930 issue, publication was suspended because of the generally depressed economic conditions prevalent. It was not until 1948 that the association attempted another publication.[67]

The athletic program through the early 1920s under Coach Corboy was moderately successful. Approximately as many games were won as were lost, and student enthusiasm remained high. However, the progress was not sufficient for Corboy, who resigned at the end of the 1925 season to begin a commercial career.[68]

Professional coaches were expensive, and in 1926 the college was engrossed in its rebuilding program. As a consequence, the administration reverted to the policy of former years in which faculty members were assigned the additional duty of athletic coaching. Professor A. Ray Van Cleave, whose academic fields were philosophy and social science, was named as football coach. Professor William Mason Jay, an instructor in English, was placed in charge of the basketball team. This was an unpopular move with the athletes, especially the football players, who wished to continue training under the supervision of a professional coach, to which they had become accustomed. Whether intentionally or not, after the change was made, Elon lost every one of the ten football games played that year, and only scored at all in one of them. Basketball fared somewhat better; victories numbered twelve and losses ten.[69]

The conspicuous number of losses exerted a strong impact on the administration, which abandoned the old system forever. In 1927 Charles Carroll, a professional from the Piedmont League, was employed as baseball coach, and scores improved. Meanwhile, the college had arranged for Douglas C. Walker, familiarly known as "Pea-head," to begin coaching the three major sports in September 1927. Oddly enough, though he came to the institution as a full-time athletic director, he also enrolled as a student, and graduated in 1931. His studies did not interfere with his main job, however. Under his direction, college sports began to rise toward a peak of achievement never previously experienced.[70]

During Walker's first year at the college, E. S. ("Johnnie") Johnson (Elon '22), at the request of the Alumni Association, compiled a list of graduates and nongraduates who had been outstanding athletes at Elon.[71] Modestly omitting his own name, he explained that each selection was "entirely my own," and presented reasons for each of his choices.[72]

From 1922 through 1931, a number of Elon players were selected for All-State Teams, and won several conference championships in the major sports.[73] After this period, faculty members who possessed athletic talent often assisted in the training of the teams, but professional coaching had become a permanent fixture at Elon. The athletic program thus established would eventually be administered by the Department of Physical Education.

During the 1920s, the college faculty continued to be represented to some extent in the municipal government of Elon College. The town was busy providing its own water supply, and making arrangements for utilities independent of the college facilities. New residential construction arose, and the addition of Johnston Hall to the orphanage increased the capacity of that institution. In the area surrounding the town, land formerly used for agricultural purposes was gradually being converted into residential use, and even a few small commercial ventures were opened.

In the summer of 1923, Thomas C. Moon, of Graham, developed a tract of real estate approximately a mile west of the town, on the north side of the highway leading to Gibsonville. A small lake, an adjacent swimming pool, a pavilion, and picnic grounds were in its center, surrounded by lots to be sold for residential purposes. A prize of $10 in gold was offered to the winner of a contest to name the park. "Moonelon," suggested by Miss Kate Mays, of Lexington, North Carolina, was the winning selection. For several years the amusement facility was used extensively for swimming, boating, and outings, which included the annual Sunday school picnic of the Burlington Christian Church.[74]

On January 12, 1928, the quiet town was aroused by a bold daylight robbery of the Elon Bank and Trust Company. The cashier, Mrs. C. M. Cannon (nee Isabella Walton, Elon '24), who was also the wife of the college's business manager, was alone in the late afternoon when a stranger walked in and requested change for a dollar. When Mrs. Cannon turned around with the silver, a gun was pointed at her. She thought this was a joke until the bandit forced her under the counter while he scooped up the $530 in sight and escaped in an automobile two accomplices had waiting outside.

The car, which had been stolen locally, was later found abandoned on N. C. Highway 100, near Whitsett, but the police found no trace of the thieves. The matter remained unsolved until February, when two people were caught in an attempted robbery in Reidsville, North Carolina, and identified as participants in the Elon holdup. They were Mrs. Nettie Jackson and Grady Pugh, who were arrested and lodged in the jail at Graham to await trial. In April Pugh escaped, but was apprehended the following month in Robeson County, North Carolina. On June 21 the couple faced trial; Pugh was sentenced to ten years in the penitentiary and Mrs. Jackson to a term of two years. This ended the story of the great bank robbery, which did not harm the institution financially, though Mrs. Cannon's nerves were doubtless shaken and the event provided the newspapers with an abundance of copy.[75]

While busily engaged in the fiscal details of administration, President Harper did not neglect his duties as an academic leader. The honorary degrees of Litt.D. from Defiance (Ohio) College and LL.D. from Union Christian College (Merom, Indiana) had been conferred upon him; and, prior to the fire, he had written five books on religious education. During the rebuilding program, he found time to add three more to the list. The president was not the only author at Elon, for Dr. Lawrence wrote a play called "For Humanity," and other members of the faculty wrote articles for publication in professional journals.[76]

In 1925 Dr. Wicker resigned from the faculty after twenty-three years of teaching to become the Masonic field secretary. The following year, the death of Dr. Lawrence removed another veteran professor from service. A normal turnover among the instructors was to be expected, but the sorrowful loss of members who had given almost a lifetime of service to Elon was a different matter.[77]

The provisions for student loans were increased during the late 1920s by funds established in honor or memory of J. Pressley Barrett, a Christian minister who edited the *Sun* for many years; E. L. Moffitt, a former president of the college; as well as J. A. Clarke and Professor M. A. McLeod, faculty member and late faculty member respectively.[78]

Among the honorary degrees conferred by the college during the 1920s were the Litt.D. degrees on J. Rainey Parker and E. L. Lawson and the D.D. on John T. Acton in 1923. The following year, D.D.'s were voted for W. D. Parry and Thomas F. Opie, and the Litt.D. for A. T. Allen. In 1926 James H. Lightbourne was awarded a D.D. degree; and Blandford B. Dougherty, founding president of the teacher's college at Boone, North Carolina, that is today Appalachian State University, honored with a Litt.D. degree. In 1927 Peter J. Kernodle received a Litt.D., and the next year the D.D. was conferred upon Nils J. Waldorf and LL.D. upon Judge Jesse F. West.[79]

At the 1928 commencement, an unusual event occurred when $100 in gold was presented to Hattie McKinney for being the first girl from the orphanage to graduate from Elon College. The gift was made jointly by Miss Louise Williams, a former matron at the institution and at the college, and Superintendent Charles D. Johnston, of the orphanage. Another unusual event of the period took place at the 1930 commencement when Mrs. R. J. Kernodle (nee Ruth Jones, Elon '06) was elected to the board of trustees, the first of numerous women to be accorded that honor and responsibility.[80]

For years the college alumni had come to feel that they needed "a General Secretary through whom they might function in a helpful way for their Alma Mater." By 1922 more than four hundred people had graduated from the institution and thousands had attended it without graduating. Many of them felt a keen loyalty to the institution and desired a central means of communication to keep them informed of each other and to keep abreast of the needs of the college. In the closing months of that year, the association took action by electing G. C. Donovan (Elon '17) as its first secretary. His duties included acting as host to visiting alumni at Elon; disseminating association news in the *Maroon and Gold* and other newspapers and periodicals; organizing local units or chapters of the alumni; recruiting new students; and soliciting funds for the college. He was also to prepare an Elon exhibit for the forthcoming meeting in Burlington of the American Christian Convention.[81]

Unfortunately, the disruption caused by the fire shortly after this office was created handicapped the new secretary, who resigned after a relatively short period in office. A successor was not elected until 1927, by which time the rebuilding program had almost been completed and conditions were more nearly normal again. George D. Colclough (Elon '26) was chosen for the position. He served until 1931, when he was elected dean and principal of the Country Life Academy, a Congregational project at Star, North Carolina. Both he and his bride, the former Sue Ella Watts (Elon '31) taught in the school for a year, after which both were engaged in educational work elsewhere in eastern Carolina for a year or so. Colclough then returned to Elon, where he was placed in charge of recruiting new students primarily, and also served to some extent as alumni secretary. From this time on, he was associated with the college in one official capacity or another, including many years of service as a trustee, for the remainder of his life.[82]

In 1927, when a union of the Christian and Congregational churches was nearing completion, negotiations were initiated by the Atlanta Theological Seminary, a Congregational institution, to move its operation from the Georgia city to Elon. The proposal was welcomed, for it would enable the college to at last have a complete theological branch. However, the officials were not able to agree upon satisfactory arrangements, and the proposition was abandoned. This did not prevent the denominational merger from succeeding, however, and in 1930 Elon's charter was amended to increase the number of the college trustees to thirty-six, six to be chosen "from the former Congregational constituency."[83]

While the academic program of the college was progressing as never before, the financial condition of the institution was declining because of the national economic depression that had begun in 1929. The amount of gifts dwindled, and many pledges could not be paid. Because of this disappointment in anticipated income, the total indebtedness had reached the sum of $487,971.34, most bearing interest that it was becoming increasingly difficult for the institution to pay. By January 1, 1931, it was almost certain that an operating deficit would exist at the close of the fiscal year in May.[84] Only additional revenue could prevent disaster. The operation of the college, dependent upon income from student tuition and charges for room and board, was entirely separate from the bonded indebtedness. The institution had managed to pay its own way successfully until the economic depression forced many prospective students to abandon plans to attend college. The enrollment shrank from a peak of 400 students to a few more than 300.

The harassed administration again appealed to the Southern Christian Convention for aid by reminding the organization that in 1928 it had voted to give Elon annually $12,750 "to pay the interest on the note of the Convention which the college holds as endowment in the sum of $112,500, and on the bonds which it holds as endowment in the amount of $100,000 out of the Convention apportionment." The first year, the college received only $7,265.56 and the second year $4,317.42 of the $12,750. Because the balance needed to be made up by gifts from individuals, a possibility that seemed remote in the future, the convention was requested to give the full amount. In addition, the 1928 convention had provided for raising $24,000 annually "as interest on the $400,000 of bonds given the college to offset its indebtedness." The delegates were informed this practice must be continued, and, if the Sunday school offerings on which it depended were insufficient, it was essential that the convention make up the deficit.[85]

The delegates were also reminded that in 1928 the convention had endorsed a "Million Dollar Campaign" to raise funds for Elon. If successful, the money was to be used to pay off the college debts and restore its endowment to the institution's use. The convention willingly blessed the continuation of this project, which was little more than an empty gesture because it was doomed to fail during the financial depression.[86] As far as the interest payments on which the college depended, prospects were remote at the time of paying them in full inasmuch as the church was having financial difficulties of its own, and the convention could not disburse funds, no matter how worthy the cause, until the money flowed into its coffers. Both Elon College and the Christian Church, like many other similar institutions, were simply victims of the times, and were forced to make new plans if they were to survive.

By this time, it had become apparent that Elon had greatly over-extended its resources to complete its rebuilding program, and numerous critics placed the blame for the distressing situation on the college president. In his defense, it should be realized that the responsibility for accepting the financial arrangements and complying with their terms rested solely with the institution's trustees. The president was supposed to make plans and recommendations, but they remained only suggestions until adopted by a majority vote of the board. At the time, its membership numbered thirty-six,[87] about equally divided between clergymen and laymen. Some of them possessed little experience in dealing with major financial matters. Others were affluent business and professional men familiar with such transactions. But the members of the board as a whole were people of sound judgment. The same was true of the Southern Christian Convention. The plans of both for Elon were executed as a matter of necessity, based upon current economic conditions at the time. All persons involved, including President Harper, were unaware that their optimistic plans were to be upset in the future by a national economic depression.

If the board could be justly criticized for its actions, it would be more reasonable to object to its spending more than half a million dollars more than first intended on its rebuilding program, and not in attempting to find means with which to pay the debt after it was

College orchestra in 1927.

made. Individual criticisms were made, as was to be expected. One was that the brick wall, for which most of the $52,000 for "entrances, grounds and walls" had been spent, was an unnecessary luxury, and others were expressed in a similar vein. It should be appreciated, however, that the donors of the Duke, Mooney, and Carlton buildings added to their original gifts to cover the final costs of the structures. This was an important factor in encouraging the officials to complete their program, despite the additional cost, instead of leaving it partially completed until more funds had been collected.

None of these extenuating circumstances enabled Dr. Harper to sit more easily in the presidential chair. Apparently not realizing the severity of the depression, then in its early stages, he felt that his denomination and individual supporters had failed him when in all probability all had been done that was possible under the circumstances. His conclusion was that he had reached the limit of his ability to continue as the institution's chief executive, and the time had come for new leadership to guide it through its crisis. When this de-

This photograph, taken in the late 1920s, shows the north gate (1923); the Power House (1906), on the left; and the North Dormitory, or Alumni Building (1912), on the right.

cision was made, in April 1931, he wrote an individual letter to each trustee in which he resigned the presidency of the college at the conclusion of the spring commencement but pledging his continued loyalty to the board and his successor in office.[88]

According to the *Maroon and Gold*, the "announcement came as a distinct surprise to his most intimate friends,"[89] and it created a sensation throughout the Christian Church. Because Harper refused to reconsider his decision, the trustees had no choice but to take action on the matter. When they met in May, a motion was made in two parts: "1. That with deep regret we accept the resignation of Dr. Harper as President of Elon College: 2. That a committee be appointed to draft suitable resolutions expressing our gratitude for faithful service." Of the twenty-six board members present at the meeting, the vote on the first part was fifteen "aye," eight "nay," and three did not vote; on the second part, the vote was unanimous.[90] The outgoing executive then presided over his last Elon College commencement. His address to the audience, made with his usual optimism, was entitled "The Best Is Yet To Be."[91] This proved to be prophetic, but many sore trials lay ahead before that desirable condition was to become a reality.

In the fall of 1932, Harper became professor of religious education in the School of Religion at Vanderbilt University. He later served as visiting professor at Boston University, the Divinity School of the University of Chicago, and Northwestern University. He moved his home from Elon College to Black Mountain, North Carolina, where he died on May 11, 1942, at the age of 62 years. In memory of his contribution to his alma mater during six years as a faculty member and twenty years as its president, his portrait hangs in Whitley Auditorium. In addition, in 1968 the new Harper Center was named for him. It is a lounge, recreation area, and dining hall connecting two dormitories, Moffitt and Staley halls, both also named for former presidents of the college.[92]

The energetic executive was primarily a scholar but he was also a man of vision. Without doubt, he built a greater Elon College from the ashes of the old, but he was trapped by circumstances he could not control that prevented payment in full for the improvements made during his administration. It remained for his successor to extricate the institution from a financial morass and save it from ruin.

CHAPTER IX

THE SURVIVAL OF THE TREE

There grew an ancient Tree upon the green;
A goodly Oak sometime had it been,
With arms full strong and largely displayed,
But of their leaves they were disarrayed.
EDMUND SPENSER
The Shepheardes Calender

Upon accepting the resignation of every previous president of the college, the board of trustees had immediately elected a successor. This was not done when Dr. Harper quit the office, which left the institution without presidential leadership for the first time since it had opened its doors. The obvious reason for this situation was the difficulty of finding a qualified person who would accept the position. The matter was deliberated throughout the summer of 1931 without any successful conclusion being reached.

The previous May, Professor John W. Barney, a faculty member who taught English, had been appointed as chairman of the faculty by the Executive Board of the trustees. Under the circumstances, the situation forced the instructor into service to some extent as acting president, a responsibility he shouldered admirably with the assistance of Dean Hook. The fall term of the college was opened in September, though under highly adverse financial conditions.[1]

The frustrated trustees realized they could delay action no longer, and turned to the church for a solution to their problem. At their request, Dr. L. E. Smith, president of the Southern Christian Convention, sent out an urgent request for full attendance at a special session of the convention to meet in Burlington in October.[2]

Late in 1930, S. C. Heindel had been employed by the college to supervise the proposed "Million Dollar Campaign." When this project was postponed because of the increasing economic depression, he was appointed as business manager to succeed Alton T. West, who had just resigned.[3] The new official prepared a complete financial report for the delegates when they assembled on the 20th in Burlington. The statement frankly explained the status of the institution in understandable detail. In summary, it listed the college's total assets as $2,232,101.08. This was composed of endowment funds in the amount of $545,693.48, the principal and income from which was pledged as collateral for loans; plant funds, which included real estate, buildings, and equipment, totaling $1,187,947.81; and the current fund, which amounted to $498,469.79.

The latter included $997.85 cash in the bank; the Southern Christian Convention bonds of $400,000, which were virtually worthless; and numerous accounts receivable of doubtful value. The liabilities included debts to banks, and included the statement that "a payment of $15,000 to retire an equal amount of the bonds was due in Richmond on September 1, 1931, but it has not been possible yet to pay it." Other items were faculty and staff salaries past due in the amount of $8,000, a total of $29,936 borrowed from the endowment and student loan funds, and $21,000 of accounts payable to 250 creditors. Some of the latter were in the hands of collecting agencies, but "a few of them had been reduced to judgment." The business manager then recapitulated, "We have, therefore, a Total Indebtedness of $487,971.34, of which practically $425,000 is bearing interest. Under present conditions, with practically no income aside from payments made by students, this is increasing at the rate of almost $250.00 per day as a result of unpaid salaries, interest, and other unavoidable expense."

The report also included another depressing statement:

> During the fiscal year of the College, beginning June 1, 1930, and closing May 31, 1931, there was an actual deficit for the 12 months period of $11,159.97; while as a result of the writing off of uncollectable items and the setting up of reserves to provide for others which are expected to be uncollectable assets, were further reduced to the sum of $22,205.49, making a total reduction or loss of $33,365.20 during the year.

The analysis concluded with a statement intended to lessen the severity of the figures it contained, if that were possible:

> *In closing*: This report is presented with the hope and faith
> that on the basis of facts herein presented there may be devel-
> oped plans for saving Elon College from its present difficulties;
> above all, that it may not lead to discouragement over present
> conditions, but rather serve as a challenge to the minds and
> hearts of the entire membership of our churches; the taking of
> a new interest, the formulation of a new program, an inspira-
> tion to new efforts.[4]

Despite this attempt at optimism, it was clear the college was not
only in desperate financial straits, but also actually hovering on the
verge of bankruptcy. Had it been a purely commercial institution, it
might have been pushed over the edge into a receivership, but fore-
closing mortgages on a college and liquidating its assets into cash
was a ponderous undertaking that financial institutions avoided if
any other means could be devised for their accounts to be collected
eventually.

Next on the agenda of the meeting was the report of the Business
Administration Committee, which clarified for the delegates the
impotency of the convention's recent efforts to aid the college. This
committee, which had been appointed in 1930 to raise emergency
funds for Elon, was composed of L. E. Smith, P. J. Carlton, John
Farmer, J. E. Kirby, Stanley C. Harrell, K. B. Johnson, H. A. Carlton,
J. M. Fix, and C. D. Johnston. This was a capable group, but it was
forced to admit that the results of its efforts to aid the trustees raise a
needed $32,000 was only $4,065.75, and "three persons have given
$1,000 each of the amount."

The committee then advanced the opinion that financial aid for
the college required two things: "*First*, we must carry the College to
the hearts of the people individually and collectively; *Second*, we
must have extensions from our creditors sufficient to allow us time
to organize, solicit, and receive funds with which to pay." To enact
these conclusions, five resolutions were recommended and adopted.
The crux of their meaning was that Elon needed a new president immediately, and it was clear that the burden of extricating the institution from its financial morass would rest to a large extent upon his
shoulders.[5]

Selection of the new official was placed in the hands of the trustees, and the convention adjourned after willingly pledging its sup-

port to the new administration in every manner possible. The delegates then dispersed, better informed as to the current financial conditions but without having solved any problems. This left the board in about the same position it had been in when the convention convened.

When Elon College had been founded in 1889, the members of the Christian Church in the South numbered less than 12,000. In 1932 the figure was more than 32,000,[6] but the denomination was still comparatively small and it had never been wealthy on the whole. The merger that created the Congregational and Christian Churches did not change the financial picture because responsibility for Elon College remained vested in the Southern Christian Convention. Raising money rapidly from the denomination during a severe economic depression was impossible, and the conventions and the trustees realized that fact, but reasons were ample to believe that the goal could eventually be won.

The board of trustees, left dependent upon its own resources, speedily came to a decision, and urged Dr. Leon Edgar Smith to accept the presidency of the college. Their choice had been born in Troup County, Georgia, on October 25, 1884, the ninth of the eleven children of John Everett and Martha Webb Smith. He attended grade school in the nearby town of Richland, where one of his teachers, D. R. Fonville (Elon '04), was influential in his decision to attend Elon College, where he could prepare for the ministry of the Christian Church. (Fonville was also a member of the board of trustees that elected Smith president of the institution.) After graduating from Elon in 1910, Smith completed his education at Princeton Theological Seminary in 1915 and earned an M.A. degree from Princeton University. After ministerial ordination, he accepted a call to the pastorate of the First Christian Church, of Huntington, Indiana. In 1919 he was called to the service of the Christian Temple, of Norfolk, Virginia, one of the most prestigious pastorates in the Christian Church and an assignment not to sever casually.

A man of practical business judgment, the minister held no illusions concerning Elon's plight, which offered little inducement to become its chief executive, but as an alumnus and trustee of the institution that had conferred an honorary D.D. degree upon him in 1919, he also felt a deep sense of loyalty and concern for his alma mater. After graduating, the clergyman had married Ella O. Brunk

President Leon E. Smith.

(Elon '07). They were the parents of Rebecca and Leon Edgar, Jr., both teenage pupils in the Norfolk schools. Because acceptance of the offer of the trustees would mean a complete change in many ways for the entire family, the consequences of such a move were necessarily carefully considered.

In Smith's opinion, Elon belonged to the Southern Christian Convention and not to the board of trustees. To assure himself as to the wishes of the entire church membership, the clergyman visited each of the five member conferences of the convention at their next annual meeting, where he learned he was the unanimous choice of all for the college presidency. Inspired by this knowledge, he then requested and received a leave of six months without pay from his Virginia church. He agreed to serve during this time as Elon's temporary president, while seeking a solution for its troubles. At the end of the period, he promised either to accept the position permanently or return to his Norfolk pastorate.[7]

In physique and personality, the new executive was almost the exact opposite of his predecessor. Harper was of medium height, slightly rotund, bland, and jovial, whereas Smith was tall, muscular, of commanding appearance, and possessed a countenance and demeanor almost stern. Harper was primarily a scholar and educator, but his successor was a clergyman and businessman. The qualifications of the latter were those most needed for Elon at the time. The trustees had unquestionably chosen a competent man for the situation, and they concentrated their efforts on persuading him to remain in the office indefinitely.

Once the decision was made, Smith acted immediately. On November 1, 1931, he arrived at Elon, where he was formally presented to the faculty and student body by Professor Barney during a chapel service. Smith then plunged into the multitudinous duties of keeping the current program of the college in operation before attacking the problems of retiring its bonded debt and paying past-due bills. Within a few days after his arrival, Business Manager Heindel, who considered the situation hopeless and was weary of being badgered by creditors with bills he could not pay, advised changing the name of the institution and making a fresh start. When this proposal was emphatically rejected, Heindel resigned and was succeeded by C. M. Cannon, the former registrar. This change placed the financial affairs of the college in the hands of two officials inexperienced in their duties, but this did not constitute a handicap because both adjusted quickly to their new responsibilities.[8]

The president was fortunate in being able to retain Josiah W. Bailey, of Raleigh, as his principal legal adviser. After the lawyer was elected to the United States Senate, Smith usually relied on C. Leroy Shuping, of Greensboro, for legal counsel. None of the executive's major decisions were made without consulting his attorneys and ascertaining the legality of his position in advance of any action.[9]

Smith's first concern was for the faculty members, who had received little pay for almost a year. This was an embarrassing situation for all, and crucial for some. Being a man of sound common sense, the diligent president was not averse to grasping at straws because any amount of money, no matter how small, would be useful and appreciated. He mailed five hundred letters to Alamance County citizens requesting a donation of three dollars from each. He received two replies: one containing three dollars and the other ten dollars. This was not encouraging, but other letters were also dispatched elsewhere. Pastors and alumni began to stress the college's need, and eventually more than $3,000 was netted in this manner. This insured operation through the fall term, at least.

Encouraged by this result, the executive continued to raise small sums in every legitimate manner possible. At the annual December presentation of "Messiah," in Whitley Auditorium, which also served as a meeting place for the College Church, Dr. Smith opened the program with a prayer. When the "Pastoral" symphony was played during the oratorio, he arranged for the ushers to take up a collection. This was a most unusual use of the instrumental number in Handel's composition, but it was continued annually during Smith's administration. The audiences, slightly amused but charmed with the high quality of the performances, usually responded liberally.[10] By means of these numerous small contributions, the president doled out partial payments of salaries to the needy faculty as fast as he obtained the money.

Recognizing that the college was also dependent upon student tuition to maintain its current operation, Dr. Smith next concentrated his efforts on increasing the student body. Enrollment had declined to an alarmingly low figure of 87. This made it imperative to attract new students immediately if they could be found. The first results were not encouraging, for many desiring to attend college lacked the means to do so. In December 1931 the situation looked bleak indeed, when the weary recruiter experienced a stroke of good fortune, for a change. During a chance meeting in Norfolk with an old friend, Dr. William M. Brown, president of the three-year-old Atlantic University, at Virginia Beach, Virginia, Smith learned that the institution had gone into receivership and would not reopen the following January. Representatives of other colleges had arranged a meeting with the student body at the Southland Hotel in an attempt to encourage as many as possible to transfer to their respective schools. Encouraged by Brown, the president attended the meeting, where he made one of the strongest sales talks he had ever delivered. He was rewarded with 37 new students for Elon, a real bonanza because it insured the completion of the 1932 spring term. Others also matriculated later, which brought the total of the student body to 257 before commencement. The college enrollment has never been so low since.[11]

After appraising the situation, Smith was convinced he could deal most effectively with the emergency if he possessed the power to act without being delayed by red tape or customary formalities. His counselor, Senator Bailey, agreed, and requested the trustees to grant this authority, at least for a temporary period. The Executive Board of the board of trustees gave its permission on December 9, 1931, in a formal statement:

> Whereas Elon College is involved in financial difficulties to a very serious degree; and whereas numerous matters are likely to arise requiring instant decision and action;
>
> Now, therefore, be it resolved that the Board of Trustees authorize and empower L. E. Smith, Acting President, to take all steps necessary in his judgment and discretion in the matter of the management of the College, dealing with the creditors, raising funds and making such arrangements as in his discretion may be necessary to the saving of the Institution, he being required only to report to this Board all his actions and transactions in writing on or before the 15th day of January, 1932.[12]

This official sanction for using his own judgment encouraged the executive to continue his plans of action for financial recovery.

By rigorous economy and wise distribution of the small income, the operation of the college continued while the president attacked another major problem. In September 1931 the Elon Bank and Trust Company had been closed by the state banking commissioner. By mutual agreement of the stockholders, the organization was liquidated, but the depositors suffered no loss. The nearest banking facilities were then in Burlington, where lawyers awaited the opportunity to attach college funds to satisfy judgments that had been rendered against the institution. Irritated but undefeated by this handicap, the resourceful president then opened an account for the college in its old Suffolk standby, the Farmers' Bank of Nansemond. Smith was then warned by his legal advisers that this account could also be attached by creditors, a possibility he circumvented by depositing the college funds in a Burlington bank in the name of Leon Edgar Smith, an account that had no claims against it. This bold move was made not to defraud creditors of their just claims, but to preserve funds for current operations until additional money could be raised to pay on the college debts. It was another one of Elon's misfortunes that the bank containing the new Smith account was closed by the comptroller-general of the United States in December 1931 because of its insolvency.[13]

Had Elon College been the only educational institution in the United States facing financial trouble at the time, it might have been far more difficult, if not impossible, to keep the faculty positions filled. However, because numerous schools were closing their doors or keeping them open only with difficulty, many professors reasoned that employment without a guarantee of full pay promptly was more attractive than no employment at all, and the staff remained at full strength throughout the crucial period. Even so, this was not easily accomplished. As often as possible, fractional parts of salaries were doled out on a percentage basis to each individual, which was all the administration could do. Even under these circumstances, the changes in personnel hardly exceeded the rate that had been normal for several years. Some of the faculty departed voluntarily, others by request, but they were all soon replaced. Usually those who departed requested that their salaries be paid in full before they left the college, but Smith only promised to continue making partial payments as fast as he was able to do so. He stubbornly refused to make a full settlement with anyone when it meant postponing needed payments to the others, a policy from which he never swerved.

Unpleasant repercussions from this situation numbered only two, and they were caused by disgruntled individuals who had been dismissed. One, who had served on the faculty only a few months, refused to turn in the grades of his students at the end of the 1931 fall term until his salary was paid in full. Upon being dismissed, he surrendered his grades and was reinstated for the following spring term. He then found other employment, and sued the trustees for his back pay, apparently even being willing to place the institution in receivership, which he was unable to do. The matter was finally compromised and the suit dropped, but it was a troublesome event.[14]

The other individual claimed he had been promised a lifetime position when he was hired in 1923 and could not be legally dismissed. The administration was not convinced by this unsubstantiated claim. Neither was it influenced by the charge made by the former instructor that faculty members were forced to return a part of their salaries to the college as a rebate, an unethical practice had it been true. Contributions from the staff had long been invited and welcomed, and a few of the personnel made them, but of their own free will. One individual who was a member of the faculty at the time has testified to this and confirmed that rebates were not demanded. However, the discharged instructor reported his grievances to both the Southern Association and the American Association of University Professors, which brought embarrassing inquiries to the administration from these organizations. Failing to achieve any satisfaction from this activity, the individual's temper cooled and he left peaceably, but he requested that the college assist him in finding another job.[15]

Both these men were hired before Dr. Smith became a part of the Elon administration. He had no means of knowing what either thought were the terms of their employment when it began, but he did know that their performance at the college had been unsatisfactory, for which reason they should be released. The president did not change his mind despite the arguments presented, and settled with both financially when he was able to do so. Most of the capable scholars on the staff who left the institution did so because they were either offered higher salaries or a wider range for their activities elsewhere. Their departure was without rancor, and some of them complimented the college program as they left for other positions.[16]

Early in December 1931 Dr. Smith attended the annual meeting of the Southern Association, in Montgomery, Alabama, accompanied by Dr. Amick, the official representative of the college to the organization. During the meeting, both were stunned by the announcement that on September 23, 1932, Elon College would be dropped from membership in the organization. One of the primary reasons for the action was that the college had been warned the previous year that its precarious financial condition must improve, whereas it had grown worse. Another factor was objection to the college system of collecting gifts from its faculty. For example, a salary would be listed at $3,000, but the employee would be notified that he would be paid only $2,700. This was a legal plan, which would probably have met with no objection from the Southern's officials had they been informed of it. However, when the matter was investigated after complaints were made, several faculty members testified they understood that the plan had been approved by the association's Commission on Institutions of Higher Learning, which actually knew nothing about the arrangement. This was reason to suspect that the payroll had been escalated only on paper to make it appear better on the annual reports. Another criticism was that the degrees listed beside two or three professors' names in the college catalogs were not identical with those they actually held; and, in one case, the source of a degree was not an approved institution. All these factors made a poor impression on the organization, which acted accordingly.[17]

Smith was unaware of any of these circumstances because they all had arisen before he became acting president of the college, nor did the association hold him responsible for the situation. In fact, he made such a good impression at the meeting that Elon was placed on the list of nonmembers, which gave it a higher status than one permanently dropped and afforded an opportunity to raise its standards sufficiently to apply for readmission to the organization. On the 7th, the president endured the unpleasant duty of reporting this academic debacle to his hardworking faculty, but accompanied it with the admonition that they must all strive together to regain their lost accreditation as rapidly as possible.[18] On this gloomy note, disastrous 1931 ended, but everyone connected with Elon College hoped for a happier new year.

In January 1932 Smith took the first step in his refinancing plan. He arranged a meeting in the Greensboro office of attorney E. S. Parker, Jr., with representatives of the institutions to which Elon

College owed large sums of money. At the conference, the president requested a debt moratorium of two years be granted, during which time requests for payments would be suspended. If granted, he promised to remain in office to devise a means of settling the accounts. Otherwise, he would return to his Virginia pastorate and leave the task for someone else to handle. After some deliberation, the financiers decided that because the president, rather than the trustees, had been given the sole financial responsibility, they would consider the matter favorably. The moratorium was granted by all but the North Carolina Bank and Trust Company, which had already instituted suit for its claim, and the Farmers' Bank of Nansemond, neither of which were demanding interest on their loans at the time. This agreement temporarily suspended pressure from the banks and gave the president time to work on future plans while also meeting the daily problems of his office.[19]

Also in January 1932 registration began for the spring term, at which time students paid their tuition and other fees by cash or with checks. The money thus collected represented the only known means of operating the college until commencement. As registration began, the president was alarmed by an anonymous message that creditors were planning to attach the funds when they were collected. Whether or not this warning was based upon fact or not is unknown, but Dr. Smith took no chances after receiving it. As rapidly as a payment was made, it was sent to the residence of the college treasurer for safekeeping until it could be deposited in the bank. In this manner, the incoming funds were protected until the registration period ended, which virtually assured completion of the term.[20]

Within a few weeks, an even more troublesome event transpired. The college endowment fund included $30,000 in bonds as security for a loan made to a commercial corporation. These had not been pledged as collateral for any loan, and constituted one of Elon's few liquid assets. To protect them, Smith turned the securities over to his secretary and gave instructions to place them in one of several suggested depositories, but not to inform him where they were until he requested the information. Fortunately, this move was made just before a deputy sheriff arrived to attach the bonds. The president informed him that he did not have them nor did he know where they were, but allowed his office and the adjacent vault to be searched in a futile effort to locate them. The sheriff then informed the official that, if the bonds were not surrendered, he was authorized to arrest the trustees and would have to take Smith into custody as one of them. The president then reminded the officer that his warrant was for "the trustees," and inquired what he proposed to do about "the other members." The crestfallen deputy, baffled by that question, returned to the county seat empty-handed, while the harassed president continued his efforts to place Elon on its feet again.[21]

When the board of trustees assembled on February 23 for its midyear meeting, the president informed the members of the Southern Association's actions, which were by then no longer news. Without bewailing what could not be prevented, Smith launched into a discussion of his intentions to regain accreditation by announcing, "Our next catalogue will carry the names of the professors, together with the degrees and the names of the institutions conferring these degrees, so that there need be no question or suspicion about them."[22]

Smith then proposed plans to aid the college to improve its stability and regain its membership. The trustees approved his recommendation to attempt the reconditioning of East Dormitory and the Alumni Building, but decided a committee should determine the needs of West Dormitory.[23] The remainder of the plans were summarized in a report later made to the Southern Christian Convention:

> . . . the Board of Trustees . . . authorized an appeal for all who could to set aside an acre of land to be known as the "College Acre," the individual farmer agreeing to plant, cultivate and harvest, and turn over to the college the gross proceeds of this one acre—also to request all Christian Churches and Sunday School in North Carolina and Virginia who would, to undertake to feed the college one day, thereby releasing money paid for board by students for other college expenses. The Board further authorized the observance of "Elon College Day" on May 24th at which time, efforts were made to undertake the budget for 1932–1933, thus removing all questions of financial support for the college this year.[24]

These relatively simple requests were made without the expectation of large sums in return, but with the hope they would produce at least a part of the assistance needed to keep the college doors open. This confidence proved to be justified.

Before the annual meeting of the convention, M. L. Patrick, a high school principal in High Point, had organized an Elon-Dollar-a-Month Club among the alumni. The recommendation of the Elon Emergency Fund Committee was then adopted by the delegates "to carry this movement to our churches, endeavoring to sign 5,000 subscribers to the plan."[25] This proposal was popular because it was within the reach of most people's resources, for which reason it rapidly gained momentum. Dr. and Mrs. Harper sent $25 for their membership, and others followed their example. The small contributions soon amounted to a sum that constituted a boon to the struggling college. These were shrewdly practical means of raising the money necessary to continue operating because other contributions had dwindled to a mere dribble on account of the depression. The Francis Asbury Palmer Fund gave the institution only $250 in 1932, an all-time low figure for that organization except for years when it made no gift at all. This did not reflect a change in the fund's policy, but a diminished income from its investments. Elon still had friends, but it was the alumni who devised the most useful means of aiding their alma mater at the time.[26]

To utilize the meager income to its fullest advantage, the strictest economy continued to be practiced. Instead of weekly, the *Maroon and Gold* was issued only every two weeks, and publication of the *Phipsicli* was canceled for the year, the only time this occurred from World War I to the present. Because many of the staff needed to rent academic robes for commencement, the faculty voted not to wear them that year. Other means were found to save money, and the students continued with their courses cheerfully under the reduced circumstances.[27]

Dr. Smith corresponded with his predecessor to discuss various aspects of college affairs. Harper was most cooperative but handicapped because, shortly after his arrival at Vanderbilt, he had lost all his papers, records, manuscripts, and books in a fire at the Divinity School. However, relying upon his memory, he compiled lists of prospective donors and supplied details of various transactions in an effort to aid his successor. The former president remained an Elon trustee until 1936, though his schedule elsewhere prevented his attending any of the board's meetings after he left the college. On one return visit, he called at the president's office, but failed to see Smith, who was away at the time. By these and other means, Dr. Harper demonstrated his loyalty to the college as long as he lived.[28]

One problem in particular on which clarification from Harper was requested concerned the status of Whitley Auditorium. Smith was shocked to discover that the initial gift to construct the building had been made in a long-range conditional manner. In 1923 Colonel Darden advanced $50,000 for the purpose as a loan, in return for which the college agreed to pay the annual premiums on a $50,000 life-insurance policy of which the colonel was the beneficiary. Upon his death, the insurance would be paid to his estate, and the loan to the college would be canceled. To guarantee performance in the transaction, $45,000 worth of bonds on the Christian Temple, in Norfolk, were taken from Elon's endowment fund and placed in escrow in a Suffolk bank. The annual insurance premiums were $2,819.80, which was practically the same as 6 percent interest on the principal borrowed. Because Darden was then in his sixties, the arrangement did not seem unreasonable to a college desperately in need of funds for rebuilding.

The money thus obtained was applied on the construction of Whitley Auditorium, and, though the $50,000 was insufficient to pay all the costs, the completed structure was publicized as an outright gift from Darden. All went well with the arrangement, however, until 1932, when Smith was surprised by the discovery of this unsuspected liability. He could find no means to pay the life-insurance premium that year, and Darden protested he was unable to make the payment himself. The president was helpless to do more, and the matter was finally settled by the colonel obtaining approximately $14,000 as the cash surrender value of the insurance policy and the remainder of the $50,000 loan from the Christian Temple bonds. This reduced the college endowment fund more than $30,000, a severe blow to sustain under the circumstances.

Another result of the unhappy transaction was that a prominent building on the Elon campus had been paid for from the general funds of the college and not by the individual acknowledged as the donor. In an effort to remedy this embarrassing situation, after Darden died in 1937 President Smith attempted to persuade his family to contribute $30,000 to make the gift realistic to some extent, but this proposal was politely but firmly declined. The entire matter was then shelved as a part of the institution's losses, and the status of the building remained unchanged.[29]

To make plans for academic expansion under the circumstances prevailing in 1932 seems incredible, but Elon College did so. In February the faculty approved holding a summer school, primarily for public school teachers seeking to renew their certificates. The instructors involved were to be paid with a percentage of the tuition collected, which separated the project from any other financial arrangements of the college. In April the state Board of Education approved the proposal, and plans were completed for courses to begin in June. Of various programs conducted during the summer months at Elon ever since its doors opened, this was the first program that granted academic credit. The 57 students who enrolled spelled success for the undertaking, which has been conducted annually from that time to the present.[30]

Among the telegrams received at Elon after the fire in January 1923 was one from L. E. Smith, which stated, "Ofttimes misfortunes are turned into blessings."[31] If he remembered these words of comfort nearly a decade later, the provisional president probably wondered if they applied to the troubles he encountered at the college. No possibility of such a metamorphosis was apparent then, or in the near future. His term of six months was nearing its end, which required him to make a decision regarding future plans. The temporary executive had discovered the college finances to be in a far worse tangle than anticipated, and he had been kept too busy with the hand-to-mouth existence of the institution to give much attention to its major obligations. Instead of improving, the national economic conditions had become increasingly worse, which made the future appear darker than ever. Because of transactions made by others, Smith had been unjustly made the target of recriminations and personal indignity that were difficult to bear. In addition, if he remained in the office, he would have to change his lifework and leave the ministry, for which he had been prepared. A less enticing position than the college presidency under these circumstances would have been difficult to imagine.

On the other side of the picture, Smith possessed three assets: the confidence of a student body that implored him through its press to remain at the helm; a faculty whose core was composed of competent educators, loyal to the college; and a firm conviction that divine providence would bless the school's effort to regain its solvent status. The minister was a fighter, and the almost overwhelming odds that would have dissuaded most men from accepting the presidential chair were a challenge that he neither would nor could ignore. Turning his back on a more comfortable situation, Smith announced his decision at the May 1932 meeting of the trustees, and became the fifth president of Elon College.[32]

Because of the growth of the community, a large percentage of the College Church membership were townspeople, for which reason in 1923 the name of the organization was changed to the Community Church. In the same year, a home was built for its minister at the corner of Haggard and Williamson avenues, and plans made to erect a church building when the congregation was financially able to do so. When Dr. Alfred W. Hurst resigned the pastorate in 1932, President Smith accepted the position on the condition that he preach no more than once each month but would be responsible for supplying the pulpit with guest ministers at other times. He was primarily responsible for liquidation of the mortgage on the parsonage, and elected to reside in it rather than in the former Harper house, which he had purchased. The entire Smith family then moved to Elon, which was convenient in the sense that the two children were ready to enter college.[33]

After these affairs were settled, Smith and several of the faculty spent the summer months soliciting new students. The work was laborious and often discouraging, but yielded 244 students for the 1932 fall term. By commencement the following spring, the number had increased to a total of 301 students for the college year.[34] The respite gained by the debt moratorium and the money trickling in, which was sufficient to provide a day-to-day existence, allowed the college to continue its operation until the close of the most crucial year in its financial history. Confident that such provisions for the program would continue, the president then began plans to attract even more students to the institution.

Smith was more personally enthusiastic over sports than any of his predecessors in the presidential office had been. An athlete himself, he liked the games and reasoned "that if you were going to play, you might as well play to win."[35] He was also conscious of the public interest in college athletics, particularly football. Elon's teams were performing creditably in baseball and basketball, but, on the grid-iron, only two games were won in 1932 and seven were lost.[36] The president was ambitious to improve this situation, both as a matter of pride, and also to offset the unfavorable publicity caused by the loss of the college's accreditation. He was also of the opinion that a good coach understood the sport, but a successful coach won games, and he was confident that D. C. Walker was already the first and could be the second.

In a conference, the coach informed the executive that the future success of football at the college depended upon obtaining better players, and these would not be attracted to the institution unless they received financial remuneration. Smith authorized Walker to obtain the essential players with the understanding that those who made the team would be charged only a token fee to attend the in-stitution. This arrangement began in 1933, and gridiron victories

1933 championship baseball team. From left to right, front row: Howard ("Smitty") Smith, Rufus ("Abby") Abernathy, Odell ("Bud") Clayton, George Chandler, Webb Newsome, and Paul Cheek. Rear rows (unspecified as to location): Lawrence Tucker, Rick Freeze, Norman Clark, Karl Milligan, Walter ("Firpo") Latham, Isaac ("Ike") Lindley, Coach "Peahead" Walker, Paul Brawley, and Norman ("Muddy") Waters.

speedily increased. The athletic progress gave the college the favorable publicity the president sought and justified his fostering of sports.[37]

There may have been means to reimburse the players, but funds for athletic operations were scarce. One football game was played in the mud at a time when no money was available for the laundering of the players' jerseys before the next game. Walker offered William H. Maness (Elon '38), the team's manager, five dollars to clean them, a price too tempting to resist in the 1930s. He resourcefully placed the forty garments in the North Dormitory showers, liberally applied soap suds, turned on the water, and ran to and fro across the uniforms. This took a considerable part of one night. The results were acceptable, and Maness received his pay, which he claimed was the hardest five dollars he ever earned.[38]

At the close of the 1936 season, Walker resigned as athletic director and joined the Wake Forest coaching staff. During his decade of service at Elon, he had made an outstanding record in all major sports (football, basketball, and baseball), including the winning of fifteen championships.[39] The honors won by various players at the time, far too numerous to list, brought increasing distinction to Elon's athletic program.[40] But it was the cooperative effort of the teams as a whole that won the contests which brought honor to their alma mater, which was, after all, the ultimate purpose of college sports.

Elon's next athletic director, engaged to coach all three major sports, was Horace Hendrickson, popularly known as "Horse." Fresh from an excellent record at Duke University, he enjoyed the good fortune to inherit well-trained squads from his predecessor, and a number of the best performers were eligible to play for another one or two years. From this advantageous beginning, athletic progress continued under the new coach. Many high honors were won, and "Horse" may have led the Fighting Christians to more honors had his career not been interrupted by World War II. When the trustees suspended intercollegiate football and baseball in 1942 for the duration of the conflict, he had little to do, and he accepted a coaching position at the University of Pennsylvania.[41] The coach was not only successful in training winning teams, but a number of his men won honors for their individual performances while he was at Elon.[42]

The most unusual of these stellar athletes was probably Joe Golombek, a 200-pound giant of incredible strength. He was once photographed pulling a heavy steamroller by means of a rope across his shoulders. He never wore a dress shirt because his collar size was 22 inches, and he could not find a ready-made garment that large. By contrast, the modern Hercules was an accomplished violinist and passionately fond of classical music. Unusually temperamental, he sometimes played his violin in the middle of the night, to the discomfiture of his roommate and neighbors in the North Dormitory. However, none of them attempted to stop his nocturnal renditions.

Hendrickson realized the giant athlete was a prima donna, and, because of his value to the team, went to extreme measures to cater to him. On one occasion, a game was scheduled in eastern Virginia, near the fullback's home. Joe decided it afforded a good opportunity to visit his relatives, so he departed ahead of the squad without permission, but left a message with Maness for the coach to bring his uniform and meet him at the game. "Horse" did so, but was so infuriated by this breach of discipline that he kept his player on the bench the entire first half. He might not have relented in the second half, but he needed the performance of the huge back.[43]

The coach finally reached his limit and suspended the temperamental player from the team for breach of discipline. Joe then entered the military service, but, at the close of World War II, returned to Elon for graduation, eleven years after he had matriculated as a freshman. He then reentered the army and was apparently content with the life of a soldier, while maintaining contact with his alma mater by correspondence. In 1954 Golombek's name appeared in the national newspapers because a body found buried in a crude grave on Long Island, New York, was identified as his by an Elon College class ring. Robbery was the suspected motive, but the facts of the tragedy remain the premier unsolved mystery connected with the college. When those who knew the man learned of his murder, their general sentiment was voiced by J. Earl Danieley, who commented, "Whoever killed Joe must have attacked him from behind, or he would never have been successful."[44]

After serving four years as football manager, Maness became as familiar to the fans as any player on the team. During that long period, he had faithfully performed his multitudinous duties, which even included taping the ankles of all the players before each game. His many friends thought that his service should be rewarded by being allowed to participate one time in an actual game. As a result, in 1932, his senior year, during the annual contest with Guilford, a steady chant began in the stands, "We want Maness!" The coach obligingly responded and, because Elon was safely in the lead, sent him in to play the last three minutes. The players cooperated by passing him the ball, never dreaming that, in the excitement of his long-awaited opportunity, he would carry it in the wrong direction, which he did. Speedy action from a teammate prevented the runner from placing the pigskin behind the wrong goalpost, the game was won, and Maness had actually played on the Elon College football team.[45]

During the progressive growth of the major sports, the popularity of tennis declined. One of the principal reasons was the lack of a proper coach to enhance the expertise of the players. This condition changed in 1930 when Professor Ross Emsinger, of the Religion Department, became the first nonstudent coach, and "tennis regained its rightful place as a minor sport in the athletic roster of the college." The following year, he departed and Hinton Rountree served as both captain and coach. Progress continued until 1942, when Professor Robert L. Westhafer, of the Mathematics Department, became the second official coach. During this period, a number of proficient players flowered, and tennis regained its position as a strong minor sport at the college.[46]

While enjoying the favorable publicity gained by winning athletic contests, Dr. Smith devised another less spectacular, but nevertheless effective, means of advertising the college. Professor Dwight Steere, director of the Music Department, organized his best vocalists into a group known as the Elon Singers. Miss Helen Chamblee, of the music faculty, served as the primary vocalist with the ensemble. Beginning in 1933, the musicians toured North Carolina and Virginia and presented their program to civic and social clubs, churches, and schools. These performances helped to raise the prestige of the institution. The annual presentation of Handel's "Messiah" was continued. In 1933 C. Fletcher Moore, then an undergraduate, played the organ for the performance, a contribution he would make for many years afterward.[47]

Advantage was taken of another opportunity for favorable publicity in 1936 when Elon "went on the air." Major Edney Ridge, of station WBIG, in Greensboro, arranged to broadcast the "Messiah" that year and offered the college time for regular Sunday afternoon broadcasts. The experience gained in these initial programs was sufficient training for a more ambitious effort. When Burlington's WBBB opened in 1941, Dr. Smith broadcast an address that introduced an Elon College series over that station each week. These presentations, which consisted of musical numbers, brief lectures, and panel discussions, became an enjoyable part of the cultural life of the area for many people, for they were popular with both the public and the performers.[48]

Academically, college affairs progressed satisfactorily throughout 1933 as far as the student body was concerned. Outwardly, the institution appeared to be operating normally, but inwardly the financial struggle for existence continued unabated. In September Smith frankly explained the conditions to W. C. Wicker, at that time president of the Eastern Carolina Conference of the church:

> We have paid one month's salaries [to present employees] and one month's salaries to the eight professors who did not

Southern Railway freight train approaching the Elon College station during the 1930s.

return to the College. We have also paid bills that accumulated during the summer. This has exhausted the money received from the students at the opening of school. I shall endeavor to raise money on the outside to pay October salaries—then I am hoping that the money from the Conferences will pay November salaries. We must balance our budget this year if we are to continue. . . . our enrollment to date is a little better than 250, which is about as it was last year and is encouraging.[49]

The necessary funds came in time, for each church conference strove to meet its quota for the college. By this means, and by his own solicitation of donations, the president met running expenses and settled a $6,000 debt with the First National Bank, of Burlington, for $600. He then continued with his plans to liquidate others.

The optimism of the executive was not shared by all concerned. After the college struggled through the opening of the 1934 spring term, some individuals expressed doubt that operations could continue after the May commencement. Smith discovered evidence of this pessimistic forecast with a rude shock. Through the newspapers, he learned that on March 23 a charter had been issued by the State of North Carolina to establish North State College. No capital stock was subscribed for the school, but its purpose was outlined:

> a. To furnish young men and young women in the environs of the college wherever located, the benefits of education beyond the elementary school level; to grant them such credentials or degrees as shall be approved by the North Carolina State Department of Education.
>
> b. To permit young men and young women to continue their scholastic education while being gainfully employed elsewhere.
>
> c. To introduce as soon and as rapidly as feasible, courses in commerce, trade and industry.[50]

The shocking part of the charter was that the principal office of the new venture was given as Elon College, North Carolina, and the incorporators were listed as Mr. and Mrs. J. Allen Hunter and Frank Johnson. Professor Hunter had been a prominent member of the college faculty since 1929, and Johnson (Elon '31) had served as a physical training instructor and proctor of the Alumni Building.

Dr. Smith was convinced that this action was part of a plot to take over Elon under a new name when the predicted bankruptcy was announced. Although this intention was denied, the irate executive considered the entire affair one of disloyalty to the institution. As a result, the trustees severed Hunter's connection with the college, though he remained a resident of the town the remainder of his life, and his wife taught a course at the institution in 1962. The conclusion of this unpleasant incident was that the charter was suspended on January 26, 1945, Elon lost one of its outstanding professors, and Smith was left more determined than ever to keep the doors of his institution open.[51]

When membership in the Southern Association was dropped, the trustees of the college appointed a Committee on Reorganization from among its members to cooperate with the president in his diligent efforts to upgrade the academic qualifications of the faculty. In 1932 the degrees held included four doctorates earned at approved institutions; ten M.A.'s; five Bachelors, two from Elon College; and one teaching certificate. In 1935, when the faculty numbered twenty-two members, there were seven doctorates; seven M.A.'s; five Bachelors, two from Elon; and one teaching certificate. This represented some progress. The effort to attract instructors with high professional degrees continued, both to improve the course offerings of the college and to regain its lost accreditation.[52]

This was not an easy task and it was handicapped by the frequency of faculty changes, two in particular. Professor Thomas Edward Powell, Jr. (Elon '19), had joined the faculty immediately after his graduation and taught biology and geology. He was made a full professor in 1923 after obtaining his M.A. degree from the University of North Carolina. This was later supplemented by a Ph.D., in biology, from Duke University. Impressed with the difficulty of obtaining specimens for science laboratory work, in 1927 he founded the Carolina Biological Supply Company, on a part-time basis. From a very small beginning, the enterprise grew to such an extent that in 1936 Powell resigned his faculty position to devote his full time to the business. History Professor Leo D. Martin, who was associated with the company, also left the college for the same reason. This change deprived Elon of two of its top professors, but both the institution and the town shared indirectly in the growth of the firm, which was to reach national significance in its field. Today the company has units throughout the United States, but its administrative office remains at the original site of the project.[53]

After the economic adjustments were made in 1932, campus activities proceeded normally because the student body was not involved in the institution's financial problems. That year, the annual May Day celebration originated. A king and queen were elected by the student body to preside over a brilliantly costumed court gathered around the traditional Maypole as a part of the outdoor festival. The colorful spectacle attracted wide local attention, both in and outside the college community.

A concession was also won to allow Saturday night parties at the college, attended by both men and women. The students then began to insist on permission to dance. They renewed their request for Halloween in 1934, but failed to prevail. As a result, the next morning the campus presented a strange sight. Many of the trees were festooned with streamers of toilet tissue, two Model T Ford auto-

Business section of the town of Elon College on North Williamson Avenue in the 1930s. A corner of the railroad passenger depot is on the left.

mobiles had somehow been placed on the porch of West Dormitory, and some purloined outhouses set up in front of the building.[54] The reason for this demonstration was clear, but the decision was not changed. The following year, when permission was again denied, the president informed the trustees, "There was an apparent threat of a student uprising just before Christmas." To resolve the troublesome matter, the faculty voted 17 to 5 in favor of allowing the students to dance. A poll was also taken among them that revealed widespread interest in this activity.[55] Smith carried this information to the trustees on February 19, 1936. After some deliberation, they voted to leave the matter in the hands of the president and the dean. Dancing was then permitted at parties, when the music was supplied by the college orchestra rather than an imported band. However, the long-protested ban was lifted permanently, though Dr. Smith insisted the social occasions be referred to as parties and not dances. The trustees did not unbend in every instance, however, for when national prohibition ended in 1933 the college charter was amended "making it unlawful to make or sell beer of any percent within the radius of a mile and a half of Elon College."[56]

An additional diversion for the students was made possible in 1937 by the acquisition of a motion-picture projector, which the versatile Dr. Hook installed in the space designed for it in Whitley Auditorium. Movies were shown on Friday and Saturday nights. A small admission fee was charged to defray the cost of renting the films and paying for the machine. Another innovation the same year was a printing press that could print the *Maroon and Gold* on the campus, and which was soon the basis for the addition of a course in journalism to the curriculum.[57]

Another concession to the students made the following year was a departure from the original college regulations. The faculty ruled that all students, regardless of creed or nationality, were required to attend chapel on Wednesdays and Fridays, but non-Protestants were excused from the Sunday morning church services.[58] This change was made because the college was attracting students from numerous religious faiths, in addition to the large number from the Congregational-Christian Churches.

As was always the case, the students were full of pranks, but none sufficiently serious to be termed hazing. Initiates into male clubs were often instructed to count the railroad ties between Elon College and the Burlington or Gibsonville railway stations, or count the bricks in the college wall. At the beginning of the 1938 fall term, by vote of the student body, freshmen were directed to wear freshman caps, but the faculty refused to allow this to become mandatory.[59] On one occasion, a duck dressed in a woman's underpants was thrown into the library through a window to the annoyance of Miss Margaret Earp, who experienced much difficulty in expelling the visitor. At another time, a cow was led into a classroom during the night. The following morning, the farmer who owned the animal located it, and remarked as he led it out of the Alamance Building, "It was the only living thing that went through Elon College without any bull."[60]

The windowsills of the classrooms on the first floor of Alamance were only a few feet above the ground. It was Dr. Wicker's custom to call the roll and then turn to write numerous problems on the blackboard. This opportunity was sometimes used by unprepared students to slide out of a window undetected. On one morning, the man who chose to make this unorthodox exit caught his foot in the cord of the window shade and was in this plight when the professor turned around. Explaining he was only attempting to regulate the shade, the culprit was solicitously released from his entanglement and escorted back to his seat, where he remained somewhat crestfallen until the class period ended.[61]

All was not mischief, however. In 1929 the North Carolina Alpha Chapter of Pi Gamma Mu, the national social science honor society, was organized at Elon by Professor Ralph B. Tower. This was the first unit of a national honor society on the campus. The thirty-three charter members were all elected from the students and the faculty on strictly a merit basis, and the chapter added distinction to the academic program of the college. The second honor society was a chapter of Delta Psi Omega, for students who excelled in dramatic production. It was organized in 1933 at the time the facilities of Whitley Auditorium were being used for an increasing number of stage productions of high caliber. One of the outstanding student stars was Kenneth Utt (class of 1942), who later was to rise in prominence on the American stage and in television.[62]

Aided by the advantage of the college owning its own printing press, a new venture in publications originated in May 1937, when the first issue of the *Elon Colonnades*, the institution's first entirely literary periodical for student writers, was published. Issued quarterly, the journal was eight by twelve inches in size, contained 27 pages, and featured a cover in color designed by L. E. Smith, Jr. Ten undergraduates composed the editorial staff under the supervision of Professor Fletcher Collins, Jr., a Yale graduate who was chairman of the English Department. The first issue contained thirty-five contributions from students.[63] Since that time, this vehicle for student expression has been published at intervals until the present as a fixture in the academic program of the college.

The advantage of the press also enabled Alumni Secretary Colclough to originate the *Elon Alumni News* in October 1937. It carried items about the college far beyond the scope of its newspaper. Although first issued as a leaflet of one page, the publication was soon expanded to a minimum of four pages, with occasional supplements, and included interesting photographic material. Its contents were not only informative to the alumni, but also served as a valuable means of stimulating the financial drives of the college among its graduates. The *News* was the forerunner of several subsequent publications under various names published by the Alumni Association.

Conferring honorary degrees, a neglected privilege for several years, was revived in 1933 when the D.D. was conferred upon Harry K. Eversull, Stanley C. Harrell, and John L. Lobinger. The following year, John G. Truitt (Elon '17), a prominent minister in the Christian Church, was awarded the D.D. degree and Havilah Babcock (Elon '18) the Litt.D. The latter taught English at the college in the early 1920s, prior to accepting a position at the University of South Carolina, where he rapidly became an author of note. He was an interesting individual who possessed a strong sense of humor. While at Elon, he became the parent of a son, and temporarily named the infant "Huckleberry Finn," to serve until he was old enough to select his own name. This eventually took place, and the boy became Havilah Babcock, Jr. In 1935 the LL.D. was conferred upon the veteran trustee Edward E. Holland, and the D.D. upon Russell J. Clinchy, a trustee from Washington, D.C.[64]

At the 1936 commencement, Richard H. Clapp received the D.D. degree; and, the following year, the same honor was conferred upon Howard S. Hardcastle and the LL.D. upon Roger Babson, the nationally known financial commentator. In 1938 the D.D.degree was awarded to three ministers of the church: John Stapleton, of Philadelphia; Walter L. McLeod, of Jennings, Louisiana; and Victor B. Chicoine, of Winter Park, Florida. The following year, Litt.D. degrees were awarded to Josiah W. Bailey and Jonathan W. Daniels, a D.Sc. degree to Thomas A. Morgan, and D.D. degrees to Robert W. Coe and Roger R. Treat. In 1940 LL.D. degrees were bestowed upon Colgate W. Darden, Jr., who had served the commonwealth of Virginia as governor, and upon Cameron Morrison, who had filled a similar office in North Carolina. H. Shelton Smith and Ruth I. Seabury were honored with the Litt.D. The latter, a native of Maine who had served as educational secretary of the American Board of Commissioners for Foreign Missions in addition to writing several books and traveling extensively in the interest of world peace, was the first woman to receive an honorary degree from Elon College.

The following year, Judge William M. Maltbie, chief justice of the State of Connecticut, was awarded the LL.D. In 1942 J. Melville Broughton, a North Carolina governor, was honored with the LL.D.; John R. Scotford the D.D.; Walter C. Rawls, of St. Louis, the degree of Doctor of Business Science; Robert H. Hinckley the LL.D.; and Miss Margaret Slattery, author and lecturer from Massachusetts, the Litt.D. This was the second time Elon had conferred such an honor upon a woman. The trustees also voted to award the degree of Doctor of Laws and Literature to William E. Sweet, former moderator of the General Council of the Congregational and Christian Churches, but he died before it could be conferred upon him at commencement that year.[65]

By the beginning of 1936, Dr. Smith had acknowledged that the only foreseeable means of liquidating the college debt was to settle with the creditors on a compromise basis, and he did not even possess the funds necessary for that purpose. Determined to make an attempt to obtain them, on May 1 he made the following proposal to the Southern Christian Convention: "That we undertake the raising of a fund sufficient to pay all the creditors of the institution, on a basis of 25% to all secured creditors and for back salaries of teachers, and 10% to all other creditors."[66] After the convention found no objection to the plan, the college executive then faced the extremely difficult task of persuading the creditors to accept its terms, for otherwise, it would be meaningless. The delegates encouraged him before they adjourned by approving a drive for $250,000 with which to

Miss Ruth Isabel Seabury, honored with a Litt.D. degree in 1940, was the first woman to receive an honorary degree from the college.

finance the plan if it should be accepted, and if the money could be raised.

With the cooperation of Floyd G. Hurst, of Norfolk, Virginia, a trustee of the college and a lawyer who was also an intimate friend, Smith explained his plan to the Virginia Trust Company.[67] After lengthy correspondence and numerous personal conferences with the institution's president, Herbert Jackson, the Elon executive was assured that the bank would assume sole responsibility for refinancing the indebtedness provided the bondholders would accept a 50 percent compromise figure. This was more than Smith had thought could be offered and spurred him to press for its approval.

To obtain a decision, a meeting was arranged between those who had purchased the college bonds from the bank and Dr. Smith. In the beginning, the session was somewhat stormy because some who attended showed little desire for settling for only a portion of their investment. The president remained calm during some heated discussion, and patiently pointed out that such settlements were being made by corporations all over the country so that creditors could salvage as much money as possible from their holdings, when the principal sums could not be paid under any existing circumstances. He also told the group that if the college were forced into bankruptcy, the cost of liquidation of the institution would probably absorb all its assets and the bondholders would receive nothing at all. This was not a pleasant task for Smith, but his perseverance was successful and the compromise was agreed upon.

In summary, the agreement worked out with the financiers was for the Virginia bank to retire loans in the amount of $20,000 from the Farmers' Bank of Nansemond, pay $21,500 for delinquent faculty salaries, $6,500 for minor claims against the college, and $142,000 to retire bonds at $500 per bond, or 50 percent, of the original value. Elon would then owe the bank a total of $190,000, bearing 4 percent interest, and payable in full within ten years. The debt was to be secured by a mortgage on all the college property, the principal and income of its endowment, and a note signed by the board of trustees, Hurst, and Smith. The reason given for requiring the president's signature was because Jackson felt that, if Smith signed it, he would personally see that it was paid.[68] The relieved executive hastened home and met his trustees on April 15, 1935, in a special session at the home of the Reverend Stanley C. Harrell, in Durham. The board unhesitatingly approved the transaction.[69]

The next step was to inform the college staff of the proposal, which was done on May 21, at a special meeting. "Following the discussion, each member of the Faculty individually signed an agreement indicating his willingness to accept 23% of the total amount owed to him by the College."[70] The president was convinced that, after this compromise, faculty salaries could be paid promptly and in full in the future, a conviction that proved to be correct. The action raised the morale of the instructors considerably, for speculation about their fiscal affairs was replaced by the knowledge of their situation and the plans being made to improve it. They were thus able to attend to their duties at the institution with renewed vigor and enthusiasm.

Other minor claims were adjusted as speedily as possible, and the suit with the North Carolina Bank and Trust Company was settled out of court.[71] Smith then concentrated on the problem of obtaining the money to pay the Virginia bank. For the first time in the history of Elon College, a professional fundraiser was employed to supervise the campaign. In January 1936 the trustees voted to employ the George W. Williams Company, of Lebanon, Pennsylvania, to manage the drive for a maximum fee of $14,000, which was to be paid from the first cash donations received. At the close of the designated period, only $66,000 had been pledged and $13,000 received in cash. The latter sum belonged to the company, and Smith was forced to make a personal loan to pay the $1,000 necessary to complete the total fee. This system of raising money proved to be a costly mistake, and the responsibility for completing the drive was left on the already overburdened shoulders of the college president.[72]

Some of the sting of this experience was diluted, however, because of the death at this time of P. J. Carlton. The longtime friend of Elon left the college a handsome bequest that reduced the total indebtedness from $190,000 to $160,000. The latter figure was quite in contrast to "the staggering amount of $704,170.84," which was the total two years previously. Fortified with this accomplishment, President Smith urged the convention at its 1936 session to emphasize the college fund drive for $250,000, "$160,000 to provide for the cancellation of the debts of the college, the remainder to meet the expenses of the campaign, the cost of necessary repairs, and to supplement our current budget that the college may go without deficit for a period during which time it will have the opportunity of increasing its endowment and in other ways increasing its income."[73]

The convention complied with the request, and also took further action:

> In 1924 this Convention authorized the issuing to the college bonds in the amount of $500,000, $400,000 to be known as Elon College bonds and $100,000 to be known as Bethlehem bonds. Later the Bethlehem bonds were returned to the Convention and were subsequently turned over to Elon College as part of its endowment. Previously the Convention had given its note in the amount of $112,500, the same to bear 6 per cent interest and to constitute a part of the college's endowment. In as much as the college has effected a plan for the settlement of its debts and is now conducting a general campaign to take care of its remaining indebtedness and in as much as these bonds are without value, therefore, be it resolved;
>
> 1. That these bonds authorized and issued by this Convention for the college be cancelled and destroyed.
>
> 2. That the college be requested to surrender the Convention's note for $12,500 and the $100,000 in bonds held as part of the endowment to the Convention.
>
> 3. That in lieu of the above the Convention give its note in the amount of $250,000 to the college, the principal of which shall be non-payable, but that the Convention assume the responsibility and bind itself to pay 4 per cent interest annually on said note. The interest is to be paid through apportionments to the churches by the Convention and to be credited on the local church's conference apportionment. This note for $250,000 is to be a part of the endowment fund of the college.[74]

The convention also complimented the Smith administration on its handling of the institution's finances, called upon all members of the church to support the fundraising, and adjourned feeling far more relief over Elon's condition than it had for a number of years.

Just as these negotiations were completed in 1936, a proposal was made by Piedmont College, a Congregationalist school in Demarest, Georgia, to merge with Elon. In 1928 Bethlehem College (Wadley,

Alabama), founded by the Christians, had become a part of Piedmont. Several conferences were held concerning the proposed new merger without definite action being taken, and the matter was finally dropped.[75]

Smith then concentrated on the campaign, which by 1939 had provided means to reduce the college debt to $120,000. Because the next year would be the fiftieth since the founding of the institution, another drive was organized under the title "Elon College Golden Anniversary Club." A donation of $50 was requested for membership in the commemorative organization. To introduce the new effort, a gala celebration of Founders Day was held on September 14, 1939, the first such occasion at the college. At a formal faculty convocation, the principal address for the occasion was delivered by North Carolina's Governor Clyde R. Hoey, after which a magnolia tree was planted on the campus to honor the memory of the original faculty of the college. Dr. J. U. Newman, then rounding out half a century of service to Elon, lifted the first shovelful of dirt. The commemorative tree, located in the angle formed by the Alamance and Mooney buildings, thrived and has since grown luxuriantly. The results of the campaign that followed were also good, especially from the alumni, but only sufficient to reduce the debt to $105,000.[76]

Time was running out, and the president determined to make one final effort to raise the needed money. On September 14, 1941, the "Elon College All or Nothing" campaign was launched and scheduled to close on January 1, 1943. This project was subject to the provision that, "If the entire amount [$105,000] is not subscribed, all unpaid pledges and all cash given with restrictions will be refunded to the pledgee or contributor."[77] A more speculative effort would be difficult to conceive, and only Smith's unbounded faith in his mission inspired him to make such a move.

The progress of the drive was so agonizingly slow that success seemed impossible. As the deadline approached, the president was advised to admit failure and refund the contributions, which he stubbornly refused to do. Efforts were redoubled, and even the smallest sums were gratefully received to add to the slowly mounting total. However, failure continued to threaten until literally the final minutes of the campaign, when several donations put it "over the top."[78]

January 26, 1943, was probably one of the proudest days of Smith's life, for he drove to Richmond and made the final payment to the Virginia Trust Company, two years before its deadline. Unfortunately, Herbert Jackson did not live to witness the event, but the confidence he had expressed in Smith's ability to pay the loan was fully justified. In appreciation, Walker Scott, the bank's current president, wrote the college executive that he had "accomplished the finest piece of work of this kind that has ever come under my observation during a long experience in the banking business." The financier also commented, "This money, of course, was raised by contributions from friends of the College, and your accomplishment has left a monument to your fine talent and energy."[79] This compliment voiced the sentiments of thousands of people who were made happy when the news was announced that Elon College was free of debt for the first time within the memory of living people.

CHAPTER X

THE PRUNED TREE

Trees, when they are lopped and cut, grow up
again in a short time, but men, once being lost,
cannot easily be recovered.
PERICLES
Lives

The administration of a college can often be compared to a steeple-chase, for as fast as one obstacle is successfully hurdled another is encountered to challenge the efforts of the rider. This analogy applies to the long term of L. E. Smith as chief executive. While he concentrated on winning the race to liberate the institution financially, other unforeseen problems arose that required immediate and decisive action.

One such emergency occurred during the last phase of the struggle to make a final settlement with the Virginia Trust Company when the college again became the victim of its archenemy, fire. In the early morning of January 17, 1942, the West Dormitory Annex, containing the dining hall, kitchen, and women's gymnasium, burned to the ground.[1] At the time, mid-term examinations were being given, for which reason Elizabeth M. Hoyt (Elon '42, who later married classmate William J. O'Connor) arose about four o'clock on the fatal morning to study. From the window of her room in Ladies' Hall, "Betty" saw the blaze in the kitchen of the building next door. Hastily throwing on some warm clothing, she ran to West to give the alarm. According to the college newspaper, the fire was discovered by the night watchman. Because it is possible that he and Miss Hoyt saw it at about the same time, both may be credited with the discovery.[2]

Miss June P. Murphy (Elon '42, later Mrs. June M. Looney) recalls, upon being aroused, seeing her window in West filled with a scarlet glow from the fire in the Annex. She also remembers the prompt action of Dean Julia Mae Oxford in arranging for the fire doors to the Annex to be closed, which confined the conflagration to that area, and efficiently supervising the exodus from the dormitory section in the main building. The male students soon began to remove furniture and other portable equipment from the rooms, while the coeds frantically threw clothing out of the windows before hurrying outdoors. Although it was soon determined that the main building would not be ignited, "there were many articles of wearing apparel still decorating the shrubbery beside the dorm when daylight illumined the scene."[3] In all this frenzied commotion, it was almost miraculous that the only physical injury to anyone was an injured ankle sustained by school nurse Helen Clodfelter (later Mrs. Sam Rankin).

The prompt arrival of the fire departments from the neighboring municipalities, aided by the parapet walls and fire doors of the main building, confined the conflagration to the north wing. Damage to the dormitory was slight, but the Annex was a total loss. Financially, the damage amounted to $40,700, of which $32,632.19 was recovered from insurance; the college suffered a loss of $8,067.81.[4]

Permission was granted to the coeds who roomed in West to take their exams scheduled for the early morning periods of the 17th at a later date, but otherwise the academic program of the college was not interrupted. The students carried furnishings and clothing back into the dormitory during the day so that the rooms could be occupied that night. Many did not sleep soundly, however, because they were disturbed by the heavy odor of smoke and the noise made by the firemen occasionally pouring water on the smoldering ruins.

Arrangements were immediately made for the students to eat breakfast and lunch at the Elon High School cafeteria and be supplied with bag lunches for the evening meal. This innovation was cheerfully accepted, and a contemporary particularly recalls Royall Spence, Jr., and Luvine Holmes enjoying their snack supper together. (Miss Holmes later became Mrs. Spence, and her husband a trustee of the college.)[5] Within a short time, a frame kitchen was erected adjacent to the east side of the Mooney Building, and the "Y" halls in the latter converted into a dining room. This arrangement served until 1951, when the kitchen was damaged by fire.[6] After that event, a war-surplus barracks was obtained from the government's Camp Butner, North Carolina, attached to the repaired kitchen after being reassembled at Elon, and used for a dining hall.[7]

During the summer of 1939, the president, exhibiting almost prophetic vision, had recognized the increasing demand for trained airplane pilots and determined that his institution should provide such instruction. At the time, 395 males and 230 females were enrolled, many of whom expressed an interest in aeronautics. Chester A. Hughes, a local alumnus of the class of 1936, had even constructed his own plane, powered by a Ford motor. Without delay, Smith applied to Robert H. Hinckley, chairman of the United States Civil Aeronautics Authority, for participation of the college in the government's Civilian Pilot Training Program.[8] Approval was granted on September 11, just eight days after World War II began in Europe.

Immediately, the curriculum was expanded to include a course in aeronautics, which included detailed instruction in the history of aviation, civil air regulations, navigation, meteorology, parachutes, aircraft, theory of flight, engines, instruments, and radio techniques. Some 35 to 50 hours of flying instruction were also offered. The course, which required a special fee of forty dollars, provided for four semester hours of credit. The students studied in groups of ten. Arrangements were made with Dover Fogleman and Conrad H. ("Bo") Jordan, at Huffman Field, in Burlington, to rent their planes and use their facilities for flying instruction.[9]

The program was placed under the supervision of Professor A. L. Hook, who felt competent to direct and teach the ground courses, but who did not know how to fly a plane. To remedy this deficiency, the veteran instructor took lessons under Fogleman and obtained his pilot's license. (Later, Hook purchased a plane and traveled in it frequently for his own pleasure until recent years.) By November 1941 more than 75 students had completed the Civil Aeronautics Course, including the flying phase. Eventually, 95 individuals, including the 75, received instructions in the ground phase.[10]

The course progressed satisfactorily until the darkening war clouds caused the government to replace its Civilian Pilot Training Program with the War Training Service, in which 40 students were instructed at Elon.[11] Within a short time, the Army Air Forces program replaced the latter training.

Immediately after Pearl Harbor, Smith offered the facilities of the college to the United States government for military training, but obtained no acceptance. However, the effects of the situation were soon felt at the institution because Selective Service began to draft both undergraduates and faculty members into military service. By November 1942, approximately two hundred students were serving in the armed forces of the country. Enrollment decreased from a total of 661 for the academic year 1940–41 to an estimated 475 for the following year. The emphasis also changed from training civilian pilots to instructing military aviators. Anxious for his college to keep up with these changes, Smith was inspired to write to Robert R. Reynolds, United States Senator from North Carolina:

> What our enrollment will be when the law lowering the draft goes into effect is extremely problematical. Evidently we shall have a lot of vacant space that could be used with profit by the government for the war effort. . . . At Elon College we can take care of two to four hundred trainees for the government, providing room, board, and instructional space. . . . I feel that these facilities should be used to further the war effort of the country.[12]

This was but the beginning of lengthy negotiations to have Elon's program in aeronautics succeeded by the authority to train pilots for the Army Air Corps. At the time, more educational institutions were available for the latter purpose than the government needed, which tended to confine approval to the largest, which possessed better facilities. However, Smith and Reynolds, aided by the latter's efficient secretary, Wesley L. McDonald, persisted against discouraging odds until approval was obtained early in 1943 for the 325th College Training Detachment of the Army Air Forces to be stationed at Elon College.[13]

On March 1, Lieutenant DeWitt D. Vickery arrived at the institution to command the unit; he was later promoted to the rank of captain. He was soon joined by three other officers, and nine noncommissioned officers and enlisted men, all from the Army Air Corps. Accommodations were arranged by renovating Mooney Building for the officers and South Dormitory (the old Publishing House), the Young Men's Club, and North Dormitory for the enlisted men. It was necessary to purchase and install $22,293 worth of equipment for the purpose. All was ready, however, by April 22, when the first group of Elon's quota of 250 trainees arrived.[14]

The prescribed course required five months time, during which more than 700 hours of study were consumed in academic and military instruction, including physical education, mathematics, physics, current history, geography, English, civil air regulations, drilling, ground work, and ten hours of flying time. Upon completion of the

Military ceremony near the O'Kelly Monument, on the south campus, during World War II.

course, the trainees were sent to army bases to complete their flight training.[15]

The college faculty taught the academic courses, and the military officers took care of the other phases of instruction. Through the newspaper, Dr. Smith requested it be made clear that "Elon's use as a training center for the Army Air Corps will in no way affect the normal college program, and that Elon will continue its regular college program with ample facilities available."[16] The result was a unique situation, which the press described as follows: "Elon College has a dual personality these days. There is an imaginary line drawn through the middle of the campus and while one side [on one side] the pre-war life of the college goes on in as near normal fashion as the times will permit, the other side has gone to war."[17] This arrangement was the result of designating the east side of the campus as the "Military Reservation." Civilian students were restricted from the area and the trainees from the west campus except during certain periods during the weekends. A special parade of the men in uniform on September 27 emphasized the military side of life at the institution and provided an interesting event for the spectators.[18]

Another marked distinction between the two phases of life at the college was that the military personnel were required to rise at 5:30 A.M., and retire promptly at 9:30 P.M., which caused one observer to remark, "North Dormitory isn't exactly the same place it was in peace time."[19]

Another innovation caused by the military program was a change in arrangements for the religious life of the students. The influx of trainees from various sections of the nation brought members of different faiths to the college. The Community Christian Church accommodated the Protestants, and services for Roman Catholics and Jews were held weekly by visiting priests and rabbis in the chapel of Mooney Building. This probably marked the first time religious services of other than Protestant denominations were held on the Elon campus and the beginning of a practice of religious toleration that is commonplace today.[20]

The wife of the commanding officer of the cadets directed the physical education program for the females. It was fortunate Mrs. Vickery was available, for there were "more girls than usual enrolled at the college." In February 1943 the *Maroon and Gold* announced that the War Department had designated Elon as a training school for the Women's Army Auxiliary Corps (WAAC), and claimed the college to be the only one in the state so far "set aside for such purposes." However, no such unit ever materialized.[21]

In August 1943 the government renewed its contract with the college, and the training program continued until 1944, when the last contingent of trainees was sent to a military base for advanced instruction.[22] The departed aviators were not forgotten, nor did all of them forget Elon. In 1945 two of them wrote a song, "Elon College Just Ahead," as a memento of their training days; other men corresponded with their former teachers on the faculty; and at least one of them married an Elon graduate.[23] The absence of men in uniform seemed strange for a while, and their departure caused a considerable depletion in the student population. Apprehensive that the public might misunderstand the situation, "Dr. Smith asked that all faculty members assist in preventing the spread of rumors, nervousness or uncertainty in regard to next year's work that may result from the withdrawal from the campus of the College Training Detachment of the Army Air Force."[24] The results of this request were successful, and the institution was soon operating smoothly on a peacetime basis.

A total of 672 pilots had been trained for the Army Air Forces at Elon. Because the government contract cannot now be located, the specific financial arrangements cannot be determined. However, the annual college audits show that in 1944 and 1945 the army paid the institution $166,263.40, most of it in cash, though a small part consisted of a credit for army improvements made on the campus and left for the use of the college. From this figure, it is evident that the program was satisfactory to Dr. Smith, who termed it a financial "life-saver." It also enabled Elon to play an active role in the winning of World War II.[25]

The army training program was only one phase of the effect of World War II on the college. When the United States became actively involved in the conflict, the students patriotically rallied to the national emergency. In January 1942 a "V For Victory Club" was organized on the campus to boost the war effort.[26] In March the *Maroon and Gold* announced that primarily because of the efforts of Emory R. Sellers, a prominent undergraduate, "Elon was the first College in the State, perhaps in the nation, to introduce the idea of Voluntary Military Training on the College campuses."[27] This was followed by the formation of the Elon College Air-Raid Organization, a unit of the Civilian Defense Organization, which supervised the first air-raid drill in the community in March.[28] Navy Day was observed at a special chapel program in October. Tribute was paid to all sailors, particularly Ensign Millard H. Piberg, killed the previous August, who was the first known Elon casualty in the Navy during the war.[29]

When the trustees met in the spring of 1942, they recognized, because of the national emergency, the probability that attendance at athletic contests would be curtailed on account of the effect of the rubber shortage on the use of automobiles. To aid the war effort, the decision was made to discontinue football and baseball for the duration of the conflict.[30] The *Alumni News* elaborated on this ruling:

> Elon College was the first school in North Carolina to abandon athletics because of the war situation. After seeing so many of the athletes leave for camp the Board of Trustees decided that the only sensible thing to do was to abandon the program until after the emergency. It is possible that basketball will be played but under no circumstances will there be athletic scholarships offered during the war.
>
> Athletes who have attended Elon will be at liberty to attend other institutions and they are eligible for participation at other schools since Elon voluntarily gave up intercollegiate athletics.[31]

Coach Horace Hendrickson resigned the following month, and accepted a position at the University of Pennsylvania.[32]

At a faculty meeting the following year, Dr. Hans Hirsch read a letter from the Coordinator of Civilian Defense, at Greensboro, congratulating the college "for having the largest percentage of Blood Donors to the Red Cross Blood Bank of any institution in the state and possibly in the nation."[33] In these and many other ways, the campus cooperated with the government's program to win the war.

Faculty members were not exempt from military duty, and by October 1943 the following instructors had either volunteered or been drafted: C. Fletcher Moore, Herbert Donaldson, and Frederick Loadwick, all from the Music Department; Howard L. Gravett (biology); Harold L. Schultz (history), J. W. Stewart (business administration); R. L. Westhafer (mathematics); and Joe Brunansky, assistant coach and director of intramural sports.[34] These were soon followed by Austin D. Sprague (mathematics) and J. L. Pierce (physical education). In addition, Miss Wilsie F. Bussell, instructor in French and Spanish, was granted a leave of absence without pay to serve the government as an interpreter. Dr. Smith commented, "We have lost a number of our more capable faculty to the war effort,"[35] but temporary replacements were made, though with difficulty, and few college courses needed to be dropped from the schedule or altered. After the conflict ended, Moore, Gravett, Stewart, and Pierce returned to their posts at Elon.[36]

In January 1943 the Elon alumni secretary published a summary of men in service:

> Elon College has a total of more than 600 alumni in the armed forces at the present time. One hundred and twenty Elon boys are in the navy. The majority of these are Ensigns or Lieutenants (Junior Grade). One hundred and five are serving as pilots in the army or naval air force. More than one hundred are connected with aviation as instructors, ground crew, photographers, bombardiers, etc. Six graduates are serving as chaplains—two in the army and four in the navy. Nearly three hundred are in the regular army, ranking from buck private to captain. Ten Elon graduates who later attended medical colleges are in the health and sanitation departments of the armed forces.[37]

In honor of these men and in memory of Joseph H. Hopkins, who lost his life in a plane crash while in training, the Sigma Phi Beta fraternity presented the college with a plaque on which the names of the men in service were listed. It was hung on the walls of Whitley Auditorium underneath the institution's service flag. Designed with the assistance of Miss Lila C. Newman, the art teacher, it was an ornamental tribute, on which casualties were fittingly acknowledged with gold stars placed beside the appropriate names.[38]

Many Elonites kept in touch with the college while they were serving in military units in various parts of the world. They visited the campus while on leave, wrote frequently to the students and faculty, and some sent back souvenirs.[39] Dr. Daniel J. Bowden, faculty adviser to the Sigma Phi Beta fraternity, used the many communications he received from the brotherhood to prepare a quarterly newsletter that was sent to all the men from the fraternity in service. When the professor became Dean of the College after the departure of John D. Messick for another post in 1944, his correspondence broadened extensively. Unable to continue the newsletter, he turned it over to Charles M. Walters, Jr. (Elon '42). As soon as communication was restored with Japan, alumna Toshio Sato wrote to a friend that her family had survived the conflict unscathed and was occupied with the task of convincing their countrymen that the Americans would not harm them during the postwar occupation of their country.[40]

The names and experiences of the many other Elon alumni and undergraduates who served in World War II are far too numerous to be listed here. Many rose in the ranks to high military office, a large number won decorations for their heroic achievements, and, regrettably, some did not return home alive. The known casualties included thirty-one men and one woman. In honor of their patriotic sacrifice, their names are inscribed on a bronze tablet on the wall of the new Alumni Memorial Gymnasium. An interesting sidelight to this memorial is that Stanley Yonkoski, declared dead after having been missing in action, was later found to be alive, but his name was not removed from the tablet. The conflict left deep scars at Elon College, as it did everywhere throughout the nation.[41]

Although the institution had been fortunate in its relations with the national government, the contract for pilot training by no means solved all its problems. Dr. Smith, admitting that the college "was out of debt, but it is not out of danger," outlined the situation to the Southern Christian Convention at its 1944 meeting:

> Elon College represents that Convention's effort to train its young people at the college level. Its history, struggles, and achievements are too well known to be rehearsed even in part. It should be said, however, and with pardonable pride, that on January 26, 1943, the last dollar of the old debts was paid. But it is a most regrettable fact that we are slipping right back into the old debt again through no fault of the College, but due to war conditions. Through the loss of students to the war effort we have put on our books this year approximately $115,000 less than in 1941–42, which means that we will realize this

year between $40,000 and $55,000 less for current expenses than in 1941–42. We ask you: What can the College do in the face of such an emergency? What will the Convention do to relieve the situation? Our college is definitely a war casualty.[42]

After having labored zealously for a decade, during which "almost criminal economy"[43] had to be practiced to free the college financially, Smith did not plan to lose the advantage so dearly won. He then explained a plan his administration had formulated to pave the way for future success instead of risking the possibility of another calamity:

In anticipation of this emergency and apparent easy money throughout the country, the College administration advocated a campaign to raise $100,000 for endowment—the amount necessary to meet the minimum requirements of the Southern Association of Colleges and Secondary Schools for a fully accredited college. Later the proposal was made and accepted by all conferences constituting the Convention that this amount be raised and used to establish the "Staley-Atkinson-Newman Memorial Foundation for Christian Education in Elon College." After due consideration it was evident that Elon College would need a much larger endowment than the additional $100,000 would provide; it was imperative that we improve our facilities and erect new buildings, such as a dining-room, gymnasium, dormitory, power house, etc. This enlarged program for the College would require a great deal of money. Consequently the College administration suggested that a campaign to raise $1,000,000 for Elon College, for endowment, improvements and buildings, be launched at once—the $100,000 previously authorized to be a part of the *Million Dollar Campaign*. This new and enlarged undertaking was authorized by a joint meeting of the Executive Board of the Convention, that the Executive Committee of the Board of Trustees of the College, the Executive Committee of the Alumni Association and representative ministers of the Convention held at Elon College on September 14, 1943. The Executive Board, as such, dissented and asked that this enlarged program be presented to the Convention for action.[44]

At the conclusion of this report, the convention endorsed the "Million Dollar Campaign," but stipulated that the first $100,000 received be assigned to complete funding of the Staley-Atkinson-Newman Memorial Foundation and that another $100,000 be allocated for the erection of a gymnasium at Elon College as a memorial "to the veterans of our constituency who served in World War I and World War II."

After this campaign was launched, the Smith administration was able to increase its efforts to attract more students and provide facilities for them. It had been correctly anticipated that numerous undergraduates who had been drafted would return to the college to complete their education. In addition, many new students were expected because of the Servicemen's Readjustment Act, popularly known as the "G.I. Bill of Rights," passed by Congress in 1944 to provide financial assistance to veterans of military service for the completion of their education. The college officials lost no time in obtaining a contract from the Veterans Administration that guaranteed payment annually in the amount of $305 per student to cover the cost of tuition, books, and supplies. This sum was in contrast with the cost to others of $275 annual tuition. The college then began preparations to accommodate as many of these students as possible.[45]

In the academic year 1945–46, registration rose to an unprecedented 678 students, 80 of whom were veterans.[46] More applications for entrance were received, but the college living quarters were filled to capacity. Seeking a remedy for this situation, in February 1946 the trustees instructed the president to apply to the National Housing Agency for the construction of facilities to house exservice personnel who might desire to enroll at Elon.[47] Within a year, the government had completed 36 of the 66 units planned, and the remainder were soon to be ready for occupancy.[48]

These apartments, ranging from one to three bedrooms each, were built of war-surplus material. In addition, a dormitory for men under construction contained four sections, in each of which were four rooms and bath facilities. The college was responsible for grading the land and providing the water and sewer connections, which cost approximately $20,000; and the government constructed the buildings at its own expense, estimated at $100,000. The units were placed in rows, the whole forming a large square. The project, located on college property just north of the campus on the road to Shallow Ford Church, was known as "Veterans' Apartments."[49]

Although responsible for the upkeep of this gift, the college profited somewhat from the arrangement by charging a monthly rental ranging from $17.50 to $22.50 per apartment. Occupancy was restricted to veterans and their families. After several years, as maintenance costs began to mount, the monthly rentals were increased to a range of $22.50 to $27.50. This assistance from the United States government proved a boon to Elon, which could not have otherwise accommodated the influx of veterans. The apartments were soon filled with occupants and remained so for several years.[50]

Because of incomplete records, the total number of those who attended Elon under the governmental program is unknown, but 80 veterans were enrolled in 1946, 412 in 1949, and 339 in 1950.[51] Neither is the total revenue derived from the "G.I. Bill" known, but from 1947 through 1949 the Veterans Administration paid the college $111,397.11, which indicated a large enrollment and was of inestimable financial benefit to the institution.[52]

When former students returned to the campus after completing their military stint, they found a number of changes in their alma mater. Students were no longer summoned to classes by the mellow tones of the old bell, but by the blatant wail of a siren, which had been installed to also serve for air-raid warnings in the area, had such occurred. The wear and tear of the war years on some of the buildings was easily discerned. This was especially true of North, which was disintegrating to an alarming degree and was no longer adequate for a gymnasium.

As the result of a detailed faculty study in 1943, the academic year had been changed to the quarter system.[53] The former fall and spring terms of four and one-half months in length and the relatively short summer term had been replaced by fall, winter, spring, and summer quarters, each three months in length. The summer program had been completely altered. Instead of offering a few special short courses for a few weeks, as formerly, the quarter was composed of two terms. The first ran from June 1 to July 9; the second from July 12 to August 14. The two terms combined were the equivalent of any other scholastic quarters. Courses in the curricula served to renew the certificates of public school teachers "and also count toward degree work" for any student.[54] Under this new system, fewer subjects were studied simultaneously by the students, but, because classes each met daily instead of on alternate days, the total for the college year was not affected. Except for the summer school, expenses for the three quarters amounted to an approximate increase of $45, which was not a significant change.[55]

A course in radio broadcasting, conducted in connection with radio station WBBB, in Burlington, had been included in the curriculum.[56] When the United States government lifted the wartime restriction on civil aeronautics in 1943, a course in aviation had again been opened at Elon the following year. It was conducted in cooperation with the Burlington Flying Service and the Burlington Municipal Airport. Students were trained to receive certificates as either private or commercial pilots. Special arrangements were made for veterans who enjoyed previous experience. Six planes were purchased for the course but because the anticipated interest proved to be of short duration, they were sold and after 1947 the course was discontinued. Only the small frame building the government had donated for the pilot training program and the tall steel skeletal tower erected beside Duke Science Building in 1941 for weather observations remained on the campus as mute reminders of the college's work in the field of aeronautics.[57]

Beginning in 1942, for four years sports were in eclipse at the college, but resumed in 1946 on the intercollegiate level. L. J. ("Hap") Perry, a former Elon star athlete, was employed as full-time coach and began to rebuild the Fighting Christians into an effective team again on a competitive level.[58]

Because of the exodus of men from the campus, in 1943 the trustees had rescinded the charters of the fraternities, but not the sororities, for the duration of the war. In May 1946, as the number of male students began to increase, the charters were restored, and the clubs again became active organizations.[59] This was a highly popular move with both sexes of the student body.

The returned veterans also found the college crowded to capacity with students. During the war, more women than men were enrolled, for which reason East Dormitory was used as a coed residence hall from 1944 until 1948, when it again became a dormitory for men. Many students were married, and no accommodations were available on the campus for couples other than the Veterans'

Apartments. In response to this situation, the administration indicated a strong preference for single students. Although married couples were not barred from enrolling, they were forced to find their own living quarters elsewhere. This policy was later altered, for a large number of the present student body are married people.[60]

Other changes had also taken place over the years. In 1946 Elon's students numbered 416 from North Carolina; 47 from Virginia; 5 from Pennsylvania; 3 each from New Jersey, New York, West Virginia, and South America; 2 each from Connecticut and South Carolina; and 1 each from six other states, the District of Columbia, and Cyprus. Religious denominations were represented by 127 Methodists, 97 Congregational Christians, 88 Baptists, 40 Presbyterians, 22 Lutherans, 17 Episcopalians, 13 Reformed, 9 Catholics, 3 United Brethren, 2 Moravians, 2 Jews, 1 Associate Reformed Presbyterian, 1 Disciple of Christ, 1 Free Will Baptist, 1 Greek Orthodox, 1 Nazarene, and 60 who were not church members. There had always been denominational diversity at Elon, but never before to this extent. The student population of the college was still primarily from North Carolina and Virginia, but only a minor part represented the denomination that founded the institution. This was the prelude to the eventual withdrawal of the church from financial responsibility for Elon, though its concern for the institution has remained vital.[61]

Another change in the religious affairs of the college occurred in 1953 when the Student Senate presented a resolution to the trustees requesting the requirement that students attend Sunday school and church each week be rescinded. Somewhat contrary to Smith's wishes, the board granted the request, though attendance at chapel, held three times each week, remained compulsory.[62] This decision was not made because the officials were no longer interested in religious emphasis, but represented an acknowledgment that the strict disciplinary measures exercised in a former generation were no longer in keeping with the independent spirit of the postwar generation. The change was not "a wholesome or helpful influence," complained the president. None of the students went to Sunday school and comparatively few attended church services. "Instead, they lounge around on the campus, often in athletic dress. It does not look like a church college on Sunday morning at 11:00,"[63] was the opinion of the disgruntled executive. Nevertheless, the ruling remained unchanged.

While the war clouds had begun to gather, the Elon administration embarked upon a new venture that it expected would be financially rewarding. Like many people reared on farms, or in other ways closely associated with agriculture, L. E. Smith was convinced that farming could be profitable. Contemplation of the $18,000 to $20,000 spent annually for food at the college gradually augmented his conviction that home production would be economical. Regardless of the financial losses incurred previously in "a similar venture," in 1939 he told the trustees, "I am convinced, however, that a farm owned by the college would be operated to a great advantage."[64] The president was sufficiently enthusiastic to obtain the board's approval, and given free rein to proceed with his plan of action.

In 1939 the college purchased 34.24 acres of land a short distance east of the town, but it was not sufficient for the extensive operation the president had in mind. The following year, a tract of 51.1 acres just north of the institution was acquired for $8,000 from the Huffines estate.[65] This purchase was financed in part with $4,300 received from the sale of the old ball park property on Haggard Avenue near the Elon College High School and some other small tracts. This sum was supplemented by a donation of $5,000 from Dr. Thomas A. Morgan, of New York City, which left a surplus of $1,000 to apply on equipment.[66] Later the same year, Oscar F. Smith, a trustee from Norfolk, Virginia, contributed $3,250, which was used to buy the 150-acre Atkinson farm, located north of the Huffines tract on the old Ossipee Road.[67] In 1941 the 55 acres known as the Oldham Farm, adjacent to the town's northeastern limits, was bought for $3,000; $500 was paid at the time and the balance at the rate of $25 per month.[68] These real estate transactions gave the college a total of 290.11 acres of land, three tracts of which contained farm buildings and considerable cleared land. After these acquisitions, Dr. Smith selected the former Atkinson and Huffines acres for cultivation and began his agricultural venture.

Zebulon H. Lynch, of Mebane, was appointed as farm supervisor at a salary of $100 per month. He moved into one of the available dwellings and with the help of his wife and two daughters, who planned to enroll at the college, began the operation. Vitus Covington, a black man, was hired for $25 per month, plus room and board, to assist with the work. Only a small amount of student help was used on the project because of the interference of World War II, but activity continued without it.[69] Being a capable carpenter, Lynch soon improved the buildings, which had suffered from neglect. Within a few months there were 500 hens in the poultry house, 18 cows in the barn, and 40 hogs in the sty.[70] Former state governor Cameron Morrison donated a Jersey bull for the herd; R. A. Coble, a hardware dealer in Burlington, gave $500 to apply on the cost of the tractor; and other appropriate gifts were received.[71]

Lynch was not only a hardworking farmer, but also an intelligent businessman. He grew produce in sufficient quantity to supply the college needs and also sell turnip greens by the hundred pounds and sweet potatoes by the load to wholesale produce dealers. By February 1942 he had used his own sawmill and tractor to cut and sell 45,000 feet of lumber, mostly hardwoods, and 50 cords of wood, thus clearing more land for cultivation. At that time, in addition to the dairy products that supplied the needs of the dining halls, the operation had cleared a $2,484 profit.[72] This was a satisfactory beginning, but the labor involved was tremendous, often including troublesome unforeseen problems.[73] In addition to directing the cultivation of the crops and caring for the livestock, the farmer was also burdened with building repairs. In 1943 he left this strenuous activity to become a United States mail carrier, but he retired from the farm operation as a successful manager.

J. L. Pierce was then employed to superintend the farming for a few months, after which the Smith administration made a contract with J. H. Ray for him to rent the two farms on shares. The college would provide the land, fertilizer, and seed; the tenant would furnish the labor, stock, and machinery; the profits would be shared equally. The college continued to own the livestock, but paid the farmer for butchering services when needed. The machinery and other necessary equipment was sold to the tenant under a chattel mortgage, and the new phase of farming began.[74]

In May 1945 the total value of the crops marketed was $9,000, from which the college cleared a profit of $3,000 after deducting $1,500 for expenses. In addition, all the pork furnished the institution for eighteen months past, plus 7,000 pounds on hand, and 50 hogs to supply the needs for the coming year were financial benefits derived from the farms. Little wonder that Smith exclaimed to the trustees, "The farm has proved a friend indeed."[75] In 1947 the college reaped a net profit of $6,283.92 in addition to "all pork for the dining hall except bacon."[76]

However, after this last satisfactory year, the tide began to turn. Mounting costs of the operation required larger expenditures annually from the college. As a result, after 1948, the farms began to lose money. Furthermore, Ray was unable to reduce substantially the chattel mortgage held by the institution on his equipment "and crops, harvested and in the field."[77] Faced with mounting losses, in 1954 the trustees voted to liquidate the program. The equipment and stock were sold, a part of the land rented to Ray for $75 per month, and Elon College closed its last venture in farming.[78] The disappointed Smith remained convinced that his original idea was sound and would have succeeded under different cirumstances. However, unable to argue against cold facts and figures, he surrendered his dream, one of the few unsuccessful projects of his lengthy administration.

In defense of the president, it must be acknowledged that, had it not been for the output of the farms, supplying the college with food under the rationing experienced during the war might have been far more difficult and expensive. In addition, the books were finally more than balanced by the increased value of the real estate holdings that had been acquired for agricultural use. The trustees adamantly refused to sell the land for many years and used portions of it for the construction of faculty dwellings and for other purposes. It eventually became a real financial asset to the college, far in excess of any losses incurred from its use for agricultural purposes.

When the farm project began, it attracted the attention of W. L. Monroe, an Atlanta, Georgia, nurseryman, who had attended Elon in 1918. In the spring of 1942, he offered to give the institution 3,000 shrubs from his stock and 7,000 more later, to be set out on the tracts by student help and sold to make money for the college. The proposal was accepted by the president, but no record has been found to show that it was ever carried out, probably because the war interfered with obtaining student help to handle the undertaking. This did not dampen Monroe's enthusiasm for the school, for he later aided it with other gifts.[79]

In 1946 W. B. Kiker, a Reidsville constructon engineer, expressed his interest in the college by offering to build it a lake, which would represent a $3,000 gift. The offer was accepted, and Kiker Lake, which became known as "College Pond," was located near the town on the former Oldham Farm. Approximately five acres were covered when the earthen dam, 200 feet long, 100 feet wide at its base and 12 feet wide at its top, was completed.[80] Stocked with fish, the attractive lake was soon enjoyed by anglers, and was a convenient place for college picnics and other outings. The school's Biology Department used it extensively as a source of marine specimens for its laboratory and for field trips for its students. It was a popular spot with many Elonites until 1972, when its waters were drained to use the land for other purposes.[81]

At the time the nation became involved in the war, faculty salaries at Elon ranged from $3,250 paid the Dean of the College to $1,300 for most instructors. Approximately $2,700 was the average remuneration for full professors.[82] During the 1940s, the administration and trustees frequently discussed establishing a system to provide retirement benefits for employees. Finally, the decision was made to pay retired faculty members who had served long enough to obtain tenure a percentage of their past salaries. The weakness in the plan was that it offered no assistance to untenured personnel or those with brief service, nor was it specifically funded. This meant that payments were not guaranteed and dependent upon the condition of the annual operating fund. Nevertheless, the arrangement was better than none at all, and went into effect during the later years of the Smith administration.[83]

Although neither the pay scale nor the retirement plan were financially impressive, they were better than previous arrangements, and Elon was fortunate in retaining a competent faculty. Moved by the loyalty of his staff, President Smith acted entirely upon his authority in 1947 by surprising each with a cash Christmas gift ranging from $10 to $20 for faculty and administrative personnel and $3 to $5 for custodians. The total expenditure, which was $526, was appreciated so much that the custom has been continued to the present.[84]

Pay gradually increased during the decade that ended in 1955, when substantial changes were necessary to meet the minimum requirements of the Southern Association for nine months of teaching. Full professors were raised from $3,600 to $4,500, associates from $3,400 to $3,900, assistants from $2,400 to $2,700. The administration absorbed this increased expense by means of a grant of

$125,700 for faculty salaries from the Ford Foundation.[85] Although the increased pay scale was not especially high, it was welcomed as adequate and bolstered staff morale.

As the busy years passed, Smith correctly concluded that effective fundraising for the college was too large an undertaking for the president, even with an assistant appointed for the purpose. To both lighten the load and produce more effective results, in 1945 he persuaded the trustees to establish the Elon College Foundation to provide financial assistance to the institution. J. H. McEwen, an industrialist from Burlington, was elected as president; Julian Price, an insurance executive from Greensboro, vice-president; and Thad Eure, North Carolina's Secretary of State, secretary-treasurer. In addition to these officers, O. F. Smith, S. T. Holland, W. Clifton Elder, and J. Dolph Long constituted the Executive Committee. The directors of the nonprofit corporation were empowered "to expend all funds received in interest of Elon College."[86] Smith's old friend, Dr. William M. Brown, was employed as director of the project.

Smith and his board hoped that the foundation would grow in importance as it raised large sums of money and guided their use, but the plan was not that effective. Numerous meetings of the officials were held for several years, but little was accomplished and the organization gradually became inactive. Because a director was no longer needed, Brown became a member of the faculty. However, several individuals made substantial personal contributions to the college, partially influenced by their connection with the foundation, which justified its brief existence, though it never became the financial agency envisioned by its planners.[87]

Although the foundation was short-lived, Founders Day was one phase of the college program that became permanent. The original celebration of the occasion in 1939 was so successful that the commemoration was repeated the following year, honoring W. S. Long, the first president. I. W. Johnson, a trustee from Suffolk, Virginia, was the principal speaker. In 1941 the third observance paid tribute to W. W. Staley, the second president, and was also the occasion for launching the "All or Nothing Campaign." The fourth celebration, held the following year, honored E. L. Moffitt, the third president. After this event, the trustees announced, "In pre-war days September 16 was observed as Founders Day. On account of the scarcity of Gas and automobile tires, it was thought advisable not to observe this historic occasion during the war." Consequently, almost a decade passed before another celebration was held.[88]

The increasing load of presidential duties forced Smith in 1946 to give up the pastorate of the Community Church, which he had held for fourteen years. He was succeeded by Jesse H. Dollar, who filled the position until 1950, after which Howard P. Bozarth served from 1950 until 1954, then William J. Andes from 1954 to 1966.[89] This change required the president to vacate the church parsonage and move next door into West End Hall, which contained several faculty apartments and had served as a college guest house, because the dwelling occupied by the Smiths was too small for official entertaining. This called attention to another Elon need, a proper house for the residence of its chief executive.

The conferring of honorary degrees continued during the war and afterward. The distinguished recipients included Jesse H. Dollar, who was awarded the D.D. degree in 1943, and Malcolm Boyd Dana, who received the LL.D. degree at the same time. The next year, Charles E. Newman and William E. Wisseman were given D.D. degrees, and Phillip S. Suffern an LL.D. In 1945 the D.D. was conferred upon Robert S. Lambert, the Litt.D. upon Ronald Bridges, and LL.D. degrees upon Charles E. Jordan and President Harry S. Truman. The latter, who was unable to journey to Elon, received the honor in absentia.[90]

Both G. D. Colclough, who served as alumni secretary in addition to his other duties, and President Smith were fully aware of the value to the college of newspaper publicity. In the mid-1930s, Page Holder and Jake Causey, two students, served as correspondents for the *Greensboro Daily News*, primarily reporting sports events at Elon. In 1937 an opportunity arose to broaden this coverage. Moses Crutchfield, who had just begun work for the *News* as a cub reporter, was also ambitious to enroll at the college as a student. Apprised of this fact, Colclough aided him to do both by arranging a plan with James F. Reynolds, the managing editor of the paper, who had attended Elon prior to World War I. Crutchfield was to reside at the college, where he could attend classes during the mornings, and devote afternoons to his newspaper work. He was not only to cover sports events, but also send out releases concerning students to their hometown newspapers, report local events, and handle all the publicity for the institution. This was the beginning of the college News Bureau, which has since been an invaluable unit of the administration.[91]

From an office in the Carlton Building, Crutchfield directed the news service until 1941, when he went into military service, and was succeeded by Edward Storey. Kent Dennan and James H. Lightbourne, Jr., and occasionally others, served as assistants. The early years of the bureau were a golden age for sporting events, for at the time the prowess of the galaxy of athletic stars at the college supplied an abundance of interesting material for the newspapers. Inspired by the experience in this field, after his military service, Crutchfield chose journalism as his profession and rose to prominence in that capacity with the Greensboro paper. He has been engaged in this connection since, except for a brief period when he served as director of the Appalachian State University News Bureau. There he was assisted by Thomas S. Corbitt, Jr. (Elon '65), the present director who succeeded to the office when Crutchfield returned to his former position with the *News*.[92]

After Storey left the post, publicity was handled by members of the English Department on a part-time basis. Professors Charles L. McClure, Russell L. Dunlap, and Hoyle S. Bruton followed each other in that order until 1949. At that time, Luther N. Byrd, a history professor and experienced newspaper correspondent, became director of the bureau and sponsor for the *Maroon and Gold*. Under his energetic leadership, in 1951 that publication was awarded first place among college newspapers on campuses of the North State Conference, the athletic association to which Elon College belonged.[93]

Beginning in 1896 an Alumni Orator had been chosen to deliver the principal address at the annual banquet of the Alumni Association (see Appendix C). N. G. Newman was the first to be given this distinction. In addition to this honor, in 1941 the custom began of choosing the Outstanding Alumnus of the year. (For a complete list of Outstanding Alumnus awards, see Appendix D.) At the banquet, the honoree was awarded a properly inscribed plaque, accompanied by a citation of his or her career that was delivered by a member of the association. The recipient then responded by an address to the gathering. This honor was first awarded to W. Clifton Elder, a Burlington industrialist, member of the class of 1925 and an energetic trustee of the college. The list of honorees that followed the initial presentation included men and women who had become prominent as authors, college presidents, scientists, teachers, clergymen, military officials, and business and professional leaders. The award was conferred annually until 1978, when its form was changed to include more than one alumnus.

Both President Smith, in 1950, and his wife, in 1957, were recipients of the prized annual Outstanding Alumnus Award, conferred with the plaudits of their friends and associates. Both had earned their prizes. Mrs. Smith, always addressed as "Lady" by her husband, had rendered invaluable aid to him in his administrative duties. Both continued with renewed vigor to work and plan for the further progress of their alma mater, and their efforts were richly rewarded.

CHAPTER XI

THE NEW GROWTH

Growth is the only evidence of life.
CARDINAL JOHN HENRY NEWMAN
Apologia pro Vita Sua.

During the Alumni Association's development of its honors program, its members, the college family, and Elon's friends far and wide looked forward eagerly to the resumption of a full-scale sports program. Although football and baseball were necessarily suspended during the war, Lacy B. Adcock coached the basketball team during the period. When the full athletic program was renewed in 1946, "Hap" Perry supervised all teams for one year. Then James B. Mallory took charge of football and baseball until 1953, after which the former was placed under Harry E. Varney and the latter under Graham L. ("Doc") Mathis. In basketball, Garland Causey, succeeded by Harold Pope, were the coaches until 1949, when the sport was added to the responsibilities of Mathis. The accomplishments of the athletes were entirely too numerous to be included here, but championships were won, individuals named to All-American and All-State teams, and athletics increased in significance as a part of the college program.[1]

An invaluable asset to the Athletic Association was construction of Memorial Stadium in Burlington during the early postwar years. Elon arranged to use this facility for football games. This made it possible to attract larger crowds of spectators, thereby increasing both enthusiasm and gate receipts. The stadium was also used for night games, which made more flexible schedules possible. Games could be planned at times when the fans were not being attracted to other contests in the area. This helped stimulate a growing patronage. Hundreds of people attended Elon's gridiron performances regularly who had never journeyed to the college to see a game. Baseball was still played at Comer Field and basketball in the Alumni Building gymnasium. The latter sport was severely handicapped because the structure was too worn by three decades of use for the best performance of the teams and too small to seat the increasing number of fans. This handicap limited gate receipts, which played a vital part in financing the college athletics, and clearly defined the program's most pressing need: a new gymnasium.

L. E. Smith, who was far more enthusiastic over sports than any of his predecessors, was keenly aware of this need, but, as a practical man, had to acknowledge that replacing the overtaxed Power House deserved priority over new construction. The administration applied itself diligently to this $132,561 project, which was completed in 1948 at its present location on the northern edge of the campus. The old building was then razed. Prior to this essential addition to the college plant, in 1946 the Alumni Association, impatient for a new gym, began raising funds with which to build one.[2]

The versatile G. D. Colclough resigned his administrative position in 1945 to become secretary of the Burlington Chamber of Commerce[3] and manager of the Merchants Association, though he continued to reside in the town of Elon College and later served as a member of the board of trustees. Upon leaving, he called attention to the increasing importance of working with the alumni. As a result of his advice, James F. Darden (Elon '43) was employed as the first full-time secretary of the Alumni Association.[4] Energetically plunging into his duties, he also accepted responsibility for raising funds with which to provide an adequate gymnasium, an undertaking that met with gradual success. By February 1949 $80,571 had been obtained in cash and pledges to offset the estimated $150,000 cost of the building. Encouraged by this progress, the trustees authorized construction to begin.[5]

Plans for the new structure were drawn by Vernon M. Kearns, Jr., who had attended Elon in 1926, as a contribution to the undertaking. Balconies and removable bleachers on three sides of the playing floor provided a seating capacity of 4,600 for games, and the addition of removable chairs accommodated more than 6,000 for assembly purposes.[6] The gym was officially opened on January 14, 1950, with a basketball game between Elon and Catawba College. Regrettably, the Christians lost to the Indians by a score of 57 to 66, but this did not constitute an unfavorable omen for the future.[7] The event was attended by the "largest gathering of press and radio representatives ever to assemble at Elon for a sporting event." Alumni, viewing the gymnasium for the first time, "were dumbfounded and could not believe that such a structure would ever be erected."[8]

The new acquisition of the college was immediately put to widespread use. According to the *Alumni News*:

> Since the opening on January 14th the building has been in use nearly every night. Burlington High School and the high schools in Alamance County have played as many of their games in the building as could be arranged by the Elon Athletic Officials. The people of Alamance County have suddenly become basketball-conscious and expectations are that it will not be too many years before the Elon College basketball squad will be playing before capacity crowds.[9]

This prediction proved to be accurate far beyond even the dreams of the Smith administration and the Alumni Association.

The Alumni Memorial Gymnasium, which cost $250,000 when completed and equipped, was dedicated on December 2, 1950, to the memory "of the known Elon alumni, who fell in battle," in World Wars I and II. A highlight of the ceremony was the gift from the class of 1950 of a bronze plaque inscribed with the names of these men and women. Presented by Richard Painter, the class president, it was accepted by Dr. Smith and was later mounted on the wall of the foyer of the main entrance.[10] An addition to the occasion was a basketball game with the North Carolina "Tar Heels." Although Elon lost by a score of 48 to 57, it was a creditable performance against one of the outstanding teams in the state.[11]

The spacious new building was not only used for athletic purposes, but for many functions that could not be accommodated in Whitley Auditorium. These included concerts by the North Carolina Symphony for the school children of the county; the Antiques Fairs sponsored by the Alamance-Caswell Medical Auxiliary; and, later, college convocations and commencements. The gymnasium was and is not only the pride of the college, but has also served as a notable addition to the educational and cultural facilities of Alamance County and the surrounding area of the state.

Darden retired as alumni secretary in 1951. The gym had been completed, a new alumni directory published, and numerous minor undertakings completed during his administration.[12] The office was then filled from 1951 to 1953 by C. Carl Woods (Elon '51), and from 1954 to 1956 by Mrs. Ruth G. Boyd (nee Lily Ruth Gamble, Elon '35). No spectacular project was under way at the time, but additional alumni chapters were organized in various areas, and general enthusiasm was maintained at a high level. In 1957 William B. Terrell (Elon '25), who had been serving as a teacher and principal in the state educational system, was chosen for the office.[13]

Relations between "Town and Gown" were cooperative during the period. In 1943 the college contributed $15,000 to the cost of a new municipal sewer system, and in 1954 the town was thanked for installing two automatic traffic lights on Haggard Avenue (State Highway 100).[14] The latter filled a real need because the once-quiet street had become a paved artery often congested with the increasing traf-

Alumni Memorial Gymnasium.

fic. Local and interstate bus lines had eclipsed the passenger trains, and private automobiles were rapidly replacing both. This posed a new problem for the town and the college: providing sufficient car parking spaces. Fortunately, because of available space, this situation did not become acute at the time.

Both the community and the institution lost some of its pioneer citizens and supporters during the Smith administration. In 1939 W. C. Wicker died; the following year, J. O. Atkinson; in 1942, J. U. Newman; in 1945, James L. Foster, Sr.; and the following year, John W. Patton.[15] Numerous others also passed from the earthly scene and left places that were filled with new names and new faces. As these changes in the ranks of citizens took place, the town, though growing slowly in size, tended to become modernized in keeping with the times, but serving as the seat of Elon College continued to be the primary reason for its existence.

Among student activities at the institution, numerous clubs were formed for members with a mutual interest, such as the French Club, the Spanish Club, the E Men's Club, and others. An attempt was made in the mid-1940s to revive the literary societies because the original ones had disbanded prior to World War II. The Dr. Johnson Literary Society for men and the Panvio Literary Society for women were organized, but they were of short duration. An abortive attempt was also made to found a society for men named in honor of war casualty Lloyd Whitley. Such organizations had seen their day and were gone forever from Elon's campus, as they were from most other colleges.[16]

Throughout his administration, President Smith never allowed his concentration on financial matters to blind him to the academic needs of the institution. A man who kept abreast of current trends, he was aware in advance of many of his officials that the universal change in conditions demanded alterations in the program of the liberal arts college. In 1941 he requested suggestions from the faculty "for making our courses more practical," and expressed the opinion, "we are fast becoming a teacher-training college."[17] Recalling trends after the first World War, Smith prophesied in 1944, "At Elon College we have always maintained a curriculum more extended than the regular liberal arts curriculum. . . . Out of this war will come a strong demand for a new emphasis upon and new additions to the usual college curriculum."[18] To meet this situation, he suggested short, practical courses in history, geography, science, business, aeronautics, architecture, manual arts, interior decorating, agriculture, dairying, and landscape gardening. Mechanics "could be added with profit."[19] He also proposed:

> More complete courses in home making, personal charm, music, dramatics, and art should be added to the cultural side of our curriculum. The demand of the future will not only be for efficiency in trades but for compelling personalities and convincing achievements in society.
>
> Our own constituency is demanding a greatly expanded curriculum in our Department of Bible and Religion. We need an instructor in Religious Education and another in rural church work.[20]

This statement to the trustees revealed Smith's concern for his church's future, a matter always uppermost in his mind while he made plans for extending the training advantages of students for occupations in secular fields.

As a result of the president's emphasis on practical education, in 1943 the trustees authorized the creation of adult courses in which citizens of the community and adjacent area could enroll either to audit the classes for their own information or to obtain college credits by taking the examinations. This proved to be a popular arrangement with the wives of the veterans, for it gave them an opportunity to study while their husbands were doing so. This program was arranged to suit the convenience of faculty and students by being conducted in the late afternoons and at night. A class lasting three hours met weekly for twelve weeks. Several faculty members, including Dr. William W. Sloan, of the Religion Department, were especially interested in fostering these courses. The offerings grew in popularity to such an extent that in 1949 the Faculty Adult Education Committee reported that four classes on Tuesday evenings and four on Thursday evenings were being conducted on the campus; and, as an extension service, two were being taught weekly in the town of Liberty, twenty miles away.[21]

While other changes were being made, one suggestion was that the requirement of four years of study for a degree might be compacted into three years. This proposal struck a discordant note with Smith, as he explained in a summary of the academic program to his trustees:

> Our curriculum at present includes a strong business department. A large per cent of our present student body is enrolled in this department. The majority of the veterans in the school are majoring in business administration. Business seems to be the most alluring field to the present generation. Teaching is not lucrative enough. The professions, such as law and medicine are too expensive in time and money for the average high school graduate. Even the youngster of today looks toward the future, "haste" becomes his watchword. The individual, however, who would be well-prepared for the responsibilities and opportunities of life must take sufficient time for preparation. A curriculum planned for the completion of the requirements for the bachelor's degree in thirty-six months is open to serious question.[22]

This statement sufficed to settle the matter permanently.

Satisfaction was widespread in 1946 when Elon College was restored to full membership in the Southern Association. This was a personal triumph for the president, who had never for a moment wavered in his efforts over the years against discouraging odds to regain this coveted status. Three years later, he was also able to announce proudly to his staff that Elon had been placed on the academically acceptable list of New York State University, which automatically carried the same rating for all institutions of higher learning in the Empire State.[23]

Inspired by the college's higher institutional rating, the administration redoubled its efforts to improve its program. The first problem on which it concentrated was excessive absence from classes. Because of the increasing number of private automobiles, many students left school early on Friday in order to make an early start on a weekend trip. Frequently their return was delayed and they missed a part or all of their Monday sessions. In addition, the campus population was so depleted at the end of each week that attendance at the cultural programs planned for those times became discouragingly low. The operation of the dining hall was also made more difficult inasmuch as the number of meals to be prepared became uncertain, which often caused an economic loss. Attempting to provide a remedy for this situation, in 1948–49, the administration restored the semester system. This was unpopular with both students and faculty, for it necessitated Saturday classes, but the attendance situation improved. Encouraged by this result, and with faith that it had become permanent, the administration restored the quarter system two years later.[24]

Another step taken was to arrange acceptance of applicants for enrollment who were satisfactorily prepared in "rithmetic," but too weak in "reading and ritin'." After much faculty debate, approval was voted for a course in remedial English for deficient students, without college credit. Each academic department was also granted permission to substitute the Graduate Record Examination, given periodically by the Princeton Testing Service, for the senior essay as a requirement for graduation. Another progressive step was a tightening in the system of faculty members advising students on their academic work. All these efforts were directed toward improving the educational benefits of the college.[25]

Significant changes were also taking place in the student body. In 1945 the two undergraduate governmental organizations, one for the men and another for the women, were combined into the Student Government Association of Elon College. The legislative authority was vested in the association as a whole, and judicial and executive powers were delegated to the Men's Senate and the Women's Council, respectively.[26] In 1948 the constitution was revised to place the legislative authority in the hands of a representative student congress, but no changes were made in the judicial and executive functions. Still not completely satisfied with the efficiency of its government, the following year the student body voted to revise it completely.

A committee of thirteen students was appointed to study the matter and draft a new constitution. The new instrument, ready in 1949, was adopted by the student body on April 26, approved by the faculty on May 2 and by the trustees on May 30. It provided for a Student Legislature composed of a specific number of elected representatives from each of the residence halls, Veterans' Apartments, and commuter day students. Judicial powers were vested in a Student Council, which possessed overall authority; an Honor Council to handle violations of the Honor System; and two Interdormitory

Councils, one for men and one for women, to rule on discipline in the residence halls. The executive powers were delegated to the president, vice-president, and secretary-treasurer of the student body. In addition, provisions were made for committees on dance, student entertainment, student orientation, and elections. Procedures were outlined for presenting petitions to the legislature, impeachment of officials, and amending the constitution. Financial support was to be obtained by assessing each student dues of fifty cents per quarter, payable before attending classes.[27]

The new bylaws authorized by the document also established the Honor System, which placed each student on his or her honor "not to cheat, steal or lie," and to report to the Honor Council any other student seen doing so. This provision eliminated monitored examinations. The instructor did not remain in the room after giving out test questions, and compliance by the student to the new rule was attested by the signing of a pledge at the end of the examination paper to the effect that he or she had not cheated nor seen anyone else doing so. Of course, this system was not perfect, but it was successful for the most part, and it proved to be one of the most useful means of building strong character and emphasizing the responsibility of the independent individual that had ever been attempted at Elon College. Its value was both emphasized and enhanced by the inclusion in the *Handbook* of a statement of proper conduct: "Under the Campus Code you are bound on your responsibility as a gentleman (lady) to conduct yourself as such at all times, and further see to it, insofar as possible, that your fellow students do likewise."[28] This constitution admirably served its purpose and was only amended in 1953 in order to increase the student dues to five dollars per year to provide the government with more money for its operation.[29]

The revised system was not only effective in improving morale, but also contributed to better relations between the students and the faculty. The change was acknowledged, in a sense, in 1957, when the faculty voted in favor of placing academic hoods over the shoulders of graduates at commencement to denote their earning a college degree. This practice was carried out, and Elon become one of the few colleges to use the time-honored symbol for B.A. and B.S. degrees. The hoods, trimmed in white and lined with maroon and gold, were attractive and popular. They enhanced the dignity with which the diploma was received, and for most students it was the only time they would ever wear the decorative colors to which they had earned title.[30]

The administration strove to recruit the best faculty members possible with the financial means at its disposal, and it was fortunate in the personnel it acquired. Besides academic qualifications, Dr. Smith only required that each belong to some evangelical church, and this presented no difficulty.[31] The individuals enjoyed ample opportunity to become well acquainted with each other because faculty meetings were held regularly and they were usually lengthy. Although no longer burdened with problems of discipline, the staff had other matters to decide in addition to hearing and discussing reports of the activities of its various members.

The proceedings were scrupulously recorded in proper detail by the faculty secretary, John F. West, of the English Department. The talented professor, who had won first prize in a state poetry contest and whose first book was published in 1951, was noted for his wit.[32] In rare instances, it was discernible in some humorous entry in his secretarial minutes, which relieved the tedium of some of the sessions when read for approval. "There was much throwing about of brains on whether we should wear academic dress on Founders Day," he wrote on one occasion, and continued, "After an hour of futile and prolix [sic] discussion, the argument died for want of a precedent."[33] The president, who liked academic regalia, probably decided the matter in the affirmative. An item on the agenda of another prolonged meeting was recorded in the same vein: "Dean Danieley and Dean Colley announced results of a meeting of some kind in Raleigh. They were so disinterested in the affair that I lost interest in their report and did not even get the name of it. Perhaps next time they will compile a mimeographed pamphlet for those interested in their extra-curricular activities."[34]

A third entry of the same type concerned the siren that served the college as a clock and was controlled by a mechanism in the Science Department:

> Dr. Sloan asked whether the siren could not be regulated so that class periods might be more consistent. His sincere question set off a chain-reaction discussion of the Fourth Dimension, during which Dean Hook explained the functions and

malfunctions of the chrono-mechanistic control center here at Elon. Implications were that the siren could not be improved upon, this century.[35]

Regardless of the secretary's pessimism, the siren was eventually adjusted and set forth its wailing notes with regularity for a number of years afterward.

In addition to other changes taking place, efforts were made to expand the services of the institution. In 1951 the Western Electric Company, of Burlington, employed 18 students to work in its plant from 4:20 P.M. until 1:10 A.M., and attend classes during the morning hours at Elon. All their college expenses were paid, and in addition each received $30 per month. Arrangements were also made for Western to send 20 of its men to the college for special study in the afternoons for five days weekly for six weeks. In 1952 this program was extended to accommodate 156 of the corporation's supervisors, who received three hours training daily for fifteen weeks. The institution was paid $50 for each of those enrolled.[36]

The Smith administration was confronted with a possible interruption of its plans for the continuing growth of Elon when the United States became involved in the Korean conflict. At the February 1951 meeting of the trustees, the president gloomily reported his apprehensions:

> War is threatening again. Young men are being called for defense. Elon students are volunteering. We have lost thirty-three boarding students since Christmas. We shall likely lose as many more at the end of this quarter, the first of March.
>
> Government officials tell us, as doubtless you have read in the papers, that we might as well prepare for not more than 50% of our student bodies for another college year. If this be the case, the situation at Elon will be tragic.[37]

At the meeting of the board in May, Smith presented concrete evidence of his cause for alarm, stating, "our present budget requires an income from 700 students." He then pointed out that the average enrollment for the year was 626, "which means that we have $51,800 less than the required amount from students to properly finance the college."[38] The college made adjustments to meet these disturbing conditions for two years, after which they were no longer necessary.

Fortunately, not only for Elon, but for the nation, the Korean conflict subsided in 1953, and enrollment immediately increased to a size sufficient to finance operations.

The conferring of honorary degrees continued to be a part of the college program. In 1946 Julian Price and Oscar F. Smith received D.B.S. degrees and D.D.'s were given to Robert S. Lambert and Stanley U. North. Two years later, John D. Messick was honored with a Litt.D., Albert Ray Van Cleave with a D.D., and Virginia's governor William M. Tuck with an LL.D. In 1949 North Carolina's governor, W. Kerr Scott, was given the LL.D. degree, Clyde C. Foushee the D.D. degree, and Lila Belle Pitts a D.Mus. degree. The following year, Ralph Bradford and Marvin E. Yount received LL.D. degrees; and D.D.'s were conferred upon Robert L. House, George W. Lawrence, Hiram E. Myers, and Arthur S. Wheelock. In 1951 LL.D. degrees were voted for J. Spencer Love, Frank L. Eversull, and Edward J. Bullock, and the D.D. for William W. Elder.

During the remainder of the Smith administration, D.D.'s were conferred upon Marvin L. Goslin, W. Millard Stevens, and Duane N. Vore, and a D.B.S. was voted for Harry L. Olden. Circumstances caused the latter to be deferred until 1953, when D.D.'s were conferred upon Chester Alexander, William L. Clegg, George G. Parker, Edward W. V. Lewis, and Henry E. Robinson, and a D.M. was given to David Barnett. In 1954 another Virginia governor, Mills E. Godwin, Jr., was honored with an LL.D. as was Aaron N. Meckel; and Edward E. Martz received a D.D. The following year, D.D.'s were given to James M. Hess and Lee R. Tuttle. In 1956 Congressman Walter H. Judd was honored with an LL.D. and George H. Shackley with a D.M. degree.[39]

The growing number of graduates posed a problem for the commencement program. The week-long festivities of earlier years had been gradually compressed into three days as time passed. On Saturday the alumni met and held their annual banquet. On Sunday morning the baccalaureate sermon was delivered, after which the afternoon and evening were devoted to musical programs and social gatherings. The graduation exercises were held on Monday. On that occasion, the president of the college presented the diplomas individually to each graduate, after which each was also given a Bible. The latter gift was contributed by the T. B. Dawson Memorial Bible Fund, established by the Dawson family.[40] While Smith was president, each received a copy of the King James version of the Scriptures, but the Danieley administration, in a spirit of tolerance, broadened the program by giving Catholics a version approved by their church and Jews a copy of the Talmud. When the ceremony was concluded, the graduates, their parents, and the faculty partook of a sumptuous lunch as guests of the college.

All these events held deep significance for both students and parents but were time-consuming and both the auditorium and the dining hall were becoming overcrowded. To relieve the situation without altering the details, in 1951 a second commencement was held in August at the conclusion of summer school. The thirty-six students who had completed their requirements during the summer session received their diplomas on this occasion, which became an annual event thereafter. This relieved the mounting congestion of the spring commencements.

The expanded activities of the institution also severely taxed the classroom space available during the day. They also offered no opportunity to those ambitious to attend college but who could not leave their employment to do so during the working hours of the day. To meet this need, in 1953 a night school was opened, separate and apart from the adult school already in operation. For five nights each week, various subjects from the curriculum were offered from 7 P.M. to 10 P.M. for the entire quarter. A class in each subject met once each week plus two or more additional meetings to make the required number of five weekly meetings, and each course was given for college credit.[41]

This extension of Elon's program spurred enrollment. The total rose from 705 students in 1953 to 1,070 in 1955, 312 of whom were in the evening school. The following year, the total rose to 1,168, of whom 663 were from Alamance County, 992 from North Carolina (including Alamance County), 89 from Virginia, and 87 from elsewhere.[42] As the total continued to rise, the trustees were reminded in 1956 that a decade earlier the board had set 1,000 students as the maximum enrollment for the college. Reluctant to lose what the institution was gaining, the board ruled that the maximum number only applied to day students and was not being broken. This clarification by the officials was satisfactory, and enrollment continued to climb.[43]

The result of this growth was that there were virtually two sections of faculty and students: those who taught and studied in the evenings and those who did so during the day. Activity continued almost around the clock, and lights blazed all night in the various buildings and on the campus, a far cry from the past, when the electricity had been cut off for the entire institution at eleven o'clock each night. As a result, Elon today has hundreds of alumni who could not have graduated without the advantage of attending classes in the evening school.

In 1952 the observance of Founders Day was revived, the fifth celebration of the occasion honoring former President Harper. A memorial tribute was delivered by the Reverend H. S. Hardcastle, and the principal address was made by United States Congressman Walter Judd. It also served as an appropriate time to launch a $2,500,000 fund drive for the college. The final commemorative Founders Day convocation under the Smith administration was held in 1955, honoring Howard B. Holmes, the first Elon faculty member to die in office. The Reverend W. Millard Stevens was selected for the memorial tribute, and Dr. Harold W. Tribble, president of Wake Forest University, for the principal address. One of the features of the program was laying the cornerstones for the McEwen Dining Hall, and two dormitories, Virginia and Carolina halls.[44]

The medals given as prizes during the early years of the college were no longer awarded annually because the funds necessary to pay for them were absorbed in the financial crisis during the depression, but scholarships continued to be added to Elon's resources. The William H. and John A. Trolinger Memorial Foundation was established by their descendents, Mrs. Isla Stratford May, and William H., John B., Parke C., and Robert E. Stratford "for the benefit of the College and worthy students of Alamance County who may attend Elon College." Mrs. Eunice E. Holland, of Suffolk, established the Christian Workers Conference Fund in memory of her husband, Colonel E. E. Holland, who was the last surviving member of the original board of Elon trustees. The income from this gift was to be used as a scholarship. The Mills and Mary Alice Luter Scholarship, created by the Luters, of Suffolk, was for the benefit of worthy students, preference being given to those from the Christian Orphanage. A fund honoring J. Pressley Barrett, a Christian minister, and another honoring E. L. Moffitt, were both to provide tuition for deserving freshmen. In addition, two student loan funds were established by J. A.

Clarke and M. A. McLeod, both former faculty members. All these funds were welcome benefits to many students to aid in paying for their college educations.[45]

The college was also assisted by financial gifts for other purposes. These included the fund in memory of Dr. J. L. Kernodle, proffered by his wife and daughter (Mrs. Attrice Kernodle Manson); the Ella V. Gray Memorial Fund donated by her son, Garland Gray; the fund given by Dr. W. H. Boone, chairman of the board of trustees, in memory of his wife, Annie Elizabeth Moring Boone; and the Oscar F. Smith Fund.[46]

Another financial transaction of importance originated in 1953 when the trustees voted to join twenty-three other privately endowed institutions in the state to form the North Carolina Foundation of Church-Related Colleges, Inc. The purpose of the corporation was to approach business and industry within the state for funds with which to supplement the current budgets of the member institutions. The plan for apportioning the money received was to allot 60 percent equally to the member colleges and 40 percent to them on the basis of enrollment. All funds handled by the foundation were to be used only for current expenses. Establishing this organization "would not prevent any school from approaching business and industry or anyone else for funds for capital improvements of any nature."[47]

Elon's president was appointed to serve as the institution's representative on the foundation, and in 1954 $1,003.00 was paid as the college's share of the initial organizational cost. As evidence of the immediate success of the corporation, the following year Elon received $3,023.46, "the largest amount" paid to any member college of the association. Following this fruitful beginning, the college received $5,514.68 for the academic year 1955–56, and for 1956–57, $10,398.03 for its proportionate share. Elon's membership was specially recognized in 1957 when two of its trustees, B. Everett Jordan and C. W. Gordon, were named by the foundation as honorary directors of the corporation. In the same year, Dr. Smith was replaced as the representative of the college by D. R. Fonville, a trustee, and W. E. Butler, Jr., the institution's business manager. The enterprise has continued to be financially beneficial to its affiliated colleges since its initial success.[48]

The growth of the institution's enrollment as a result of increased financial aid for students and a more flexible program soon brought the administration face to face with an acute housing shortage. Accommodations had simply not been expanded to correspond with a student population that had doubled in size. The facilities on the campus and in the Veterans' Apartments were filled to capacity. In addition, students were quartered in the old Bank Building and in several dwellings owned by the college, distinguished by such names as Cedar and Oak lodges and Carlton and Atkinson houses, but this solved only a minor part of the problem. The latter house was severely damaged by fire in 1949, which added to the gravity of the situation.[49] To inspire action on the part of the trustees, the president frankly told them, "To build a student body with contented and paying students who will remain on the campus until graduation, living conditions must be acceptable." Smith then added, "We need and must have, if possible, four new dormitories and a new dining room."[50] These needs were too urgent to wait for the results of a lengthy fund drive. The obvious solution was to borrow the neces-

Fire at the Atkinson House in 1949. The structure, located just south of the railway tracks, was then used for student housing.

sary money, proceed with construction, and repay the loan as contributions were received.

In agreement with this plan, the trustees authorized the president to seek construction funds. Smith then followed his most promising lead by applying to the federal government's Housing and Home Finance Agency for a $625,000 loan to be used for erecting new buildings and improving old ones. The negotiations that followed proved to be so involved with details that months lengthened into years before the agency rendered its decision. Finally,, the period of agonizing uncertainty ended in 1955 when the loan was approved, enabling the college administration to begin planning the details of the project.[51]

By means of the borrowed funds, in 1956 Virginia Hall, for women, was constructed on the site of the old West Dormitory Annex, and Carolina Hall, for men, on the eastern side of the campus. This program aroused a spirit of cooperation among the friends and supporters .of the college. The churches of the Southern Convention undertook the raising of $300,000 with which to repay the loan. The furnishings for the former were donated by Burlington Industries and for the

Professor J. E. Danieley, Mrs. Iris Holt McEwen, and President Smith at the laying of the cornerstone of McEwen Dining Hall in 1956.

latter by Dr. and Mrs. John R. Kernodle, of Burlington.[52] The generosity of Mrs. Iris H. McEwen, of Burlington, supplemented the building of the McEwen Dining Hall, named in memory of her husband, James H. McEwen, a former trustee of the college. This gift released a substantial part of the loan funds for use in renovating West Dormitory and other structures.[53] These additions to the physical plant facilitated operation of the institution, but still more room was needed.

For many years, the college had generously supplied the Southern Convention with space for its headquarters. In 1956 these offices were located in Ladies' Hall. When fire gutted the South Dormitory that year, the remnants of that building and the lot on which they stood were offered to the convention as a gift, provided the structure was rebuilt to serve as the organization's headquarters. The offer was emphasized by the announcement by the college that it could no longer supply office space on the campus. After consulting with engineers, the proposal was rejected by the convention as impractical for it, and the college then cleared the debris from the lot without any plans for its further use at the time.[54]

The loss of the building, small as it was, increased Elon's need for

Campus May Day fete in the 1950s.

another men's dormitory. Encouraged by the increasing donations to use in repaying its first governmental loan, the college applied for another in the amount of $250,000 to be used for construction. This was granted without the delay formerly encountered. A gift of brick worth $5,000 from James M. Cheshire (Elon '38), president of the Sanford Brick Company, aided the project, and the new building began to rise in 1957 on the eastern side of the campus.[55]

In the course of these transactions, it was noted that Elon's corporate charter had been encumbered with nine amendments. Control of the institution originally had been vested in the Christian Church, which ceased to exist as such in 1931 when it became a part of the Congregational-Christian Churches. The ninth amendment, enacted in 1945, made the proper change in the denomination's name and also specified that the thirty-six trustees should "be chosen from persons nominated by The Southern Convention of Congregational-Christian Churches or its legal successor, twenty-four of whom shall be members of the Congregational-Christian Church." This broadened the official board extensively because formerly all trustees were required to be members of the affiliated denomination. Because of the numerous changes, the instrument of authority had become unwieldy, and some of its provisions were in need of additional clarification. Under the circumstances, the trustees decided the best solution was to discard the old charter entirely and arrange for the writing of a new one. Thad Eure, who was both chairman of the board of trustees and North Carolina's secretary of state, drafted the new charter, which was adopted on March 24, 1956, without a dissenting vote by the college trustees.[56]

The really significant changes in the new constitution included the provision that "The name of the agent therein [of Elon College] and in charge thereof upon whom process against said corporation may be served is Dr. L. E. Smith, President, or his successors in office." This inclusion was probably the result of Smith's early experiences with the college finances and was intended to prevent some future misunderstanding. A more important addition was the specification that "the Corporation and the college that it owns and operates shall at all times be under the general control of the Southern Convention of Congregational-Christian Churches." This statement spelled out for the first time exactly who owned the institution and was responsible for its welfare. Another change was the method of electing the trustees:

> Those trustees in office on and after July 1, 1956, shall serve the terms for which they were elected. The Board shall at the expiration of such terms elect their successors for four year terms from persons certified to it as nominees of the Convention and any and all vacancies for any cause must be filled by the Board from persons so nominated."[57]

This made the officials virtually a self-perpetuating board.

The significance of the new charter was that it constituted a decisive step toward making Elon autonomous. In the future, the church would be related to the institution, but it would not be the denomination that owned the college. This was not an isolated revolutionary change, but similar to many taking place nationwide during the same period. Neither was a rebellion against religion indicated. The fact

Alamance Building, viewed from the south gate, in the mid-twentieth century.

was that many colleges were founded by churches no longer able to financially maintain the expanding institutions, which needed to seek assistance from other sources, and had to be autonomous to do so.

Because of the numerous projects completed or under way, Dr. Smith decided in 1954 as his seventieth birthday approached that it was time to turn the reins of Elon's administration over to a younger driver. When he broached the matter to his trustees, they prevailed upon him to retain the office until the building program was more nearly completed and a suitable successor for the presidential chair selected. He agreed to do so, and did not officially retire until June 30, 1957, after having been elected president emeritus of the college, the only Elon executive who had ever been honored with that title.[58]

In his final report upon leaving office, Smith called attention to the endowment of $680,000, which had increased from $231,000 the previous year, and to approximately $600,000 additional invested funds of the college. In summary, he reported:

> The student enrollment has increased to such an extent that to protect the accreditation of the college it is necessary to transfer most of the invested funds to the endowment fund. This will give a total of more than $1,200,000 invested from which we received last year a total of $40,537.13 for the support of the college, making a grand total of $81,051.13 for the support of the college, or 29.7% of the cost of operation and 70.3% from student tuition fees, room, rent, and board.[59]

A student body of 1,634 made it possible for the college to operate on a sound financial basis. This presented a striking contrast to the situation existing when Smith had taken office.

Shortly before he retired, Smith was privileged to assist in dedicating the new Church History Room in the library. This was an attainment long dear to his heart. In 1936 the Southern Convention had designated Elon College as the official custodian of its historical records. This action was attributable largely to the efforts of Wilbur E. MacClenny (Elon '97), the convention historian.[60] Following this action, material was sent to the college, where it was stored in a room known as the Church History Room in the Carlton Library Building, but no arrangements were made to classify and display the data.

After this initial move, years rolled by with no further action. Exasperated by this neglect, in 1952 the librarian, Mrs. Oma U. Johnson, personally appeared before the Southern Convention to register a complaint:

> The Church History Room, although a prized part of the College Library, should be a great strength and a prized possession of the entire denomination, and especially of the Southern

James M. Waggoner (Elon '55), editor of the Maroon and Gold, *and the college printing press.*

Convention. To become what it should and could, it will be necessary for the Convention to lend its sponsorship and aid.

Immediate Needs—Filing cabinets, book cases, and display cases for storage; Lesser items such as folders, envelopes, mending material, catalog material, etc.; a part-time custodian, who should be a person who is both vitally interested and familiar with the church and Convention. The duties of this person would be to acquire a copy of all publications of the denomination, of the programs of all important church meetings, all printed books and pamphlets about church leaders, watch the newspapers for church items of permanent value, classify and file all material, and prepare a catalog of it.

In its present condition, the material in the Church History Room is not adequately preserved, and in almost no order.[61]

This plea obtained no response until 1955, when the Woman's Convention of the church voted financial support for the project. This inspired the organization of the Historical Society of the Southern Convention the following year to assist the women in their endeavor. The organization appointed a committee composed of Mrs. Johnson, Mrs. William W. Sellers, and convention Superintendent William T. Scott to coordinate the effort. As a result of this revived interest, the room was properly furnished and equipped. Mrs. Johnson was named custodian to catalog the priceless material contained in the collection, and on May 12, 1957, the new room was officially dedicated. Because of the expertise and dedication of the custodian, and the assistance of others, the collection soon became available for reference and research, thereby fulfilling the purpose for which it was intended.[62]

As a parting gesture to the president, the trustees named the men's dormitory then under construction the Leon Edgar Smith Hall; and Smith's portrait, a striking likeness, was hung in Whitley Auditorium opposite that of his predecessor, Dr. Harper. A scholarship was also established in Smith's honor by an initial gift from John T. Kernodle, of Richmond, Virginia. Additional contributions were later made to the fund, the income from which is used for the aid of worthy students. Mrs. Smith was complimented by the Elon College Garden Club, which planted a maple tree in her honor near the western gate of the campus.[63]

Upon retirement, the Smiths moved to Virginia, where their fifty-three years of married life ended in 1965 with the death of Mrs. Smith. As a fitting tribute to her memory, her husband established the Ella Brunk Smith Memorial Fund, the income from which was to "provide a cash award each year to the young lady who, in the judgment of the faculty upon recommendation of the Department of Religion, has made the greatest contribution to the moral and religious life of the campus."[64]

Later, the president emeritus married Mrs. Muriel C. Tuck, and resided in Virgilina, Virginia. Even in his retirement, he frequently visited Elon and attended meetings of the trustees, church conferences, and other functions until advancing age curtailed his traveling. Despite this handicap, his concern for the institution's welfare and progress continued to be his primary interest. He passed away on August 19, 1975, at the age of 90, just three weeks after the death of his second wife. His funeral was conducted in Whitley Auditorium, and he lies at rest in Elon's Magnolia Cemetery.[65]

L. E. Smith served a longer term than any other president of Elon College, and his achievements were phenomenal. He restored the college to financial stability from impending bankruptcy, doubled the size of its physical plant while improving it throughout, and more than trebled the extent of all its activities. At their meeting on May 27, 1957, the trustees paid him the following tribute:

> With vision, courage and rare ability, coupled with an enthusiastic loyalty to this college and to the cause of Christian Education, Dr. Smith set about his task with vigor and energy which has lasted until this day. He faced every challenge and made of it an opportunity. His disappointments led to new avenues of service. With faith in God, the future beckoned him on. He chartered his course, set his sights and diligently pursued his goals. Because of him, the history of Elon College gives us all ample reason to be proud. Its present strength and character hold much promise for the years ahead.[66]

CHAPTER XII

THE EXPANDING SHADE

The kindliest thing God ever made,
His hand of very healing laid
Upon a fevered world, is shade.
THEODOSIA GARRISON
Shade

During the last year of Smith's administration, the search by the trustees for a new executive culminated with election of Dean of the College James Earl Danieley. The sixth president was a native of northern Alamance County, born July 28, 1924, the son of Henry Hubbard and Grace Elizabeth Mansfield Danieley. After spending his youth on his parents' farm, he attended Altamahaw-Ossipee High School, then graduated from Elon College in 1946, and was immediately employed by his alma mater to teach chemistry. During a leave of absence from faculty duties, extending from June 1950 through the fall term of 1952, and by summer studies, the young instructor earned two graduate degrees, the M.A. in 1949 and the Ph.D. in 1954, from the University of North Carolina, at Chapel Hill. In 1953 he was made Acting Dean of Elon College, and the following year was confirmed in the position permanently. In addition to his administrative duties, he continued to teach chemistry, and was on leave for postgraduate studies in that field at Johns Hopkins University, in Baltimore, when elected to the presidency.[1]

In 1948 Danieley married Verona Daniels, of Beaufort, North Carolina, an Elon student who had served as Dr. Smith's secretary since 1941. After graduating from the college the following year, Mrs. Danieley taught Spanish at Elon College High School for one term. While her husband was in graduate school at Chapel Hill, she was employed by Vernon Crook, the university's business manager for athletics. At the time the dean became the institution's president, the couple had two children, Ned, named for his godfather, Professor N. F. Brannock, and Mark. Later, the family was increased by the birth of a daughter, Jane.[2]

The new executive was a tall man of large frame, in the pink of physical condition. His youthful appearance was not modified in the least by his thin hair, a forerunner of baldness within a few years. His frequent broad smiles and hearty laughter demonstrated a jovial disposition, which enabled him to conduct even the most serious business as a pleasant experience rather than a gloomy transaction. Reared on a farm, he was an expert horticulturist, as evidenced by his productive flower and vegetable gardens.

After their marriage in 1948, both Danieleys changed their membership from the Methodist Episcopal Church to the Congregational-Christian Churches. The young professor rapidly rose to prominence by becoming a deacon in 1949, then was elected chairman of the Laymen's Fellowship of the Southern Convention and a member of the board of directors. Subsequently, he became president of the National Laymen's Fellowships, in addition to serving on various denominational committees. When the United Church of Christ was formed, Danieley served as the first chairman of the newly established Council on Lay Life and Work for two two-year terms.[3]

Dr. Danieley was adequately prepared physically, intellectually, and spiritually for the responsibility he undertook when he became one of the youngest college presidents in the country at the age of thirty-two. He also possessed an advantage none of his predecessors had enjoyed. Because of the relatively brief period between his undergraduate days and his elevation to the executive chair, he had participated in the college program within recent years both as a student and faculty member. This gave him a fresh and intimate awareness of the attitudes of both students and teachers, as well as an understanding of their strengths and weaknesses. This knowledge proved to be an invaluable asset as he administered his multitudinous duties.

The young executive was fully aware of his responsibilities. "The presidency of a college is not a position, but a calling," he stated.[4] Recognizing this concept and expressing his devout religious beliefs,

President J. Earl Danieley.

his first act upon taking office on the morning of July 1, 1957, was to request divine guidance for his administration. This was done in a public prayer service, afterward observed each year Danieley held the presidential office.

On that summer morning, the "Service of Prayer and Meditation" in Whitley Auditorium was attended by approximately 250 people. Professor John Westmoreland played the organ for the occasion, special music was rendered by a double quartet of students, and the entire congregation joined in the singing of the hymns. As planned by Danieley, the Reverend William J. Andes, minister of the Community Church, conducted the litany, "For Our College and All of Its Life." He invoked divine blessing not only for the president, but also for the faculty, students, and all phases of the institution's life. On behalf of the board of trustees, Chairman Thad Eure spoke briefly on "The Assurance of Our Help."

After the program was concluded, Eure and Andes, joined by D. R. Fonville, secretary of the board of trustees, A. L. Hook, Dean of the Faculty, Jerry Loy, president of the 1957–58 student body, Martin Garren, president of the Southern Convention, and William B. Terrell, executive secretary of the Alumni Association, escorted Danieley to his office, where he began his presidential duties. No president of the college has ever begun his term of office under more solemn and dignified circumstances nor viewed his task with a more serious sense of responsibility.[5]

A college president always has his problems, and Danieley had his share. However, those encountered during the early years of his administration were the problems of a smooth operation and not those of a crisis or impending disaster. This enabled him to contemplate the needs of the entire college program without needing to concentrate on one demanding segment. At the same time, though the institution was enjoying a comfortable financial status, it was not sufficiently affluent to speculate in expensive experimentation or reckless expansion. Its resources had to be carefully safeguarded, and its income nurtured for its progress to continue. Danieley knew this, and proved to be a good watchdog, but he was also ambitious to supply the needs of the college. He, therefore, made both the objectives of his administration: expansion and debt control. Fully aware that the college required a steady annual enrollment of new students, he believed one way to attract them would be to provide more individual benefits for those already studying at Elon. This gave him a third objective: greater growth of the individual. The first president of the college in a quarter of a century who was also a teacher, he experienced no trouble deciding where to begin.

In Elon's early years, most of the male students had enrolled to study for a profession and the females to become either teachers or cultured housewives. This was not entirely the case in 1957, when many attended college simply because they were financially able to do so and entertained few, if any, preconceived plans for the use of their education after it was acquired. Danieley also realized that entering college was a traumatic experience for many students because they became part of a different environment from that to which they had been accustomed. Many needed assistance in making decisions that would vitally affect their careers, and some needed a helping hand when a stumbling block was occasionally encountered. To assist the aimless prepare for some special work after graduation and to mature properly while in school, the president moved to make individual counseling a basic part of the college program. This service began immediately, and Dr. C. Robert Benson was employed as professor of education and freshman counselor, beginning with the 1957 fall term.[6]

The new faculty member, then in his mid-thirties, was a native of Rowan County. After graduating from Catawba College, Salisbury, North Carolina, he had earned both the M.A. and Ph.D. degrees from the University of North Carolina.[7] He served as principal of the Graham High School, where he assisted with the athletic coaching program, until 1953. He was then connected with the Winston-Salem school system until he came to Elon.

Benson was not only qualified academically, but was also familiar with the local area, young students in general, and athletes in particular. At this first faculty meeting, he explained that his function as counselor was not to replace other officials, such as the Dean of Men and the Dean of Women, nor to assume their duties, but to plan a more detailed system of guidance for individual students. This would begin with the assignment to each faculty member of a list of students to advise. Meetings were then to be scheduled between the advisers and their groups, at which time "each faculty member should convince his advisees that he is a person they can come to for help and advice."[8]

The counselor then made it clear that the extended guidance system was to include general counseling for individuals, in addition to academic advice:

> Dr. Benson said further that all faculty members are advisors at all times, whether they realize it or not. He said that Elon College is much larger than the schools most of them [the students] come from, and that they are away from home for the first time and they need security.
>
> He said that these students are going to be guided in the next few months, if not by the faculty, then by the wrong kind of outside acquaintances.[9]

This explained the enlarged duties of the staff and the increased concern of the administration for the college student body.

In conjunction with the guidance program, an effort was made to assist graduates who had become interested in specific vocations find situations suitable for their qualifications. Although the college had never assumed the responsibility of obtaining employment for its students after graduation, it had always been concerned about their future, though assistance in that respect had been primarily confined to the efforts of individual faculty members. This changed in 1957, when the Placement Service was opened under the supervision of Professor Hook.[10] Although the institution still did not become responsible for finding jobs for its graduates, every possible effort was exerted to do so. Arrangements were made with commercial and industrial organizations as well as with the government, to send their representatives to the campus to discuss employment opportunities in personal interviews with the students. The army, navy, marines, and air force also took advantage of this opportunity to seek recruits. The immediate success of this plan was summarized in 1961 by the president:

> One of the genuine satisfactions we as faculty members experience is the knowledge that our graduates are having no difficulty in finding desirable employment or opportunities for further study. Toward this end we have expanded our placement office and are now offering this service to all our graduates. We are also spending more time and effort in helping our students to obtain assistance for graduate study.[11]

With this statement, the Placement Office became a permanent part of the college operation.

After serving a year as counselor, Benson was elevated to the office of Dean of Students, in which he continued to oversee the entire guidance program. His accomplishments did not pass unnoticed by

West Dormitory in the 1950s.

other institutions, for he left Elon in 1961 to assume broader college administrative responsibilities elsewhere.[12] He was succeeded by Dr. Hook for a short period until the program's phases were combined under the direction of Alfred S. Hassell (Elon '57), former registrar, who became Dean of Student Personnel Services.[13] Hook then returned to his cherished science classes.

Shortly after Danieley became president, Horace H. Cunningham, who had served as chairman of the Department of Social Science and professor of history for several years, was appointed as Dean of the College. His undergraduate training had been at Atlantic Christian College, "a liberal-arts church college," and he brought to his new office a "thorough grounding in that tradition."[14] He had risen to the rank of captain in the army during World War II, prior to completing a doctor's degree in history. The new official was both an outstanding scholar and an efficient administrator. Sympathetic with the counseling program, he cooperated in every manner possible to foster it. Furthermore, he championed more explicit requirements both for enrolling and earning a degree at Elon.

For a number of years, freshmen had been required to attend an orientation program at the beginning of the fall term. During that brief period, they were given tours of the campus, briefed on the college system, and presented with a copy of the *Student Handbook*. This booklet contained the constitution and bylaws of the Student Government Association, various regulations, and other information applicable to students. Also, during the fall quarter, they were required to attend short classes twice each week, at which time further instruction was given in such subjects as rules, regulations, study habits, and recreational opportunities. Each student received a quarter of an hour of college credit for this course.[15]

In 1957 the entire introductory program, including the classes formerly required, was combined into Freshmen Orientation Week. At the end of the period, the new undergraduates were required to pass a test on the contents of the *Student Handbook*.[16] This prevented many future cases of students pleading ignorance of the rules when one was broken. During the week, provisions were also made for the faculty to conduct tests in mathematics and English to determine whether or not the students were properly prepared in either of these subjects to meet Elon's standards. If a deficiency were revealed by this method, the student needed to take a noncredit remedial course in the subject. An example of such a course was remedial reading, opened in 1948.[17] These methods helped to solve problems of qualification and classification.

During orientation, the freshmen were also required to don maroon and gold caps, or "beanies," and wear them until the second football game of the season was won, or until Homecoming Day, whichever was first. Because the headgear had to be purchased from the Student Government Association, the treasury of that organization was boosted. Later, October 1 was set as the terminal date for wearing the caps, but after 1973 the regulation was rescinded.[18]

The indoctrination period was also concurrent with another new feature, Freshmen Religious Orientation Week. The Reverend George Alley, minister of the Suffolk (Virginia) Christian Church and a trustee of the college, served as the first "visiting resource leader" for this new program. It has been described in detail:

> A meeting was held with the faculty on Sunday evening, September 15, at which time Dr. Alley spoke. A discussion period and a social hour followed. During the week of September 16–20, Dr. Alley spoke to the day class freshmen at 10:10 a.m. each day. The same service was held for the evening class freshmen at 7:00 p.m. In addition to these services, he met with each of the ten sections of the freshman orientation and held discussion groups in the parlor of West Dormitory in the evenings. He was available during afternoon hours for conferences with students.[19]

It was the consensus of the opinions of both faculty and students that the week was "exceptionally helpful," which for awhile inspired plans to repeat the program annually.

As a result of Cunningham's recommendations, which were approved by President Danieley and the faculty, in 1959 Elon began using a national testing service to screen prospective students and evaluate the progress of those admitted to the institution. The rule was adopted that scores of the Scholastic Aptitude Test (SAT) of the College Entrance Examination Board must be submitted by all applicants for admission to the college. The ruling also stipulated, "Through satisfactory achievement in Advanced Placement tests, freshmen may receive a limited amount of credit in advanced placement in the following fields: biology, chemistry, English, history,

Latin, mathematics and physics." This was a distinct advantage to graduates of high schools that featured a wide range of curricula, and prevented an unnecessary duplication of study in many cases. The following year, the College Entrance Examination was made a universal requirement of all applicants for admission, and became one criterion for calculating predicted grade-point average, which was the basis for enrollment at the college. This made testing during orientation no longer necessary.[20]

As a requirement for graduation, a senior had to take either a comprehensive examination or write an acceptable essay on his major subject. In 1957 this rule was amended to permit the substitution of the Graduate Record Examination for the former requirement, if the professor in the student's major subject approved. However, regardless of individual or departmental preference, the faculty voted that all seniors must take the examination "during the last quarter of study before graduation." The results of the testing were then used in the counseling program of the major department involved, the dean's office, and the Placement Office.[21]

The next step in enhancing scholastic achievement was the authorization by the administration of a Faculty Committee on Academic Standing. This was established in response to the following recommendation from Dean Cunningham:

> The College expects all students to maintain normal academic progress toward graduation. This means that at least a "C" average is necessary to satisfy its academic requirements. Students falling below a "C" average in any term will have their records reviewed by the Committee on Academic Standing. Such Committee . . . may either warn or place these students on academic probation.
>
> Students on academic probation will be expected to achieve a term average of "C" in two probationary terms. Those making satisfactory progress will be removed from probation by action of the Committee on Academic Standing. On the other hand, those whose work fails to show adequate improvement will be asked to discontinue their studies.
>
> Students who are dropped for failure to maintain normal academic progress are not eligible to be considered for reinstatement until one academic term has elapsed. Requests for

reinstatement will be considered by the Committee on Academic Standing.

Students and their parents are notified officially when the former are placed on probation, continued on probation, and removed from probation.[22]

In addition to the dean, faculty appointed to serve on this important committee included Dr. Ferris E. Reynolds and Professors William T. Reece, John D. Sanford, and Paul S. Reddish.

To coordinate this rating system, uniformity was necessary. Dr. Danieley complained that the use of the semester system in the night school and the quarter system for the day classes caused considerable confusion. In response to his request, the board of trustees voted for the entire college to use the six-day semester system beginning September 1, 1959.[23] Also, the same year, by vote of the trustees, the summer commencements, which had never been more than one-day affairs, were moved from Whitley Auditorium to the Community Church. The baccalaureate sermon was delivered in the morning, and the graduation exercises held in the afternoon. Because the church was air conditioned and the auditorium was not, this was a popular move for all concerned with the August event.[24]

The Danieley administration also introduced a new phase in the religious life of the college. Although he was not an ordained clergyman, he was as concerned for the spiritual welfare of the students as any of his predecessors had been. Two courses in religion were required of all undergraduates, and attendance at religious chapel two times each week was mandatory. Feeling that this kind of regimentation did little to touch the private life of each student, the president sought to provide spiritual guidance for the individual by appointing a college chaplain, or campus minister. In 1960 the Reverend John S. Graves (Elon '50) was chosen for this responsibility, which was added to his duties as Professor of Religious Education.[25]

The appointee could hardly have been more wisely selected. An energetic bachelor, who possessed an almost unbelievably cheerful disposition, the popular "Reverend Johnny" knew everyone—students, faculty, townspeople—and was accepted by all. He responded promptly to any call, no matter what the hour or how great the inconvenience. His love of humanity was sincere and encompassing, but the students were his primary concern. He counseled the per-

The Reverend John S. Graves, college chaplain for many years.

plexed, comforted the troubled, admonished the slothful, encouraged the weak, praised the industrious, and prayed for everyone. In case of a death, he made the necessary arrangements and often traveled to the funeral, regardless of the distance or personal sacrifice involved. His efforts left an indelible mark on those who knew him because he used his divine calling to make life happier and more spiritually abundant for Elon students.[26]

To further the Danieley program, it was necessary to retain a competent faculty and an efficient staff. To assist in doing so, additional fringe benefits were devised for the college employees. At a 1958 meeting, the trustees approved a group hospital insurance plan with the Home Life Insurance Company, of New York, in which 40 percent of the premium for each staff member would be paid by the institution and 60 percent by the individual. This was a popular opportunity for protection at a relatively low cost, which was to prove a major financial asset to many of those covered by its provisions.[27]

The president was quite concerned over the college retirement plan then in effect because it was not funded, which meant that payment could not be guaranteed. Under his leadership, on October 7, 1959, the trustees approved an arrangement with the nationally known Teachers Insurance and Annuities Association. The plan's specifications and the accompanying option were then announced:

> Those employed prior to September 1, 1958, who choose to remain under the plan of retirement then in effect may do so; those employed prior to September 1, 1958, who choose to join the TIAA plan contributing 3% of their salary, may do so; Elon College will contribute 6% in those cases with the express agreement that the retirement pay received from TIAA which has been purchased by contributions by the College will be added to the amount the person received from social security and from Elon College to give the "one-half salary amount" guaranteed by the plan to such persons upon retirement; and, persons who were employed by the College after September 1, 1958, may join the TIAA plan after one year of service (except where, because of rank, immediate participation has been made an agreed upon condition of employment); participation is required after completion of 3 years of service and attainment of age 30.[28]

This arrangement removed the shadow of uncertainty from the minds of the college officials, and proved to be satisfactory to most employees.

The total enrollment at the college in 1962 was 1,259 students, 1,015 in the day classes and 244 in the evening. The faculty serving full time was composed of 47 men and 14 women. Their average age was approximately 41 years, and 16 of them were Elon graduates. Faculty salaries had advanced from an average of $4,257 in 1957 to $5,279. Several of the staff had served the institution for a lengthy period, including Dr. Hook, since 1914; Miss Lila C. Newman, since 1924; Professor C. Fletcher Moore, since 1934; Professors P. S. Reddish and Luther N. Byrd since 1945; President Danieley, Professors Ferris E. Reynolds and J. C. Colley and Business Manager W. E. Butler, Jr., all since 1946. The President, Dean, Director of Develop-

North Dormitory, on the site of the present Powell Building, being razed in 1958. President Danieley is standing at the corner of the building.

ment, Director of Student Personnel Services, Business Manager, and Registrar were all Elon graduates. Together they formed the nucleus of a happy group who loved their alma mater and bent every effort to accelerate her progress.[29]

To assist the president in procuring funds, in 1960, the Development Office was established. Its first director was Robert C. Baxter (Elon '56).[30] Equipped with a law degree from Duke University, the new official was an excellent choice because he was able to advise many prospective donors about the legal aspects of gifts in addition to performing legal services for the college. Shortly after he entered upon his duties, Dr. William T. Scott, the retired superintendent of the Southern Christian Convention, was appointed as Director of Church Relations, to solicit financial support from individuals and churches of the affiliated denomination. By action of the trustees in 1958, the title of Field Secretary was changed to Admissions Counselor. Samuel L. Webster, Jr., who had followed Roger Gibbs in the office, resigned the next year and was succeeded by William R. Ginn, who filled the post for several years.[31]

Danieley no more escaped Elon's old bugaboo, fire, than did his presidential predecessors. On December 15, 1958, a blaze was discovered in the chapel of the Mooney Building. Another occurred in the same room on January 10, 1959. According to the insurance settlement, the damage for both amounted to $13,860.40. It was indeed fortunate that the entire structure was not burned. Arson was strongly suspected, but never proved, though a student left the college as a result of the unhappy incident.[32]

Following the first Mooney fire, the administration began extensive changes in the physical plant. Because no practical use had been found for the former Publishing House building, its charred remains were removed, and the adjacent former Bank Building was rented to the Vikon Chemical Company, a local commercial enterprise. The Club House was sold in 1958 for $100, and, after the buyer removed the structure, the site was used for a parking lot.[33] North Dormitory (old gymnasium), considered too dilapidated for further renovation, was demolished in 1959. The following year, Ladies' Hall met the same fate for the same reason.[34] Financial arrangements were then begun to construct New Dormitory for women on its site. The first floor was completed by November and temporarily roofed over. A gift of more than $100,000 from Dr. and Mrs. William W. Sloan, anonymous at the time, made possible addition of the second and third floors the following summer. The building was later renamed Sloan Dormitory in honor of the principal contributors to its construction.[35]

In return for a lot in College Park as a site for a new parsonage, the Community Church gave its old one to the college, and the house was moved from the corner of Williamson and Haggard avenues to 106 West College Avenue. It was converted into the college Home Economics Demonstration House, including living quarters for an instructor and several students majoring in home economics. The faculty member in charge of the function was Mrs. Mary G. Butler until 1962, when she was succeeded by Miss Edith Brannock. After the Demonstration House was moved from its former location in Cedar Lodge, the latter was equipped to serve as the College Infirmary.[36] Dr. Robert Watson moved his office from the Carlton House

Ladies' Hall. Sloan Dormitory now occupies the site. Photo by Professor A. L. Hook.

to the new facility, which he shared with Dr. Philip R. Mann (Elon '54). Plans were also made to remodel East Dormitory and lay a new floor in the Alumni Gymnasium.[37]

The first floor of the Mooney Building was converted into a Student Union, in which the snack shop was operated by Slater Food Service. This organization had also been placed in charge of the dining hall in an effort to improve efficiency. However, this change was not made smoothly. The first manager, Miss Helene M. Urban, and her assistant, Miss Hannelore Schwarzenbach, were technically trained to use cooking measurements with precision, and the Slater employees were not. Because the latter made no progress in adapting to the new method, the quality of the food began to decline and much of it was unpalatable. This state of affairs could not, and did not, exist very long because the students rose in revolt. Presenting a show of force never before exhibited by the undergraduates at the college, they marched to the West End Building, where the president lived at the time, to register their complaints. By the cooperation of Burlington police, under Chief Alfred Garner, with the local authorities, order was maintained; results were obtained overnight, and, under the new manager, John C. Wells, the food improved immediately. Of course, the students growled about the fare as they probably always will, but their criticism was no longer serious. The college also received favorable publicity in the area because its dining hall became a popular place for civic clubs and similar organizations to hold luncheon and dinner meetings. The student waiters were "well organized in providing alert service," according to Editor Howard White of Burlington's *Times-News*, and "the meals are outstanding."[38] Catering to outside organizations as a sideline also financially benefited the institution.

The old emergency Dining Hall next to Mooney then provided a triple service because its three sections were used to accommodate faculty offices; a men's dormitory; and the printing press, which had been located in the Mooney Building. The boisterous antics of the male residents in their part of the building occasionally disturbed the relative calm of the professorial sanctums; and, when the press was in operation, it shook the entire structure to the accompaniment of a thunderous roar. But the occupants were happy, for they anticipated better quarters in the near future.[39]

Elon's Alumni Association continued to support the administration's program loyally. Homecoming Days, Parents Days, Founders Days, and commencements were usually attended by a representative number of association members. Among the many sons and daughters of the college making meritorious progress in their careers, one in particular achieved a distinction that reflected credit on his alma mater. Colonel James S. Cook, Jr., a native of Graham (Elon '37), was serving as chief of the Heraldic Branch, Office of the Army Quartermaster General, in Washington, in 1959, when Alaska became a state. It was his responsibility to submit the designs for the new forty-nine-star national flag to President Dwight D. Eisenhower for his selection. After the choice was made, Cook assisted in raising the chosen banner on the White House flagpole. Within a few months, Hawaii was granted statehood, and the colonel repeated the process, but with the fifty-star flag. These performances earned a citation from the president for the colonel's "work related to the designing and adoption" of the two flags.[40] Elon College is pardonably proud that one of her sons played such an intimate part in the design of the flag that flies over the nation today and of its immediate predecessor.

During the later years of the Smith administration, the trustees occasionally discussed providing a more suitable home for the college president, but no action was taken. The subject was revived in 1961, when the time seemed favorable to proceed with the project. A committee composed of Mrs. J. H. McEwen, George Colclough, and Royall Spence was appointed by the board to work with Vernon E. Lewis, the architect, and Dr. Danieley in planning the house. The following spring, the trustees voted to remove the old Carlton House from the corner of Haggard and O'Kelley avenues and use that site for the structure. On February 2, 1963, the contract was let for construction, which began immediately, and the Danieleys moved into their new home in August.[41]

The two-story brick residence, which featured tall columns at its front entrance, was designed to harmonize with the architecture of the other college buildings and made an imposing addition to the town. In addition to the private quarters for the family, ample room was available for formal entertaining and accommodations for a few overnight guests. The attractively landscaped grounds, by a vigorous application of the president's "green thumb," soon contained a rose garden that lured many visitors to admire its beauty. The college was

justly proud of the first official home it had provided for its chief executive, and its first occupant thoroughly enjoyed being its tenant.

While the building program was under way, an extremely important academic matter required attention. The Southern Association
of Colleges announced a new method of rating its members. Once in
each ten years, an Evaluation Committee would be sent to inspect
the institution and report its findings. Prior to its visit, a detailed
self-study had to be made of the college's entire operation and several copies sent to the organization's headquarters. This posed a formidable task for a new executive who lacked any precedent for guidance, but Danieley determined Elon's valuable membership in the
organization would not be jeopardized because of the exacting new
requirements. He cannily requested that the college evaluation take
place early in the ten-year period of visitations. The request was
promptly granted. Authority was given to begin compiling the self-
study record on October 8, 1958, with the understanding that by
November 1960 it would be completed and all in readiness for the
committee's visit.

Official home of the college president.

To serve with him as a steering committee for the project, the president appointed Deans Cunningham and Benson as well as Professors C. Fletcher Moore, William T. Reece, Arnold C. Strauch, and Mrs. Frances Longest. Arrangements were also made for Dr. Guy Snavely, executive director emeritus of the American Association of Colleges, and Dr. Goodrich White, chancellor of Emory University, to serve as consultants during visits to the college.[42] This proved to be a wise move because these experts rendered valuable assistance in the undertaking.

Within the allotted time, the grueling task of making the study was completed; and in February 1961 the Evaluation Committee members, under the chairmanship of Gus E. Metz, assistant to the president of Clemson College, South Carolina, arrived at Elon. Several days were then filled with conferences, meetings, interviews, and various inspections. The committee was pleased to find that the teaching load did not exceed sixteen hours per faculty member, in accordance with the association's rules, but strongly advocated an increased number of higher academic degrees among the faculty. This criticism particularly applied to doctor's degrees. Although the overall salary average had increased 19 percent since 1949, the remuneration was still considered too low by the evaluators. They also concluded that additions to the library were imperative to properly serve the needs of the increased enrollment. The committee also recommended that the interiors of several buildings be redecorated, and advised better police protection for the institution. These improvements were all to be completed before the next decennial evaluation. The general consensus of the inspectors was that Elon was progressing favorably. The ordeal ended with the result that the college retained its accreditation for another ten years as a member in good standing of the association.[43]

After the committee departed, no time was lost in acting upon its suggestions. One of Danieley's first acts as president had been to pay the Globe-Wernicke Company $11,973.00 to complete the stacks on the library's upper level. In 1960 Dr. Susan G. Akers, dean emeritus of the School of Library Science of the University of North Carolina, had been employed to serve one day each week as a consultant. At the close of the next year, Theodore E. Perkins, the librarian, reported a total of 54,489 volumes in the collection, 1,403 acquired by purchase, 716 by gift, and 367 by binding. Phonograph records totaled

2,073, and pictures 1,785. The total circulation had been 29,187 for the year. Within a few months following the inspection, 2,326 volumes were added.[44]

Even though the evaluators had not been unduly critical of Elon's musical equipment, the college Music Department was not satisfied with its facilities. The Skinner pipe organ in Whitley Auditorium was thirty-six years old and badly worn from almost daily use since its installation. Supported by "contributions and pledges from some interested friends of the College,"[45] the blessing of the administration was obtained for a major renovation of the instrument. Dean Moore, who was also chairman of the Department of Fine Arts, in collaboration with Ray C. Euliss, an enthusiastic organist from Burlington, planned the specifications and tonal design for the project. Under the supervision of W. K. Dowling, of Atlanta, Georgia, the old organ was thoroughly cleaned and releathered. The twenty-six ranks of the instrument were also supplemented by fifteen new ranks, all of which included more than 2,600 pipes. A new console was purchased from the Reuter Organ Company, and by the spring of 1962 the project had been completed.[46]

On April 8 the new instrument was dedicated in a formal ceremony, presided over by President Danieley and participated in by chairman of the trustees Thad Eure; Clifford Hardy, president of the student body; Dean Moore; and Professors Reynolds, Graves, and Charles Lynam. The recital that followed was played by the world-famous Virgil Fox, and dedicated "To the Glory of God and the Joy of Mankind," in honor of Dean Moore, "Scholar, Musician, Devoted Teacher, and Friend." This was an appropriate tribute to the man who originated the renovation and contributed many hours of mental and physical labor to its fulfillment. Some of the large number who attended were unable to even gain access to the packed auditorium.[47] The event was one of the highlights in the musical history of the college.

Near the end of the Smith administration, new student awards gradually replaced those that had necessarily been discontinued during the lean financial years. Many of the new prizes consisted primarily of money rather than medals, and were given for overall accomplishment rather than specific performance. These consisted of the W. L. Monroe Christian Education and Personality Awards, given in memory of Dr. W. A. Harper and in honor of Dr. John G. Truitt, an alumnus and prominent clergyman in the Christian Church, to the male and female students showing the most personal improvement; the Stein H. Basnight Trophies, for outstanding work in Bible studies and performance in college athletics; the George Shackley Awards to the two students showing the most improvement in piano and in organ, respectively; and the two awards given in memory of Jerry D. Strader, one for outstanding work in Christian education and the other for accomplishment in student dramatics.

During the Danieley administration, the Underwood Company gave a gold medal to the most proficient student in business education; Sigma Mu Sigma, a service fraternity, originated the William Moseley Brown Award to the outstanding senior; and an award was given by the Student Government Association to the individual who contributed the most valued service to the student government. To these were soon added the Somers Prize Essay Award, offered by Chaplain Lester I. Somers and Mrs. Doris L. Somers, for the best es-

Dr. A. L. Hook receiving Outstanding Alumnus Award in 1963 from Dr. Robert W. Truitt.

say submitted to the Department of Philosophy and Religion. Other prizes were the P. E. Majors Club Award to the leading major in physical education and the Dudley Ray Watson Award to the most proficient student in business administration.

These awards had formerly been presented at the spring commencement, where the increasing number was adding congestion to a program already lengthy. Furthermore, few of the undergraduates remained for the closing exercises and missed witnessing the honoring of fellow students. Because of these reasons, in 1958 the administration established Awards Day, to be held annually in the late spring, at which time practically all the presentations were made during an assembly of the entire student body. This change accomplished the desired objective of increasing interest in the program among the students.[48]

Under the leadership of Dr. Cunningham, the North Carolina Alpha Chapter of Pi Gamma Mu in 1959 began awarding the official Scholarship Medal of the society to Elon's outstanding student in social science. It was presented to Richard Kopko, the first recipient, at a chapter dinner, but was afterward included in the Awards Day ceremonies.[49]

The old Ministerial Association was replaced in 1967 when the Mathatians were organized by Dr. Reynolds for students planning "to enter the Christian Ministry, Religious Education, Social Service or Medical Missions." The group's purpose was to "discuss special problems in connection with church vocations and to plan and take part in service and field projects."[50] After Professor Graves had arranged for completion of the inspiring John U. Newman Memorial Prayer Room on the second floor of the Alamance Building in 1967, the organization held its weekly meetings there. About 1970 the organization disbanded.

The administration also established the Order of the Oak in 1962 "to recognize superior scholarship, to encourage intellectual achievement, and to foster the liberal and critical mind." Eligibility required at least junior rank, good character, and a cumulative average of 3.30 quality points per semester hour.[51] In the spring of 1968, the organization became the Elon College chapter of Alpha Chi, a national society that had been founded in 1922 for the recognition of superior scholarship among college students.[52]

During the first several years of Danieley's incumbency, a number of specific bequests were added to the endowment fund. These were listed by the names of their donors or by the name of the person in whose memory or honor they were given. Included were the John M. Campbell, Harry K. Eversull, W. J. Ballentine, D. R. Fonville, Sr., H. L. Bondurant, J. H. Register, Virginia B. Kernodle, and John M. McLean funds. New memorial scholarship funds to aid deserving students were given in memory of David M. Helfenstein, Sue B. Macon, N. F. Brannock, Howard B. Holmes, Sadie V. Fonville, John W. Barney, L. E. Smith, Helen M. Parkerson, Charlotte A. Hebard, and Andrew Morgan. The last of these was a tribute to a black employee of Elon for many years who was accidentally electrocuted while engaged in some work at his home.[53] Student assistance was also provided by a fund established by the Burlington Elks Club, and by the National Defense Education Act of 1958 Loan Fund. Assistance from these sources aided many students laboring under financial difficulties to complete their education.

In 1958 authority and financial support was granted by the Student Government Association to establish the Elon College Liberal Arts Forum. Its purpose was "to stimulate interest in the liberal arts and to promote and foster a spirit of inquiry" among the students, principally through "the medium of scholarly lectures." The first members of the forum were students James P. Elder, Etta Britt, and Daniel Gee; and Professors James Hess, William M. Brown, Richard Haff, and Clarence Carson.[54] Concerts, art films, seminars, and debates were also sponsored by the organization. Enthusiasm dwindled after Elder graduated in 1960, but was renewed vigorously three years later when he returned to the college as a member of the history faculty.

By means of increased financial support, scholars from colleges and universities in the United States and abroad were brought to the campus. In 1966 a cherished dream was fulfilled by the holding of "a week-long symposium devoted to humanistic studies."[55] The lectures during the period were interspersed with indoor and outdoor concerts, luncheons, dinners, seminars, and receptions. The symposiums were continued for several years aided by patrons from Burlington and elsewhere. Some of the distinguished participants were: Dr. Osborne B. Hardison, Jr., director of the Folger Shakespeare Library; Dr. Francis B. Simkins, historian from Longwood College; Dr. Paul Gross, professor of chemistry at Duke University; Dr. Alfred G.

Engstrom, professor of Romance languages at the University of North Carolina; and James J. Sweeney, director of the Houston Museum of Fine Arts. These inspiring events, in modified form, have been continued as an annual feature of Elon's cultural offerings.

Coincident with the founding of the Liberal Arts Forum, the Pi Gamma Mu Society began to sponsor an annual lecture by a visiting scholar. The first was delivered in 1959 by Dr. Fletcher M. Green, of the University of North Carolina history faculty. Among the long list of guest lecturers who followed were historian Richard Watson, of Duke University; Bernard Boyd, of the Department of Religion at the University of North Carolina; and, from the same institution, historians Hugh T. Lefler, popularly known as "Mr. North Carolina," and George B. Tindall; and from Tulane University, Hugh F. Rankin. The last of these, after graduating from Elon in 1959, had achieved national recognition for the numerous books he had written on historical subjects.[56]

During the early 1960s, the college was privileged to appoint a faculty member and spouse as its representatives to take part in the program of the Danforth Associates. This activity, sponsored by the Danforth Foundation, was designed to strengthen "informal student-faculty relationships through faculty entertaining in their homes, encourage faculty counseling of students at the level of friendship, and to deepen faculty and student dimensions through the fine arts, worship and the involvement in extra-campus community life." Elon's first representatives were Dr. and Mrs. John Sanford. After their four-year term, they were succeeded by Professor and Mrs. Roy Epperson, and later by Professor and Mrs. J. Wesley Alexander. At occasional district meetings, the associates pooled their ideas and fostered new ones. Upon their return, Elon's representatives put these into practice, which benefited the college family.[57]

Elon was one of the seventeen colleges that organized the Piedmont University Center in 1962 to pool their resources in obtaining cultural programs that no one of them individually could afford. Each member institution paid $1,500 per year in dues, the total of which was supplemented by grants from the Babcock Foundation, of Winston-Salem; the Z. Smith Reynolds Foundation, from the same city; and the Fund for Advancement of Education, a Ford Foundation affiliate. By bloc booking, a dozen prominent scholars were engaged annually. From this list, each member could select several to appear at its institution for a moderate fee. A library of twenty-nine educational films to be loaned to the colleges was soon in readiness. Two research grant programs were conducted: one to finance projects approved by the Center, and the other to supply matching funds for each college to disburse among its faculty for work on higher academic degrees.[58]

The member institutions appointed representatives to serve on the Center's various committees. These met at Reynolda House, the palatial Winston-Salem home of the R. J. Reynolds family, which was also made available to the organization for use as its official headquarters. The members, in addition to Elon College, were Agricultural and Technical, Belmont Abbey, Bennett, Catawba, Davidson, Greensboro, Guilford, High Point, Johnson C. Smith, Lenoir-Rhyne, Livingstone, Mars Hill, Pfeiffer, Salem, Wake Forest, and Winston-Salem State.[59]

The scholars who lectured at Elon under the auspices of the Center included Dr. Lawrence R. Thompson, professor of English at Princeton, Dr. George E. Mowry, dean of the Division of Social Sciences at the University of California, Dr. Peter Bertocci, professor of philosophy at Boston University, Dr. Dewey W. Grantham, professor of history at Vanderbilt, and Dr. Sylvester Broderick, professor of African studies at the University College of Sierra Leone. Numerous others of the same caliber made visits to Elon that were both educational and inspirational.[60]

During the late 1960s, the support of the foundations dwindled as they became more deeply enmeshed in other projects, and the Center was phased out for lack of finances with which to operate. Most of its equipment, including visual-aid material, was turned over to the Association of Independent Colleges, which was the successor to the Council of Church-Related Colleges. The unavoidable dissolution of the Center was a distinct loss to the cultural programs of the member institutions because it had been used advantageously while in operation.

Apart from these programs, the Danieley administration invited an occasional guest to Elon. One of the best known of these was Gerald R. Ford, at that time House Minority Leader in the United States Congress. He spent most of one day at the college. His formal lecture received rapt attention, and the students participated enthusiastically in the discussion session. Years later, those who were present on the occasion recalled it with pride when Ford was elevated to the White House.[61]

All the various presentations at Elon were supplemented by the programs of the annual lyceum. It was responsible for the appearance of outstanding instrumentalists and vocalists, as well as various musical groups.[62] For an institution of its size and limited financial means, the college provided an excellent cultural program without admission charge for its family and the public in general. Interspersed among these offerings were numerous social affairs arranged by the Student Government Association, the fraternities, sororities, and clubs. If any Elonite was bored because of lack of anything to do besides study, it was his or her own fault.

Literary interest came to the fore in 1962. After a lapse of several years, *The Colonnades* was revived under the supervision of Professor Franke J. Butler; Nancy Butler served as editor-in-chief.[63] Another feature was the addition to the faculty of Manly W. Wellman, a prolific author from Chapel Hill, who conducted a course in creative writing for a selected group of regular and special students and continued it for eight years. This academic addition immediately attracted ambitious writers of fiction. As a result of this offering, two authors were produced whose works were accepted for professional publication. D. McKay, of New York, released *Head into the Wind* in 1965 and *Shadow on the Water*, in 1967, both by Mrs. Dorothy R. Barnwell. In 1973 the Moore Publishing Company, of Durham, marketed *Tide's Rising*, by Mrs. June S. Strader. Many others who never achieved publication profited from the course.[64]

Under the Danieley administration, the awarding of honorary degrees continued. In 1957 an LL.D. degree was awarded to William T. Scott, and D.D.'s to George D. Alley, Rickie E. Brittle, and James F. McKinley. The following year, a D.D. was given to William J. Andes, and LL.D.'s were conferred upon Thad Eure, North Carolina's secretary of state and chairman of the Elon College board of trustees, and Walter A. Graham. The same degree was awarded in 1959 to William C. Friday, president of the University of North Carolina, and to Curtis Schumacher. The next year, a Litt.D. was awarded to Lucy M. Eldridge, a D.Sc. to A. L. Hook, and an LL.D. to United States Senator and Elon College Trustee B. Everett Jordan. In 1961 James H. Lightbourne, Jr., and Frank R. Hamilton received D.D.'s and Lewis E. Spikes an LL.D.

Academic procession on Founders Day, 1962. North Carolina's Governor Terry Sanford leads. He is followed by U.S. Vice-President Lyndon B. Johnson and Elon President Danieley.

The regular observance of Founders Day also continued, and in 1962 attracted more attention universally than had any of its predecessors. The reason was that, in addition to conferring an LL.D. on U.S. Congressman Charles R. Jonas, the guest speaker was Lyndon B. Johnson, vice-president of the United States. A visit from an official of such high rank was a noteworthy honor for the college, and the event attracted widespread attention. Johnson landed with his entourage on the campus in a helicopter, and spent most of the day there. The degree of Doctors of Laws was duly conferred upon him, after which he delivered a speech primarily on foreign affairs that was heard by the largest crowd ever assembled at Elon up to that time. It might have been even larger had it even been dreamed that within a year the speaker would be the president of the nation. Another "red letter" day was added to the college's history.[65]

While the academic and cultural fields were expanding, the trustees of the college became concerned with the increasing expense of athletics. To avoid any embarrassing financial entanglements, the board ruled that, beginning with the 1958–59 season, the maximum

Audience listening to U.S. Vice-President Lyndon B. Johnson's address on Founders Day, 1962. From left to right, front row: W. C. Elder, Ralph H. Scott, John R. Kernodle, Horace Kornegay, and Samuel J. Ervin, Jr. Second row: Allen E. Gant, Clyde W. Gordon, T. S. Earp, and Royall H. Spence, Jr.

quotas for grants-in-aid "be set at 33 for football, 12 for basketball, and five for baseball. These were to include all partial grants and were to be given under the direction of the faculty Committee on Athletics."[66]

In addition to Elon, the North State Athletic Conference was composed of Catawba, High Point, Pfeiffer, Atlantic Christian, East Carolina, Guilford, Lenoir-Rhyne, Western Carolina, and Appalachian State Teachers College. Representatives from each of these institutions planned the operation of the conference. However, the financial participation of each school was controlled by its president. In 1960 these executives formed the Presidents' Group to keep the cost of athletics compatible with their budgets and to maintain competition on the same level for all.

This aim was accomplished by a mutual agreement for each member institution to grant a similar number of scholarships. Such an arrangement assured keeping intercollegiate athletics on an even keel throughout the conference. Elon's Danieley served as second president of the group, which continued to maintain its policy, though it was not always popular with the conference officials. In 1963, after several changes in the membership, the name was changed to the Carolinas Intercollegiate Athletic Conference.[67]

While these negotiations were being conducted, several changes were made in the coaching staff. Varney, in football, was followed in 1960 by George M. Tucker for four years, then for one year by Gary B. Mattocks, who had been Tucker's assistant and track team coach. In 1959 Mathis was succeeded in basketball by William R. ("Bill") Miller; he filled the position for the ensuing nineteen years. Mathis was also followed as baseball coach by Dr. John D. Sanford, who chaired the Department of Health and Physical Education and served as Director of Athletics. Dr. "Jack" was the only Ph.D. to serve full time in these offices. The chairman, who also held the rank of professor, and the other coaches, who were assistant professors, also taught the many sections of the physical education courses. These were numerous because every student at the college was required to take at least two of them. Under the training of these competent men, a new galaxy of Elon stars arose.[68]

The college was justly proud of its athletes, whose efficient teamwork as a group made stellar performances by individuals possible. At the same time, the young president was not satisfied. He envisioned a physical education program that would not be confined to the participants in the three major sports and classes conducted by the coaches, but one in which every Elon student could actively engage. He began early in his incumbency to devise plans for acquiring the necessary facilities to make this benefit possible. This was an ambitious undertaking, but its purpose was worthwhile, and the goal would eventually be won.

Evidence of the changes that had gradually taken place among Elon's officials was revealed in the personnel of the board of trustees. In 1962, the thirty-four men and two women who were members included two clergymen, six physicians, seventeen business men, one practicing attorney, two bankers, four engaged in government service, and four who lacked a specific category. Only sixteen were Elon alumni. Of the religious denominations represented, twenty-seven were Congregational Christians, three Methodists, three Presbyterians, two Episcopalians, and one Baptist.[69] The average age of the trustees was approximately fifty-seven. These facts disprove an idea prevalent among many uninformed people that the board, and therefore the college, was officially dominated by its affiliated church and its alumni.

In fact, on June 25, 1957, just five days prior to Danieley's initial prayer service, years of negotiations were concluded by the merging of the Congregational-Christian Churches with the Evangelical and Reformed Church to found the United Church of Christ. Several years were then required to complete the intricate governing details of the new denomination. These were completed by 1965, in which year the Elon trustees directed that the college charter be amended to change its denominational connection to "the Southern Conference of the United Church of Christ." The newly created conference, which replaced the old Southern Christian Convention, was organized at Elon College in 1966 and immediately moved its offices to Burlington. The Reverend James H. Lightbourne, Jr. (Elon '42), its chief executive, was given the status of an ex officio member of the college board of trustees.[70]

Although presiding over the college was his primary duty, Danieley also exhibited enthusiastic loyalty to the town. Born nearby, he was proud to be a resident of the municipality he knew so well, and was sincerely concerned about its welfare. At his first faculty meeting as president, he made this attitude clear. "Let us become an integral part of the Elon College community," he challenged. "Let us come to know the townspeople and break down forever any feeling that college professors are somehow different from other people and do not belong in a normal and average community."[71] This statement of his sentiments was heeded especially by some staff members residing within the town's corporate limits and was effective in smoothing relationships between "Town and Gown."

A spirit of cooperation was evident in 1959 when the trustees authorized the president "to develop jointly with the town a sanitary landfill on the college farm for refuse disposal."[72] This solved a vital problem for the community and was an economical measure for all. Also, during the 1960s, faculty members W. Jennings Berry, D. D. Atkinson, and H. H. Cunningham served on the town board of commissioners; and Cunningham, Gilbert C. Latham, Louis Wilkins, and Mrs. J. E. Danieley were members of the town planning and zoning board.[73] When the Southern Railway decided to raze the Elon station in 1961, college and municipal officials cooperated by not opposing the move. In return, they were rewarded with permission to use a strip along the northern side of the tracks for parking.[74] This was a boon to the college because the space was used almost entirely by students.

The dismantling of the railroad station marked the close of an Elon era, as observed in the *Alumni News*:

> The favorite spot of countless students in the good old days has gone from the scene. The railroad station was removed several months ago. Only green grass and shrubbery mark the spot, but many memories linger. The joy of going "down to the station" to meet the train (girls chaperoned, of course); the anticipation of meeting the trains in September to see who was coming back since nearly everyone traveled by train; the farewells in May as students departed for the summer vacation months. But these days are gone forever for the old station is gone and only two trains daily—one east, one west—and if you want to ride, you flag![75]

The loss of the station meant little to the students of the 1960s, many of whom had never boarded a train, but it was the loss of a landmark to the "old-timers." Significantly enough, it was the railroad that had been mainly responsible for the location of the college at Mill Point in the first place, but its importance to the institution no longer existed. Soon the two remaining passenger trains were discontinued, and evening events at the college no longer needed to be scheduled at a quarter past eight in the evening to avoid interruption by the eight o'clock passenger train. The thunderous freights that frequently pass along the track disturb lectures a few minutes, as they always have, but no one minds the distraction. Both the college and the railroad are where they are apt to remain, and they learned long ago to live in peace with each other.

Although the Danieley administration had completed the construction program begun by Dr. Smith, and added one new building to it, more room was needed. The interior of the Mooney Building, so often rearranged for new occupants, once again underwent a revamping. The Department of Languages moved to the third floor, where it was equipped with one of the most modern language laboratories in the state. It contained "28 student positions, with two

Razing the railroad station in 1961. Photo by Jack W. Lambeth.

tape channels, one phonograph channel, and an intercommunication system." The student positions used a dual-channel tape recorder and were equipped "for listening to master tapes, for work with special tapes, and for recording."[76] The Department of Religion filled the entire second floor, and the first floor housed the Student Union. The space in the latter was suitable only for a small snack bar, campus shop, and student post office. Both the Student Government Association offices and the infirmary were elsewhere and some distance apart. No lounges or recreation rooms were available for the use of the student body. This was especially inconvenient for commuters because they were forced to carry all the material they would have to use during the day around in their arms, and sorely needed some accommodations for their comfort.

The lack of student lounge resources was noticed by the Reverend Thomas E. Bollinger, rector of the Episcopal Church of the Holy Comforter, in Burlington. He obtained the approval of President Danieley for the women of his parish to establish a student coffee house by renting an apartment in Oak Lodge, the former Harper home, for the purpose. Under the direction of Mrs. William S. Chandler, assisted by Mesdames William DeR. Scott, Roger Gant, Jr., W. Clary Holt, and others, an attractive suite of rooms was tastefully decorated and opened for the use of students and faculty in 1963 under the name of the All Saints Coffee House. The hospitality of the ladies in charge was rewarded by a patronage that soon overflowed the limited capacity of the house. The program was then enlarged by setting up a chapel in one room in the apartment. The Reverend Harry Woggon, assistant rector at the Burlington church, held services there and also spent much of his time mingling with and counseling the students. He left at the end of one year because of budgetary curtailments, but the coffee house continued its service until after the new Student Union was occupied in 1966.[77]

In addition to space needed for the students to use as gathering places, the library had outgrown its quarters in the Carlton Building and could expand no further. It was also essential that a new dormitory for men be provided, and several of the old buildings needed extensive repairs and refurbishing.

Obviously a construction program that would meet the needs of the college would require a large sum of money. Happily, in the mid to late 1960s greater financial assistance from the federal government became available than ever before, and Elon officials promptly took advantage of it. As the seventy-fifth anniversary of the founding of the institution drew near, the time seemed propitious for a major fund drive. The trustees approved a plan proposed by Danieley to instigate a Diamond Anniversary Fund drive to raise $600,000. One-third of this sum was to be used for renovation, repairs, and improvements in the Duke, Whitley, Mooney, Carlton, and Alamance buildings. Another third was to be endowment for faculty salaries; and the remaining third, endowment for scholarship purposes.

The campaign was placed in the hands of Paul Frazier, a representative of Ketchum, Inc., professional fundraisers. He was ably assisted by Director of Development Baxter and Director of Church Relations Scott. To supplement the approximately one-fourth of the funds needed that were being supplied by a governmental grant, they obtained the balance within a reasonable time and put the funds to use where they were needed.[78] The results were gratifying, but not one foot of space had been added to the physical plant and more buildings had become a necessity.

When the anniversary campaign was initiated in November 1963, additional objectives were also announced for a long-range development program. These were $350,000 for a library, $275,000 for a men's dormitory, $200,000 for the housing of married students, $125,000 for physical education facilities, and $450,000 for additional endowment. When the Diamond Anniversary goal was attained, the time seemed appropriate to begin the long-range plan. The project began when a contract was negotiated with the United States Secretary of Housing and Urban Development for the sale of $835,000 Elon College Dormitory and Student Center Bonds of 1965. The money was to be used to construct "a dormitory building to house 150 men students and to construct a new student center building to include a snack bar, campus shop, clinic, student organization offices and lounges, with the necessary appurtenant facilities."[79] Shortly after this action, a federal grant was sought with which "to build a new library with a seating capacity of 611 students and space for 124,000 books."[80] Determined not to overlook any opportunity, the trustees also authorized the president "to file a preliminary application with the North Carolina Commission on Higher Education Facilities for a grant of $120,000," with which to construct a physical education building equipped with a swimming pool.[81]

Events moved with sufficient speed for construction to begin immediately on two of the buildings. The south driveway to the campus was closed so that a quadrangle could be formed; the new Student Center would face the Alamance Building across a grassy lawn. The attractive brick, two-story building, featuring a terrace on its western end, was complete in every respect. It contained a snack bar, campus shop, lounges, conference rooms, recreation rooms for games and television viewing, a clinic, post office, and offices for the Student Government Association.

On Parents Day, November 5, 1966, dedication ceremonies were held for the completed William S. Long Student Center and the tripartite men's dormitory, whose sections were named Brannock, Hook, and Barney, respectively, to honor those veteran professors.[82] On the same day, ground was broken for the new library. A unique feature of the gala occasion was the presence of North Carolina's

Trustees at the ground-breaking ceremonies for the Long Student Center in 1965. From left to right: George D. Colclough, Thomas S. Earp, Chairman of the Board Thad Eure, W. D. Rippy, and J. Hinton Rountree.

Governor Dan K. Moore, who introduced the principal speaker on the program, Virginia's chief executive, Mills E. Godwin, Jr. The presence of these two officials was a reminder of the harmony that had always existed between the two states in founding and supporting Elon College, a situation that has never changed. After Moore expressed his pleasure "that Elon is moving steadily forward in its efforts to serve young people in the best tradition of Christian higher education," Godwin paid a special tribute to the administration and "to all those who have had a part" in the expansion program. He continued, "The dormitories, and the library that is to follow, have already been dedicated to an extent far beyond the power of a visitor. We commit them to their proper function realizing that they signify the dedication of those who conceived the need, who planned the details, and who contributed of their resources to the final fulfillment."[83]

The speeches of both distinguished speakers were loudly applauded by the large crowd of interested visitors, who also rejoiced over the building program's progress. Although a long road would obviously have to be traversed before the costs were paid, there was every reason to expect that this could and would be accomplished.

CHAPTER XIII

THE MATURE TREE

The tree of deepest root is found
Least willing still to quit the ground.
HESTER LYNCH THRALE (PIOZZI)
Three Warnings

The governmental grants-in-aid programs, which enabled Elon College to take such giant strides in construction during the 1960s, were accompanied by several restrictions governing the use of the funds. One of these specified that "the officers and agents of the College operating housing and related facilities shall not discriminate in the use and occupancy of such facilities on account of race, color, creed, or national origin."[1] The board of trustees voted to accept this provision along with the other requirements. This created a special problem because Elon, like practically all other southern educational institutions, had never admitted black people. Of course, some other races and nationalities had attended the college—almost from the day it opened its doors—and their relations with the administration and the rest of the student body had been highly amicable. For example, no alumna of the institution ever participated to a more outstanding degree in campus affairs than the Japanese Toshio Sato.

The desegregation policy that the national government adopted in 1954 had aroused bitter criticism and resentment in many areas, particularly in the southern states. Private schools were not affected by the law unless they were receiving grants, but the terms of these were explicit in their requirements. The general public was not aware of the necessity for complying with these terms, and the admission of black students to colleges formerly restricted to whites could be strongly opposed by institutional supporters. For that reason, the outcome of such a situation could be extremely unpleasant, to say the least. At any rate, Elon officials did not need to wait long before learning how the college would be affected by the changed national conditions.

During the spring of 1963, Paul deMontaigne, a native of Martinique, was a faculty member at Palmer Institute, a black school located midway between Elon College and Greensboro, at Sedalia. To pursue a planned graduate program, he needed several undergraduate courses, and applied for entrance to the evening school. Danieley personally admitted him, and, concerned about possible repercussions, escorted him to the first meeting of the class for which he had registered. The president made a brief statement about tradition being broken and the beginning of a new policy that he hoped would be harmonious for all concerned. It was. After his speech, the students concentrated on their study of the history of Western civilization under Professor Jon Wendt, and paid no special attention to the new student. The next day, the news media made no mention of the incident, and the relieved president, breathing a sigh of relief, turned his attention to other problems.[2]

However, deMontaigne did not return to the college after attending his first class, which caused Dr. Danieley to drive over to Palmer to ascertain the reason. The student informed him he had discovered his financial means were insufficient to pay for the courses he wished to take. The president then told him to resume his studies because funds could be found to assist him. The black man did so, and his fees and tuition were contributed by several generous faculty members.

DeMontaigne also enrolled for a religion course, where his entrance after his initial appearance attracted no more attention than his presence had done in the history class. The young black man, whose French was better than his English because of his nationality, was received in a friendly manner by his fellow students, and he completed the work he needed. Elon had taken the first step in racial integration.

In the fall of 1963, Glenda K. Phillips, an honor graduate of a high school in Burlington, registered as the first black day student at the college. A talented musician, she promptly qualified for Elon's marching band, which was rapidly becoming distinguished under the supervision of Professor Jack O. White. Illness prevented her from completing her college work; this left the honor of being Elon's first black graduate to Eugene E. Perry, of the class of 1969. By that time, more than a dozen blacks were members of the student body, a number that rose to 174 in the ensuing decade.[3]

During this transition, which was accompanied by violent repercussions at many institutions, only one incident occurred at Elon based on race, and it was a mild one. The black students requested the Department of Social Science to include a course on black history in its curriculum. At a conference attended by the petitioners and Dean Moore, Department Chairman Durward T. Stokes ex-

Eugene E. Perry, class of 1969, the first black person to graduate from Elon.

plained that neither the proper material nor a qualified instructor was available to teach such a course. However, he announced that a number of books and periodicals pertinent to black culture had been added to the library collection and that suggestions for others would be considered. This apparently satisfied all but the one student responsible for the idea.[4]

During the late 1950s, considerable apprehension arose in collegiate circles over the possible influence of communism among faculty members. To prevent the spread of this doctrine, visiting speakers were carefully screened before being invited to the institution. No special concern was aroused at Elon on the subject, but President Danieley, always a stickler for an explicit policy, requested the trustees to clarify their position in the matter. In response, on October 7, 1959, upon the motion of G. D. Colclough, the board approved a statement on academic freedom:

> 1. Freedom to teach the truth as he sees it is the privilege and responsibility of the teacher, without which there is no hope of sound education. A teacher has no right, however, to be protected by this principle if he teaches the overthrow of the principle or of the system out of which it springs.
>
> 2. Sound education is founded on Christian principles and reflects the spirit of democracy, which declares certain rights to be inalienable: the right of trial by jury and of fair treatment, the right to worship God according to conscience, and to vote according to conviction. The conscientious exercise of these rights shall in no way affect the status or tenure of a member of the faculty of Elon College. However, Elon College does consider it entirely proper to consider the person's religious views and his church affiliation when employing faculty members.
>
> 3. Freedom to search for the truth and to publish the results of research is fundamental to the promotion of higher learning. Elon College encourages the publication of the results of faculty research.
>
> 4. It is recognized that the Board of Trustees of Elon College has the "power to elect . . . professors . . . ," "the power to prescribe and direct the course of study . . . ," and to determine the policies of the College. However, in accordance with well-

established principles by which sound educational procedure is
guided, the Board of Trustees of Elon College, as a matter of
policy, has delegated matters of administration to those
charged with the administration of the College and matters
concerning the instructional program to the faculty of the
College.[5]

The president was reassured by this policy statement, which clearly
defined his authority to handle any matters that might arise concerning academic freedom at the college.

Although affairs remained calm at Elon, the fear of Communist
influence increased within the state. In 1963 the General Assembly
passed the "Speaker Ban Law," which forbade any state-supported
college or university to permit the use of its facilities for speaking by
any person to whom the following conditions might apply:

(A) Is a known member of the Communist party; (B) Is known
to advocate the overthrow of the United States or the State of
North Carolina; (C) Has pleaded the Fifth Amendment to the
Constitution in refusing to answer any question with respect
to Communism or subversive connections or activities, before
any duly constituted legislative committee, any judicial tri-
bunal, or any executive board of the United States or any
state.[6]

This act caused a furor throughout the state, especially among the
colleges it supported. They feared that the Southern Association of
Colleges and Schools would take away their accreditation on the
grounds that freedom of speech was being violated. Relief came in
1965, when a special session of the legislature repealed the law. Nevertheless, some apprehension remained.

As events soon proved, communism was not the most serious
threat to campus placidity. It was the increasing unpopularity of U.S.
participation in the Vietnam civil war that was the major cause of
student and faculty unrest. At first, resentment toward the government's military policy was indirectly responsible in part for an asser-
tion of individual independence to a greater extent than previously
exhibited. This was evident during the fall term of 1962, when the
Student Government Association began monthly publication of *The
Campus Crier*, "for the information and entertainment of all stu-

dents."[7] The issues, composed of eighteen to twenty mimeographed sheets of typescript, contained properly written news articles. The first staff was composed of editor Carol Tragesar; assistants Gail Hettel, Al Baer, Allen Tyndall, Stanley Switzer, Denyse Theodore, Marion McVey, Lee Clarke, Melvin Shreves, Peter Smith, and Jack DeVito; and typist Carol Boyle.[8] None of these individuals were radicals or nonconformists. However, the staff members obviously felt less restraint than had they been writing for the *Maroon and Gold,* which probably would not have published an article criticizing dining hall food that appeared in the *Crier.*[9] The amusing manner in which the article was written did not veil the writer's purpose of criticizing the college cuisine, always a favorite target for student protesting, but it was hardly an attack on administrative policy.

Despite the light vein of the article, the *Crier* was neither a joke sheet nor a crusading publication at first, but a newsletter. Beginning with volume IV, the format was changed to a printed six by ten inch pamphlet of ten pages, which was more attractive than the former typescript but considerably reduced in contents. Gradually, the contributors became primarily concerned with criticizing the administration or providing humorous entertainment, but they failed to achieve outstanding success at either and in 1968 the publication was discontinued.[10]

Some of the young faculty members, who had attended less disciplined institutions than Elon, openly encouraged the students in their rebellious attitude toward the college rules. The main targets of their protest were compulsory chapel attendance, the ban on alcoholic beverages at the school, and coed dormitory restrictions. Violations were frequent, but punishment was not severe because the Honor Court was usually sympathetic with the defendants.

During the fall term in 1965, the group of students and a few faculty members composing the foremost "liberals" clashed with the college officials. Acting on its own initiative, the group invited James Wilson, a member of the Student Peace Union at the University of North Carolina at Chapel Hill to speak on "The New Student Left" at the college. When this meeting was publicly announced, the administration pointed out to the group that to invite a visiting speaker to the campus without official approval was a violation of the institution's rules. In the case at hand, permission was refused because "Wilson's organization had recently picketed the Special Warfare Center at Fort Bragg, calling for withdrawal of American armed forces in Vietnam."[11] The controversy aroused by this action was still boiling at the time, and President Danieley wished to keep his school clear of it.

After the planned meeting was canceled, a few members of the group responsible for the incident defiantly met in a third-floor room of the Carlton Building, where they heard Wilson speak anyway. What he said exerted little effect and was not publicized to any extent, but the action could hardly be ignored. Those involved were severely reprimanded and warned that a similar action in the future would not be tolerated. This policy was explained in detail to the trustees by the president:

> Communications media have given great publicity to efforts on behalf of students and faculty members to sponsor speakers without the approval of the college and university administrators. Our students and some of our faculty members have read the news and, although they consider themselves non-conformists, they feel compelled to conform to the styles being set by "liberals" on other campuses.
>
> This administration has taken a positive stand. No meeting is to be held on this campus which has not been scheduled on the Dean's calendar in the regular manner. No meeting involving an outside speaker is to be scheduled without approval of the administration or its representative.
>
> It is not our purpose to close the door to any speaker but it is our responsibility to screen programs which are planned for this campus to determine, to the best of our ability, whether they will make a positive contribution to the total educational program of Elon College. This program includes the intellectual, the cultural, the social, and the physical lives of our students. The policy permits and encourages a wide variety of visitors. However, it excludes the rabble-rouser and those of his ilk who have no contribution to make to our students or to this institution.[12]

The *Crier* promptly accused Elon policymakers of refusing "to all a true spirit of free enquiry to exist on the campus,"[13] but no further attempt was made to bring speakers to the institution without proper approval.

These circumstances would have been troublesome enough for the administration even if the faculty had included no dissenting members. In 1965 thirteen of the instructors organized an Elon chapter of the American Association of University Professors (AAUP). This organization of national prominence probably should have been represented at the college earlier. However, it had not been, and the circumstances of the time in which it was organized gave the president grounds to consider the move an attack against his administration.

Danieley reported this fully to his trustees:

> This organization, known to most of us as the AAUP, has stated its objectives to include efforts to raise faculty salaries, to protect academic freedom, and to assist members of the teaching profession whose right to academic tenure has been threatened. These are worthy objectives. Personally I yield to no one in my desire to see our faculty members paid reasonable and fair salaries. I am committed to the idea of academic freedom exercised within the framework of responsible campus citizenship. I strongly support reasonable regulations protecting the academic tenure of the individual professor. From the standpoint of these general objectives I am in sympathy with this organization. However, I should point out that in many instances the local chapter of AAUP has become the "official critic." It is the "anti-administration" group—it is automatically against the plans, programs, projects, and efforts of the administration.
>
> Our chapter has in its membership a group committed to the objectives as stated by the Association. There is also a group of critics who are ready and willing to protest whatever we try to do. The administration of Elon College is prepared to deal fairly, patiently and sympathetically with each individual member of the faculty and with the faculty as a whole. It is also prepared to cooperate to the limit of its ability with any group of faculty members constituting a chapter of a recognized professional organization.[14]

After announcing the organization of the chapter, Danieley clearly stated his position in the matter:

As your president I sincerely regret any situation which may arise which will tend to divide our faculty, fragment our efforts, or dissipate our energies. We are committed to the idea of an academic community and we believe that the small college can and should be an ideal place to study, to teach and work. It may well be that there are members of our faculty who have found or will discover that they are not in sympathy with the aims and objectives of this institution. If such is the case now, or in the future, this administration is prepared to render such assistance as is reasonable and proper to the end that any competent faculty members who may be caught up in such a situation may find positions on other campuses where their education and experience can be utilized more effectively and where they will be able to make a more significant contribution.[15]

After this unequivocal statement, several faculty members eventually sought employment elsewhere. Because of the spirit in which it was founded, the AAUP chapter did not grow significantly, nor was it very active for a while, though it has remained in existence ever since as a mutually beneficial faculty organization.

Although almost everything connected with the controversial Wilson visit to Elon soon became an unhappy memory, the incident was indirectly responsible for a useful addition to the college plant. An impressionable student, specially interested in history, became convinced that the institution needed a history seminar room. It could be used for private meetings that would not need to be approved as public programs, would be useful in teaching the history courses, and would be convenient for entertaining guests of the Liberal Arts Forum.

Blessed with far more than the average amount of worldly goods, the student decided to finance the project, under the following conditions: the project would be planned by Professor James P. Elder, Jr., the donor's teacher, who would also carry a key to the completed room; and keys would also be entrusted to the college president and the chairman of the Department of Social Science, in which history was an academic division. These provisions were intended to leave control of the room virtually in the hands of the history staff.

The administration accepted the proposal to renovate, decorate, and furnish a room in the Carlton Building "to be 'first class' in every respect." Otto Zenke, Inc., a distinguished firm of interior decorators from Greensboro, was employed for the purpose. The completed project was a panelled room of rare charm, furnished throughout with costly antiques. The room was air-conditioned, and provided with a moving-picture screen that was concealed in a niche when not in use. The cost was in excess of $20,000. A brass plate on the door identified the facility as the "History Seminar Room."[16] This inspiring setting was immediately put to the use intended by the generous donor, who preferred to remain anonymous. The officials in charge were generous in allowing the room to be used by the trustees for their meetings and for other purposes that did not conflict with the history program. It was not used for any gatherings that would not have been officially approved for any other room in the college, and it was one in which the entire college was proud.

The faculty had increased in size proportionate to the student body. Although many of the staff were neighbors, living close to each other within the town of Elon College or nearby, the homes of others were scattered about over Alamance and Guilford Counties, as well as elsewhere. The result was that some of them were barely acquainted. The annual dinner, or picnic, at the beginning of the fall term was the only social occasion during the entire year when all the families were together at the same time, though the Elon College Women's Club's monthly meetings created some congeniality for the females.

To improve the situation, in 1967 the college opened a Sunday buffet lunch on the second floor of McEwen Dining Hall for staff members, their spouses, and their guests. This was a brilliant success because a large number became regular weekly diners. The result was that families of almost strangers, or no more than casual acquaintances, came to know and like each other better, which proved to be a valuable morale builder for the institution. The occasion was so enjoyable that some couples drove quite a distance each Sunday to lunch with their friends.

Knowledge of the arrangement soon became widely publicized, which caused a nearby restaurant proprietor to accuse the college of operating a public lunchroom without a license to do so. This charge was not true and could easily have been contradicted, but, rather than engage in a public controversy, the administration closed the buffet. This deprived the college personnel of an opportunity to mingle socially that has never been replaced. The spirit of friendly understanding and cooperation generated by the lunches was of far more value than the delicious cuisine that accompanied them, and constituted a benefit that was sorely missed.[17]

Another progressive phase of the Danieley program was the holding of occasional retreats for a few key students and administrators. A favorite place for such meetings was the Assembly Grounds, at Blowing Rock, in the western section of the state. Later, the Seven Devils site, near Boone, was used, where a special feature was breakfast cooked by the president. In October 1968 the group numbered thirty, half students and the other half from the administration. They met to become acquainted, make plans for the year, and discuss mutual problems. "This was a much larger group than we have had in recent years," commented the president, who explained, "but we felt it essential to include a number of persons who are serving their first year in positions of administrative responsibility." The various meetings scheduled at these gatherings were considered sufficiently rewarding to justify an annual repetition of the event ever since.[18]

While efforts continued to maintain student-faculty harmony, funds became available for improving the interiors of several of the buildings. Foremost on the list was the long-awaited renovation of the Duke Science Building. At the close of the spring term in 1966, to give the workmen ample room, the equipment and portable furnishings from the structure were stored in old East Dormitory. This move was the occasion for general rejoicing because the science faculty had seldom discarded anything. In addition to that currently used for instruction, the equipment included the mechanism from Dr. Hook's office that regulated the college bell, an old airplane motor left over from World War II days, and other items that consumed so much floor space in Duke that room for the students was sometimes cramped. Everything was packed into the historic old dormitory, but it was tragically gutted by fire on the evening of July 4, 1966.[19]

The local and neighboring fire departments, which arrived promptly, extinguished the blaze, but not before the contents were ruined by smoke as well as water and the walls of the building weakened. The frame South Building, directly in front of East, was providentially saved because, had it ignited, it would have burned like tinder. As on other occasions, arson was strongly suspected, but never conclusively proved. During an official investigation that lasted three days, the offices in South Building were closed, to the discomfiture of their faculty tenants, and all to no avail, after which the matter was dropped.[20]

New equipment could be purchased to replace that which had been lost in the fire, but a worse tragedy was the loss by faculty members of lecture and research notes and papers that could not be replaced. Aid was soon forthcoming to equip the newly renovated Duke Building as soon as news of the faculty needs circulated. The Smith Foundation, of Norfolk, sent $25,000; "equipment valued at more than $17,500" was given by the Western Electric Company through its College Gifts Program; the Esso Education Foundation contributed $5,000; Vikon Chemical Company sent $200; the Smith, Kline, and French Foundation gave $500; Monsanto sent $400; individuals donated $80; and other contributions were expected later. "These gifts," Danieley told the trustees, "along with insurance proceeds should make it possible to re-equip our science department very adequately."[21]

After somewhat lengthy negotiations, the insurance carriers paid the college $109,058.49 for the loss sustained. Because restoration of the old building was deemed impractical, it was razed and the site made into a paved parking lot.[22] It is questionable as to whether or not a fire should be termed "a blessing in disguise," but, if so, the blaze at old East came very close to justifying that description, inasmuch as the eventual results represented a college improvement.

While the Science Department was being refurnished, Elon's general construction program made consistent progress. By the 1968 spring commencement, the mammoth new Library, located parallel to the west campus wall, had been virtually completed. The three-story brick structure was arranged for open-stack library service, and provided study seats for 610 persons, including 236 private study spaces. In addition to stack room for 124,000 volumes, there were listening devices for recordings and tapes as well as viewers for microfilm reading. The first floor, or basement, contained a room for periodicals and one for storage. The second, or main floor, accommodated the offices, circulation desks, catalog, and newspaper reading space. On the third floor was a large room for classes, lectures, or meetings as well as a handsome Church History Room. The entire structure was air-conditioned.[23]

The administration conceived the idea of moving, or attempting to move, the book collection from the Carlton Building into its new home in one day. This could only be accomplished by sufficient manpower, and no machinery was available for such a purpose. Many who cooperated with the plan secretly doubted it could be accomplished in such a short time, but misgivings were not spoken aloud. Monday, July 15, 1968, was designated as Elon Library "Move-In Day." Each person carrying ten loads of books was promised a card for each trip. Ten cards, or tickets, would entitle the holder to a steak supper to be served on the campus at the close of the day. To obtain the assistance of the summer school students, classes were suspended and all offices closed on Monday, the moving day. This turned out to be a mistake because most of the students went home on Friday and did not return until Tuesday morning, after the mov-

President Danieley leads move of library from the Carlton Building to the new McEwen Library.

ing had been completed. Nevertheless, a crowd estimated at 200 or more persons visited the college for a part or all of the day to assist in the project.

Moving began promptly at 8:30 A.M. Dr. Danieley supervised the systematic removal of the books from the shelves in Carlton, while Theodore E. Perkins and Guy R. Lambert, librarian and associate librarian, respectively, directed the shelving of the volumes in the new building. Mrs. Durward T. Stokes passed out the tickets to the carriers at the completion of each trip. The Pepsi-Cola Bottling Company, of Burlington, contributed free cold drinks from a stand on the campus—a refreshing service because the weather was blistering hot. One student, Roger Slaughter, a man of powerful physique, traveled at a slow run to chalk up fifty trips in order to win supper for his entire family. Residents from the Children's Home (changed from Christian Orphanage in 1956), townspeople, alumni, and faculty all participated. The Reverend Hoyle L. Whiteside, a Lutheran minister from Burlington, brought his family to Elon for the day to carry books. Dr. John G. Truitt came early with the identical wheelbarrow he had used to carry books into Carlton when that library opened in 1924. He made one trip to the new building, which was as much as the aged clergyman was physically able to do, but his presence stim-

Cookout in front of McEwen Library at the close of library moving day.

ulated others in their endeavor. Lester W. Johnson, manager of the Western Electric Company, in Burlington, arrived with a number of his employees and manfully carried their share of the heavy loads.[24]

Everyone enjoyed a hearty lunch as guests of the college, which was the only interruption in the moving process during the long day. In the afternoon, the temperature became hotter, the books grew heavier, and the carriers moved more slowly, but none abandoned the task. The appearance of many became ludicrous because light-colored shirts and dresses became streaked with multi-colored hues as the dye from the book covers stained the wet clothing and bare arms of the carriers. Protesting muscles ached and everyone was weary, but the line continued to move. At 5:05 P.M., everyone heaved a deep sigh of relief when they heard the announcement from the officials that the last of the 67,000 volumes had been shelved in their new home. The carriers were hot, dirty, tired, and hungry, but proud of their accomplishment. Everyone except the cooks immediately relaxed while the steaks were being grilled. All revived sufficiently to eat. The crowd dispersed soon after the meal.

There has never been a more cooperative occasion at Elon College before or since. The event attracted widespread attention, which brought area news media to the campus. Dr. Danieley, who stopped stacking books while he was interviewed by the newspaper, radio, and television representatives, paid a tribute to the occasion: "Move-In Day will come in later years to be an historical occasion, just as the Move-In Day of 1924 when the present Carlton Building, housing the library since that time, was opened."[25] Librarian Perkins said, "It seemed impossible to think that all this work could be done in a single day. I remember that not long ago one college library in our state closed down a few weeks to handle such a transfer, and their task wasn't much larger than the one here."[26] Of course, a lot of work remained to be done in checking the books to insure their proper order in the stacks, but their laborious transfer from one building to another had been accomplished. This enabled Elon's new $700,000 library to open for service the following morning.

While the final plans for the library were being approved in 1966, the trustees decided at their March 9 meeting that a number of opinions for present and future institutional needs would be advantageous and authorized a Long-Range Planning Committee. Members were J. L. Crumpton, T. S. Earp, W. D. Rippy, and Royall Spence, trustees; Wesley Alexander, Paul H. Cheek, Allen Sanders, and Durward T. Stokes, from the faculty; Noel Allen, Mary Faust, Carol Lupinacci, and C. V. May, Jr., students; and Robert C. Baxter, C. Fletcher Moore, and Theo Strum, from the administration. Dr. Danieley served as an ex officio member of the group.[27]

The committee did not become active until the following year, when it held several meetings during April and May in one of the recreation rooms of the William S. Long Student Center.[28] Ignoring rank and freely expressing their opinions, the members pooled ideas and discussed the pros and cons of various suggestions. The resulting central plan conceived for the future was, therefore, a product of all segments of the college family, which was the intention of the organizers. The project was concluded before the close of the spring term and the report placed in the hands of the trustees.[29]

In arriving at its conclusions, the committee first considered statistics for 1967–68, which revealed a total of 1,355 day students, 737 of whom were dormitory residents and 618 commuters. These students came from twenty-three states and five foreign countries. The total dormitory capacity of 724 was insufficient for the number requesting residential accommodations. Enrollment in the evening school had gradually shrunk from a peak of 542 to 99 students. Based on these figures, the committee recommended:

 1. Dormitory Students
    RECOMMENDATIONS:
        1. Elon College should remain a relatively small college in order to continue to provide an emphasis on the importance of the individual student.
        2. The College should move toward a dormitory enrollment of 1000 students with an additional 600–700 commuter students in the day classes. This means providing additional dormitory facilities for approximately 200 women and 100 men students.
        3. The addition of 300 dormitory students means that additional dining facilities must be provided—a new facility to be the most desirable approach.
 2. Commuter Students
    RECOMMENDATIONS:

4. The College has an important role as a community college. It should begin to raise admissions standards gradually for commuters keeping in view two important factors:

a. The need to serve the community.

b. The image in the community of an institution which admits those who are unable to gain admission to other colleges.

3. Evening Classes

RECOMMENDATIONS:

5. Evening classes should be continued, possibly on a modified schedule, with students who are registered in day classes permitted to register for courses which are scheduled regardless of the time of the day the courses are given.[30]

The committee also favored arranging for a group that possessed proper expertise to appraise the curriculum concerning possible revision. The new Library would be sufficient for the institution's needs when completed, but laboratory space for the science classes was found to be crowded. The planned Classroom-Office Building would solve that problem because its third floor was to be reserved for the use of the natural sciences. Gymnasium classrooms, a heated swimming pool, and a second lake were included in the overall plan, which also included replacement of the dilapidated Veterans' Apartments with a baseball field, continued renovation of the running-track, and additional tennis courts. Provisions for more automobile parking space were also strongly urged.

Another phase of the long-range planning was to develop College Park to provide new faculty homes. A system was proposed for this desirable project:

It is recommended that the College make building lots (especially those in College Park) available to faculty persons for the purpose of home construction; that the faculty member satisfy in full one-tenth of the cost of each lot each year he teaches and that the lot would become the property of the faculty member at the end of the ten-year period of service. It would be understood that if a faculty member decided to sell the house, the College would have the opportunity to purchase and, in the event the faculty member leaves before the end of ten years, he would pay the remaining cost of the lot.[31]

The park was the area of residential lots lying between Trollinger, O'Kelley, Atkinson, and Woodale avenues, south of the railroad tracks. Many faculty members took advantage of the inducement to build in this choice location, and soon attractive brick residences began to rise throughout the area.

The committee also approved college membership in the Southern Association of Colleges and Schools, the North Carolina Association of Colleges and Universities, the American Council on Education, the Association of American Colleges, the American Association of University Women, the Council for Higher Education of the United Church of Christ, the National Commission on Accreditation, and the North Carolina Foundation of Church-Related Colleges. The receipt by Elon of $253,838.58 as its share of the income of the latter organization during the fourteen years of membership was complimented by the committee. Last but not least, recommendations were made to increase the percentage of the staff holding doctorates, continue the advance in faculty salaries, provide greater opportunity for the faculty to work toward higher degrees as well as honors, and provide a plan of study sabbaticals in addition to the summer plan then in operation in cooperation with the Piedmont University Center.[32]

The college officials approved the long-range plan in general by taking action on some of its provisions immediately. The recommendations of the committee served as the guidelines for institutional development for the next decade, and were eventually carried out in their entirety. This study was one of the most satisfactory student-faculty-administration projects ever conducted at Elon College, and was the precursor of similar studies.

In line with the recommendations of the planners, in 1968 a new complex of buildings was completed on the north campus. Staley Hall, fronted by an ornamental lake, served as a residence for 200 women; Moffitt Hall housed 100 men; and Harper Center, containing a lounge, recreation area, and dining hall, connected the two dormitories. The complex was a commodious, attractive architectural addition to the college plant. Plans were then made for expansion of the gymnasium and erection of the Classroom-Office Building, the latter to stand on the approximate site of the old North Dormitory (Alumni Gym). These additional accommodations placed Elon in a strategic position to take advantage of an unusual opportunity that arose at the time.

On March 8, 1968, an announcement was published in Virginia and North Carolina newspapers that Frederick College, in Portsmouth, Virginia, had been given by its founder-owner, Fred W. Beazley, to the commonwealth of Virginia. In the future, the institution was to be operated as a two-year community college. Seven years earlier, the philanthropist had purchased an abandoned marine supply depot, where he opened the school as a four-year liberal arts college. For a number of reasons, the original plan for independent operation had been changed, though the Beazley Foundation still supported the institution financially.

When J. E. Danieley read this news, he realized immediately that the rising juniors and seniors at Frederick would need to complete their work at another college to obtain a degree. Without unnecessary delay, on the 12th he telephoned Dr. Ernest Wood, president of the Virginia school, to offer full credit at Elon for "students' work as it stands, including D's," if any who were recommended for admission to Elon by the Frederick College administration wished to make the transfer.[33] On the 18th, Danieley and Dean Alfred S. Hassell visited Frederick, showed slides of Elon, described the institution, and discussed the situation with students. At the close of a busy day, 165 applications had been made for entrance to Elon. This was not the final total, which the press announced as 210 in May.

Upon returning from his successful mission, Danieley informed his trustees:

> This is very important to us from two standpoints: (1) It shows a willingness to cooperate with other institutions and to assist students who face difficult days which are entirely beyond their control. (2) It will give us a fair number of upperclassmen in spaces which otherwise will of necessity be assigned to entering freshmen. . . .
>
> The entire Frederick story is highly unusual, but it now appears that we will be able to be of tremendous assistance to many of the students and that their coming to Elon will be

distinctly advantageous to our program. We will continue to work with the administration at Frederick and with their students and offer assistance to them in any way which seems in the best interest of the students there and Elon College.[34]

In adopting this attitude, the Danieley administration figuratively "cast its bread upon the waters" because Frederick College was backed financially by $6 million or more from the Beazley Foundation. Of the more than 200 students who transferred to Elon College, 118 graduated. The foundation provided approximately $225,000 in scholarships for these students. As an act of gratitude, Dr. Danieley served as special assistant to the trustees of the organization in 1972 without remuneration,[35] and the Beazley Foundation reciprocated with an unrestricted gift of $50,000 to Elon. The transfer plan was beneficial to students and officials of both Frederick and Elon colleges.

While arranging accommodations for the influx of new students, the faculty concluded a study of the semester system as it then existed. After the Thanksgiving and Christmas holidays, the students returned for a period of two to three weeks, during which they were primarily occupied with the examinations that concluded the fall term. They then enjoyed another recess of a week or more. The spring term, which then began, was interrupted by the Easter holiday. As a result of this schedule, vacation periods were too close together during the fall term for the best academic results.

After a thorough study of the subject, the faculty made a recommendation, approved by the trustees in the spring of 1968, that placed the college on a 4-1-4 system.[36] This meant that classes would be held only five days each week. Those on Mondays, Wednesdays, and Fridays would meet for fifty minutes, and those scheduled for Tuesdays and Thursdays would be eighty minutes in length. The fall term would end when the Christmas holiday began. Immediately after the holiday, the month-long winter term would begin, during which a student would enroll for only one course. At its conclusion, no recess would occur but the spring term would begin immediately. The elimination of the intersemester holidays and the shortening of the examination period made it possible for the academic year to end two or three weeks earlier than formerly.

This plan was popular from its inception. It also provided an advantage never before possible for the faculty. The winter term furnished a perfect opportunity to present travel-study courses and facilitated other innovations. During the first "mini" term, in 1969, Professors James P. Elder, Jr., and S. E. Gerard Priestley collaborated in a course on British history in which they conducted a group of approximately 50 students and townspeople to England for the month. Professor Suzanne Hooper led a small group of her French students to France. Professor Durward T. Stokes originated a course in North Carolina history that featured daily visits to historic sites in the state. Professor Donald J. Kelly took a group of physical education enthusiasts to the mountains on skiing trips. As time passed, other faculty and other disciplines cooperated in these unusual offerings. These included Professors Carole W. and George W. Troxler, Dennis Beskow, Robert G. Blake, Frederic T. Watts, Jr., Martha S. Smith, Mary Ellen Priestley, Betty K. Gerow, David M. Crowe, Jr., Richard T. Apperson, C. Fletcher Moore, Terrell W. Cofield, and others who were more or less engaged in the travel courses each year.

Another advantage of the one-month term was that a subject failed by a student in the fall could be repeated successfully during the winter and the individual would be prepared to enter the second phase of the course in the spring term. Otherwise, making up the deficiency would have had to wait until summer school or the next fall term. It was distinctly advantageous for the student to study the course the second time without such a delay. "We are happy with the program," announced the president, who also commented, "Psychologically, the faculty senses a healthy satisfaction that we are leaders in a movement to improve education and a motivation to seek new ways to stimulate learning."[37]

In keeping with this line of thought, two other innovations were introduced to Elon at this time, in the Department of Social Science. Both were conceived by Professor Stokes. One, intended to ease the classroom shortage and scheduling difficulties, was the lecture-seminar type of classes for freshmen. An unusually large enrollment, usually 75 to 100 students, were permitted in these courses. At two class meetings each week, the professor delivered formal lectures. The class was then divided into sections containing a maximum number of fifteen students. Each group met weekly with a senior, a major in the subject being taught who had been selected by the professor in charge of the course to assist him. At these meetings, the professor and his assistant took turns conducting planned discussions of the subject matter, question-and-answer sessions, and oral and written testing. In this program, many of the students engaged in more personal participation than in a class of smaller size conducted by the routine conventional method. This was a special advantage to the Department of Social Science, which accommodated the second largest number of majors in the college.[38] However, when completion of the Classroom-Office Building relieved the shortage of space, the program was abandoned.

The second innovation was the introduction of special topical studies planned by each instructor in the field of his expertise. The offerings numbered 351 were taught by assigned reading requirements and the writing of a term paper. The number 491, in addition to being used for the travel courses, also designated a seminar course, taught by discussion, reading, and writing a research paper. Classes of both the reading and seminar types were limited to a maximum number of fifteen students who were majors in the field studied. Almost every college faculty member yearns to teach the subject he had pursued in graduate school, and this plan provided an opportunity for him to do so. It also compensated for the tedium of teaching numerous lower-level survey courses. The instructor also enjoyed the privilege of changing his topic each semester because the course subjects were only announced for these numbers at registration and not printed in the college catalog. The arrangement also allowed the serious advanced student to benefit from a wide range of instruction in his or her chosen major study. This program was advantageous to several departments at Elon, though the Department of Social Science utilized it far more extensively than any other.

Another practice that appealed to many professors was the college's liberal policy of paying one-half of the expenses of a faculty member to attend a professional meeting, or all the expense if the individual was an official of the group or presented a paper on the program at the meeting. This encouraged participation in the scholarly organizations of the country, and was responsible for a certain amount of publicity through office-holding and publication. The college was not a university with a stern "publish or perish" club held over its faculty, but the institution did assist and reward the academic progress of the individual as much as possible. The principal duty of a faculty member was to teach undergraduate students as effectively as possible. Other pursuits in the field of learning, such as writing articles or books or serving as a guest lecturer, were secondary, but nevertheless appreciated. The college also paid for the typing of a Master's thesis or a doctoral dissertation compiled by its instructors. In these and other ways, the administration encouraged academic progress among its instructors. It was the generous application of this policy in a day when opportunities for college employment were plentiful that enabled Elon to retain personnel of high caliber throughout the period.

Dr. Carolyn J. Zinn organized the Contemporary Affairs Symposium in 1969 as a political science feature. It presented some interesting programs, including lectures by Senators William Proxmire and Wayne Morse.[39] In 1970, over the protests of Donald Tarkenton, the student president of the symposium, the Student Senate merged financial support of the organization with the appropriation for the Liberal Arts Forum. This in effect spelled the finish for the symposium, and the program of the forum notably advanced. Some interested citizens of Burlington generously assisted in entertaining the distinguished guests the latter organization brought to the campus, but student government funds paid a substantial part of the tab for the expensive dinner parties and receptions that accompanied their visits. These social activities aroused criticism among some students whose fees helped pay the bills and who were not particularly interested in the forum's presentations. Finally, in August 1969, a petition signed by more than twenty disgruntled undergraduates was addressed to the administration "requesting a complete report and audit of the Student Government finances."[40] This request could hardly have been ignored, and the officials promptly authorized investigation.

A special committee to deal with an audit of the Student Government Association (SGA) was appointed under the chairmanship of Professor Janie E. Council and consisting of college Business Manager Butler and students Cary Allred, Morrow Miller, and Bill Walker. A local certified public accountant, Roy Apple, was employed to make the audit. His report, delivered on September 8, and later published in the college newspaper, was somewhat of a revelation to most of those who read it. During the 1960s, each student had paid a $10 Student Government Association Fee annually at registration. In the academic year 1968–69, these amounted to a total of $31,360. Added to this sum, income from sale of newspaper ads, sale of souvenirs at Homecoming, and admissions to dances and entertainments swelled the total to $39,680.30 for the Student Government to spend. This figure was ridiculously large to be disbursed at the discretion of a few students, and it was only fitting that publicity be given to the transactions. From the treasury, $9,600.17, or almost one-fourth of the funds, had been given to the Liberal Arts Forum, but only $1,975.51 had been appropriated for the Contemporary Affairs Symposium. The remainder of the money had been spent on student concerts, dances, and entertainments. No misappropriation of funds had occurred, but a more systematic system of bookkeeping was sorely needed.[41]

As a result, the student officials accepted a plan drawn for them by Apple for making an annual budget and using an improved method of handling their financial affairs. This improved system had already been put into practice by early 1970, when the student authorities held a budget meeting:

> February 19, the Student Senate assembled to approve a revised budget for the 1969–70 SGA fiscal year. The greatest amount of controversy arose from the Liberal Arts Forum.
>
> SGA Pres. Lee Loy prefaced the discussion of the new budget by saying, "The SGA has done little for the majority of the students this year; it has appealed only to a small minority of individuals. I feel what they want is more entertainment in the form of a big Spring Weekend. The students have been forgotten too long." After some heated discussions on the budget, Mr. Loy's wishes came true. The largest amount of money was cut from the LAF budget, and is presently at the figure of $5,008.24. This is compared to the last year's budget of $9,600.17. The amount allowed for Spring Weekend expenditures is $10,136.75.[42]

This was still a generous appropriation for the forum, which continued to conduct its annual programs, but on a modified scale. The patronage of Robert Model, a former member and an alumnus of the college, and several generous families in the area were invaluable to the continued existence of the organization. It probably represented a wiser expenditure of money than the payment of large sums to "name" bands to bring their "rock and roll" music for spring weekends. However, the funds belonged to the students and it was their prerogative to determine how they would be spent. Regrettably, however, the Contemporary Affairs Symposium was lost in the shuffle of student politics and financial arrangements.

Once these matters were settled to the satisfaction of all but a few, the college was in the best position in its history to progress in peace and harmony, but this was not possible. As at most American institutions of higher learning at the time, a segment of the student body was rebelling against the college authority. They resented compulsory chapel attendance more strongly than ever, protested the prohibition of alcoholic beverages on the campus, decried the strictness of women's dormitory regulations, advocated restriction of the Long Student Center to any use other than student activities, sought establishment of a college radio station, and complained about the dining hall.[43]

Danieley was determined to carry out to the best of his ability the regulations established by the college trustees and entrusted to him for execution and enforcement. A teetotaler, he was strongly opposed to the use of alcoholic beverages and even refused to attend forum and symposium dinners when he learned they would be served. This attitude irked the complaining undergraduates, who not only disagreed with the executive on the consumption of alcohol, but also blamed him for all the disciplinary measures they did not like. "A few students are spending a considerable amount of time working on 'the administration', which they and I both realize means 'the president,'" reported Danieley to his board. "They characterize me as conservative . . . a term which I don't consider nearly as uncomplimentary as those who use it when they 'work me over'" was his sensible reaction to this opposition.[44]

The next result of student unrest was the success of the crusaders in persuading the Student Government Association to sponsor a campus newspaper. On October 15, 1968, the first issue of *Veritas* was published. Obviously, its sponsors considered the *Maroon and Gold* to be solely the organ of the administration, for they labeled the new paper as "E. C. News—Liberated Press." In the first issue, SGA president Noel L. Allen explained the reason for the new venture:

VERITAS represents something very special—something that
is new to Elon and unique to the majority of small schools. It
is designed to be immediately separate from both the S. G. A.
and the College Administration. Though it will exist as
an S.G.A. committee this year, next year its editors will be
elected in a student body election and hopefully after this edition, it will be financially independent.

I am a strong believer in freedom of the press, even when it
hurts. No issue can ever be skirted, but a level of objective
criticism must be maintained. To be meaningful and lasting,
VERITAS must use well researched commentary and be always
willing to weigh publicly both sides of any concern. It can
never let itself be either the college's or the S.G.A.'s "administrative voice."[45]

The staff was composed of coeditors Randall S. Spencer and Barton
C. Shaw, associate editors David Spicer and Earle White, sports editor Charles T. Butler, layout editor Raymond R. Sorrell, and advertising manager Linda L. Long. Reporters were Richard Beam, Jay Fisher,
Thomas Harris, Cheryl Hopkins, Catherine Mangum, Denny Mc-
Guire, Edward McGinnis, John McConnell, Carrol McKinney, Morrow Miller, Ann Peterson, Nancy Reger, Barbara Waugh, and Lindsey
Wyatt. Some of these students were seriously interested in journalism; others expected the paper to be a healthy contribution to campus life; and a few were active protesters, only interested in a vehicle
with which to criticize the administration.

An inkling of the influence of the latter was apparent in the "Com-
pendium," published on the first page of the initial issue:

In the best interests of this student community the new
S.G.A., at the request of its president, has taken a step from
which others, whether through laziness or fear, have heretofore retreated. It has instituted this new, liberated campus
newspaper. Rapport between the S.G.A. and the students and
within the student body itself has long been absent and has
resulted in a climate which breeds social indifference and academic callousness. This situation is as unhealthy to the col-
legian pursuing a liberal education as is the distance which
exists in this college between students, professors, and admin-

istrators. As long as this prevails, liberal education is impeded, even infected.

Discussion of issues on campus is symptomatic of interest in and eventually regard for the institution and conditions existing therein. And without a valve which will open rapport, discussion can only be limited in scope, uninteresting, ineffective. To serve as this valve, then, is the end VERITAS hopes to achieve.[46]

When publication began, the college administration made no move of any kind to oppose the project. Danieley, who firmly believed in the old adage that, if given sufficient rope, the culprit would eventually hang himself, said nothing except evaluating the paper in his March 1969 report to the trustees:

> The paper is supported in part by Student Government fees and very largely by local advertisements. It has served as a medium for attacking college policy, promoting student unrest, criticising persons in the administration and on the faculty, and publishing a few "dirty words" by reprinting articles from a campus on the west coast. The claim is that this is a free, uncensored press and no one who has read it would disagree with the claim. We believe that it has won only mild approval from most students and disapproval from quite a significant group. With only two or three significant exceptions we have chosen to ignore the paper.[47]

Officialdom exercised good judgment in its attitude. Because the newspaper failed to become financially independent and the more serious members of the staff quit the project, in November 1969 publication ceased of the original *Veritas*.

The failure of the short-lived newspaper to foment a revolution did not suffice to dissuade the protesters from attempting other methods to defy authority. It had been the custom for the dining halls to serve a steak dinner on Saturday night, at which male students were requested to wear coats and ties. On the evening of April 12, 1969, the troublemakers defied this rule and were consequently denied entrance to the cafeteria by Dean of Students W. Jennings Berry and his assistant P. W. Benton. Forthwith, forty students signed a petition listing their grievances and then marched across the campus to present it to the president at his home. He promised to provide a reply to them in his office on Monday morning. The requested changes were an end to Saturday dress regulations, discontinuance of involuntary chapel, and revision of drinking regulations and women's rules.[48]

On Sunday, April 13, many students boycotted the cafeteria, and a group numbering between 100 and 150 staged a sit-in in front of McEwen. At six o'clock in the evening, SGA President Allen and Treasurer Russell Schetroma addressed the participants in front of the Long Student Center. Afterward, another petition, little different from the first, was drafted and delivered to the Danieley home. The number of marchers was estimated at 300 to 500 by Allen and approximately 125 by Danieley.

The patient executive calmly received the petition, and, as promised, replied to the students on Monday. He informed them that a student committee would revise the coat-and-tie regulation; smoking would continue to be prohibited in cafeteria and classrooms; the women's rules would be revised; the established committee of the board of trustees would report on chapel revisions; and the sunbathing rule would be revised in a manner "acceptable to the major-

Fiftieth reunion of the class of 1926, held at the scene of its gift to the college of a new gazebo for the old campus well.

ity of our students."[49] This compromise temporarily calmed the troubled waters for all except the leading protesters, who then sought other issues to which they could devote their talents for creating turmoil. During the fall term of 1969, they found one—one that appealed to a group of students whose level of protest went way beyond the subjects of neckties at meals and sun-bathing procedures.

On September 25, the new SGA President, William Y. Comninaki, wrote the faculty that his association had decided to join the National Vietnam Moratorium on October 15, and requested its support of a boycott of classes on that date.[50] This protest movement throughout the country had arisen in opposition to the escalation of U.S. participation in the Vietnam War, which was becoming increasingly unpopular throughout the nation with students and others. Numerous males of draft age frankly admitted they were enrolled in college in an effort to obtain deferment from military service, and Elon had its share of them.

In his reply to the request on behalf of the faculty, Dr. Danieley explained to Student Government officials that "we will not attempt to interfere in any way with peaceful, orderly demonstrations or protests which do not disrupt the normal activities of the college," but he also asserted, "Elon College will continue to operate on a normal schedule on Oct. 15 with all classes and laboratories meeting as scheduled." The executive also acknowledged that, "although several faculty members might like to cooperate with you, as faculty members we have no choice but to fulfill our obligations to our students and to hold our classes as scheduled."[51] This ruling was not universally popular, but was challenged only by C. Michael Smith, an assistant professor of English, who announced he did not plan to meet his classes on the day of the moratorium. Although warned that the consequences of this action might be severe, he persistently refused to abandon his intention. It was somewhat paradoxical, though, that he did arrange for colleagues to include his students in their classes on the day of protest.

The college newspaper described the beginning of the moratorium: "The day began with a silent vigil at 8:45. About 90 students gathered along the sidewalk between Alamance and the Student Center. Faculty members such as Professors Michael Smith and Phillip Owens, Dr. W. W. Sloan and Dr. and Mrs. Priestley joined."[52] At 10:45 a crowd estimated at 150 persons gathered around a platform on the campus to hear speeches. Barry Simpson, Craig Mc-Creary, and President Comninaki explained the purpose of the moratorium. Dr. Sloan was applauded for stating, "I don't think we can be Christian and advocate war." Professor Smith then delivered the keynote address. Following the oratory, the group adjourned for the next phase of the program, which took place in Burlington.[53]

Those who participated there assembled near the YMCA, where they were joined by students from Williams and Jordan Sellars high schools. About 180 strong, they marched up Main Street and turned down to the post office. There they observed a period of silent prayer, after which they sang "We Shall Overcome" and dispersed.

During the afternoon at the college, more speeches ensued as well as another rendition of "We Shall Overcome." Events climaxed in the evening with a memorial service held in the Elon College Community Church. The meditation, based on the theme "Let There Be Peace," was presented by Dr. Danieley. "Today has been a highly unusual day in the life of this country, in various places, for a great variety of reasons, millions of citizens have in their own way made a witness for peace."[54]

Most of the students and faculty paid little or no attention to the program that day while they went about their regular duties, but they were pleased that it was conducted in an orderly, dignified manner. Recognizing this, the president expressed his "deep appreciation to all our students for the mature and responsible manner in which the October 15 protest was observed on our campus." He also commented, "I was tremendously impressed with the fact that most of our students attended classes as scheduled," and stated, "The evening worship service was a period of great inspiration to me."[55]

The moratorium might have been respectfully listed among Elon's interesting events had it not been for one jarring note: the authority of the institution had been flouted when a rule was deliberately broken. That damaging fact could not be ignored. The breach of discipline was common knowledge, for which reason the outcome was awaited with keen interest. On October 17 President Danieley suspended Professor Smith from his faculty duties and directed him not to meet his classes until the Executive Committee of the board of trustees could meet on October 22 to decide on his dismissal "for breach of contract."[56] The action was based upon the presumption that the professor had violated his contract in refusing to carry out his specified duties, and did not in any way concern freedom of speech or civil liberties of the individual. Faculty members were allowed to fail to meet their classes in cases of a death in their family, illness, or attendance at a professional meeting, and not for other reasons unless by special permission. Failure to meet classes when permission to do so had been denied in advance could hardly be excused.

Smith challenged the legality of the presidential action on the grounds that his academic freedom had been violated and that he had been denied the privilege of freedom of speech. This controversy provided grist for the mills of the news media, and publicity soon spread from the local newspapers to the national press. Both the American Civil Liberties Union and the American Association of University Professors (AAUP) became interested in the affair. On behalf of the latter, Professor William Van Alstyne, of the Duke University Law School faculty, visited Elon, glanced at the facts of the situation, and contended that the AAUP had no case. Nevertheless, Smith retained Professor Daniel Pollitt, of the University of North Carolina Law School faculty, to represent him, after which Danieley arranged for Professor Francis Paschal, of the Duke University Law School, to serve as counselor for the administration.

When the Executive Committee of the board of trustees met on the 22d, it approved the suspension of the instructor but frankly criticized the president for not also stopping his pay. The latter stoutly defended his action on the premise that allowing the salary to continue might enhance a speedy, peaceful settlement of the controversy, and he was correct. In a special meeting on November 9, the trustees were brought up to date:

> President Danieley read the following: I am today releasing to the press the following statement: "Since Professor Michael Smith has now given me satisfactory assurances that he intends in the future to meet his classes, I have terminated the suspension which I instituted on October 17. Professor Smith has authorized me to release the following statement on his behalf."
>
> STATEMENT OF ASSISTANT PROFESSOR C. MICHAEL SMITH
> My actions in calling off classes for the Moratorium on October 15, 1969, sprang from my deepest convictions about the

tragedy of the Vietnamese war and the opposition to the current U.S. military policy in South East Asia. I followed the dictates of my conscience and could do no other. At the same time, realizing both the responsibilities of Elon College in assuring that classes meet as scheduled and that due to my suspension my students have already suffered an interruption in the normal course of their education, I do not intend to call off classes in the future without the permission of the Chairman of the English Department. It may be, in some future unknown situation, that my conscience and my judgment of the then Chairman of the English Department will not coincide. If that unlikely situation ever does arise, I would then have no recourse except resignation.

My case has resulted in difficulty for me, the faculty, the students, and the administration of Elon College. I would hope that a further result would be a restudy of academic due process and faculty governance on our campus.[57]

The board then voted to reinstate Professor Smith, and the controversy at Elon College roused by the moratorium ended.

When this settlement was announced, everyone expressed exclamations of relief except a few diehards, who refused to be pacified in any manner. However, they bided their time quietly for a few months until March 1970, when the faculty contracts for the next year were issued. Smith did not receive one, which was not unexpected, and two other instructors were released who had nothing whatever to do with any controversy. One, who taught English, was not progressing toward a required higher degree. The other was an instructor in dramatics, which was being phased out of the institution's curriculum. It had been a fruitful department, but, "because of the high cost of the program and the low attendance, it was costing the College approximately $10.00 for each person who saw a dramatic performance."[58]

Protesting the alleged unfair treatment of all three, on March 6, 1970, a new version of *Veritas* appeared. Its format was crude, it was poorly reproduced somewhere off campus from faulty typescript, and it was distributed by a few students. The publication was not sponsored by the Student Government Association, but was apparently an independent undertaking of several students and one named faculty member, all listed as "The Comrades." The contents were vulgar, inflammatory, crude, and vindictive. Even doctored photographs were included, which cruelly lampooned certain individuals. When Dr. Danieley later saw the paper, he said it "contained language which is not in keeping with the aims, objectives and practices on the campus of Elon College."[59] The president was a genial man, but he could be pushed only so far, and the new publication exceeded the limit. However, as it happened, he did not have to deal with the unpleasant matter personally.

In acknowledgment of International Education Year, Gerald Read, professor of comparative education at Kent State University, organized a month-long world tour for educators and Dr. Danieley joined the group. The timing was shrewdly planned for the paper to make its initial appearance while the president was away on this trip and Dean Moore was judging a music contest in South Carolina. However, Dean Strum rose to the occasion. On the day of the first issue, four of the contributors were summoned to appear before an administration committee the following day to answer charges of printing obscene material and circulating it on the campus. They appeared, but were suspended from school because they refused to stand trial on the charges.

Moore hurriedly returned to the college, where he was immediately bombarded with requests for interviews by all branches of the news media and with questions from almost everyone else. The harassed dean stoutly upheld the administration's demands, and on the 10th the accused changed their attitude and were turned over to the Honor Court. The following day, the second number of the *Veritas* appeared, but it contained no obscene words. On the 18th, the four staff members, who had been found guilty as charged, were placed on probation for the remainder of the semester. Five days later, the third number of the so-called newspaper was sold on the campus, after which no more issues appeared. This virtually ended organized student unrest of any consequence at Elon College.[60]

President Comninaki, who had tried to please the administration and all divisions of his constituents without pleasing anyone, including himself, on December 8, 1969, resigned his office. Frustrated, disillusioned, emotionally upset, and physically unwell, he also quit school, even though he had completed most of the requirements for graduation. Vice-President Lee Loy stepped into the chief executive office of the Student Government Association, and affairs began to return to normal.[61]

Some disciplinary changes were made at Elon, as they were elsewhere, but these were in the process of natural evolution when unrest became pronounced. If anything, desired changes were delayed, not hastened, by the activities of the protesters. The results had proved that forceful defiance of authority was not the best way to obtain reforms. As it was, Elon was fortunate in facing no more serious disturbances than the controversies related because military and police units were patrolling some campuses in the state where buildings had been set on fire and damaged while mobs were dispersed with tear gas. In the final analysis, the integrity and morality inherent in the characters of the majority of Elon students were on the side of law and order, which was a tribute to the institution's standards.

The leaders of the rebellion either graduated, left the college by choice, or flunked out. Only the "hippies" remained, and these were not necessarily synonymous with the protesters. A number of the leaders in the opposition to discipline scorned the unkempt long hair, ragged dungarees, and dingy sweatshirts that some of their colleagues preferred, and many other students who embraced this fashion were only interested as spectators in protest demonstrations. It was a phase of American life that was not confined to college students or to youth. Men of all ages began to grow beards, mustaches, and long hair, and women and girls wore miniskirts and let their hair hang freely down their backs. The old heads at the college were patient, for they knew this phase would run its course, and, when the pendulum swung in the reverse direction, only the future could reveal the extremities of the next craze.

CHAPTER XIV

THE MAJESTIC TREE

Towers and battlements it sees
Bosom'd high in tufted trees
JOHN MILTON
L'Allegro

While the officials were being provoked by the activities of an obstreperous minority of the student body, the other affairs of the college were by no means neglected. The president's office was busier than it had ever been. The Classroom-Office Building and the Physical Education Building, which was to house the new indoor swimming pool, were both under construction. The Carlton Building and Whitley Auditorium were undergoing extensive renovation. The latter's stage was enlarged; the organ console moved into the capacious new orchestra pit; the entire lighting system improved; and comfortable cushioned seats replaced the old wooden benches, which had always made their occupants feel they were tilted slightly forward. Although the seating capacity was not increased, the rearranged facility was far more useful for presenting musical and dramatic performances.

These and other worthwhile projects required large sums of money for construction, and, despite generous governmental grants-in-aid, a large amount had to be borrowed. The retirement of this debt, plus the ever-present need for increasing the endowment, made a major fundraising effort mandatory. The Diamond Anniversary Fund and the smaller Loyalty Fund had both been successful, but amounted to far less than the $3 million goal set for the next campaign. In 1967 negotiations were completed with Tamblyn and Brown, a firm of professional fundraisers from New York, to conduct the E-4 Campaign (Elon Expands Its Educational Excellence).[1] Adrian Hoffman was the company representative sent to Elon to supervise the program, which soon began.

The first phase was solicitations by the Advanced Gifts Division, which on October 16, 1968, made an encouraging summary of its progress and listed the following completed and proposed solicitations:[2]

Government grants	$781,049.00
Trustees	223,300.00
Parents of students	100.00
Faculty	1,040.00
Corporations and foundations	256,600.00
Alumni	1,500.00
Friends	22,487.50
Churches and organizations	250.00
Total	$1,286,326.50

After this report was proudly delivered, the second phase of the program began. This consisted of solicitation by the Major Gifts Division. Fortunately for the college, two Burlington Industries executives, William L. Fayle and R. Cruse Lewis, agreed to serve as chairman and associate chairman, respectively, of this part of the drive. While it was under way, guest speakers were invited to the campus to address campaign rallies held to generate enthusiasm. These included Archie K. Davis, of Winston-Salem, chairman of the board of directors of the Wachovia Bank and Trust Company, and Dr. Martin L. Shotzberger, president of Catawba College.[3]

As the months passed, successful campaign solicitations became more and more difficult, but the unceasing effort was rewarded occasionally. In December 1968 Tamblyn and Brown's contract was renewed for an additional six months. At the conclusion of this period, in May 1969, $1,528,000 had been raised, including "amounts pledged to the Library Building Fund and government grants on the classroom-office building and physical education division." On May 31, 1970, the fund totaled $1,703,000, but this was little more than half the original goal.[4] Prospects for reaching the $3 million mark seemed remote, but the college president and his associates stoutly refused to close the campaign. Their long, hard labor had made them as determined as former President Smith when he launched the "All Or Nothing Campaign," and they refused to consider failure even as a possibility.

Under the leadership of J. L. Crumpton, chairman of the Campaign Steering Committee, the project was reorganized with the consultative assistance of the firm of Gonser, Gerber, Tinker, and Stuhr, of Chicago. Dr. Robert Stuhr visited Elon each six weeks to aid in evaluating the effort, give advice on techniques and possible projects, and assist in planning the work and training personnel. Elon was fortunate in enjoying the services of such an expert consultant, and the results were proportionately rewarding.[5] The Loyalty Fund, which had received $12,963 from 521 contributions in 1969–70, was continued as the Annual Fund. A system was devised for acknowledging gifts in print by naming the donors as members of clubs. The range of the Century Club was $100–$500, the Oak Club, $500–$1,000, and the President's Club, $1,000 upward.[6]

Dr. Danieley arranged to devote more of his time than previously to personal solicitations, and the renewed effort to reach the original goal began. A legacy from the William L. Monroe estate maturing just at the time was encouraging, and progress slowly but consistently accelerated.[7] In June 1972 Chairman Crumpton was able to exultantly announce the almost incredible fact that the drive had gone "over the top!" More than 150 donors, workers, faculty, and staff celebrated this final attainment of $3,010,816 at a victory luncheon. Congratulations were read from Chairman Eure, of the board of trustees, and Governor Robert W. Scott, among others, while everyone relaxed with pleasure after having accomplished the seemingly impossible.[8]

While plans were being made during the autumn of 1970 to reorganize the flagging E-4 project, the Southern Association of Colleges and Schools had announced that its decennial self-study visitation of the college was scheduled for the following year. Professor Winfred Meibohm, of the Department of Social Science, was assigned the editorship of the voluminous self-study report of the institution required in preparation for the event. Administrative personnel who were assigned significant responsibilities in completing it included Deans Moore and Strum, Dr. Baxter, and W. E. Butler, Jr. Faculty members who assisted by serving on the steering committee were Professors James Overton, Allen Sanders, Robert Delp, Janie Council, Durward T. Stokes, Eleanor Moffett, Jo Williams, and Wesley Alexander.[9]

The lengthy task was completed in August 1971, and the visitation committee arrived on September 26 for its investigation. Dr. Jack Suberman, dean of the College of Humanities of Florida Atlantic University, chaired the committee. He was assisted by Dr.

North Carolina's Governor Robert W. Scott accompanied by chairman of the Elon board of trustees and North Carolina Secretary of State Thad Eure at Founders Day in 1969. Professor C. Fletcher Moore is in the background.

Thomas Spragens, president of Centre College, of Danville, Kentucky; Dr. Thomas Kreider (English), of Berea College; Dr. Gilbert Lycan (history), of Stetson University; Dr. Lillian C. Manley, executive director of the Alabama Consortium for the Development of Higher Education; Dr. George C. Taulbee, associate dean of the College of Arts and Sciences of the University of Houston; Dan M. King, librarian at Kentucky Wesleyan College; D. L. Vaughan, treasurer of the University of the South; Dr. J. Allen Norris, acting dean of Rollins College; and Dr. David T. Kelly, associate executive secretary of the Commission on Colleges of the Southern Association.[10]

This group remained at the college for three days, during which time its members checked records; talked with students, faculty, staff, and employees; visited classrooms, dormitories, the library, and other buildings; and in general thoroughly inspected the condition and the status of the institution from both the standpoint of its records and the testimony of persons involved in the operation. Before Dr. Suberman left the campus, he gave an oral report to Dr. Danieley that he considered "highly satisfactory."[11] The formal written report of the visitation committee was not acted upon officially until December 13, 1972, when the association's Commission on Colleges met in New Orleans. At that time, Elon's self-study was approved, and the accreditation of the institution reaffirmed for a period of ten years.[12]

In its report, the committee recommended that, during the decade scheduled to elapse before the next visitation, the college concentrate upon raising the number of doctorates on its faculty. The standards of the association required that, in senior colleges, at least 50 percent of the teaching faculty in humanities, social sciences, and natural sciences possess educational preparation equivalent to one year of advanced study beyond the master's degree and at least 30 percent must hold the doctor's degree. In any discipline in these fields in which a major concentration of courses was offered, at least one quarter of the faculty must hold the doctor's degree in that discipline. Elon barely met the requirements for the faculty at large and did not meet the requirements in some of the departments in which majors were offered. The visitors also urged the college to "recruit its faculty from a wider area, choosing fewer appointees who have studied at Elon or only one university," and to support financially and otherwise encourage faculty research and publication. Faculty members were also encouraged to "rethink the objectives" and the offerings of their departments "as they relate to the aims of Elon College."[13]

The investigators also suggested that careful thought be given to the admissions policy of the institution and "its implications for the future of the College," and frankly stated that more remedial work was needed if students continued to be admitted "with the type of educational background as those now enrolled." The committee also recommended that the annual Elon audit be certified and conform to the format of the College and Business Administration Manual published by the American Council on Education. The report concluded by predicting that the new organizational and committee structure adopted by the college would "bring a greater latitude of freedom to the students and a stronger voice for the faculty in setting policies for the College."[14] All these recommendations were seriously regarded by the administration, and steps were taken immediately to act upon them.

The "new organization and committee structure" at Elon, to which the visitation committee referred in its report, was the product of a new set of faculty bylaws adopted with the approval of the trustees in the spring of 1970. The provisions of the new rules were not elaborate, but were more democratic than those in the past. All faculty members were eligible to vote in faculty business meetings except those "elected by the Board of Trustees with a teaching load of fewer than eighteen hours in the current academic year." The crux of the organizational system was the creation of an Academic Council, composed of nine elected faculty members who enjoyed voting power, and the college president or his designee as a nonvoting member.

These representatives were elected for two-year terms of office on the following plan:

> One member shall be elected from each of the following divisions into which the departments of instruction are organized: (1) Humanities; (2) Mathematics and Natural Science; (3) Social Sciences; and (4) Physical Education, Health, and Teacher Education. In addition, five at large members shall be elected by the Faculty. . . . To serve as a voting member of the Academic Council, a faculty member must be a voting member [of

the faculty] under the terms of these bylaws, must have two years of service on the Faculty, and must hold the rank of assistant professor or above. No more than two members of the Faculty whose principal duties are administrative may serve on the Council at any one time.[15]

The powers and responsibilities of the group were also specified:

> The Council shall deliberate on any matter within the province of the Faculty for the purpose of formulating general policy for approval or disapproval by the Faculty. Those matters which are the responsibility of standing committees shall be referred to the appropriate committee. . . .
>
> The Council shall serve as a hearing committee, when hearing is to be held, in cases involving the dismissal or suspension of a faculty member or charges of unprofessional conduct against a faculty member.[16]

In addition, the council served as the nominating committee for the elective members of the faculty; acted in an advisory capacity to the president; and developed, maintained, and published "upon adoption by the Faculty," a set of professional standards.

The bylaws also provided for permanent committees on Academic Standing; Curriculum; Library; Lyceum; Student Affairs; Teacher Education; Athletics; Faculty Research; Religious Life; Judicial Review; and Fraternities, Sororities and Service Organizations. All these were to be composed of members elected from both the faculty and the student body. An article was included on "Rights and Responsibilities of Faculty Members."

Its section on academic freedom was the 1940 statement on that subject agreed upon by the Association of American Colleges and University Professors, adopted verbatim:

> (a) The teacher is entitled to full freedom in research and in the publication of results, subject to the adequate performance of his other academic duties; but research for pecuniary return should be based upon an understanding with the authorities of the institution.
>
> (2) The teacher is entitled to full freedom in the classroom in discussing his subject, but he should be careful not to intro-

duce into his teaching controversial matter which has no relation to his subject. Limitations of academic freedom because of
religious or other aims of the institution should be clearly
stated at the time of appointment.

(3) The college or university teacher is a citizen, a member of a
learned profession, and an officer of an educational institution.
When he speaks or writes as a citizen he should be free from
institutional censorship or discipline, but his special position
in the community imposes special obligations. As a means of
learning and an educational officer, he should remember that
the public may judge his profession and his institution by his
utterances. Hence he should at all times be accurate, should
exercise appropriate restraint, should show respect for the
opinions of others, and should make every effort to indicate
that he is not an institutional spokesman.[17]

Another section required loyalty of the faculty to the college, specified that "governmental activities and outside employment" should
not interfere with the primary duties of the educator, and stated that
ethical and professional standards be established and upheld.

The principal changes introduced by these bylaws was the election of committees that had formerly been appointed by the administration, and the establishment of the Academic Council. The
entire plan originated during the turmoil over Professor Smith's suspension. The new system satisfied the unhappy element of the faculty, and the majority of the professors were more or less indifferent
to making the change and exhibited no strong preference for or
against the matter. Unquestionably, the new system gave the faculty
more voice in administrative matters, and it also provided a fertile
seedbed for campus politics, which had never previously been extensive at the college. At any rate, the system had become established,
and President Danieley informed the trustees on October 20, 1970,
that it was working smoothly.[18]

As a result of the increasing number of important events connected with Elon's program and the accelerated pace with which
they occurred, attention was invited to customs and fixtures that
had become outmoded. One of these was the timing of the *Maroon
and Gold*, which had constituted a serious problem for several years.
This was because the contents of the paper were a week old when

the issues were distributed, which made it virtually impossible to use "as a means of communication to students and faculty regarding current events." In the spring of 1970, the course in journalism was removed from the college curriculum, and, because of the tremendous cost involved, publication of the school newspaper was discontinued. The old printing press, once the pride of Elon, but worn to the point of being held together with baling wire, and the faith of its student operators, was retired from service. Its weekly roar was heard no more under the oaks, for the college no longer had a newspaper. Instead, a one-page mimeographed *Communicator* was distributed on Tuesday containing copy turned in to the editor the previous day. This proved to be "an effective means of communication" and was continued on a permanent basis.[19]

Yet, sentiment was expressed on the campus for the *Maroon and Gold* either to be revived or to be replaced. College officials were aware of this feeling, but memories of *Veritas* were fresh in their minds and they declined to sponsor the project. Instead, they called attention to the student fees of $25 collected annually, which produced a total of $43,000 that was turned over to the SGA for its senate to spend. Under these circumstances, the student body possessed the means to finance a newspaper and had permission to publish one "provided it follows the guidelines of acceptable journalism and is in keeping with the general philosophy and traditions of Elon College." However, no action was taken on the matter at the time, and the *Maroon and Gold* and the old press became a part of the institution's historic past.[20]

Relations between Elon and the Southern Conference of the United Church of Christ, which had ever been cordial, received a special emphasis from the college in this period. In 1966 a Committee on Southern Convention History delegated Dr. William T. Scott, a United Church minister, to write a history of the Christian Church, which founded Elon. He promptly began accumulating data, but ill health prevented him from completing the task. The college then salvaged what appeared to be a doomed project by offering the services of Durward T. Stokes, one of its history professors and a friend of Dr. Scott, to collaborate with him in further research and the writing of the book. Shortly after this arrangement was completed, Scott died suddenly, and the assignment was left in the hands of his associate. This was disconcerting, but the college administration made generous concessions to relieve the situation, and *A History of the Christian Church in the South* was published in 1973. Had it not been for the leadership of President Danieley and the contribution of his administration, the book, which was acclaimed as a valuable addition to American church history, might never have been written.[21]

In the field of music, numerous advances were made during this period. In the 1960s Professor Jack O. White organized the band into four units: marching band, concert band, stage band, and the Emanons. The latter was really a jazz ensemble whose odd title was derived from "no name" spelled in reverse. This unit came into national prominence in 1964, when it was invited to play at the New York World's Fair. The successful engagement was rewarded with an invitation to return the next year, and it was accepted. In 1970 the Emanons played in Europe for USO programs; and, as a result of arrangements made by the United States embassy in Luxembourg, performed at the annual grand ball in that country. Five years later, the musicians played a return engagement for a similar event. In 1972, under the sponsorship of the United States Navy and its unit, the All-American Entertainers, the band visited Puerto Rico and other countries. The marching band division became an indispensable part of football games, and provided an excellent spectacle for the audience at half time.

A talented trumpeter himself, White also founded the Brass Clinic, a week of special instruction in the brass instruments held annually for students of high school and college age. This summer

Professor Jack O. White and the Emanons.

program grew through the years until it required eight instructors to teach the fifty-odd students enrolled.[22]

Within a short time after assuming office, Dr. Danieley had become impressed with a book entitled *Memo to a Faculty Member*. Its author was Professor Earl J. McGrath, a prominent leader in the Institute of Higher Education at Columbia University. The theme of the book was the relation of a college curriculum to institutional finances, and it was similar in content to *Memo To A College Trustee* (1959), by Beardsley Ruml and Donald H. Morrison. The conclusions drawn from these and similar books was that most American colleges would experience difficulty surviving in the future unless their curricula were trimmed to a few more than the basic courses required for their majors. This would eliminate special studies attracting only a comparatively few students, which were usually given at a financial loss. A program condensation would also often enable the institution to operate with fewer faculty members, thus lowering the payroll and aiding the effort to keep tuition as low as possible. Because of the influence of the opinions of these authors, a presidential order was issued at Elon for each department to revise its offerings, subject to the approval of the Curriculum Committee.

Compliance with the instructions was much more thorough in some departments than in others, but the overall result showed some degree of progress toward the administration's goal. The matter then remained more or less in abeyance until 1970, when many independent colleges were in dire financial straits, though Elon was not one of them. Another curriculum revision was then ordered, and specific guidelines were delineated. Thirty-three course hours was to be the maximum requirement for a major in each department, and thirty were to be preferred. Only two or three courses in addition to the number required for the major were to be offered in each department. Seminar courses could be continued, but they should be offered less frequently than previously. In addition, the core curriculum that was required of all students was to be stripped of many of its specified studies. They were to be replaced by elective courses chosen by the individuals.

This mandate caused a turbulent reaction. Many faculty members, faced with the changing of requirements that had been the standard for many years, did not conscientiously approve the action. Others simply did not wish to abandon pet courses or programs in the interest of economy. They preferred for the athletic appropriation to be cut instead. Other instructors were pleased, for they considered any change an improvement. The mechanics involved were also a major chore because sixty-one hours were being offered in one subject, fifty-one in another, and the new quota was exceeded in almost everything taught. To choose which courses to eliminate from all that were considered important was no easy decision, but it needed to be made.

Throughout the winter and spring, the Curriculum Committee met frequently. Time after time, departmental chairmen revised lists of offerings, vowing no more courses could possibly be eliminated, only to be told that the new figures were the maximum. This required a further revision and additional elimination before the report could be accepted. The strain began to wear on the committee members because the lengthy sessions, some held at night, were in addition to their regular classroom work.

Finally, the grueling chore was completed. The departments had adjusted to their new requirements. More significant to the faculty as a whole was the elimination from the core curriculum of requirements for foreign language, history, social sciences, and economics, as well as a reduction in the math-laboratory science requirement. Only the formerly specified courses in English and religion remained unaltered, the latter more because of the insistence of the trustees than of the faculty. The B.S. degree in chemistry had been dropped, though the B.A. degree in that subject was retained. The major in home economics had been removed from the curriculum, though courses in the subject were still offered, and drama had been dropped entirely. No major had previously been offered in the latter subject, but courses had been conducted and plays presented under the direction of two professors, who also taught speed-reading courses.

Other changes were of less importance, but as a whole the alterations in requirements and offerings were revolutionary. Many were unhappy with the new system, some even predicting it would be temporary, but it was nevertheless placed in operation. In all fairness to the Danieley administration, it must be realized that similar changes were taking place in institutions of higher learning all over the country at the time, and the general results were very much the same. Just how much credit is attributable to this revision is a matter of speculation, but, for some years after its adoption, Elon was one of the few colleges in the state operating in the black financially.

At the time, when courses were being deleted from the curriculum, "Current Issues" was added. Academic credit was given for the program, which was conducted with students in small groups, working under a faculty leader, to engage in mature, scholarly deliberation of some of the key issues before the American people. The administration was convinced that this type of approach should characterize the educational world, and that solutions to some of the "more vexing problems" might be found "if more people were willing to seriously examine their own positions and to engage in meaningful discussion with those who think otherwise."[23] Dr. John G. Sullivan was the pioneer professor of the new offering.

Regardless of the enviable status of the college, Dr. Danieley shared the concern, if not actual alarm, of many leaders in higher education over the rising cost that accompanied financial inflation. Unlike state-supported institutions, independent schools lacked guaranteed budgets, nor any means of obtaining them. This made their future financial security uncertain. In recognition of the importance of this matter, the Elon official accepted an appointment from Governor Robert W. Scott to serve on the state Legislative Study Commission on Student Financial Aid. Although already loaded with major responsibilities, the commissioner gave a full measure of time and energy to the new assignment, which were eventually rewarded. Danieley had served without success in a similar capacity under the previous governor, Terry Sanford, but was quite willing to continue his efforts.

At the October 1970 meeting of Elon's trustees, Danieley reported on his stewardship and solicited their support of his convictions. He had strongly championed the effort to obtain financial aid from the state for college students "regardless of the institution which they choose to attend" because he considered this program "vital and necessary." The president thought such aid should be based upon the needs of the individuals. He also explained:

> In addition to this program which has been recommended by the Commission, I also feel strongly that the time is approaching when some means must be found whereby the State can be of definite financial assistance to the private institutions. My

own preference is for a contract plan whereby the State would pay a given amount to each institution for each North Carolina resident who is a bona fide student at that institution. These are two separate propositions. One to aid the student; the other to aid the private college. I favor both propositions and invite your careful consideration and support of these proposals when they are considered by the General Assembly in the 1971 session.[24]

This statement was acceptable to the Elon president's colleagues, for it echoed their sentiments, and all worked zealously to reach their goal.

Governor Robert Scott, state Senator Ralph Scott, who was also an Elon trustee, and other influential legislators supported the commission's efforts, which were rewarded during the 1971 session of the legislature. Under House Bill 780, the private colleges were allotted a fixed sum of money from the state, to be used for aid for each resident of North Carolina enrolled as a student in the fall of 1972 in excess of the number enrolled in 1970. Senate Bill 732 provided $575,000 to be disbursed on a pro rata basis to the private institutions for North Carolina students enrolled for the regular academic year. In Elon's case, this meant $25 for each of the approximately 1,000 North Carolina residents expected for the coming year. Also under this legislation, the college qualified for a grant of $34,600 to be used specifically as scholarships for worthy students who were North Carolina residents. When the final adjustments were made, Elon received $34,711.30 for the purpose.[25]

This program, which enabled the private college to be more competitive, was also an economy for the state because it utilized the existing private institutions by giving them financial support rather than spending larger sums for new facilities at government-owned schools to accommodate the state's student population. As a result of this program, the board of governors of the University of North Carolina recommended funding at the rate of $75 per student by the 1973 General Assembly, whereas the North Carolina Association of Independent Colleges and Universities requested funding at a level of $200 per student. The latter was based upon the conviction that it would prove to be "the most logical and reasonable approach" to providing financial aid to the state's youth who wished to attend private colleges.[26] This marked the beginning of a program of state aid to individuals for education in the independent schools, which has continued since and has been expanded to larger grants for this purpose.

For the purpose of keeping in more intimate touch with the college, another democratic step in its administration was taken by the trustees at their October 15, 1969 meeting. They voted to initiate the custom of designating two recent graduates of the institution to serve on the board. This innovation was to begin by electing an alumnus of 1968 for a one-year term and one from the next class for a two-year period. After 1971 a member of the graduating class of the preceding year would be elected to serve two years. As a result, two recent graduates would sit on the board at all times. Eligibility was to be limited to those whose academic standing was in the upper 10 percent of their class.[27]

At the board meeting in April 1970, the first two trustees were elected under this plan. They were W. Parke Herbert (Elon '68) for a one-year term, and Gerry S. Oxford (Elon '69) to serve two years. A recent graduate has been elected to the office annually since, which has proved to be a popular move.[28]

The concern expressed over the future financial position of the college was a reflection of the changed responsibility for the maintenance of the institution. "There is some uncertainty about the future pattern and amount of church support," Danieley warned his trustees. He also reminded them that Elon received no regular support from the national denomination, though the college had been allocated $35,000 annually for the past several years in the budget of the Southern Conference of the United Church of Christ. Catawba College, of Salisbury, North Carolina, had also been supported to the extent of $50,000 per year, as arranged by the Evangelical and Reformed Church before the formation of the United Church of Christ.[29]

In 1972 these plans were changed. Each institution was given $8,717.18 from the national offices of the church, and both were allowed the opportunity to apply for a supplemental grant. Elon took advantage of this privilege to request aid for her minority students. The Southern Conference included $40,000 in its budget for distribution to the two colleges. By an agreement with Dr. James H. Lightbourne, Jr., the conference executive, Dr. Martin Shotzberger, president of Catawba, and Elon's President Danieley, 60 percent of the sum was to be divided equally between the two institutions and 40 percent prorated to them on the basis of enrollment. This was accepted, though it meant in essence that the two institutions would experience more than a 30 percent decrease in support from the churches, "including total receipts from the Conference and the General Synod."[30] It also emphasized the fact that Elon College, though still church-affiliated, had not been church-supported for years, which made the college officials responsible for its financial operation. This situation was a result of the denominational mergers, and not of a deliberate plan for the church to abandon its responsibility.

Among the multiplicity of events that crowded the second half of the Danieley administration, the one which probably attracted the most universal attention was the expansion and renewed progress of the athletic program. This new phase of accomplishment began on December 21, 1966, when the board of trustees, meeting in a special session, named Shirley S. ("Red") Wilson as head football coach and assistant professor of psychology.[31] He was a native North Carolinian who held an M.A. degree from the state university and had served in the United States Navy during World War II. After his discharge, he had been phenomenally successful in coaching football at Virginia and North Carolina high schools. When he came to Elon from Fayetteville High School, Wilson brought with him his two assistants, Dwight ("Mickey") Brown and Jerry Tolley, to serve in the same capacity at the college. Alan J. White, acting chairman of the Department of Physical Education, was also an associate coach on the new staff.[32]

Shortly after "Red" Wilson arrived at Elon in January 1967, he obtained the part-time coaching assistance of the famous former University of North Carolina All-American Charles ("Choo Choo") Justice. The new group then plunged into its duties, and the star of the Fighting Christians soon began to rise to new planes of brilliance.[33]

In addition to their work in football, Jerry Tolley served as tennis coach and "Mickey" Brown supervised the wrestling team, which had originated in 1968 under the coaching of Professor Paul Sebo. Jerry Drake supervised the baseball squad, and in 1973 Charles Harris organized a soccer team. In addition to the track team, and in line with its program, a cross-country team was organized by Frederic T.

Watts, Jr., in addition to his duties as associate professor of political science.[34] Tony Radovitch assisted in basketball and coached the golf team until later succeeded by William Morningstar. After his second session of service, Coach Wilson was made athletic director, and Donald J. Kelly became chairman of the Department of Physical Education.[35]

When a team attains the level of any kind of "bowl" contest, it naturally occupies the limelight in the college athletic program, but other sports brought honors to Elon in addition to football. The college created a well-rounded sports program that achieved commendable progress in all fields and spectacular success in a few.[36]

During this expansion of sports, female athletes emerged into greater prominence than ever before, in large measure because of the arrival at Elon of the talented Yow sisters from nearby Gibsonville. Kay Yow coached the first women's basketball team authorized for intercollegiate participation, beginning in 1972. That same year, a volleyball team she organized began intercollegiate competition under the direction of Barbara Yarborough. Miss Yow also formed a softball team, which began playing in intercollegiate games in 1977 under the coaching of Mary F. Jackson.[37]

Performance in the three sports was good, but in basketball it was amazing. The records broken by the stellar playing of Wanda Wilson and the two Yow sisters, Susan and Deborah Ann, attracted national attention. Today, the three Yow sisters are coaches: Kay at North Carolina State University, Susan at East Tennessee State University, and "Debbie" at the University of Kentucky.[38]

In March 1973 President Danieley reported "another outstanding year in the field of intercollegiate athletics. He praised the progress in the major sports; the newly introduced soccer, cross-country, and wrestling; and women's sports, which included softball and volleyball. He was also pleased with the prospects in golf, in tennis, and in track.[39]

This period also featured a galaxy of stars. They were so numerous that only the most outstanding one can be mentioned here. Richard E. McGeorge, captain of both the football and basketball teams, in addition to being a capable golfer, made athletic history at Elon.[40] Coach Wilson acclaimed the grid star "the greatest football player I have ever coached." It was also because of his accomplishments that McGeorge became the first Carolinas Conference player "to ever be the first choice of a professional football team." It was a coincidence that at almost the same time the Elon star's name was chosen for national honors, it was also drawn by Selective Service for military duty. McGeorge left school to serve his stint in the army, then returned to the college in 1971 for the one final semester necessary for graduation. He received many tempting offers from professional sports organizations, but chose the one from the Green Bay Packers, and played with them through the 1978–79 season.[41]

The all-around success of Elon athletics inspired the establishment of a Sports Hall of Fame to honor the stars, coaches, and backers of the Fighting Christians. In September 1972, President Danieley requested Moses Crutchfield, Bill Hunter, Professors A. L. Hook, Luther Byrd, and Howard Richardson, and the Reverend James Waggoner to serve as a committee to decide upon criteria for membership and plan the method for inductions. Tyrone Rowell, director of Alumni Relations, was requested to serve as coordinator for the committee, and Melvin L. Shreves, director of the News Bureau, to supply information from the records pertinent to the nominees.[42]

The committeemen, who responded to the idea with enthusiasm, soon completed their work. Selections for the honors were to be made in secret from nominations sent to the faculty Athletic Committee. It was deemed advisable to select a limited number of faculty members and coaches in addition to the players honored annually. The initial ceremony took place on Homecoming Day in October 1972 in Whitley Auditorium. On that occasion, momentous in its significance to many in addition to the sports enthusiasts, nine were inducted into the new order in the presence of a large audience. Dr. Hook, "Friend of Elon Athletics Since 1914," was fittingly chosen to head the list, which included two coaches as well as six athletes.[43] Each individual was presented by a speaker, who outlined his athletic career before presenting him with a suitably inscribed plaque. The inductee then gave the college a personal memento, such as his old football helmet, jersey, baseball glove, ball, or similar item that had been associated with his sports participation. The program proved to be immensely popular, and thus another Elon tradition was founded. (For the entire list of inductions to the Hall of Fame to the present, see Appendix E.)

The roll of those who have been inducted has followed no chronological pattern or gradation of fame though it is obvious that an effort has been made to honor some of the oldest former stars and coaches. In some cases, it has been regrettably necessary to award the plaque posthumously to a wife or some other appropriate representative of the honoree. The authorized committee makes the annual selections from the nominees submitted for the award. Judging from its past history, the Hall will eventually list all the Elonians prominently connected with the college sports program, for the number of inductees grows faster than the emergence of stars.

Throughout the Danieley presidency, Founders Day was celebrated frequently, though not annually. Among the distinguished speakers on these occasions were the Reverend Ben M. Herbster, president of the United Church of Christ; the Reverend Franklin H. Littell, professor of church history at Chicago Theological Seminary; Vermont C. Royster, editor of the *Wall Street Journal*; Governor Robert W. Scott, of North Carolina; and Fred W. Baise, Jr., one of the astronauts who had journeyed to the moon. The latter was of special interest to the college family because of the universal atten-

The marching band, led by Professor Jack O. White, during the 1970s.

tion attracted by the space program. While present at the college, Royster was awarded an L.H.D. degree and Governor Scott an LL.D.[44]

In 1973 the attention of the nation was also focused on American military personnel being released from North Vietnam prison camps. Captain Jeremiah A. Denton, Jr., of the United States Navy, was one of those who had survived the brutal treatment received during several years of incarceration. He accepted the invitation to speak at Founders Day because his son, James S. Denton, was president of the Elon College Student Government Association. Two other released prisoners who attended the commemoration were air force Major Norman A. McDaniel and navy Commander Eugene B. McDaniel, who were no kin to each other. The latter had been known as "Red" when he graduated from Elon in 1955, after serving as captain "and an all-conference choice" on the college's championship baseball team. He had also become acquainted with Denton while they were in the same prison in Vietnam.[45]

President Danieley, Captain Jeremiah A. Denton, and his son, James S. Denton, on the campus, Founders Day, 1973.

By pure coincidence, the date set for the college celebration was the same day later designated by the national government when restrictions would be removed and the POWs allowed to relate their experiences to the public. Because three prominent ones were together at Elon on that occasion, interest increased to a sensational level. Arrangements were soon made to handle the situation satisfactorily. After the college program at which Denton gave his address was concluded in the morning, the three men agreed to give an account of their experiences to the news media representatives at two o'clock in the afternoon, the hour the governmental ban was removed. Not since the visit of Vice-President Lyndon B. Johnson, if indeed then, had such an assortment of reporters and their equipment assembled in Whitley Auditorium to record the event. The revelation of the atrocities to which the three had been subjected was almost incredible to civilized hearers, especially when described in the comparatively serene setting of the Elon campus. It was a day of national, possibly international, significance, and a thrilling page in the annals of the college.

Other honorary degrees voted by the college trustees during Danieley's presidency included an LL.D. to George J. Kelley and a D.D. to Clyde L. Fields in 1962, a D.D. to Robert M. Kimball and LL.D.'s to Susie M. Sharp and Charles F. Myers, Jr., in 1963, and a D.D. to Walstein W. Snyder and an LL.D. to Archibald K. Davis in 1964. The next year, North Carolina Governor Daniel K. Moore received an LL.D. and Mary Duke Biddle Semans a L.H.D. degree. In 1966 Robert L. Dickens and Nathan H. Yelton received LL.D.'s and Charles Colin a D.M. The following year, Alexander R. Burkot was awarded a HH.D. degree, Stanley C. Donnelly a D.S. degree and D.D.'s to Robbins E. Ralph and Kenneth D. Register. In 1968 Thomas E. Powell, Jr., took a D.S. degree, Martin Ritt a D.F.A. and Royster the degree already mentioned. The following year, a D.D. was given to Robert B. Marr and LL.D.'s to John L. Crumpton and Roy E. Rollins, in addition to the honor presented to Governor Scott.

In the latter years of the Danieley administration, Iris H. McEwen, donor of two major buildings on the campus, was awarded an L.H.D. degree in 1970, in addition to an LL.D. given to Reid A. Maynard and a D.D. to Hoyle L. Whiteside. The next year, William E. Taylor was recognized with an LL.D. and D.D.'s were conferred upon Porter W. Seiwell and Joseph Taylor Stanley. The latter was a minister of the

President Danieley and Mrs. McEwen in front of the Iris Holt McEwen Library.

United Church of Christ and the first black man to be so honored by Elon College. The following year, a D.D. was given to Melvin H. Dollar and LL.D.'s to Donnell S. Holt and Congressman L. Richardson Preyer.[46]

College presidents always have many "irons in the fire," and the more personal attention given to each, the more satisfactorily it heats. Furthermore, the expanded use of the airplane, in addition to other forms of modern transportation, enabled Danieley to visit more places himself than had been possible for any of his predecessors. The amount of travel thus involved set a grueling pace, which was the cause for his occasionally confiding to a friend that he expected to leave the executive office and return to the classroom before he passed his prime. Official duties were also made increasingly difficult in the early 1970s when the president began to suffer from a painful back ailment. After extensive hospitalization, the trouble was diagnosed as a ruptured disc. This was followed by successful surgery, but months elapsed before recovery was complete. It was at this time that the official decided to retire from his administrative office.[47]

Danieley's physical condition gave him food for serious thought, but it was not the reason he resigned his presidency. His decision was based on a number of factors:

> At the end of this year, I will have completed 16 years as Elon's president. Several years ago the national average for the term in office of college presidents was determined to be about 8 years; it is less than that today.
>
> It is difficult to determine precisely when a person should retire. Certainly, one must consider the situation both from the standpoint of the institution and personally: (1) The College is in good condition—the E-4 Fund Campaign has been successfully completed; the Self-Study report is in and should be approved in December; the building program is essentially finished; renovation of older buildings will be completed in the summer of 1973; the enrollment is good and prospects continue to be good; the faculty substantially meets accreditation requirements; and the reputation of the College is good and improving.
>
> (2) The situation seems right from the personal standpoint—

I am 48 years old and in reasonably good health—some back problems persist; I am a committed teacher and wish to return to teaching; I have the necessary vigor and enthusiasm to study to prepare to do a good job; and

I strongly desire more free time for study, writing, hobbies, family. The list of factors could be much longer. Suffice it to say, in consideration of all factors involved, I have concluded that there is not likely to be a better time than this year and, therefore, I am announcing my intention to retire as of June 30, 1973, and requesting the Board of Trustees to permit me to return to my status as a full-time member of the teaching faculty of the College as of the beginning of the fall semester of 1973.[48]

This resignation was accepted and the request accompanying it granted by the trustees on October 18, 1972. The board then ruefully began plans to search for a replacement. The faculty and administrative staff were frankly shocked, even dismayed, by the totally unex-

Ex-President Danieley conducting a class.

pected announcement. The public was also surprised by the decision. However, Danieley had made his choice. When he gazed out of the window of the office where he had labored so many years as an administrator, a gleam came into his eyes as he focused them on the Duke Science Building, which housed the chemistry laboratory he had long been forced to neglect.

The retiring president could take deep pride in his administration's accomplishments. The entire physical plant had been renovated, modernized, and reequipped. Seven major buildings had been added, two of which were sprawling complexes of three divisions. The value of the college property had increased to $9,571,888; the endowment to $2,928,862; and 1,753 students were enrolled.[49] The indebtedness was $3,421,996, which was being retired satisfactorily.[50] Fully accredited, the institution had every reason to anticipate a bright future. Under these circumstances, the president-chemist could return to his test tubes and Bunsen burners knowing that the sixteen years away from the laboratory had been used advantageously for the college.

CHAPTER XV

THE FRUIT OF THE TREE

Even so every good tree bringeth forth good fruit.
MATTHEW 7:17

While Danieley's unexpected resignation was still a topic of current conversation, the wheels were set in motion to find his successor. The search methods were far more democratic than ever before. Although the final decision rested in the hands of the college trustees, various students, faculty, administrators, alumni, and friends of the institution were consulted for suggestions and opinions. Several names were mentioned unofficially in connection with the office until the late spring 1973, when the announcement was made that James Fred Young had accepted election as the seventh president.

The 38-year-old educator had been born in Burnsville, North Carolina. He attended Mars Hill College prior to graduating from Wake Forest University in 1956 with a Bachelor of Science degree. The following year, he earned a Master's from the University of North Carolina at Chapel Hill, and seven years later completed a Doctor of Education at Columbia University. Between the two periods of graduate study, he served six months in the United States Army. Later, he pursued additional studies at Appalachian State University, East Carolina University, and the University of Virginia. In addition to winning scholastic honors during his academic career, he also found time to play baseball and basketball, and engage in journalism.[1]

While completing his advanced studies, Dr. Young had been employed in the public school system of North Carolina. He was especially familiar with Alamance County, for he had served as assistant superintendent of the Burlington city schools from 1964 until 1968. During his service in this office, he attracted statewide atten-

President J. Fred Young.

tion by writing "Collective Negotiations for North Carolina Teachers?" which was published in *Popular Government* by the Institute of Government at Chapel Hill.[2] He also became involved in local religious and civic affairs, including service as president of the Alamance County Community Action Program, and he was selected for "Outstanding Young Men in America," an enviable distinction.

In 1968 Young became associated with the public schools in Lynchburg, Virginia. After three years there, he moved to Richmond to fill the post of Deputy Superintendent of Public Instruction of the commonwealth of Virginia. During all these years, the educator continued to play an active role in state and local affairs, and filled a number of important positions. His professional reputation had advanced to a high degree when he was called from his office in the Old Dominion to become Elon's chief executive.[3]

Mrs. Young, the former Phyllis Johnson, of Wendell, North Carolina, was also a graduate of Wake Forest University and had taught in the public schools for several years. While her husband was connected with the Burlington schools, she had attended Elon College as a special student and taken a number of courses that could be useful in changing her type of teacher's certificate, if ever desired.[4] The Youngs were the parents of three children: Alan, eight; David, four; and Jane, three. This provided an interesting coincidence because the first two families to occupy the college president's home included three children, two boys and a baby sister named Jane. Because the family had changed residences fairly often, it moved into its college home with ease and immediately became a part of the community. The Youngs enjoyed renewing old acquaintances and making new ones. The president, young in body as well as in name, specially enjoyed the proximity of the gymnasium and its equipment for keeping physically fit as well as the nearby golf course, where he could relax from the arduous duties of his office.

Dr. Young was the first president of the college without a previous connection with the institution nor membership in the school's affiliated religious denomination at the time of his election to office. However, one of his first public acts before taking over the post was to accompany Professors Robert W. Delp and Stokes to the annual meeting of the Southern Conference of the United Church of Christ, at Catawba College, in Salisbury, North Carolina, to become better acquainted with the denomination.[5] Shortly afterward, he transferred his membership from the Baptist Church, in which he had been reared, to the United Church of Christ, in compliance with the institution's rule that the chief executive should belong to that denomination—a requirement that has since been abandoned. Joining the Community Church at Elon constituted another gesture of good faith and intended cooperation on the part of Young.

Elon's seventh president was the first to take office who did not face some glaring deficiency in the institution and its programs that demanded immediate attention. The college was operating smoothly, like a machine in good condition that only needs further tuning to increase its service. No previous chief executive of the school had enjoyed such an opportunity. Dr. Young clearly realized this, and he diligently studied means of taking full advantage of the situation.

The principal problem of institutions of higher learning at the time was the maintenance of financial stability. Elon was operating

Postgraduation joy. Governor James E. Holshouser, Jr., congratulates a student while President Young looks on.

Carolina Dormitory fire, 1975. Photo by David Rolfe. Courtesy,
Burlington Daily Times-News.

in the black, and its new president intended that it should continue to do so. The traditional ceremony of inaugurating a new president, though impressive, was both expensive and time-consuming. Young economized in both respects and also expressed his personal preference by banning the usual procedure and becoming the first new administrative head of the college installed without a formal inauguration. Although he assumed the presidential duties on August 1, 1973, he was not formally installed until a luncheon on October 17. On that occasion, in the presence of more than 250 trustees, faculty and staff members, and student leaders, Board Chairman Thad Eure administered the oath of office, in which Young pledged to "uphold the honor, integrity, Christian ideals and character" of the institution. In a brief address, he acknowledged his responsibilities and challenged all the friends of Elon everywhere to join him in the dedication of their "fullest individual and collective efforts to the preservation and extension of the ideals and concepts that are the foundations of Elon College." In so doing, all would then be "worthy of our noble heritage and our great responsibility." This concluded the sim-

Trustee and state Senator Ralph H. Scott receiving honorary Doctor of Laws degree at 1976 commencement from President Young. On the left is Vice-President for Academic and Student Affairs James A. Moncure.

ple ceremony, which had been presided over by Royall H. Spence, Jr., chairman of the Presidential Selection Committee.[6]

Realizing that tuition collected would have to supplement income from other sources if a financial deficit were to be avoided, Young scrutinized the admission of new students carefully. Because of the broader flexibility in required studies, an increase in the number of college-age youth in the area, the convenient location, and the up-to-

President Young and Dean Theo Strum chatting with students during one of the special social hours on the campus.

date facilities, applications for entrance to Elon rose astronomically. Because most applicants were admitted, the student body population climbed within three years from approximately 1,800 to 2,150 for the 1976 fall term. Of this latter number, 1,379 were from North Carolina, 493 from Virginia, and the remainder from New Jersey, Maryland, Florida, New York, Delaware, South Carolina, Pennsylvania, "and 17 other states and nine foreign countries." Of this increased influx, 1,225 resided in dormitories, which severely taxed the campus housing facilities. Most rooms designed for two occupants housed three, and the dining halls were crowded to capacity.[7]

After thoroughly surveying the details of the operation, Dr. Young reorganized the administration's structure to correspond with his plan of action. He arranged for the appointment of Dr. James A. Moncure as Vice-President for Student and Academic Affairs, to head the scholastic program. The new official had served as a professor of history and dean of University College of the University of Richmond, in the capital city of the Old Dominion, and was prepared by a wide range of experience for the office he assumed on March 1, 1974. His duties included "responsibility for all internal affairs of the college" as they were related to student personnel and instruction, while providing "leadership in program and staff development."[8]

When Danieley retired, Dr. Moore had resigned as Dean of the College to teach exclusively in the Music Department. Dr. Strum, who had served as Dean of Instruction, then filled the office until 1976, when Dr. M. Christopher White succeeded her. S. Carlysle Isley, of Burlington, was appointed as Director of Development, succeeding Charles A. Hutcheson. W. Jennings Berry became Director of Counseling Services, and was succeeded as Dean of Student Affairs by William G. Long, who had served as Dean of Men at the University of North Carolina until 1967, and from that year until 1974 as Dean of Student Services at Kalamazoo (Michigan) College.[9] Dean June M. Looney then officiated for two years as Associate Dean of Students, after which the office was combined with that of Long's duties and she returned to the teaching of psychology on a full-time basis. Other changes were made from time to time in addition to these major administrative realignments. Although Young remained the final authority, he allowed his appointees considerable latitude in the exercise of their duties and devoted his time and energy primarily to increasing the endowment and financial resources of the college.

Former President Danieley accomplished a metamorphosis in reverse, so to speak. This was a feat many did not believe possible, but by August 1, 1973, he had changed back from the dominant outspoken executive he had been for sixteen years to the smiling, affable professor of chemistry he had formerly been. If his opinion was desired by the new officials, he was prepared to give it. Otherwise, he remained silent on administrative affairs and aloof from their operation while devoting his time generously to his students. Such a change in status might have been difficult for many, but, from all appearances, the chemistry teacher accomplished it with ease.

J. Fred Young was Elon's first president whose graduate studies had been entirely in the field of education. Long, Staley, and Smith had been Christian clergymen; Moffitt, Harper, and Danieley had been trained in other academic disciplines. Thus, the new executive possessed the ability to consider learning as an overall project, not confined primarily to one field, which was the real purpose of the liberal arts institution. The graduate schools sought to produce specialists; the four-year colleges endeavored to graduate well-rounded citizens.

The president's concepts were succinctly expressed in an article entitled "Student Life Program Undergoing Changes," written by Dr. Moncure:

> The commitment to educate our youth in mind, body and spirit in this planetary global village requires every resource that can be mustered for the cause. The academic process, still the vital core of the learning enterprise, is being subjected to careful scrutiny and gradual modification to increase learning efficiency.
>
> Student life is undergoing, and must continue to undergo, fundamental change. A relatively passive support system twenty-five years ago, it is now becoming a conscious integral component of the process of human development. Only the beginning of this college activity area is in sight! Academic and student life are truly one ball of wax and an alert college is one that is upgrading the total learning environment.[10]

The academic official continued with an explanation of Elon's effort to meet the challenge:

Human nature does not provide for problemless individuals, much less societies, yet civilization is a measure to some extent of the ability of individuals and institutions to solve problems or build ways around insoluble situations. At Elon great effort is being made to provide its students with maximum growth opportunities and experiences.

The place of the small liberal arts school in the future rests in the quality of student life. The mammoth universities will have faculties certainly as good as those in the small colleges, but the behemoth institutions cannot provide the life style, the maturing environment that a small college can offer. Elon College knows this and is doing something about it.[11]

This statement summarized the goals of the administration, and steps began to be taken early in 1974 to expand the college program and operation to conform with it.

To gain the advantage of expert opinions and assistance in the development of his program, Dr. Young proposed establishing the Elon

Students playing in the electronics piano laboratory of the Music Department.

College Presidential Board of Advisers. At their October 1974 meeting, the trustees authorized the project, the purpose of which was "to assist the President in the defining and interpreting of Elon College's aims, objectives, and programs to its public and to gain acceptance for them and to advise the administration regarding the College's programs." This was to be accomplished by board members fostering the long-term objectives of the college as a church-related institution, encouraging student recruiting, reporting to the administration "the acceptance or non-acceptance of specific College programs," and recommending ways to improve the effectiveness of the entire operation.[12]

Without delay, the president appointed twenty-nine members to the new board. The alumni included Ray C. Euliss, Maurice Jennings, Ernest Koury, C. Almon McIver, Dr. Philip R. Mann, and Max Ward, all of Burlington; Dr. M. Cade Covington, of Sanford; James F. Darden, of Suffolk, Virginia; the Reverend Beverly M. Currin, of Pensacola, Florida; G. T. Holmes, of Badin, North Carolina; Miss Marjorie Hunter, of Washington, D.C.; Robert B. Smithwick, of New York City; A. G. Thompson, of Lincolnton, North Carolina; and Dr. Daniel T. Watts, of Richmond, Virginia.

The other members were Laurence A. Alley, of Elon College; Mrs. Alyse S. Cooper, Ralph M. Holt, Jr., James W. Maynard, the Reverend James W. Morrison, Mrs. Maxine O'Kelley, Dr. Brank Proffitt, and Mrs. June Strader, all of Burlington; Dr. James D. Glasse, of Lancaster, Pennsylvania; the Reverend Robert M. Mitchell, of Pawtucket, Rhode Island; Mrs. Sarah Rhyne, of Graham; Renold Schilke, of Chicago, Illinois; Irwin Smallwood, of Greensboro; and Dr. Edwin G. Wilson, of Winston-Salem.

The board held its first meeting at the college in January 1975, where it was organized after an inspiring address by Dr. Bruce Heilman, president of the University of Richmond. "All of these people have a deep interest in Elon College and are willing to become more involved in its planning and progress," announced Young, who correctly anticipated that their contributions would be of increasing value to the institution.[13]

Another plank in the administration's platform was continued modernization and expansion of the curriculum. By 1975 a number of new offerings were being announced in the college catalog. The Department of Community Services and Allied Health was established under the direction of Dr. Frances R. Marlette. The purpose of this four-year interdisciplinary study was to "prepare students for work in mental health, vocational rehabilitation, prison counseling, welfare administration and other governmental services."[14] This unit, whose name was later changed to the Department of Human Services, attracted 94 majors the first year it opened. In 1979 this number had increased to 177 students.

Another addition was creation of the Department of Military Science, offering two- and four-year programs for male and female students. This result of several years of endeavor was made possible by arranging to affiliate with the U.S. Reserve Officer Training Corps (ROTC) unit already in operation at State Agricultural and Technical University, in Greensboro. Elon became the eighth college in the state offering the program at the time. Because some of the classes and other exercises in the course were held at the university, the Elonites needed to commute back and forth in order to participate. Completion of the full program was rewarded by a commission as second lieutenant in the United States Army. Special financial assistance was also available to those who enrolled. The program immediately attracted forty students, a number that has remained about the average ever since. It might have been larger except for the prob-

Students engaged in the college's Human Services program.

lems of attending some classes at such a distance from the campus.[15]

More interesting courses were also designed for the winter term. In addition to those conducted by Coach Kelly at the French-Swiss Ski College in the North Carolina mountains for skiing instruction as well as the annual trips to England, groups were led on a tour of Palestine by Dr. M. Christopher White and to Russia by Dr. David Crowe. Professors Durward T. Stokes and George W. Troxler enlarged the visits to Carolina historic sites, and other appealing offerings varied from year to year.[16]

Curriculum stimulation was also accompanied by a successful drive to organize chapters of more national honor societies on the campus. By 1978 Phi Alpha Theta, in history, Beta Beta Beta, in biology, Epsilon Beta Epsilon, for economics and business majors, and Sigma Sigma Epsilon, for Secretarial Science students, had been established. In addition, the Elon College Leadership Honor Society was replaced by the Elon College Circle of Omicron Delta Kappa, the organization founded in 1914 to recognize and encourage "the achievement of exemplary character and superior quality and leadership, and to cooperate in worth-while endeavor and join with faculty members on a basis of mutual interest, understanding and service." Thirty-six faculty members and students were inducted into this organization when it became a part of the institution's program.[17]

Scene at Greek Week, a period of frolic in the spring.

In January 1974 the trustees were moved by the increase in student organizations and enrollment to establish the Communications Media Board, composed of representative student members. Its purpose was to govern campus communications by newspaper and radio. As a result of this action, in October, in conjunction with the Student Government Association, publication began of *The Pendulum*, a biweekly tabloid. It was coedited by Deborah Cochran and Patricia Lynch, and Dr. Mary E. Priestley served as adviser. The aims of the paper were announced in its first issue: "We intend to report events which are important to both the students and the faculty, to develop a channel by which students and faculty members may voice their opinions, to dispel rumors by gathering all the facts and to insure their validity before the article is printed. However, we do reserve the right to edit all work to insure a high quality of journalistic writing."[18] Housed in a Long Student Center office containing "a drafting table, a T-square, and two typewriters,"[19] the project was meagerly equipped but manned by a dedicated staff, and became a permanent part of the college scene.

Periodically after the pioneer Elon radio venture was destroyed in the 1923 fire, a few enthusiasts advocated the installation of a modern station at the college. No action was taken until 1969, when the Student Government Association appointed Donald Perkins to the

Students arriving at the beginning of the school year.

chairmanship of a Radio Committee, which consisted also of Robert Truitt and Barry Simmons. Because funding was provided by the student treasury, the project was planned and ready for launching within three years, but then was stalemated inasmuch as no location for the station was authorized in the college plant. Enthusiasm was revived in 1975 by Robert Hurst and other students, and rooms were assigned to the enterprise in Harper Center. With the generous assistance of Jack Starnes and the staff of station WBAG, the Federal Communications Commission was requested to license WELN-FM at the college. Some changes needed to be made in the application while delays were encountered in Washington, but the students persevered in reaching their goal. Finally, they were rewarded and on December 8, 1977, the new 10-watt educational radio station WSOE was formally opened at Elon.[20]

The maximum range of the station was approximately twenty miles. Broadcasting periods were the afternoons and evenings of the school working week. The programs included "pops" music played from albums of records, campus news, and educational presentations, some of which were prerecorded. In time, documentaries, profiles, and similar features were added.

While arrangements to open the station were dragging along slowly, a course in communications was opened under the direction of Mrs. Marjorie Long. When broadcasting began, the course was absorbed by two new ones in the subject, conducted under the supervision of the English Department. These were introductory and operational courses. An average of 15 to 20 students have enrolled for these annually. Another student group, of similar size, has devoted personal service to the operation of the station since it opened. This served as their contribution to the Student Government Association's function at the college. When this volume went to press, WSOE was planning a change from 10 to 100 watts in order to comply with government regulations. This will improve the facility in a number of ways when it has been completed.[21]

During the last weeks of 1974, Professor Steve Caddell, the campus minister, aided by Dean William G. Long, established the Black Cultural Society of Elon College. Although membership was open to all students at the school, the purpose of the organization was to "provide social atmosphere for the Black students on the campus." This was to be achieved by fostering "understanding and a sense of unity" among them, encouraging "a greater awareness and appreciation of the culture of Black people," and combatting any inequalities or injustices concerning them at the institution. The society was organized under the cochairmanship of Rodney Evans and Donald McLaughlin. They were encouraged in their endeavor by the Reverend Marvin Morgan, an Elon alumnus who had completed his theological training at Duke, and by guest speakers on the programs of their meetings.[22] Attendance averages twenty-five.

When Professor James P. Elder, Jr., departed in 1973 for employment with the Folger Shakespeare Library, in Washington, D.C., Dr. John Sullivan succeeded him as sponsor of the Liberal Arts Forum. It continued to present outstanding programs and to constitute an important part of the intellectual life of the college.[23]

Another active organization on the campus was the chapter of the Society for Advancement of Management (SAM). It had been popular with business majors since it had been chartered in 1966. Fred Busick was its first president, and Professor James Toney was its sponsor. Under succeeding advisers, Professors Douglas Crouse and Janie Council, respectively, it annually brought speakers prominent in the world of business to Elon. Dr. Edward H. Rudow, a psychol-

Black Cultural Society, 1980.

ogist with the Farr Association, and Edward M. Herron, Jr., chairman of the board of Eckerd Drug, Inc., were typical of the caliber of lecturers.[24] In 1976 the organization originated the custom of recognizing the outstanding SAM member of the year with a plaque inscribed as the Janie E. Council Award. The membership also donated a trophy case to the college Business Department, and it is installed on the second floor of the Alamance Building. The chapter has also been active in numerous other ways on the campus.

Speakers brought to the campus by the Public Affairs Committee of the college included William Kuntsler, Julian Bond, and Frank Reynolds. Because of the inspiring leadership of Elena Scott, student chairman of the committee, the Student Government Association was persuaded to cooperate with it in sponsoring a lecture by the fa-

Elon elementary education major engaged in practice teaching.

mous consumer champion Ralph Nader. On the evening of October 30, 1974, the Alumni Memorial Gymnasium was crowded to capacity to hear him express his views. The occasion was a highlight among the platform appearances of speakers at the college.[25]

Nader's visit also increased interest in the Public Interest Research Group (PIRG), which he had founded. The purpose of this national nonprofit organization was to promote consumer protection by providing an opportunity for college students "to take action on problems of pollution, discrimination, consumer fraud, health care, and deception."[26] Two months after the lecture, North Carolina Public Interest Research Associate Peter Brown conferred with Elon students in regard to forming a unit on the campus. Groups were already active at Duke, St. Andrews, Wake Forest, and Davidson, and the proposal was favorably received by the Elonites. However, the project had to be approved by the institution's board of trustees and the Student Government Association. In the latter case, the decision would be made by a student referendum. If the vote was favorable, two dollars of each student's tuition payment would be assigned to PIRG for its operation. If an individual objected to this use of his money, it would be refunded upon request.[27]

Randell B. Flynn, who was elected president of the project, arranged for October 13 to be election day. The vote was favorable and on the 22d, the trustees approved establishment of the new organization. Coming at a time when the rising prices caused by financial inflation were a national worry, PIRG attracted some enthusiastic members. In December a survey of comparative grocery prices was published for public information and followed by additional studies later. Other activities devoted to consumer protection kept the group busy, and it served a worthy practical purpose at the college.[28]

The laudable beginning of the Young administration, so pleasing in general, was marred by one jarring note. The new president was intensely interested both in the expansion of the institution's plant and its adjacent municipal surroundings. He was aware of the numerous benefits a prosperous city can provide that are impossible for a small town with a low income from taxes. This was especially true at Elon, where the college and the Children's Home, which comprised more than half the real estate, were exempt from the payment of property taxes. Water and sewer extensions had been slowly made with difficulty, and other improvements were often delayed or

The old college water tank, ornamented with student painting,
being razed in 1979.

postponed indefinitely. Under these circumstances, a proposal to merge the town with the city of Burlington did not seem particularly unreasonable. Under the impression that officials in both municipalities desired such a move, Dr. Young openly endorsed the proposition.

Another factor was particularly attractive to the college officials. The city of Burlington could not legally join the institution financially in constructing such facilities as a fine arts center, an auditorium, or a football stadium in another municipality even though they were for the use of the public and the college. Whereas, if the town merged its identity with that of the city, no legal barriers would exist to such projects in the future. This was another, and perhaps the strongest, reason for the approval of the merger by the Young administration.

Discussion of the plan was placed on the agenda of a January 8, 1974 meeting of the Elon College board of aldermen. Because a large attendance of citizens was anticipated, the officials convened in the Parish House of the Community Church, which was filled to capacity. In addition to Mayor T. E. Smith, Aldermen W. Jennings Berry, M. E. Campbell, Kenneth Clem, Noel Inge, and Robert Olsen were present, plus Town Attorney Robert Baxter, Town Engineer Larry Alley, and Town Clerk Mrs. Roxie Hetzel. The merger proposal was presented by Ira Drake, president of the Burlington-Alamance County Chamber of Commerce, who pointed out that the move would be beneficial to Elon because the town was pressed to provide adequate services to citizens inasmuch as resources, including the tax base, were limited; it depended upon Burlington for sewage treatment; depended upon wells for its water supply; and needed more municipal services. Drake contended Burlington could supply them at no additional cost.

Regardless of the possible advantages these suggestions portrayed, the heated discussion that followed their presentation was conclusive evidence that the majority of Elon College's citizens did not desire a merger with their neighboring municipality. A petition containing 286 names was also introduced in protest of the proposal. After considerable argument, pro and con but mostly con, the board adjourned and announced it would meet again on January 22 for further consideration of the matter. On that date, action was postponed indefinitely, and the subject completely dropped. The controversy caused a breach in relations between the town and college that only time would heal, but business transactions were not interrupted. After the college renewed its annual agreement to pay the town $3,000 for the special police patrol of the somewhat isolated north campus and a similar sum for municipal services, it joined the municipality in making plans to celebrate the United States Bicentennial.[29]

The unpleasantness of the controversial episode was eclipsed during the year that followed by several major gifts to the college. Dr. J. H. R. Booth, of Baltimore (Elon '15), gave the institution property in Wake and Lee counties conservatively valued at $400,000. Another donation, one of the largest sums of money ever left to the institution by an individual, $184,743, was from the estate of Lizzie B. Turner, of Isle of Wight County, Virginia. The veteran trustee Dr. John L. Crumpton, and his wife, Pretto B. Crumpton, of Durham, donated their country estate of 23 acres of land, containing a handsome dwelling and a four-acre pond, to Elon. The administration decided to utilize the $125,000 property as the "Crumpton Conference Center," to serve as an ideal place "for seminars, retreats, picnics, and special meetings." No time was lost in taking advantage of the rural location for these purposes.[30]

Major gifts also included the 48,315-volume library of the defunct Stratford College, in Danville, Virginia. The collection, appraised at

Crumpton Conference Center.

$750,000, was presented to the college by Royall H. Spence, Sr., and his wife, Dolly L. Spence, their daughters, Mary Spence Boxley and Dolly Spence Dowdy, and their son, Royall H. Spence, Jr. This magnificent donation doubled the size of the Elon College library and made it the fourth largest in the state among private institutions. Only those at Duke, Wake Forest, and Davidson surpassed it in size.[31]

In addition to the books acquired by this gift, Elon also received the card catalog, shelving, study carrels, tables, and chairs from the Stratford library. Because of the foresight that had been shown in planning the Iris Holt McEwen Library, space was ample for the new collection and its separate catalog. Each volume contained a bookplate marked "The Spence Collection." President Young considered the contribution of this family of friends and alumni to be one of the most significant in the history of the institution. "The library is the heart of the College academic program," he asserted. Librarian Theodore E. Perkins was also highly pleased inasmuch as the housing of the collection as a unit already cataloged made the material available to faculty and students without delay.[32]

In the same year, the library received another distinction when it was designated as the national library of the American Theatre Organ Enthusiasts. It thus became the official depository of the organization for music, scores, cue sheets, pictures, and similar material connected with the instruments used in theaters before the advent of talking pictures.

Dr. Paul M. Abernethy, of Burlington, president of the Piedmont Chapter of the Enthusiasts, enlisted the aid of his fellow members in a service to the college that extended over a period of about five years. This was the installation in the gymnasium of a large organ, obtained from the Paramount Theatre in Charlottesville, Virginia, and presented to Elon by Hugh M. Cummings, Sr., of Burlington. Placed high in the balcony over the playing floor, it was played officially for the first time by Professor Richard T. Apperson at Freshman Orientation, in September 1978, and the second time for commencement the following spring. The organ was a joy to all concerned because for the first time a musical instrument was available that provided sufficient volume to fill the huge expanse of the gymnasium. It was a valued piece of equipment, obtained through the generosity of friends of the institution.[33]

Elon College Community Church.

The facilities of the library were further enlarged in 1976 by a gift from the Rockefeller Foundation of a hundred records of American music. These traced the history of the United States through its music. Elon was selected to receive this special limited-edition collection "because of its commitment to musical education and scholarship and for the College's ability to make the recordings accessible to a large public." This was another tribute to the planning of the building, which had been equipped for such a project when it was constructed. The records, since acquisition, have been available for public listening at the McEwen Library.[34]

Ever alert for advantageous real estate transactions, in 1974 the trustees authorized the payment of $2,500 per acre for the 43-acre Caddell property, adjacent to the north campus. Approximately a year later, the college sold its farm (the Atkinson tract) in the Shallow Ford community for $173,682, which represented a substantial profit.[35] The college had always held ample land for expansion in a northern direction, and the acquisition of the Caddell tract immeasurably enhanced this option.

To exercise this advantage judiciously, a contract was made with Lewis Clarke Associates, landscape architects and estate planners of Raleigh, to devise a master plan for land use and future campus development.[36]

On October 22, 1975, Wayne McBride, a representative of the firm, presented the completed study to the board of trustees. In addition to preserving the existing college plant, it proposed the addition of a driving range, athletic field house, community center and recreation area, a fine arts center, an infirmary, additional parking space, and a lake with adjacent boathouse. This plan, favorably received by both the college and town, constituted the guide for future campus growth.[37]

While optimistic plans were being formulated for the future use of the institution's campus, a revolutionary change was being made in the age-old policy regarding the college's off-campus property in the town. On February 12, 1974, Larry B. McCauley, Sr., Director of the Physical Plant, reported to the trustees that the college owned twenty-eight houses, nine of which were mortgaged. Because of increasing cost of maintenance, in addition to the outmoded construction of some of the dwellings, he was convinced it would be profitable to sell some of the structures outright and to demolish others in order to use their sites for different purposes.[38] It was apparent to the officials that supplying housing for the faculty to rent was no longer a necessity because changed conditions enabled each family to select a house suited to its own requirements in nearby residential areas. For these reasons, McCauley's suggestion was adopted for the college "to reduce its rental property to the most reasonable

Members of the board of trustees in front of McEwen Library at the meeting on March 4, 1981. From left to right, front row: *Samuel E. Scott, Thad Eure, Mrs. Emily H. Preyer, Joseph M. Copeland, Roger Gant, Jr., Venetia Toren Everett, R. Leroy Howell, and Thomas B. Sain.* Second row: *G. Melvin Palmer, W. D. Rippy, Woodrow W. Piland, A. G. Thompson, John Robert Kernodle, and G. Thomas Holmes, Jr.* Third row: *Jape E. Rawls, Jr., Walter L. Floyd, Royall H. Spence, Jr., C. Max Ward, W. Millard Stevens, and Maurice Jennings.* Last row: *Wallace L. Chandler, Thomas E. Powell, III, Reid A. Maynard, President J. Fred Young, Lula B. Helvenston, Clyde L. Fields, and Ralph H. Scott. Members not present were: Rex G. Powell, J. Harold Smith, Frances Wilkins, Ramsey E. Cammack, James H. McEwen, Jr., Bernadette McMullen, J. L. Crumpton, Sherrill G. Hall, Richard J. Holland, Ernest A. Koury, Sr., James B. Powell, J. Hinton Rountree, and Mary T. Semans.*

extent possible."[39] Action began immediately. Some houses were placed on the market and several demolished.

This new policy, though it had its critics, aroused no strong objections, but the use of dwellings formerly rented to faculty members to house fraternities and sororities did become a bitterly controversial matter. During the latter years of the Danieley administration, fraternities had been allowed to move their headquarters from the club rooms in Mooney Building to houses in town rented from the college. No organized opposition to this move had been made by the townspeople, though it may not have been universally popular.

At the time the trustees adopted the new policy for college property, based on the McCauley report, their attention was directed to Title IX of the Higher Education Amendments of 1972, which required off-campus housing to be provided for sororities if it was made available for fraternities.[40] In compliance, the tenants were soon removed from several of the institution's houses so that they might be prepared for occupation by the female organizations. By

Spring commencement ceremony in Alumni Gymnasium. Vice-President Moncure is at the podium, and President Young, in the center of the rostrum, is preparing to present a diploma to an approaching graduate.

the same means, fraternities were also moved into more commodious quarters. This caused a centralization of headquarters for the Greek letter groups, most of which were "located within a one block radius of each other."[41] Although the neighborhood involved in this concentration was "a mixture of business, apartments, and single family housing," Dr. Young acknowledged, "It is understandable that some of the residents might oppose fraternity and sorority housing in the area." This was prophetic because the move was challenged by opponents on the grounds that it violated the town's zoning law. The administration then stoutly defended its interests, for the plan supplied housing for 60 students, from which the overcrowded college received an annual income of approximately $150,000 in tuition and fees.[42]

The growing dissension was based on the local zoning law that authorized only single-family housing in the northwestern quadrant of the town. The argument was whether or not a fraternity or sorority fitted this category. This was obviously a question on which opinions could, and did, differ. To settle the problem of legality, the college requested the town board to change the zoning restrictions to remove any conceivable barrier to student housing in the area. The aldermen considered this request at length, and the college and town made other efforts to effect a compromise.[43]

In the spring of 1977, the smoldering issue burst into flame. The opponents of the college policy vehemently complained at the town hall and through the press that the student housing had become a public nuisance. They cited the noise created by parties late at night, violations of automobile parking rules, littering lawns and streets with beer cans and other debris, and the use of loud and vulgar language. It was charged that wholesalers' trucks delivered beer by the case to the fraternity houses, where it was apparently consumed to excess. It was also alleged that the houses contained coin-operated pinball machines, which constituted business being illegally operated in a residential zone.[44] These were the principal allegations, which were undoubtedly based on fact to some extent but did not represent the true picture.

The aldermen yielded to the pressure of their irate constituents on April 25 by declaring that the house behind the president's home and another near the church were being unlawfully used for student housing. Inasmuch as this aroused no action on the part of the college, the municipal board announced in July that legal action would be taken to enforce its decision. The administration then turned the matter over to the college attorneys and prepared to contest the action.[45]

At a hearing on July 29 before Judge William T. Graham, the town sought an injunction to force the college to cease using the six houses in question for student quarters until the case should be tried in court. This was denied by the judge on the grounds that a possible zoning infraction for a relatively short period would not damage the municipality. As for objectionable behavior constituting a nuisance or unlicensed business being operated, the town ordinances covered such misdemeanors and these could be enforced on the student violators.[46]

After this episode, the college's lawyers were successful in having the case removed from state jurisdiction by a transfer to federal court. This ended the legal battle because a compromise was effected before the case ever came to trial. The college imposed stricter regulations on the fraternities and sororities, and promised they would be enforced.[47] Timothy M. Moore and Bernard B. Carr, president and vice-president, respectively, of the Student Government Association, Senators Robin Moser and Annette Metcalf,

Art class.

Charles Hopkins, president of the senior class, and Steve Eanes, presidential aide, met with the aldermen in a round-table discussion of means for "town and gown" to enjoy more harmonious relations in the future.[48] This was indeed a diplomatic gesture of value on the part of the students and the municipal officials. The college then agreed that several houses would no longer be used for student quarters, but that others were to be permitted to retain this status, at least for a reasonable period of time. In addition, pinball machines, jukeboxes, and other objectionable equipment would be removed from the fraternity houses, and an effort made to curb objectionable behavior.[49] These agreements ended the lengthy battle, in which both sides had suffered unpleasant publicity, heavy expense, and damaged personal feelings. It also clarified the fact, if any doubt ever existed about it, that a successful future would be possible only if the college and the town worked together as one unit, and not as two separate organizations. The value of this conclusion may have justified the controversy in the final analysis.

One of the factors that contributed significantly to the compromise was the decision of the trustees on September 29 to sell the town two lots on Williamson Avenue across from the United States post office as a site on which to build a new Elon College town hall. The site included the house rented to the Kappa Sigma fraternity, which was vacated, then razed. This removed another one of the causes for complaint. The trustees considered the appraisal price of $30,500 offered by the town for the tract to be "unrealistic in view of current property values, but that the offer is being accepted because the Executive Committee members consider this an ideal site for a Town Hall, want to cooperate with the Town Board to bring about total community improvements, and as a step to resolve other matters of mutual concern." The transaction was completed with the condition that, if the town ever sold the property, the college would have the right to repurchase it "at current prices."[50] This sale of real estate was another example of working together for the mutual benefit of all, and set a worthy example for future activities of the two organizations.

A minor clash between the administration and the town arose in 1978 over the acquisition of the vacated town of Elon College's Middle School plant, which was owned by Alamance County. The college desired the property for future expansion and the town for recreational purposes. The contest for ownership culminated in December, when the college paid the Alamance County school authorities $114,000 for "a gymnasium in fair condition, 23 classrooms, a large auditorium, library rooms, a teachers' lounge, a kitchen and cafeteria." The structure, named the East Building, supplied space for wrestling, dancing, storage, maintenance work, and facilities to support outdoor activity on the two playing fields.[51]

In comparison with the town's past ordinances, a revolutionary change occurred in 1975, which was advocated by neither the municipal nor college officials. For some time, changed state laws had permitted beer for off-premises consumption to be sold in the town's stores. In April the proprietor-renter of the former Garrison's Soda Shop applied for a license to sell beer for on-the-spot consumption. This had been prohibited by local law. During the controversial period that followed, the Elon College ordinance was declared unconstitutional by the state's attorney general, and the Alcoholic Beverage Control Board approved the application that the aldermen had rejected. The coveted authority was then granted because there seemed to be no other choice in the matter.[52] Students and others were then able to quench their thirst with beer at any one of the four taverns that were established after sale of the beverage was legalized.[53] As a result, it was necessary for the town to hire a man "to pick up trash and beer cans that do not make it to the containers" on the streets and parking lots.[54] Otherwise, the end of prohibition has made no noticeable difference in the life of the town and college.

Inspired by downtown renovations in other cities and towns, and aided by a federal Public Works Grant of $186,000, in 1977–78 the municipality of Elon College carried out a beautification project of major proportions in the two-block business section of North Williamson Avenue. Beginning on the north side of the railroad tracks at the corner where Dr. and Mrs. S. E. Gerard Priestley had opened the Priestley Art Gallery, new sidewalks of brick replaced the former concrete ones to West College Avenue on one side and to Haggard Avenue on the other. Between newly planted willow oaks and flower beds, Charleston style benches were placed alongside handmade wooden trash receptacles. All the buildings were repainted in Williamsburg colors. Thus, an attractive space was provided in which pedestrians could relax or more safely cross the streets by means of the new crosswalks. It was a major accomplishment.[55]

As the year 1976 dawned, Elon College joined the nation in celebrating its Bicentennial. The cross-country track team, composed of Robert Merceron, Jay Grandin, Preston Ruth, John Hinkle, Wayne Bumgardner, and Dosie Comer, coached by Professor Frederic T. Watts, Jr., went to Hillsborough, where it was presented with an official Bicentennial flag. The athletes then ran in relays the thirty miles to the college, where their arrival was applauded by the enthusiastic crowd that had assembled to see the banner hoisted upon the campus flagpole by state and institutional officials.[56]

In the same year, an unhappy event introduced the Young administration to Elon's ancient enemy, fire. On the evening of April 9, a blaze broke out on the third floor of the Carolina Dormitory. All the 140 male residents vacated the building without injury except one, who broke an ankle jumping from a window. The conflagration, caused by an accident, was swiftly controlled, but not until damage amounting to approximately $40,000 had been done.

The concern of Alamance County for the welfare of the college

Elon track team arriving at the college from Hillsborough in 1976 carrying the Bicentennial flag. From left to right: Robert Merceron, Jay Grandin, Preston Ruth, John Hinkle, Wayne Bumgardner, and Dosie Comer. Coach Frederic T. Watts, Jr., is in the background.

was evident when David Cauble, the county fire marshal, arrived on the scene, accompanied by equipment and personnel from the Burlington, Mebane, Haw River, Swepsonville, E. M. Holt, Gibsonville, Altamahaw-Ossipee, Eli Whitney, Graham, Snow Camp, Pleasant Grove, Elon Volunteer, and Elon Rural fire departments. Never before in the history of the institution had so many protective units been on hand in time of need, and it was comforting to many spectators who remembered blazes in the past that could not be extinguished.[57]

The existence of two Elon companies resulted from some firemen leaving the town's official organization, the Volunteers, and forming the Elon Rural Fire Department, headquartered just outside the corporate limits. (Because of the confusion in identity, the name of the new company was later changed to the Boone Station Fire Department.) The younger group, while seeking financial support first from the town and then from the county, became a rival of the older company and thus both responded to fire alarms in the same area. It was a unique situation for a small community to accommodate two competing groups of firefighters. It existed until a court decision in 1978 caused the younger organization to disband. Meanwhile, the college had been in no way involved in the controversy, but diplomatically, and with sincerity, sent letters of thanks to both groups for assistance at the dormitory fire.[58]

This calamity, which could have been far more serious, did not appreciably deter the march of events. It was during this festive year of 1976 that President Young explained to his board of trustees a Master Plan he had devised, after much thought, for the long-range needs of the college. Its enactment depended upon raising a large sum of money, to be used for the following purposes: [59]

I. Campus Plan	$1,200,000
A. Athletic Fields and Field House	
B. Parking and Site Development	
C. Refurbishing Present Buildings	
II. Academic Scholarships	$1,200,000
III. Planning for Fine Arts Building	$ 100,000
IV. Fine Arts Building	$3,000,000
Total	$5,500,000

The advice and support of persons "close to the College" was sought at 25 small "cultivation dinners," which provided overall encouragement.[60]

The trustees voted unanimously to "authorize and direct the President to plan, organize, and conduct a capital funds campaign for $5.5 million." They also approved the presidential recommendation that Wallace L. Chandler be appointed as general chairman of Phase I, the campaign to raise the first $2.5 million of the total goal. The appointee, a resident of Richmond, Virginia, was senior vice-president of Universal Leaf Tobacco Company, Inc., a 1949 graduate of Elon, a trustee of the institution, and one of its most loyal alumni. It was fortunate for the college that he accepted the fundraising responsibility.[61]

Under the professional guidance of Ketchum, Inc., through its campus representative, William Melvin, the PRIDE Campaign was planned. The name was an acronym for the slogan "Providing Resources for Institutional Development at Elon." The Phase I drive was opened by Dr. Young, who summarized the life of the college over the years by periods:

> *The Founding Phase,* from 1889 through 1923, when the foundation was laid.
> *The Survival Phase,* from 1923 through 1947, when the College was recovering from the disastrous fire of 1923, the ravages of the Great Depression, and the scars inflicted by World War II.
> *The Growth Phase,* from 1947 to the present, when the major share of the campus was built, the curriculum expanded, and enrollment grew to the present student strength of 2,150.

The executive then concluded, "The College is now entering a fourth phase, one that will build on the past to bring an even higher level of excellence to the faculty, students, curriculum and campus."[62] This concise introduction launched the "Covenant with Quality" program.

Spurred by the enthusiastic efforts of divisional leaders Dr. Jo Watts Williams, Roger Gant, Jr., Maurice N. Jennings, C. Almon McIver, Ernest A. Koury, Julian P. Griffin, A. G. Thompson, G. Melvin Palmer, Sherrill G. Hall, Laurence A. Alley, and Thomas B. Sain, the solicitations were successful.[63] In less than two years,

$2,601,974.71 in cash was raised, and more than 1,100 individual do-
nors made pledges. More than 64 percent of the total contributions,
or $1,624,650, came from the people of Alamance County, a con-
crete testimony of local loyalty to the institution. The sentiments of
the administration were voiced by Director of Institutional Relations S. Carlysle Isley. He said the officials were pleased, but not surprised, because "people have always been receptive to supporting
Elon College."[64] After this phenomenal success, Phase II planning
began.

The momentum produced by the PRIDE Campaign generated the
spirit of giving outside the organized solicitations. The donations
that resulted included real estate, paintings, musical instruments,

A new graduate.

trees, shrubbery, books, records, tapes, stocks, bonds, and an airplane.[65] Alan Smith, the college electrician, and Dr. Charles Harris restored the clocks in the tower of Alamance to service after years of disrepair. In 1978 the class of 1953 celebrated its silver anniversary by giving an electronic carillon system to play inspiring musical selections as the hours are announced by the clock's chimes.

The class of 1926 replaced the worn wooden college well house with a brick gazebo in a small court. The 1954 graduates donated a landscaped court adjacent to the O'Kelly Monument and equipped it with benches and shrubbery. The class of 1918 furnished a prayer room in the Whitley Building, and the classes of 1928 and 1929, respectively, furnished seminar rooms in the Alamance and Mooney buildings. The 1927 alumni refurbished and decorated the small dining room in McEwen, and other substantial contributions were made to the college plant.[66]

The generous support of the academic program, expressed by the numerous gifts, came to a climax on March 8, 1978, when Dr. Thomas E. Powell, Jr., endowed a chair of biology with a $250,000 donation. This magnificent donation from an alumnus, former faculty member, and founder of Carolina Biological Supply Company, was the largest of its kind in the history of the college.[67] Following close behind this contribution, five sons of the donor, Thomas E., III, Samuel C., James B., Joseph E., and John S., gave a major portion of the sum necessary to pay for the Classroom-Office Building. The purpose of this generosity was to honor their aunt, Miss Caroline E. Powell. The college officials acknowledged this intention by appropriately changing the name of the building to that of the honoree.[68] Financial support for the college expressed in such large gifts and numerous smaller ones elevated the spirits of the Young administration, and the many friends of Elon were confident that the future would continually grow brighter.

While these impressive gifts were being made to the academic phase of the college program, athletics were by no means neglected. Back in 1936, Webb Newsome, an all-around Fighting Christian star, promised President Smith he would return some day to build an adequate playing field for his alma mater. On March 7, 1977, though Smith did not live to witness the event, the 42-year-old promise was kept with a gift of $50,000 to build the Webb Newsome Athletic

Field on the north side of the campus.[69] On April 29, 1978, fitting ceremonies were held to open the completed project, which has been in regular use ever since.

In 1979 Maurice and Ernest Koury, industrialists of Burlington, provided funds to build the John A. Koury Field House adjacent to Newsome Field. This $350,000 facility, which honors the father of the donors, was still under construction when this volume went to press. When it is completed, the college athletic program will be properly equipped for all the sports.[70]

Another boon for the Physical Education Department was received in 1978. The Belk-Beck group of department stores contributed $50,000 to complete payment for the "olympic-size indoor swimming pool," in honor of A. Vance Beck, one of their executives. The presentation was made by Allen V. Beck, Jr., and the pool then appropriately named for his father. Their generous gift, located inside the B. Everett Jordan Gymnasium, was in almost constant use for physical education classes, general recreation, and as a base for both the Elon College Swim Club, a student organization, and the

Members of the Powell family at the ceremony in 1979 naming the former Classroom-Office Building the Caroline E. Powell Building. From left to right: *Thomas E., III, Joseph E., Samuel C., Miss Caroline E., Thomas E., Jr., James B., John S., and William C.*

Elon Swim Association, a community organization.[71] Students, staff, faculty, and townspeople have all enjoyed the A. Vance Beck Swimming Pool, one of the most popular college facilities.

While the financial prosperity of the institution was progressing, the academic program was also being broadened. One of the most unusual features of the expanded offerings was the Academic Skills Program, opened in the 1975 fall term. This laboratory project was designed for students who possessed adequate mental capacity but were handicapped with the inability to read with sufficient speed, take proper notes in class, and write acceptable papers. The major components of the program were reading comprehension, writing skills, mathematics, and counseling. These were designed to facilitate the regular college courses and not serve as a substitute for them. The establishment of this department was the result of a general realization that many of the nation's youth were deficient in these skills. After considerable deliberation, Elon was one of the colleges that early took remedial steps in the matter, a practice now common to most institutions of higher learning.[72]

Mrs. Rachelle Johnson, of Florida State University, was engaged to design and conduct the laboratory the first year of its operation. She was succeeded by Mrs. Betty Maness. The new facility, housed in the Mooney Building, was used by 145 students during the 1976−77 academic year and by 247 the following year. Dr. Moncure's prediction seemed correct that the program would "provide the expertise and individual attention some students need to enable them to enjoy a successful experience in college as they seek to fulfill their academic aspirations." The laboratory was also a precursor to a more elaborate program that followed within a few months.[73]

The zealous efforts for continued improvement were richly rewarded in June 1977, when the institution received the largest financial boost in its history. This was a $2 million grant from the government's Advanced Institutional Development Program, under the provisions of Title III of the Higher Education Act. This impressive sum was to be used for assisting students "with a wide range of abilities to achieve their personal development potential," enhancing the talents of minorities, encouraging nontraditional students, and fostering "the ability of the College to achieve these objectives."[74]

The plan, usually referred to as the AIDP, was funded by the grant extended over a five-year period. The activities that were included, which advanced Elon's program extensively, were described in detail by President Young:

Curriculum Revision to ensure that students of varying abilities are served effectively. Major curricular areas will be reviewed and strengthened; course content will be updated; and teaching methods will be diversified.

Learning Resources Center to provide academic support services. These services will consist of development courses in reading, writing, and mathematics; tutoring; a laboratory with equipment and materials to provide for self-paced learning; audio-visual materials and services to the faculty; and computer terminals and instruction.

Academic Enrichment Program to enable talented students to pursue graduate and professional studies successfully. This program provides for early identification, counseling, special academic enrichment seminars and courses.

Pre-Professional and Career Program by securing higher accreditation for Business Administration, Community services, and Allied Health, thus increasing opportunities for students majoring in these fields. Career programs within other fields, such as teacher education, will be modified and strengthened to offer better career options. Work Experience Internships will be expanded.

Career Planning Program to assist students, commencing in the freshman year, to identify career interests and opportunities. Students will develop personal plans and academic programs with the assistance of diagnostic testing, counseling, mini-courses, and other resources providing current information on career fields. Upward mobility will be encouraged.

Student Life Enrichment Program to ensure that campus life is an effective part of the educational process. This program will provide for student-to-student counseling; enriched activities, particularly for commuter students; and a strengthened residential life program.

Program for Non-Traditional Students to provide special services that are of a special benefit to these students. Area business people will be trained for management advancement opportunities; special courses, programs, and schedules will be provided to enable non-traditional students to complete their education.

Institutional Research and Administrative Improvement to strengthen institutional leadership and management. An office of Administrative Services will be strengthened to provide information for program analysis and review. Extensive administrative training programs will be conducted to strengthen support services.

Planning, Management, and Evaluation System to enable administrators to assess needs and measure performance on a systematic, long-term basis. This system will include Management by Objectives, Budget Planning and Control, and Management Information.[75]

This plan, divided into nine categories, comprised the academic emphasis of the college administration for the period, and no time was wasted in its activation.

To comply with the regulations of the United States Department of Health, Education and Welfare (HEW), which established the rules for its agency, the United States Office of Education, a coordinator had to be employed to administer the AIDP program. In July 1977 Dr. Daniel N. Moury, former associate director of the Office of State Colleges of the New Jersey Department of Higher Education, was selected for the responsibility. The college then planned to use $1.1 million of its own funds to supplement the grant and thus expand the scope of its potential benefit for the institution.[76]

The project began with the renovation of the entire first floor of the Mooney Building to serve as the Learning Resources Center. The move replaced the old Academic Skills Laboratory with the most modern scientifically designed equipment available for administering the various AIDP phases. Dr. Jo Watts Williams, from the faculty of the Education Department, was appointed as director of the Center, and she was provided with capable assistants. The faculty then was occupied in fulfilling the requirement of HEW to redefine the departmental objectives and work out other future plans to carry out the program.[77]

For at least a decade before the new program was initiated, a noticeable number of students, older than the average undergraduates, had attended Elon, especially the evening school. These were in addition to the large number of public school teachers who were engaged in renewing their certificates, usually in the summer school. Although some of the "non-traditional" students were interested only in specific studies, most of them sought to earn degrees. The class of 1964 included at least five middle-aged graduates, including one 56 years of age. Of these, three became public school teachers, and two went to graduate school, then engaged in college teaching. In 1976 the graduates included a group of employees of the Burlington Police Department, all past the standard student-age bracket.

In 1978, under the AIDP program, a special workshop was planned to prepare adults for returning to the classroom and aiding them in every manner possible. This program was broadened to include all persons past the age of 23 years, and was not specifically designed for those who had attained middle age. The facility was opened under the supervision of Geraldine Fox, of the English Department faculty. She was succeeded after the first year by George R. Lentz, Sr., the present director.[78]

This innovation, which was immediately popular, was broadened by redesign to the Continuing Education and Adult Extension program. Both regular and special courses were offered, including "Personnel Administration," scheduled for October 1979 at a location in Burlington for the convenience of many who were interested. In 1979 a total of 219 nontraditionals were enrolled, approximately a fourth of whom were approaching or in the category known as middle age.

One of the special results of the varied AIDP program was the college's first television course. Conducted by Drs. James H. Pace and Carole Chase, chairman of the Department of Religion and associate professor of religion, respectively, the subject of the thirteen weeks of study was the religions of the world. The weekly lectures, discussions, and tests were broadcast over WUNC-TV, Channel 4. A total of fifty-one students completed the course, but it was not repeated because of scheduling difficulties.[79]

Many of the institutional accomplishments that were being made as the decade of the 1980s began can be attributed to the faculty. Expanding as it did, it grew increasingly cosmopolitan, and the percentage of its members holding higher degrees rose. These new ideas and talents enriched Elon's programs. More than ever before, the faculty became involved in institutional governance, operation, and planning. Each department agreed upon objectives to guide future activities, and conducted a student evaluation of the faculty to provide more accurate information for study.

Faculty participation not only played a major role in the broadening of the academic advising of students, creation of academic internships, and establishment of a computer system, but also contributed to winning the coveted AIDP approval. This high-level cooperation between the administration and faculty is a major asset to the college, and constitutes a substantial base for future growth.

While more academic innovations were being devised and the administration finding funds with which to pay for them, athletics at the college were forging ahead at a fast pace. The golfers, under Coach Morningstar, and the baseball players under coaches Bobby Jones (Elon '62) and Robert D. McBee, won honors as did the wrestlers, soccer team, and the Golden Girls in basketball.[80] In December 1973, the football team won the National Association of Intercollegiate Athletics (NAIA) "bowl" playoff game, but lost the final decisive contest. Nevertheless, Melvin Shreves happily wrote, "Never before in the history of Elon College has more than one player been named to an All-American team," but in that year of jubilation, Glenn Ellis, Nick Angelone, John Muir, and Fred Long all made the grade.[81] In keeping with the plaudits merited by his players, Coach Wilson celebrated his forty-sixth Elon win, surpassing the 45 victories "posted for the great 'Peahead' Walker."[82]

Because enviable progress continued to follow for several years,[83] the public was shocked in June 1977 when Wilson's resignation was announced.[84] Failure in accomplishments was not a reason for the move because, during his Elon career, "Wilson had built a national small college power," and become highly acclaimed as a coach.[85] This record qualified "Red" to become head football coach at Duke University, and he took "Mickey" Brown with him as a member of his staff. Jerry R. Tolley was then placed in charge of the football team.[86]

A somewhat different type of athletic honor came to Elon in 1977 when Melvin L. Shreves, Sports and Public Information Director of the institution, received the Clarence "Ike" Pearson Award for being NAIA's Sports Information Director of the Year. The Elonite had won numerous awards for his writing previous to the high honor bestowed upon him at the NAIA convention, in Kansas City, Missouri, and had achieved merited distinction for both himself and the college.[87]

The efforts of the new football coach, Tolley, were rewarded in 1978 when his team faced the "Rams" of Angelo State, San Angelo, Texas, in the NAIA finals. President Young accompanied the players south and "brought down the house" at the pregame banquet with a witty quip:

> "According to the press reports, the Christians are about to be sacrificed again. We were about to forfeit the game," he told a group of some 300 people, including players. "But then I remembered a biblical reference about the time Abraham was about to sacrifice his son Isaac to the Lord.
>
> But the Lord stayed Abraham's sword arm, whereas Abraham exclaimed that an offering must be made, what could be sacrificed?
>
> 'And the Lord said,
> I have prepared a ram for you.'"[88]

Unfortunately, the Christians were not so merry twenty-four hours later. Despite a valiant effort, they met defeat. They were discouraged, but nevertheless proud for having won their way to the final game.

The ultimate reward came in 1980. In Burlington Stadium, a week after defeating East Texas State University on December 13 by a score of 14 to 6 at Commerce, Texas, the Elonites triumphed over Northeastern State University, of Oklahoma, by a score of 17 to 10 to win the NAIA, Division 1, football championship. This was the only national championship the Fighting Christians had ever won, and it generated jubilation among the student body. Another result of the victory was that Tolley was elected as the association's National Coach of the Year.

In September 1979 the school had been surprised at the resignation of "Bill" Miller as head basketball coach. The reason given was that, after forty years of coaching and playing, "the enjoyment was gone." The veteran leader retired gracefully, after winning many honors and a host of friends. He was succeeded by his assistant, William ("Bill") Morningstar, and plans for future achievements on the court continued without interruption.[89]

In 1977 Thomas L. Bass, Jr., was succeeded as Director of Alumni and Parent Relations by William R. Ginn, whose duties also included participation in the operation of the Development Office. The *Alumni News* was changed to *The Magazine of Elon*, but remained a valuable factor in the effort to maintain the high level of contact that had been made with the alumni.[90]

Another honor came to the college in 1977, when Tim McDowell, the Director of Public Information and Public Relations, was appointed to fill the vacancy in the state House of Representatives caused by the resignation of Judge W. S. Harris, Jr. McDowell not only completed the unfinished term of his predecessor, but won a two-year term on his own at the next election. He is the second employee of the college to represent Alamance County in the General Assembly.[91]

Elon continued to be fortunate financially. In 1977 a low-interest, long-term government loan of $633,000 was obtained for use in renovating the men's dormitories, which was completed in the summer of 1979. The following year, "The Oaks" was built at a cost of $522,000 on the North Campus. This modular-type, wood-perimeter-framed dormitory houses 144 students and is equipped with a lounge, laundry, study, and vending-machine rooms. In the same year, a low-interest government loan of $2,800,000 was obtained, and plans were made to use the funds for additional dormitory con-

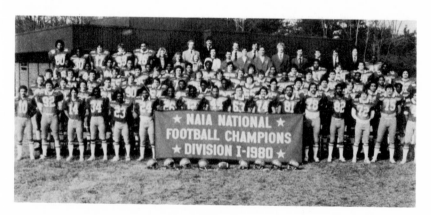

The "Fighting Christians" of 1980, NAIA national football champions.

struction. Numerous gifts, consisting of smaller sums, were also received, and they were deeply appreciated.[92]

The college benefited substantially again in 1979, when the Z. Smith Reynolds Foundation, Inc., approved a grant of $350,000 for the institution. The funds were to be used for a deferred gifts program, in which Catawba, Mars Hill, Meredith, Pfeiffer, and Saint Augustine's colleges would participate with Elon. The details of the operation were explained by President Young:

Though each institution in the consortium has endeavored
to attract deferred gifts, administrators feel that a much greater

Tim McDowell, Director of Public Information and Publications, appointed to the House of Representatives of the North Carolina General Assembly in 1977, elected in 1978, and reelected in 1980.

return can be realized from an organized effort to train selected individuals who can devote their full time to contacting potential donors.

Present financial constraints on private education make such an investment difficult or impossible for a single institution. With the support from the Z. Smith Reynolds Foundation, however, these six colleges can initiate deferred gifts programs which within a few years will become a valuable source of continued revenue.[93]

The program was planned for three years and expected to be yielding a financial profit by the end of that period.

Awarding honorary degrees continued under the Young administration. In 1973 the trustees voted a D.S. for John R. Kernodle and an LL.D. for Nelson Ferebee Taylor. In 1976 a D.H.L. was conferred upon Renold O. Schilke and LL.D.'s upon Ralph H. Scott and North Carolina's governor, James E. Holshouser, Jr. In 1978 an LL.D. was awarded to Isabella W. Cannon and a D.C.S. to Clyde W. Gordon, Sr. The following year, Henry W. Bray received a D.D., Rex G. Powell a D.C.S., William W. Sloan a D.H.L., and North Carolina's governor, James B. Hunt, Jr., an LL.D. degree.[94]

By 1979 Elon had mushroomed since the 1930s. In 1933 President Smith had supervised 29 faculty members and operated with 10 administrators. In 1979 the college was staffed with 145 faculty and approximately 97 persons serving in administrative capacities, aided by more than 60 secretaries and assistants. An elaborate computer system had been installed and other modern equipment procured to expedite the many details of operation.

Change had again been reflected in 1976 by another amendment to the college charter. The phrase "under the general control" was changed to "affiliated with" the United Church of Christ. The maximum number of trustees was raised to thirty-eight, "two of whom shall be youth trustees to serve two-year terms," and one-fourth of the total was required to belong to the United Church. However, in 1978, twenty were members of that organization, thirteen were Alamance County residents, eight were from Virginia, five from states other than North Carolina or the Old Dominion, one was a black, three were women, three were ministers, and nineteen were Elon alumni.[95] These statistics eloquently demonstrate that Elon College serves both its local geographical area and students from afar. It is an institution tolerant of religious convictions and governed by a democratic board of officials.

As the 1970s ended and Elon began to move into the decade of the eighties, the Young administration, which had solidified and matured, was well prepared to meet the fresh challenges to higher education that were inevitable as the nation entered a new phase in its history.

◆§ CHAPTER XVI §◆

THE ENDURING TREE

Each year to ancient friendships adds a ring,
As to an oak.
JAMES RUSSELL LOWELL
Under the Willows

Nine decades have passed since the five representatives of the Christian Church stood in the grove at Mill Point contemplating the site for a college. Farsighted as they were, it is doubtful if they envisioned the sprawling institution that stands there today. The twenty-five major, handsome buildings, conservatively valued at $25 million, which constitute Elon College today, and the 2,500 students thronging its campus would have been difficult to imagine in 1889. If the committeemen did expect such growth from the seed they were planting, they proved to be prophets indeed. It is more plausible to suspect that they realized more keenly the struggle that would ensue in founding the institution rather than the results of that act nearly a century in the future.

The five founders would doubtless be surprised, possibly shocked, to discover that their beloved Christian Church had lost its individual identity after two denominational mergers had made it a part of the United Church of Christ. They would also be amazed to learn that the college they were planning was affiliated with but not owned by the church, and that only 5.2 percent of its student body were members of that denomination. They would be pleased, however, to know that a minimum of religion courses is required of all students and that a college chaplain has been maintained, but they would be appalled at the freedom allowed the students as compared with the customs prevalent in 1889.

The quintet of churchmen could also indulge in pardonable pride for the part their church had played in making a liberal arts education under Christian leadership available for its youths. They could also feel justified in their attitude that higher learning should be made possible for both men and women, which was Elon's policy from its beginning. The state of North Carolina supported an outstanding university for its males, but in 1889 had made no provisions for the education of females. It remained for the Christian institution to become one of the early leaders in the state offering coeducation. This liberal attitude toward higher education for women was a cardinal principle of Elon College when the institution was conceived, and it has always been a rewarding part of the school's operation.

Whether unfortunate or not, however, some of the plans of the founders were fulfilled but others were not. It was a major disappointment to the devout church leaders that a theological seminary was never established at the college nor a chair of theology founded, but this was counterbalanced by the fact that the college sent many of its graduates to seminaries elsewhere in preparation for their careers in the Christian ministry. Many could not have completed the lengthy requirements had it not been for the basic training they received at Elon.

The campus in the early 1970s.

Senior Oak.

Furthermore, the town did not become the permanent center of Christian Church activities that was the dream of the founders, but this was largely attributable to economic reasons. The publishing venture was a failure, as it was destined to be wherever located, because the denomination was too small and too financially handicapped to make it a success. The Southern Conference found more suitable quarters for its office in Burlington, and moved it to that city. However, the Christian Orphanage was a success from its founding and still renders a valuable humane service. Also, the town has attracted numerous denominational leaders and others to join its residents after retirement from duties elsewhere.

Despite the failure of some of the roseate plans for the growth of denominational functions, the town of Elon College has always been the primary location for church and civic gatherings, conventions, Chautauquas, lyceums, study programs, committee meetings, and similar purposes. Its facilities have ever been courteously extended and its hospitality enjoyed. These activities, in addition to those of the college, have kept the town and the institution busy with the many visitors and their programs. These advances of both the institution and the municipality have far outweighed any disappointments over plans that failed to mature as expected.

Most of all, the pioneer churchmen would be pleased to learn of the thousands of Elon alumni who have carried throughout the world the training they absorbed under the maroon and gold banner. Their creditable records are legion and praiseworthy. They have honored their alma mater and provided valuable contributions to the world in every field. They are also noted for their loyalty to the institution, and constitute the real backbone of its stability.

In a day when gloomy predictions are being made concerning the future of the independent college because of declining population and diversified educational interests, Elon is holding its own. The success of the Young administration in enlarging the endowment and maintaining financial solvency, added to the accomplishments of its predecessors, has enabled the institution to maintain financial stability. The emphasis on curriculum adjustment, programs of widespread general appeal, and creditable athletic performances are attracting students in a steady stream and bid fair to continue to do so.

The founders would see today few objects that they gazed upon in

1889, but the Senior Oak would be one of them. Then a sapling, now a huge tree, it symbolizes by its healthy growth the growth of the college from one unfinished building to its present impressive plant. A visiting speaker on one Founders Day described an Elon oak as "unwedgable,"[1] in tribute to its strength, and so it has proved to be. Ancient trees eventually succumb to the ravages of time but young sprouts replace them, and it is this renewed growth supplementing the old that shelters Elon College.

APPENDIX A

CONSTITUTION OF GRAHAM COLLEGE

The General Convention of the Christian Church does hereby make and ordain the following Constitution for the government of said Institution:

ARTICLE I. The said College, with all its appurtenances, shall be owned by the General Convention of the Christian Church.

ART. II. The affairs of the Institution shall be under the management of a Board of fifteen Trustees, who shall be members of the Christian Church. The majority of the Board of Trustees shall form a quorum for the transaction of business. They shall hold office as hereinafter specified, or until their successors are elected. Said Trustees shall have power to do, perform, and execute all duties, acts and trusts incidental to such institutions, except such as are specially reserved to the Faculty.

Of those first elected, one-third shall hold office for two years, one-third for four years, and the remaining third for six years. Afterward all elections shall be for six years. Upon the happening of the death, resignation or incompetency of any member of the Board of Trustees, or upon his supercedure, the remaining members shall fill the vacancy thereby occasioned. If any member of the Board of Trustees shall become incompetent to act in that capacity, or if he shall become unable to discharge, or shall persistently neglect the duties of that office, he may be superceded by the other members of the Board, and thereupon his functions shall cease. A two-thirds vote shall be necessary to effect such a supercedure.

ART. III. The permanent officers of the Board of Trustees shall be a President, a Vice-President, a Secretary and a Treasurer, all of which officers shall be elected by the Trustees, from their own number, for the term of one year, and shall perform the duties and be invested with the powers usually appertaining to said officers in such institutions.

ART. IV. The Trustees shall meet annually on the day next preceding that of the Commencement of the College, for the purpose of electing persons to the offices then to be filled, and for the transaction of such other business as may be necessary, and may meet also on their respective adjournments.

Special meetings of the Trustees may be called by order of the President, Vice-President, or any three of the Trustees, by publishing notice thereof four weeks in the SUN. Such meetings shall be holden at the College Building.

ART. V. The Board of Trustees shall have power to adopt such By Laws, Rules and Regulations, not inconsistent with the "Act of the General Assembly" incorporating this Institution, hereafter to be obtained, as may from time to time seem to them proper, and to appoint such subordinate officers, agents and employees as may be necessary for the interest of the Institution, and prescribe their rights, duties and liabilities.

ART. VI. The Board of Trustees shall elect a Faculty, consisting of President, Professors and Tutors, and shall fix their salaries, per agreement, and the price of tuition in the Institution.

ART. VII. The donation made for the purpose of securing the location of the College shall all be expended in the purchase or appropriation of College grounds, building purposes and incidentals thereto, and shall constitute no part of the Endowment Fund.

An Endowment Fund shall be set apart, never to be diminished, the interest only to be used, which fund may be increased by charitable bequests and donations.

ART. VIII. The Trustees shall be entitled to three cents per mile for the distance necessarily traveled in going to and returning from all meetings of the Board legally called or holden.

ART. IX. The management, discipline and government of the pupils and students in the departments of said College shall be entrusted to the President and Faculty of said Institution.

ART. X. The Board of Trustees shall obtain a charter from the next legislature of the State in which it may be located, securing to the College all the rights and privileges usually obtained by such Institutions, and shall devise and procure a corporate seal for said Institution, by which all its public and appropriate acts and documents may be authenticated.

ART. XI. These articles may be amended, or changed at any annual meeting of the Trustees, by two-thirds of the members present voting in the affirmative.

BY-LAWS OF THE BOARD OF TRUSTEES
OF GRAHAM COLLEGE

The General Convention of the Christian Church does hereby make, ordain and establish the following By-Laws, Rules and Regulations:

ARTICLE I.

SECTION 1. The Trustees shall meet annually at the time and place prescribed in the Constitution. It shall be the duty of the President of the Board to give at least one month's notice of such meeting, in such manner as he may think best.

SEC. 2. All elections of Trustees shall be by ballot, and the candidate or candidates receiving a majority of all the votes cast shall be declared duly elected. Certificates of election shall in all cases be made out, signed by the presiding officer and Secretary, and entered on the record of the Board. Such Trustees so elected shall be notified by the Secretary of their election, and shall serve for one year, or until their successors are elected.

SEC. 3. The Trustees should be selected from the list of persons recommended by the General Convention, but in case of failure on the part of the General Convention to recommend such persons, then the Trustees are to be guided by their own judgment, and the interests of the Institution.

SEC. 4. All the officers of the Board shall be elected for one year, and shall serve until their successors are chosen.

ARTICLE II.

SECTION 1. For the election of President, Secretary, Treasurer, or any member of the Faculty, the concurring vote of a majority of all the Trustees shall be necessary to a choice; in the transaction of other business of the Board, a majority of the Trustees present shall be competent to the transaction of such business.

SEC. 2. The following shall be the order of business at each session of the Committee, unless otherwise ordered:

I. Reading, correcting and approving the minutes of the preceding session of the Board, and also of the proceedings of the Executive Committee.

II. The report of the President, with the report of the Secretary, Treasurer, and Agent.

III. The reports of Commissions.

IV. Other business which may have precedence in the order in which it shall be presented.

SEC. 3. The President of the Board shall have all the privileges of a Trustee, but shall not participate in debate while himself occupying the chair. Upon each vote by ayes and nays his name shall be called last.

SEC. 4. The final vote upon all questions of business shall be taken by ayes and nays and entered upon the Record, and at the request of any three Trustees, any vote shall be so taken and entered. All elections by the Board shall be by ballot, unless otherwise ordered.

SEC. 5. Motions to adjourn shall at all times be in order. The previous question, motions to take from and lay on the table, and motions to adjourn shall be decided without debate. Each day shall constitute but one sitting of the Board.

ARTICLE III.

SECTION 1. The Board of Trustees may at any regular meeting appoint a committee, to be designated the Executive Committee, to serve between the meetings of the Board of Trustees. Said Executive Committee shall consist of five Trustees, of whom the President of the Board shall be one, and President also thereof.

SEC. 2. Said Executive Committee shall have full power to do and transact all affairs and business which the Board might rightfully do, and which shall be necessary to be transacted in the interim between the meetings of the Board, subject, however, to the revision and approval of the Board: *Provided* that the proceedings of said Executive Committee shall have full force and effect until the next meeting of the Board. But such disapproval shall in no case amount to the violation of any contract made and entered into by said Executive Committee.

SEC. 3. The Executive Committee shall meet as often as may be deemed necessary upon the call of the President, and due notice being given to each of its members.

SEC. 4. A majority of the Executive Committee shall constitute a quorum for the transaction of business.

SEC. 5. The Rules of Order in voting and the other transaction of business shall be the same for the Executive Committee as for the Board itself.

ARTICLE IV.

SECTION 1. The officers of the Board shall be allowed such compensation for services as shall be fixed by the Board.

ARTICLE V.

SECTION 1. *Duties of the President.* The President shall preside at all meetings of the Board and of the Executive Committee, and shall sign the daily proceedings of each, when properly entered and approved. In the absence of the President, the Vice-President shall perform all the duties of the President. The President, however, may call any member to the chair temporarily, and also in case of the absence of the President and Vice-President the Board or the Executive Committee may appoint a temporary chairman.

S E C. 2. The President shall be the general financial agent of the Institution and shall see that all its funds are properly accounted for, and promptly paid or secured, according to the provisions of the By-laws, rules, orders, and directions of the Board or the Executive Committee.

S E C. 3. He shall be the General Superintendent of the affairs of the Institution, directing and managing the same according to the provisions of the Constitution and By laws, rules, orders and directions of the Board or the Executive Committee.

S E C. 4. He may appoint any temporary agent the better to carry out and effect the above objects, subject, however, to the approval of the Board of the Executive Committee.

S E C. 5. The President shall sign all orders drawn upon the Treasurer, and all deeds, bonds, notes, and all agreements and contracts of the Institution.

S E C. 6. He may at any time require the Secretary, Treasurer, Faculty of the College, or any agent of the Board, to make a report in writing in reference to any or all matters in their charge respectively.

S E C. 7. He may temporarily fill any and all vacancies which may occur in the offices of Secretary or Treasurer, until the meeting of the Board or the Executive Committee.

S E C. 8. The President, at each annual meeting of the Board, shall make thereto a full report in writing of the state and condition of the affairs of the Institution, and of the operations and transactions of the same during the fiscal year next preceding such report, and shall, together with his report, present to the Board all such reports as may have been made to him by the Secretary, Treasurer, Faculty of the College, or Agents, as he may deem necessary for the information of the Board.

S E C. 9. The President shall see that all the loans of funds and all property of the Institution are well secured against any loss or injury.

ARTICLE VI.

S E C T I O N 1. *The Duties of the Secretary.* The Secretary shall have the care, custody, and keeping of all the books and papers of the Board, except such as shall be required to be kept by other officers or agents thereof. The books and papers in the Secretary's office shall at all times be open to the inspection of the Board, the Executive, or to any committee of the Board, or to any one of the Trustees.

S E C. 2. The Secretary shall keep a book in which he shall promptly record full and complete minutes of all the acts and proceedings of the Board and of the Executive Committee.

S E C. 3. The Secretary shall issue and attest all orders drawn upon the

Treasury and shall also attest all deeds, bonds and other contracts and agreements; and to such as shall require a seal to give them validity, he shall also attach the seal of the Institution.

S E C . 4 . He shall be the Book keeper and Accountant of the Board. He shall keep separate and distinct accounts of the different funds of the Institution with the Treasurer, the Agents, the borrowers of funds, and with all other persons having business transactions with whom account should properly be kept.

S E C . 5 . The Secretary shall receive and receipt for all moneys paid to the Institution, and shall enter the name on the books to their proper accounts. He shall also pay over all such moneys to the Treasurer, taking his receipt for the same, designating to what fund all such moneys belong.

S E C . 6 . The Secretary shall, at every annual meeting of the Board, make a full report in writing of the state and condition of the books, accounts, and other matters in his charge, up to the close of the fiscal year.

S E C . 7 . The Secretary shall faithfully hand over to his successor, or to the Board, or to the Executive Committee, or to the President when demanded, all the records, books, papers, and all other articles and things in his hands, care or keeping, by virtue of his office, belonging to, or in any wise appertaining to the Institution.

ARTICLE VII.

S E C T I O N I . *The Duties of the Treasurer.* The Treasurer shall receive and receipt for all moneys paid to him by the Secretary. He shall safely keep all moneys and faithfully disburse the same upon the proper orders drawn upon the Treasury.

S E C . 2 . He shall keep a register of receipts given, and of orders paid. The receipts shall show the date, number and amount, the person to whom paid, and the fund out of which the same was paid.

S E C . 3 . He shall keep the necessary books, in which he shall post, in a concise and proper manner, his accounts with the Institution, keeping a separate and correct account of the different funds of the same.

S E C . 4 . No money shall be drawn from the Treasury, or paid out by the Treasurer, but upon an order drawn by the President and attested by the Secretary.

S E C . 5 . The Treasurer shall, at every annual meeting of the Board, make a full report in writing of the condition of the Treasury, of the different funds, separately and in the aggregate, up to the close of the fiscal year.

S E C . 6 . The Treasurer shall deliver over to his successor in office, or to the Board, or Executive Committee, or President, when demanded, all the books, papers, moneys, or other articles or things belonging or appertaining to the Institution in his hands, care or custody, by virtue of his office.

SEC. 7. The Treasurer shall give bond and approved security in an amount to be fixed by the Board or the Executive Committee, for the faithful performance of his duty.

ARTICLE VIII.

SECTION 1. *Of the Educational Fund.* All moneys belonging to the Endowment Fund that may be, or shall come into the hands of the Treasurer, shall be promptly loaned out or disposed of by the President, as the Board of Trustees may from time to time direct.

ARTICLE IX.

SECTION 1. *Of the Funds of the Institution.* All the funds and means shall be divided into two classes, to be designated and known as the Endowment Fund, and Building and Incidental Fund.

SEC. 2. The Endowment Fund shall consist of the whole of all such gifts, grants, donations and bequests to the Institution as by the terms of the gifts, grants or bequests may be made or designated, as to or for the use of said Endowment Fund. The said Endowment Fund shall in no case be expended or diminished, except in case of forfeiture or actual loss; but shall be kept, retained and preserved as a permanent fund for the endowment of the Institution, and shall be put at interest and secured, as in the wisdom of the Board they may think best.

SEC. 3. The Building and Incidental Fund shall consist of the whole of all donations given to secure the location of the College, all receipts for tuition in the Institution, all the interests arising from the Endowment Fund, the whole of all gifts, grants, donations and bequests made or to be made to the Institution to which, by the terms of the gifts, grants, donations and bequests, no other direction is or may be given.

SEC. 4. The Building and Incidental Fund is chargeable with any and all sums and amounts paid or to be paid for or on account of the College grounds, the buildings and improvements made or to be made thereon for the Institution, all the apparatus and furniture for the use of the Institution, all the necessary books and stationery for the use of the officers and agents of the Institution, and for the salaries of President, Professors and Tutors of the Institution, the compensation of all officers and agents of the Institution, and for fuel, lights, etc., for the use of the Institution.

Article X.

Section 1. *Duties of the Faculty.* The Faculty of the Institution shall, by its President, at each annual meeting of the Trustees, make a full report in writing, showing the state and condition of the Institution, and its operations during the fiscal year, noting by name the cases of peculiar merit; and also presenting, as far as can be prepared, a catalogue of the then current session of the Institution.

Article XI.

Section 1. *The Fiscal Year.* The fiscal year shall commence . . . .

Sec. 2. These By-Laws may be altered or amended by the Trustees, at any annual meeting, by a two-thirds vote in the affirmative.

In order to make a provisional arrangement for conducting the business hereby given in charge to the Board of Trustees, and until the first regular meeting of said Board, we now appoint . . . . President of an Executive Committee, ... Treasurer, ... Secretary, and . . . . and . . . . members thereof. These persons shall constitute an Executive Committee, as provided in Art. III of the above said By-Laws, and shall hold their offices by virtue hereof until the first meeting of the Board of Trustees, and no longer.

AN ACT TO INCORPORATE ELON COLLEGE

The General Assembly of North Carolina do enact:

SECTION 1. That W. S. Long, J. W. Wellons, W. W. Staley, G. S. Watson, M. L. Hurley, E. T. Pierce, W. J. Lee, P. J. Kernodle, J. F. West, E. E. Holland, E. A. Moffitt, J. M. Smith, J. H. Harden, F. O. Moring and S. P. Read, and their associates and successors, be and they are hereby created a body politic and corporate to be styled the "Board of Trustees of Elon College," and by that name to remain in perpetual succession, with full power to sue and to be sued, to plead and be impleaded, to acquire, hold and convey property, real and personal, to have and use a common seal, to alter and renew the same at pleasure, to make and alter from time to time such bylaws as they may deem necessary for the government of said institution, its officers, students and servants: Provided, that such by-laws shall not be inconsistent with the Constitution and laws of the United States and of this State. Also, to have power to confer on those whom they may deem worthy such honors and degrees as are usually conferred in similar institutions: Provided further, that said trustees shall not be individually liable for their acts and doings as trustees.

SECTION 2. The affairs of said College shall be under the management of a board of fifteen trustees who shall be members of the Christian Church. A majority of the board shall form a quorum for the transaction of business. Said trustees may convey real estate by deed, under their common seal, executed by the president and secretary of said board. They may hold office as the general convention of the Christian Church may specify or until their successors are elected. Said trustees shall hold their first meeting at Mill Point, in Alamance County, on the . . . . day of . . . . , 1889; afterwards, they shall meet on their own appointment; but of necessity, the president, with the advice of two trustees, may call a special meeting of the board, or any five members of the board may call such a meeting by giving notice to each member in writing at least ten days before the time of meeting.

SECTION 3. That said institution shall remain at the place where the site is now located, in Alamance County, Boone Station Township, at the place now called Mill Point; and shall afford instruction in the liberal arts and sciences. And the trustees may, as they shall find themselves able and the public good requires, erect additional departments for such other branches of education as they may think necessary or useful.

SECTION 4. That the board of trustees shall from time to time appoint a president and other officers and instructors, and also agents of the institution, as may be necessary; and shall have power to displace or remove any or either of them for good and sufficient reasons; also fill vacancies which occur in the board by resignation, death, expiration of term of office, or otherwise, among said officers or agents, and prescribe and direct the course of study to be pursued in said College and its departments.

SECTION 5. The president of the College shall be ex-officio a member of the board of trustees and president of the same, and in his absence the board shall elect one of its own members to preside for the time being, and if any of said trustees shall be permanently appointed president of said College, his office as trustee shall be deemed vacant and the board of trustees shall fill the same.

SECTION 6. That said College and the said trustees shall at all times be under the control of the general convention of the Christian Church.

SECTION 7. The board of trustees shall faithfully apply all funds by them collected and received according to their best judgment in erecting suitable buildings, supporting the necessary officers, instructors and agents, and in procuring books, maps, charts and other apparatus necessary to the well being and success of the College.

SECTION 8. The treasurer shall always, and all other agents when required, before entering on the duties of their appointments, give bonds for the security of the corporation and the public in such penal sums as the board of trustees may direct, and with such sureties as they shall approve.

SECTION 9. Property to the amount of five hundred thousand dollars held by said trustees for said College shall forever be exempt from taxation.

SECTION 10. That it shall not be lawful for any person or persons to set up any gaming table or any device whatever for playing at any game of chance or hazard, by whatever name called, or to gamble in any manner, or to keep a house of ill-fame, or to manufacture spirituous or intoxicating liquors or otherwise to sell or convey for a certain consideration to any person any intoxicating liquors, within one and a half miles of said College; any person who shall violate any of the provisions of this section shall be guilty of a misdemeanor.

SECTION 11. That all property, real and personal, and all choses in action that have been or may hereafter be conveyed, given, granted or devised, or that may have in any manner come or may hereafter come into the possession of said trustees for Graham College, shall vest in and belong to said trustees of Elon College, and the said trustees for Graham College are authorized to make or cause to be made such conveyances as will vest in said trustees for Elon College the title of all property heretofore conveyed, given, granted or devised to them, or which has in any manner come into their possession for Graham College, or that may hereafter be conveyed, given, granted or devised to them, in any manner, or come into their possession for said Graham College.

SECTION 12. That this act shall be in force from the date of its ratification.

Ratified the 11th day of March, A.D. 1889.

AMENDMENTS 1909

SECTION 1. That section two of chapter two hundred and sixteen, Private Laws of one thousand, eight hundred and eighty-nine, be amended by striking out the word "fifteen" in line two of said section between the words "of" and "trustees," and inserting in lieu thereof the word "eighteen," so that said section shall read: "The affairs of said College shall be under the management of a board of eighteen trustees," instead of fifteen, as now written.

SECTION 2. That this act shall be in force from and after June fourth, one thousand, nine hundred and nine.

Ratified this 26th day of February, A.D. 1909.

AMENDMENTS 1913

SECTION 1. That section one of chapter one hundred and thirty-nine Private Laws of one thousand, nine hundred and nine, be amended by adding after the words "instead of fifteen, as now written," "but the quorum shall remain eight as provided in section two, chapter two hundred and sixteen, Private Laws of one thousand, eight hundred and eighty-nine," so that the said section shall read: "The affairs of the said College shall be under the management of a board of eighteen trustees, but the quorum shall remain eight as provided in section two, chapter two hundred and sixteen, Private Laws of one thousand, eight hundred and eighty-nine."

SECTION 2. That if any merchant, druggist, liveryman, agent or vendor of merchandise or commodity of any kind whatsoever shall sell the same on credit to any minor member of the student body of said College, while a student of the College, without the consent in writing of the President or Dean of said College, or of the parent or guardian or person standing in loco parentis of said student, such sales and contracts of sale without written consent, are hereby declared void and uncollectible. The provisions of this section shall not apply in case of board, room rent and medical attention, nor medicines furnished upon the prescription of a physician or surgeon practicing according to the laws of North Carolina.

SECTION 3. That this act shall be in force from and after its ratification.

Ratified the 27th day of January, 1913.

AMENDMENTS 1915

SECTION 1. That section two of chapter two hundred and sixteen Private Laws of one thousand, eight hundred and eighty-nine, be amended by striking out the word "fifteen" in line two of said section, between the words "of" and "trustees," and inserting in lieu thereof the word "twenty-four," and adding after the word "trustees" in the said line and section, "but the quorum shall remain eight as provided in section two, chapter two hundred and sixteen, Private Laws of one thousand, eight hundred and eighty-nine," so that the section shall read: "The affairs of the said College shall be under the management of a board of twenty-four trustees, but the quorum shall remain eight as provided in section two, chapter two hundred and sixteen, Private Laws of one thousand, eight hundred and eighty-nine."

SECTION 2. That this act shall be in force from and after its ratification. Ratified the 30th day of January, 1915.

AMENDMENTS 1917

SECTION 1. That section nine of chapter two hundred and sixteen, Private Laws of one thousand, eight hundred and eighty-nine, be amended by striking out the words "five hundred thousand," in line . . . . of said section between the words "of" and "dollars," and inserting in lieu thereof the words "five million," so that the section shall read, "Property to the amount of five million dollars held by said trustees for said College shall forever be exempt from taxation."

SECTION 2. This act shall be in force from and after ratification.

AMENDMENTS 1923

The Board of Trustees of Elon College in regular annual session, a corporation of North Carolina, on this 28th day of May, A.D. 1923, do hereby resolve and declare that it is advisable that the charter of Elon College be amended pursuant to a resolution of the Southern Christian Convention, adopted May 3, 1923 as follows, to wit: "We recommend that the Secretary of State of North Carolina be requested to amend the Charter of Elon College so as to permit a total of thirty (30) trustees instead of twenty-four (24) as at present, with a quorum of ten (10) instead of eight (8) as at present."

AMENDMENTS 1930

The Board of Trustees of Elon College, a corporation of North Carolina, on this 18th day of February, A.D. 1930, do hereby resolve and declare that it is advisable that section two of Chapter 216, Private Laws of 1889 and section six Chapter 216, Private Laws of 1889, be amended as follows:

That section two of chapter two hundred and sixteen, Private Laws of one thousand, eight hundred and eighty nine, be amended by changing the first two sentences of that section to read as follows: "The affairs of said College shall be under the management of a board of thirty-six Trustees who shall be chosen from persons nominated by the Southern Christian Convention or its legal successor. Thirty of these Trustees shall be members of the Christian Church and six of them members of the Congregational Church. Twelve members of the board shall constitute a quorum for the transaction of business" instead of "The affairs of said College shall be under the management of a board of fifteen Trustees who shall be members of the Christian Church. A majority of the board shall form a quorum for the transaction of business," as now written.

That section six of chapter two hundred and sixteen, Private Laws of one thousand, eight hundred and eighty-nine be amended by changing said section to read: "That said College and the said Trustees shall at all time be under the control of the Southern Christian Convention or its legal successor," instead of "That said College and the said Trustees shall at all times be under the control of the General Convention of the Christian Church" as now written.

AMENDMENTS 1944

The Board of Trustees of Elon College, a corporation of North Carolina, on this 22nd day of May, A.D. 1944, do hereby resolve and declare that it is advisable:

1. That each and every amendment to the charter of this corporation (Chapter 216, Private Laws of North Carolina, 1889), whether by acts of the General Assembly or by procedure under the general corporation laws of North Carolina, be repealed.

2. That Section one of said chapter be amended to eliminate from the presently styled corporate name "Board of Trustees of Elon College" the words "Board of Trustees of" and the word "the" before the quoted corporate name, so as to make the corporate name of this corporation—"ELON COLLEGE."

3. That Section two of said chapter be amended by striking out the first two sentences in said section and substituting in lieu thereof the following: "The affairs of said college shall be under the management of a Board of Trustees consisting of thirty-six members, who shall be chosen from persons nominated by The Southern Convention of Congregational-Christian Churches or its legal successor, twenty-four of whom shall be members of the Congregational-Christian Church. Twelve members of the Board shall constitute a quorum for the transaction of business."

4. That said chapter be amended by striking out the words "General convention of the Christian Church" wherever they appear and substituting in lieu thereof the words "Southern Convention of Congregational-Christian Churches or its legal successor."

ALUMNI ORATORS, 1896–1954

Year selected	Name	Year of graduation
1896	Nathaniel G. Newman	1891
1897	Elijah Moffitt	1893
1898	Herbert Scholz	1891
1899	S. E. Everett	1893
1900	S. M. Smith	1895
1901	J. E. Rawls	1896
1902	Walter P. Lawrence	1894
1903	John P. Lee	1896
1904	E. D. Summers	1899
1905	I. W. Johnson	1898
1906	Charles H. Rowland	1900
1907	Mrs. Bessie S. Cheatham	1898
1908	George F. Whitley	1902
1909	C. E. Newman	1899
1910	Miss Jennie T. Herndon	1896
1911	William A. Harper	1899
1912	D. R. Fonville	1904
1913	Mrs. J. K. Ruebush	1901
1914	H. E. Rountree	1903
1915	A. W. Andes	1906
1916	Mrs. Charles T. Moses	1907
1917	J. Adolphus Long	1905
1918	George O. Lankford	1907
1919	Mrs. William A. Harper	1899
1920	S. E. Everett	1893
1921	G. C. Davidson	1904
1922	Mrs. E. A. Crawford	1916
1923	Stanley C. Harrell	1909
1924	H. Shelton Smith	1917
1925	Mrs. Leon E. Smith	1907
1926	Havilah Babcock	1918
1927	J. L. Crumpton	1917

1928	Mrs. H. P. Powell	1922
1929	C. C. Howell	1908
1930	William T. Scott	1924
1931	Mrs. R. S. Rainey	1923
1932	H. Lee Scott	1923
1933	Alonzo C. Hall	1910
1934	Mrs. Rose H. Holder	1925
1935	Fred F. Myrick	1914
1936	P. E. Lindley	1920
1937	W. F. Warren	1910
1938	Roy S. Helms	1923
1939	John R. Ingle	1911
1940	Thomas H. Franks	1909
1941	J. Clyde Auman	1918
1942	C. J. Felton	1912
1943	W. J. B. Truitt	1917
1944	Mrs. W. E. Wisseman	1928
1945	*No annual alumni meeting held*	—
1946	Mrs. William T. Scott	1924
1947	William R. Turner	1932
1948	Mrs. John G. Truitt	1926
1949	David W. Shepherd	1920
1950	I. W. Johnson	1898
1951	Thomas E. Powell	1919
1952	Mrs. Russell Bradford	1917
1953	C. J. Peel	1915
1954	Mrs. Gwendolyn P. Fogleman	1927

OUTSTANDING ALUMNUS AWARDS, 1941–1980

Year selected	Name	Year of graduation
1941	W. Clifton Elder	1925
1945	Mrs. Mamie H. Leathers	1902
1946	Dr. John D. Messick	1922
1947	W. G. Stoner	1923
1949	George D. Colclough	1926
1950	Dr. Leon E. Smith	1910
1951	Mrs. Clara Lucile J. Herr	1918
1952	Walter J. Wilkins	1916
1953	Dr. W. H. Boone	1894
1954	Mrs. Rose H. Holder	1925
1955	Dr. A. Liggett Lincoln	1910
1956	John T. Kernodle	1908
1957	Mrs. Leon E. Smith	1907
1958	Dr. J. Earl Danieley	1946
1959	Dr. Havilah Babcock	1918
1960	Dr. H. Shelton Smith	1917
1961	Dr. Robert W. Truitt	1941
1962	Dr. John R. Kernodle	1935
1963	Dr. Alonzo L. Hook	1913
1964	Dr. T. E. Powell, Jr.	1919
1965	Judge Eugene A. Gordon	1941
1966	Dr. J. L. Crumpton	1917
1967	L. J. ("Hap") Perry	1923
1968	Judge William H. ("Bill") Maness	1938
1969	Dr. Daniel T. Watts	1937
1970	A. G. Thompson	1941
1971	Robert E. Lee	1946
1972	Miss Marjorie R. Hunter	1942
1973	Dr. C. LeGrande Moody, Jr.	1938
1974	Clyde W. Gordon, Sr.	1926
1975	Dr. Durward T. Stokes	1964
1976	Rev. Joyce B. Myers	1959

1977	Royall H. Spence, Jr.	1942
1978	*Distinguished Alumnus Award*	
	Wallace T. Chandler	1949
	Capt. Eugene B. McDaniel	1955
	Oka T. Hester	1937
	Young Alumnus of the Year Award	
	Samuel Story, Jr.	1969
	Citizens Service Award	
	Laurence A. Alley	—
1979	*Distinguished Alumnus Award*	
	Marvin Moss	1954
	Frank Hayes	1942
	Young Alumnus of the Year Award	
	Gerry Oxford	1969
	Carolyn Little	1969
	Citizens Service Award	
	Roger Gant, Jr.	—
1980	*Distinguished Alumnus Award*	
	Jesse H. Meredith	1943
	Martin Ritt	1936
	Young Alumnus of the Year Award	
	Sally Ann O'Neill	1970
	R. Wayne Weston	1971
	Citizens Service Award	
	Thomas E. Powell III	—

ELON SPORTS HALL OF FAME

INDUCTEES, 1972–1980

OCTOBER 1972

Dr. Alonzo L. Hook, *"Longtime Friend of Elon Athletics"*
Douglas C. ("Peahead") Walker, *coach*
L. J. ("Hap") Perry, *football, basketball, baseball*
Salvatore M. ("Sal") Gero, *football*
James M. ("Jack Rabbit") Abbitt, *football, basketball, baseball*
Henry T. ("Pete") Williams, *football, baseball*
Anthony ("Tony") Carcaterra, *football, basketball, baseball*
Robert L. ("Jack") Boone, *football*
E. S. ("Johnny") Johnson, *football, basketball, baseball, track*

MAY 1973

James L. ("Hank") Hamrick, *basketball, baseball*
Gilbert ("Gil") Watts, *baseball, basketball*
Jack Gardner, *basketball, baseball*
Hollis Atkinson, *basketball, baseball, track*
C. V. ("Lefty") Briggs, *baseball, basketball*
C. C. ("Jack") Johnson, *basketball, baseball, track, coach*

OCTOBER 1973

Lou F. Roshelli, *football*
E. Hal Bradley, *football, basketball*
C. Lynn Newcomb, *football, track*
John U. Newman, Jr., *baseball, basketball*
Gordon A. Kirkland, *football, baseball*

OCTOBER 1974

Robert C. ("Bob") Browne, *football, basketball, baseball*
Arnold E. Melvin, *football*

Talmage ("Tal") Abernathy, *baseball*
A. Roney Cates, *basketball*
George W. Wooten, *football, track, golf*

OCTOBER 1975

H. Jesse Branson, *basketball*
Moses D. ("Dick") Caddell, *football, basketball, baseball*
Bunn Hearn, *baseball, coach*
Wilburn E. ("Webb") Newsome, *football, baseball, boxing*
Roy E. ("Country") Rollins, *football, basketball, track*

OCTOBER 1976

Curry E. Bryan, Jr., *football*
Henry A. DeSimone, *football, baseball*
Zeb S. Harrington, *football, baseball*
C. Benjamin Kendall, *basketball, baseball*
Albert Mastrobattisto, *football*
Willie K. Tart, *football, track*
Lloyd E. Whitley, *basketball, tennis*

OCTOBER 1977

Arthur F. Fowler, Jr., *baseball, football, basketball*
James R. ("Nick") Thompson, *baseball*
Delmer D. ("Dee") Atkinson, *basketball*
N. B. ("Muddy") Waters, *football, baseball*
Dan Long Newman (*posthumous*), *basketball, football, baseball*
Daniel P. ("Rusty") Jones (*posthumous*), *tennis*
Dr. Howard R. Richardson, *football*

NOVEMBER 1978

Burgin W. Beale, *football, baseball*
Garland Causey, *football, basketball, coach*
Joe Golombek, *football, basketball, boxing*
Sherrill G. Hall, *baseball*
J. Mark McAdams, *football, basketball*
Paul A. Roy, *baseball, basketball*
Henry R. Walser, *football*

NOVEMBER 1979

Russell T. ("Shine") Bradford, *basketball*
Paul C. ("Lefty") Cheek, *basketball, baseball*
Walter C. ("Firpo") Latham, *basketball, baseball*
Graham L. ("Doc") Mathis, *football, basketball, baseball, coach*
Richard E. McGeorge, *football, basketball*
Robert J. ("Bob") Stauffenberg, *football, track*

NOVEMBER 1980

Howard L. Briggs, Sr., *baseball, football, basketball*
Paul F. Briggs, *baseball*
Horace J. Hendrickson, *coach*
Walter L. Hobson, Jr., *basketball, baseball*
Wade E. Marlette, *football, basketball, baseball, track, cross country*
David A. Mondy, *golf, basketball, track*
Joseph B. Newman, *football, basketball, baseball, track*
John C. Whitesell, *football*

I. PREPARING THE SEEDBED

1. Wilbur E. MacClenny, *The Life of Rev. James O'Kelly* (Raleigh, N.C.: Edwards and Broughton, 1910), 84–104.

2. Durward T. Stokes and William T. Scott, *A History of the Christian Church in the South* (Burlington, N.C.: Southern Conference of the United Church of Christ, 1975). Pages 27–46, 50–54, and 60–61 describe the organization in detail.

3. Stokes and Scott, *Christian Church*, 313, lists all of O'Kelly's known publications. The book referred to is William Guirey's *The History of the Episcopacy, in Four Parts: From Its Rise to the Present Day* (Privately printed, n.p., n.d., but in circulation by 1800).

4. William H. Turrentine, "History of Christian Education in Alamance County," an unpublished manuscript in the Church History Room (hereafter cited as CHR), in the library of Elon College. This room contains all the existing records and historical material of the Christian Church in the South.

5. Peter J. Kernodle, *Lives of Christian Ministers* (Richmond, Va.: Central Publishing Company, 1909), 113.

6. *The Hillsborough (N.C.) Recorder*, February 5, 1836.

7. *Hillsborough Recorder*, August 1, 1839.

8. *The Christian Palladium* (Union Mills, N.Y.: Christian General Book Association), June 15, 1841.

9. *The Christian Sun* (Hillsborough, North Carolina, and other locations in North Carolina and Virginia), February 12, August 27, 1851. See also Sallie W. Stockard, *History of Alamance* (Raleigh, N.C.: Edwards and Broughton, 1900), 87. It is possible that Nelson planned to close his seminary at the end of the spring term in 1851, which may have been one reason Mrs. Kerr moved to Graham to conduct her school, or both institutions may have been in operation at the same time, which seems unlikely in a town so small. Nelson was a Presbyterian.

10. Proceedings of the North Carolina and Virginia Christian Conference, 1828–56, session of 1841, unnumbered pages, hereafter cited as NC&Va. The minutes of several of the conferences were published in pamphlet form. These, along with the original Minute Book, and a typed copy of it made by Wilbur E. MacClenny are all in CHR.

11. NC&Va. 1845 session.

12. NC&Va. 1849 session.

13. *Hillsborough Recorder*, August 15, 1839; Kernodle, *Lives*, 228–229.

14. NC&Va. 1849 session.

15. Typescript, prepared by Wilbur E. MacClenny, of the minutes of the Eastern Virginia Christian Conference, 1830–59, CHR, 135, hereafter cited as EVa. After the typescript of these and other church records were made, the originals were destroyed when the library at Elon College was consumed by fire on January 18, 1923.

16. Office of the Alamance County Register of Deeds, Alamance County Courthouse, Graham, N.C. (hereafter cited as ACRD), Deed Book I, 720.

17. NC&Va. 1850 session.

18. NC&Va. 1846 session; *Sun*, December 1, 1846.

19. *Sun*, July 16, 1851.

20. *Sun*, October 6, 1852.

21. Ibid.

22. ACRD, Deed Book I, 306. On December 3, 1850, John R. Holt paid Mary Long fifty dollars for one acre in Graham "on Main Street north from courthouse." See also Wilbur E. MacClenny, "The Evolution of Elon College," *Sun*, October 12, 1939, 5; and Kernodle, *Lives*, 229. Both of these sources agree that Holt's school was located in the present 200 block of North Main Street. Records show that the property of the institute, which later became Graham College, was situated in the 300 block of present South Maple Street.

23. NC&Va. 1853 session.

24. Kernodle, *Lives*, 227; Stokes and Scott, *Christian Church*, 117; *Sun*, November 30, 1855.

25. EVa. 1857 session, 117.

26. *Sun*, May 15, 1858.

27. ACRD, Deed Book 4, 164. The deed includes the details of incorporation.

28. Kernodle, *Lives*, 330; *Sun*, July 9, 1858.

29. *Sun*, January 21, 1859.

30. ACRD, Deed Book 4, 164. Because Harden had sold the church the lot on which to build the institute in 1850, this larger tract must have been adjacent to the first tract rather than the one described in the deed as the land "whereon Graham Institute now stands."

31. EVa. 1859 session.

32. *Minutes of the Thirty-Sixth Annual Session of the North Carolina and Virginia Conference, Held at Hank's Chapel, Chatham County, N.C., October 10th, 11th, and 12th, 1861* (Suffolk, Va.: printed at the Christian Sun Office, 1862), 6; Kernodle, *Lives*, 330–331.

33. ACRD, Deed Book 4, 165.

34. ACRD, Deed Book 4, 528.

35. *Sun*, October 19, 1922; data from tombstones in Linwood Cemetery, Graham.

36. *Sun*, November 23, 1922. Of the Long family, William and Daniel became clergymen-educators; George, a physician; Jacob, a lawyer; Benjamin F., a judge; Joseph enlisted in the Confederate army and was killed at Chancellorsville; John moved to Missouri where he was a prosperous farmer and became the father-in-law of John U. Newman, who joined the Elon College faculty; and Elizabeth married J. N. H. Clendenin and assisted her brothers in the operation of their school in Graham.

37. *Minutes of the Thirty-Fifth Annual Session of the North Carolina and Virginia Christian Conference, Held at Pleasant Hill, Chatham County, N.C.* (Suffolk, Va., Southern Christian Book Concern, 1860), 15.

38. W. W. Staley, "A Modest Recognition of a Worthy Man," *Sun*, November 23, 1922; ACRD, Book of Marriage Records I. The earliest county marriages are listed on typed sheets in the back of the book. In copying from the original handwritten record, the name was erroneously read and transcribed as "William A. Long" instead of "William S. Long."

39. *Minutes of the Forty-Second Annual Session of the North Carolina and Virginia Conference, Held at Union Chapel, Alamance Co., N.C., Nov. 5th, 6th, 7th, 8th, and 9th, 1867* (Suffolk, Va.: Christian Board of Publication, 1868), 15.

40. "Dr. Long's Career as Teacher Spans Three Score Years," *Raleigh News and Observer*, October 22, 1922, reprinted in *Sun*, November 23, 1922.

41. *The Christian Annual*, 1870, NC&Va. session, 24–25. Beginning in 1870, the minutes of the member conferences and of the General, or Southern, Christian Convention (hereafter cited as SCC), if it met that year, were published in the Christian Sun office and bound in a volume known as *The Christian Annual*, hereafter cited as *Annual*.

42. *Annual*, 1870, NC&Va. session, 24.

43. Ibid.

44. *Annual*, 1870, EVa. session, 7.

45. ACRD, Deed Book 6, 213.

46. *Annual*, 1873, NC&Va. session, 68.

47. *The Alamance Gleaner* (Graham, N.C.), April 23, 1878.

48. *Annual*, 1873, NC&Va. session, 42. See also Milo T. Morrill, *A History of the Christian Denomination in America* (Dayton, Ohio: Christian Publishing Association, 1912), 287–289; and David F. Jones, February 8, 1929, to Mrs. H. Turrentine Stokes (Mrs. William T. Stokes, Jr.), in the possession of the author.

49. *Gleaner*, August 13, 1878.

50. *Laws and Resolutions of the State of North Carolina Passed by the General Assembly at its Session of 1881* (Raleigh, 1881), 776.

51. *Gleaner*, May 30, 1881.

52. Ibid.

53. Typescript of an interview by William T. Scott of Mrs. Lawrence, 1964, CHR.

54. *Gleaner*, May 30, 1881; *Annual*, 1884, 62, 69; Stockard, *Alamance*, 87.

55. Stokes and Scott, *Christian Church*, 121.

56. *Annual*, 1895, SCC, 1894, 19.

II. PLANTING THE SEED

1. *Annual*, 1883, General Convention, 1882, 28.

2. Ibid., 29.

3. *Annual*, 1887, General Convention, 1886, 18.

4. Daniel A. Long, *Sketch of the Legal History of Antioch College* (Dayton, Ohio: Christian Publishing Association, 1890), 17–18.

5. *Annual*, 1887, General Convention, 1886, 23–25.

6. *Annual*, 1889, General Convention, 1888, 17; *Gleaner*, July 7, 1887.

7. *Annual*, 1889, General Convention, 1888, 17.

8. *Annual*, 1888, NC&Va. Conference, 1887, 47; *Annual*, 1888, EVa. Conference, 1887, 41.

9. *Annual*, 1889, General Convention, 1888, 17.

10. Ibid., 20.

11. Ibid., 20.

12. Ibid., 22.

13. Ibid., 22–23.

14. Ibid., 22.

15. *Sun*, September 27, 1888.

16. *Sun*, January 17, 1889.

17. *Sun*, July 5, 1888. According to recorded deeds, the owner of the land at Mill Point usually spelled his name "Trolinger," but occasionally as "Trollinger." The latter spelling is most often used today. In 1871 the North Carolina Railroad had been leased to the Richmond and Danville Railroad. Later, the line was acquired by a new corporation and became the Southern Railway.

18. *Gleaner*, November 1, 1888; *Sun*, November 11, 1888.

19. *Gleaner*, January 10, 1889.

20. Ibid.

21. *Gleaner*, January 3, 10, 1889; *Sun*, January 11, 1889.

22. *Sun*, September 16, 1889.

23. *Gleaner*, January 24, 1889.

24. *Gleaner*, July 28, 1892.

25. Mary L. and T. H. Mackintosh, *Town of Elon College: A Brief History* (Elon College, N.C.: Town Bicentennial Commission, 1976), pages unnumbered. The spelling of "Boon" gradually became "Boone."

26. Records of Appointments of Postmasters, 1832–September 30, 1971, North Carolina, Vol. 49, 1877–89, 4, on file in the National Archives, Washington, D.C.

27. *Sun*, January 24, 1889.

28. *Sun*, January 3, 1889.

29. Will S. Long, "The College Is Founded," *Sun*, October 5, 1939.

30. *Sun*, January 3, 1889.

31. *Sun*, January 24, 1889.

32. *Private Laws of North Carolina, Session of 1889* (Raleigh, 1889), Chapter 216.

33. ACRD, Book of Deeds 13, 547–560.

34. Mackintosh, *Town of Elon College*.

35. *Sun*, April 11, 1889.

36. Minutes of the Town Board of Elon College, Book C, 77, Book E, 51, on file in the town hall.

37. *Sun*, September 16, 1889.

38. ACRD, Book of Deeds 13, 585–586, 602; ACRD, Book of Deeds 14, 530.

39. Mackintosh, *Town of Elon College*; Long, "College Is Founded."

40. Mackintosh, *Town of Elon College*; Records of Postmasters, Vol. 69, 1889–1930, 3–4, 5–6; *Private Laws of North Carolina*, 1893, 486.

41. Long, "College Is Founded."

42. *Sun*, September 16, 1889.

43. *Sun*, May 26, 1889.

44. *Bulletin of Elon College, Twenty-Third Annual Announcement for 1912–1913 and Catalogue of 1911–1912*, 14. The *Bulletins* were published quarterly each year, one issue being the Catalogue Number, hereafter cited, respectively, as *Bulletin* and *Catalogue*. The library maintains a file of all surviving issues of these publications, as well as all other college publications subsequently cited, plus the various alumni publications that were published by the Alumni Association. See also MacClenny, "Evolution of Elon College."

45. *Catalogue*, 1911–1912, 16; *Sun*, May 16, 1889.

46. Long, "College Is Founded."

47. *Sun*, July 18, 1889; *Gleaner*, May 25, 1889.

48. *Sun*, May 18, 1889.

49. Ibid.

50. Long, "College Is Founded."

51. *Sun*, July 14, 1910.

52. S. M. Smith, "Elon College Fifty Years Ago," *Sun*, July 24, 1941, 5. Two articles bearing similar titles were also published in the *Sun*: December 11, 1941, 13–14, and April 30, 1942, 13. All three are hereafter cited as Smith, "Fifty Years."

53. N. G. Newman, "Elon College in 1890," *The Maroon and Gold*, January 27, 1923, 14. This publication was for many years the official newspaper of the college.

54. Smith, "Fifty Years"; *Sun*, July 24, 1941, 5.

55. Long, "College Is Founded."

56. *Alumni Directory*, 1931, 7, 8, 10; Elon College, N.C., Registration Book, 1890–1902, on file in the library; Hoyle S. Bruton, "Elon College Means Much to Education," *Burlington (N.C.) Daily Times-News*, May 9, 1949; *Catalogue*, 1911–1912, 78; *Catalogue*, 1901–1902, 43; *Elon Alumni News*, April 1943.

57. Long, "College Is Founded"; *Catalogue*, 1901–1902, front page.

58. *Catalogue*, 1911–1912, 14; *Annual*, 1891, General Convention, 1890, 31; *Sun*, September 4, 1890.

59. *Annual*, 1891, General Convention, 1890, 30; *Sun*, January 8, 1891, 2.

III. THE SEEDLING

1. *Catalogue*, 1890–1891, 17. See also Registration Book, 1890–1902. Elmer Newman and Maud Klapp were only nine years of age when they registered.

2. *Catalogue*, 1890–1891, 18; Registration Book, 1890–1902. C. C. Williams was forty-three years of age when he registered.

3. *Catalogue*, 1890–1891, 25.

4. *Catalogue*, 1890–1891, 1891–1892, 1892–1893, unnumbered front pages. See also Proceedings of the Faculty of Elon College, N.C., Book I, 63–64, hereafter cited as Proceedings. Inserted between these pages is a printed revised list of the faculty for 1892–1893, evidently published after the catalog was issued. This list indicates that Durham and Miss Cushman were replaced by Scholz and Miss Price prior to the opening of the fall term. The Proceedings of the Faculty through Book VI are on file in the library;

subsequent proceedings are on file in the president's office. See also *Gleaner*, June 26, 1890, which names the original faculty.

5. Proceedings, Book I, 69; *Catalogue*, 1901–1902, 44.

6. *Gleaner*, June 4, 1891.

7. Proceedings, Book I, 78.

8. *Sun*, June 11, 1891, 217.

9. Ibid.

10. *Catalogue*, 1901–1902, 44.

11. *Sun*, June 11, 1891, 217; *Catalogue*, 1890–1891, 16.

12. *Catalogue*, 1901–1902, 44. See also *Bulletin of Elon College, Alumni Directory*, 1931, 93. For additional data on the Reverend C. J. Jones, see Stokes and Scott, *Christian Church*, 230.

13. *Sun*, June 9, 1892, 1.

14. *Catalogue*, 1899–1900, 43.

15. *Catalogue*, 1899–1900, 43.

16. Proceedings, Book I, 3, 12, 23, 39, 48.

17. Proceedings, Book I, 33, Book II, 41, 45.

18. Proceedings, Book I, 8, 12, 14, 23, 53, 79. The faculty did not possess the authority to confer degrees, but could recommend recipients for earned and honorary degrees to the trustees, who were usually but not always guided in their actions by the faculty requests. In 1894 the board was requested to confer the degree of Doctor of Divinity upon O. J. Waite, of Fall River, Massachusetts, but no record has been found to indicate the action ever took place.

19. Proceedings, Book II, 44.

20. *Catalogue*, 1890–1891, 15–16.

21. Proceedings, Book I, 6, 8–10, 47, 55, 58, 59, 77, and 139.

22. Proceedings, Book IV, 20.

23. *Catalogue*, 1890–1891, 13; *Annual*, 1895, SCC, 10.

24. Proceedings, Book II, 30.

25. *Gleaner*, May 18, 1893.

26. Smith, "Fifty Years," *Sun*, December 11, 1941.

27. *The Elon College Monthly*, October 1892, 20–21, June 1891, 26–27, hereafter cited as *Monthly*.

28. *Monthly*, April 1893, 24–25, June 1893, 32–33, March 1894, 19.

29. Proceedings, Book I, 8.

30. *Monthly*, June 1891, 1–2.

31. *Monthly*, June 1891, November 1892, June 1893, October 1894, April 1895, front covers.

32. *Monthly*, March 1894.

33. *Monthly*, April 1895, November 1892, covers.

34. *Catalogue*, 1890–1891, 12.

35. *Monthly*, December 1891, 53–54.

36. Proceedings, Book I, 89; S. M. Smith, "The Elon of Early Days," *The Elon Alumni Voice*, Vol. I (May 1928), No. 2, 30–31.

37. Smith, "Early Days," 31.

38. *Catalogue*, 1890–1891, 14–15.

39. *Monthly*, June 1891, 22.

40. Emmett L. Moffitt, "The Original Faculty of Elon College," *Sun*, September 21, 1939, 4–5.

41. *Annual*, 1891, General Convention, 1890, 31.

42. ACRD, Deeds of Trust Book 12, 149, 205, 281; Book 13, 187, 201, 204.

43. Newman, "Elon in 1890."

44. *Monthly*, May (April), 1893, 23.

45. *Sun*, February 25, 1892, 104; March 10, 1892, 129; April 1, 1892, 219.

46. *Sun*, June 29, 1893, 377.

47. *Sun*, July 10, 1893, 5.

48. *Sun*, December 22, 1892, 727.

49. *Gleaner*, December 14, 1893.

50. *Gleaner*, January 29, 1891.

51. *Annual*, 1895, General Convention, 1894, 10.

52. *Sun*, January 10, 1894.

53. *Elon College Alumni News*, May 1967, 5.

54. *Gleaner*, August 3, 1924.

IV. THE SAPLING

1. Levi Branson, *Branson's North Carolina Business Directory* (Raleigh: 1892); *Monthly*, June 1891, December 1892, March, October, December 1894, April, December 1895; *Gleaner*, September 15, 1892.

2. *Sun*, July 2, 1891, 4.

3. Proceedings, Book I, 100; Book II, 36, 65.

4. *Sun*, January 12 (1), February 2 (2), 1899. The distance requested by the petitioners could have been no less because the charter of the college prohibited the manufacture and sale of alcoholic beverages within one and a half miles of the institution.

5. *Sun*, February 2 (2), 9 (2), 16 (2), 1899.

6. After her husband died, Mrs. Staley married Archibald M. Cook. The children by the first marriage were William W., Letitia, and Lydia Staley; by the second, Duncan, George, Netta, Robert N., and John M. Cook. The last named graduated from Elon College in 1896, then married Irene Johnson, a faculty member.

7. *Sun*, October 13, 1932, 6; *Gleaner*, November 23, 1882.

8. *Sun*, October 13, 1932, 6.

9. *Annual*, 1903, SCC, 1902, 19.

10. *Sun*, June 14, 1894, 2, October 13, 1932, 6.

11. Proceedings, Book II, 18; Book III, pages unnumbered.

12. ACRD, Deeds of Trust Book 19, 153. See also Deeds of Trust Books 12 (149, 205, 281) and 13 (187, 201, 204).

13. *Annual*, 1897, SCC, 1896, 13–14.

14. *Annual*, 1899, SCC, 1898, 15.

15. Ibid.

16. Ibid.; *Sun*, April 26, 1916, 13.

17. *Annual*, 1901, SCC, 1900, 20.

18. Proceedings, Book II, 119.

19. *Annual*, 1901, SCC, 1900, 19–20.

20. Ibid., 20.

21. *Annual*, 1887, General Convention, 1886, 25; 1891, General Convention, 1890, 35; *Sun*, May 29, 1890, 2.

22. *Gleaner*, June 25, 1896.

23. *Gleaner*, January 30, 1902; *Annual*, 1903, SCC, 1902, 16, 35.

24. *Gleaner*, November 13, 1902; *Sun*, June 11, 1902, 1.

25. *Annual*, 1903, SCC, 1902, 22.

26. *Annual*, 1907, SCC, 1904, 14.

27. *Gleaner*, April 14, 1904; ACRD, Deeds of Trust Book 24, 208. The loan of 1895 was renewed by the execution of a new deed of trust in 1898, and it was this instrument that was satisfied by Staley's payment.

28. *Annual*, 1903, SCC, 1902, 22; *Annual*, 1907, SCC, 1904, 14.

29. *Annual*, 1903, SCC, 1902, 18–23. The amount of the deficit was erroneously printed as $8,413.54.

30. *Annual*, 1903, SCC, 1902, 23.

31. *Annual*, 1907, SCC, 1904, 13.

32. Proceedings, Book III, May 19, 1902, unnumbered page.

33. Proceedings, Book III, May 21, 1905, unnumbered page.

34. Proceedings, Book III, May 29, 1905, unnumbered page.

35. *Gleaner*, June 8, 1905.

36. *Alumni Directory*, 1931, 11, 13, 14.

37. *Sun*, June 14, 1905, 4; October 13, 1832, 6; October 16, 1941, 6.

38. Proceedings, Book II, 56, 109; *Catalogue*, 1897–1898, 21–22; *Alumni Directory*, 1931, 29.

39. *Sun*, June 10, 1903, 4; *Gleaner*, August 27, 1896.

40. *Catalogue*, 1897–1898, 64.

41. *Sun*, July 4, 1895, 3; *Catalogue*, 1897–1898, 14.

42. *Catalogue*, 1897–1898, 64.

43. Ibid., 12; Proceedings, Book II, 60, 109; *Phipsicli*, 1913, unnumbered front page; *Catalogue*, 1901–1902, 44; Proceedings, Book III, May 29, 1903.

44. Proceedings, Book II, 126; Book III, October 19, 1904.

45. *Monthly*, December 1894, 39.

46. *Monthly*, October 1894, 20.

47. *Catalogue*, 1897–1898, 13; Proceedings, Book II, 110; *Elon College All Sports Record Book*, compiled by James M. Waggoner in 1965 and updated in 1972 and 1978 by Waggoner with the publication assistance of Melvin L. Shreves and Gary F. Spitler (Elon College, N.C.: Elon College Sports Information Office, 1978), D-37. Waggoner, who originated this record, has also supplied to the author data not included in the book but which was based on the notes he made during twenty-five years of research on Elon athletics. These notes contain an account of the first baseball game by a participant.

48. Proceedings, Book II, 126.

49. Proceedings, Book III, March 12, 1903; *Sports Record Book*, D-37.

50. Proceedings, Book III, March 16, 23, 1903, March 21, 1904, February 5, 1905.

51. Proceedings, Book IV, 104.

52. Proceedings, Book II, 140.

53. Proceedings, Book III, November 11, 1904; Newman, "Elon in 1890."

54. Proceedings, Book II, 137.

55. *Sun*, June 11, 1902, 4; *Annual*, 1903, SCC, 1902, 23; *Annual*, 1907, SCC, 1904, 14.

56. Proceedings, Book I, 100, Book III, April 22, 1901, March 28, 1904.

57. *Sun*, June 11, 1902, 4, June 3, 1903, 4, June 8, 1904, 4, June 7, 1905, 5.

58. *Gleaner*, June 28, 1894. Bandy's name is erroneously spelled "Dandy" in the article.

59. Proceedings, Book II, 18; Stokes and Scott, *Christian Church*, 127, n57.

60. *Sun*, June 7, 1905, 4.

61. *Catalogue*, 1897–1898, unnumbered front page.

62. *Catalogue*, 1901–1902, unnumbered front page.

63. *Alumni Directory*, 1931, 7; *Catalogue*, 1902–1903, unnumbered front page.

64. *Catalogue*, 1900–1901, 1901–1902, front page in each.

65. *Gleaner*, August 18, 1904; Proceedings, Book III, September 19, 1904; *Sun*, August 31, 1904, 2. Presumably the college charter that was draped in mourning was a framed copy, hanging in a conspicuous place in the Main Building.

66. *Sun*, March 25, 1903, 4; Proceedings, Book III, September 2, 1903, June 2, 1904. Lincoln had charge of the Academic, or Preparatory, Department,

during his senior year and therefore was a faculty member prior to his graduation, in June 1904.

67. Proceedings, Book II, 69, 95.

V. THE GROWING TRUNK

1. *Album of Christian Ministers, Churches, Lay Workers, and Colleges* (LeGrand, Iowa: n.p., 1915), 85.
2. ACRD, Deeds of Trust Book 33, 177.
3. Proceedings, Book IV, 71.
4. ACRD, Deeds of Trust Book 35, 479.
5. *Sun*, June 13, 1906, 4.
6. *Bulletin*, August 1907. Running, or stretcher, bond was a type of brick work more in vogue in 1905 than at the present. No header bricks were visible from the outside, though the outer wall was built against a rough brick inner wall. When the lathes and plaster were applied to the interior, the walls of West were approximately sixteen inches thick. See also *The Burlington* (N.C.) *Daily Times-News*, January 17, 1942.
7. *Bulletin*, August 1907.
8. Alonzo L. Hook, now dean emeritus, has been associated with the institution ever since he entered its freshman class in 1909. During an extended series of interviews, he has provided to the author many historical facts about the college, including the playing of basketball on the court in West Dormitory. His reminiscences have also been taped by the college and are on file in the library. The interviews and reminiscences are hereafter cited collectively as Hook, Interviews.
9. *Bulletin*, August 1907; *Annual*, 1909, SCC, 1908, 21; *The Elon College Weekly*, January 4, 1911, hereafter cited as *Weekly*; *Sun*, January 9, 1907, 4–5.
10. *Bulletin*, August 1907; Interview series, William B. Terrell (Elon '25), who worked at and resided in the Power House when he was a student. His reminiscences have been taped by the college and are on file in the library. The interviews and reminiscences are hereafter cited collectively as Terrell, Interviews.
11. *The State Dispatch* (Burlington, N.C.), August 3, 31, 1910; *Sun*, August 11, 1909, 4, July 6, 1910, 4; *Annual*, 1911, SCC, 1910, 19.
12. *Weekly*, October 4, 1910.
13. *Weekly*, November 9, 1910.
14. *Annual*, 1907, SCC, 1904, 13.
15. *Annual*, 1909, SCC, 1908, 23; *Annual*, 1913, SCC, 1912, 18.
16. Interviews, Mrs. E. B. Huffine and Mrs. Floyd Whittemore, 1978;

Newman, "Elon in 1890"; *Annual*, 1909, SCC, 1908, 21; *Catalogue*, 1912–1913, 29; Proceedings, Book VI, 192.

17. *Sun*, October 4 (4), November 1 (4), 1905.

18. Proceedings, Book IV, 19, 22–23, 32; *Sun*, June 14, 1911, 3; *Alumni Directory*, 1931, 16.

19. Proceedings, Book IV, 78, 145; *Sun*, June 10, 1908, 8, June 9, 1909, 5; Proceedings, Book VI, 68. Because of the loss of many early Elon records by fire, this list may not be complete.

20. *Sun*, October 4, 1905, 2.

21. Proceedings, Book IV, 190–192.

22. Ibid., 192, letter from Harper to the literary societies inserted in the minutes.

23. *Gleaner*, October 17, 1907.

24. Proceedings, Book IV, 67. The issue of January 1908 (Vol. I, No. 3) is the only extant copy of the periodical.

25. *Sun*, February 2, 1910, 5, February 9, 1910, 4.

26. *Gleaner*, October 17, 1910; *Sun*, February 2, 1910, 5; *Weekly*, February 15, 1910.

27. *Dispatch*, February 16, 1910.

28. *Weekly*, May 23, 1911; *Maroon and Gold*, March 30, 1962, 2–4. The *Maroon and Gold* later succeeded the *Weekly*.

29. *Gleaner*, May 21, 1908; Proceedings, Book IV, 68–69, 77, September 9, 1907, 185; *Sun*, June 9, 1909, 1, May 31, 1910, 4; *Weekly*, May 31, 1910. R. M. Morrow, Jr., was born in 1894 and died 2 years later. The donor's daughter, Deloris (Mrs. John H. Barnwell), graduated from Elon in 1922 and then served for several years on its faculty as an instructor in domestic science. See also *Sun*, March 19, 1927, 2. When Dr. Morrow died, he bequeathed the college $10,000 in his will.

30. *Sun*, June 16 (4), 23 (4), 1927. See also *Sun*, October 25, 1934, 9, for an account of Wellons' participation in the Civil War and his attendance at the execution of Nat Turner. See also Terrell, Interviews.

31. *Sun*, June 13, 1906, 4.

32. Proceedings, Book IV, 160.

33. *Weekly*, March 8, September 13, 1911. Before 1911, nothing is known of the history of the Ministerial Association, composed of ministerial students or those who planned to follow that profession.

34. Proceedings, Book IV, 97–103.

35. Proceedings, Book V, 106, 108, 120–123.

36. Ibid., 109–113.

37. *Weekly*, February 15, 1911.

38. Proceedings, Book V, 51, 95, 165, 171; *Sun*, June 10, 1908, 8, June 9, 1909, 5, June 14, 1911, 7; *Weekly*, May 31, 1910.

39. *Sun*, June 9, 1909, 5.

40. *Sun*, June 8, 1910, 4.

41. Proceedings, Book IV, 78–80.

42. Ibid., 129–130, 154.

43. Ibid., 163–164.

44. *Sun*, July 31, 1908, 5; Hook, Interviews; *Weekly*, February 1, 1911. This site was between the present residence of Mrs. George Colclough and the Elon Middle School, on Haggard Avenue. The tennis court built by President Moffitt beside his residence, which later became the property of Charles D. Johnston, was never owned by the college, though the students were allowed to use it. The proximity of this practice facility may partially account for several of Johnston's sons becoming Elon varsity tennis players. The court was on the site of the present United States post office.

45. Proceedings, Book V, 30.

46. Ibid., 26–27; *Sports Record Book*, D-37. At the time, there were two divisions of Bingham Academy, one at Mebane and one at Asheville. The institution was eventually consolidated into the latter division.

47. Proceedings, Book V, 83, 85.

48. Ibid., 142.

49. Ibid., 130; *Weekly*, March 8, 1910.

50. *Weekly*, March 8, 1910.

51. Proceedings, Book V, 147, 151.

52. Hy Turkin and S. C. Thompson, *The Official Encyclopedia of Baseball*, 2d rev. ed. (New York: A. S. Barnes and Company, 1959), 183.

53. *Weekly*, March 1, 1911.

54. Ibid.; Proceedings, Book VI, 47; Turkin and Thompson, *Encyclopedia of Baseball*, 184.

55. *Sports Record Book*, D-37.

56. Proceedings, Book V, 124–125.

57. *Sports Record Book*, A-41.

58. Proceedings, Book V, 127. The date of this meeting was incorrectly entered by the secretary of the faculty as October 5 instead of November 5.

59. Proceedings, Book V, 128.

60. Ibid., 129; *Sports Record Book*, A-41.

61. Proceedings, Book V, 130; *Sports Record Book*, A-41.

62. *Weekly*, March 8, 1911.

63. *Weekly*, March 22, 1911.

64. *Gleaner*, December 3, 1908; *Weekly*, October 4, 26, 1910, March 8, 27, May 3, 1911.

65. *Sun*, September 28, 1910, 9; *Weekly*, October 4, 1910; Proceedings, Book V, 84. In 1909 Sipe Fleming, a freshman, umpired a women's game and was reprimanded by the faculty for doing so.

66. *Weekly*, May 24, 1911.

67. *Weekly*, April 19, 1911.

68. *Weekly*, April 5, 19, May 31, 1911.

69. *Weekly*, May 31, 1911.

70. *Weekly*, February 2, 1900.

71. *Gleaner*, January 31, 1907; Staley Wicker to Mrs. T. H. Mackintosh, January 21, 1976, in the possession of Mrs. Mackintosh, who resides in the town of Elon College.

72. *Gleaner*, December 19, 1907; *The Elonian*, Vol. I (January 1908), No. 3, 126.

73. *Gleaner*, June 18, 1908; Interview, Mrs. T. H. Mackintosh (nee Mary Graham Lawrence), 1978. Her reminiscences have also been taped by the college, and are on file in the library. The interview and reminiscences are hereafter cited collectively as Mackintosh, Interviews.

74. *Gleaner*, January 5, 1905; *Annual*, 1907, SCC, 1904, 44; *Annual*, 1909, SCC, 1908, 6–9; Stokes and Scott, *Christian Church*, 212–214.

75. *Gleaner*, January 21, 1909.

76. *Monthly*, June 1893, 29.

77. *Monthly*, April 1893, 21; *Sun*, October 31, 1895, 2; *Annual*, 1936, SCC, 69.

78. *Weekly*, April 26, June 28, 1911.

79. *Sun*, December 22, 1909, 9; *Dispatch*, January 5, 1910; *Weekly*, February 15, 1910, January 11, 1911.

80. *Weekly*, January 11, 1911.

81. *Sun*, June 28, 1911, 6. Data supplied by the Grand Lodge of the Ancient Free and Accepted Masons of North Carolina.

82. Office of the Alamance County Clerk of the Court, Book of Wills 4, 92–97; *Sun*, June 28, 1911, January 18, 1923; *Gleaner*, August 22, 1907.

83. *Annual*, 1909, SCC, 1908, 22.

84. *Sun*, June 9, 1909, 1.

85. *Sun*, June 8, 1910, 5.

86. Proceedings, Book III, June 2, 1905, Book IV, 80, 180, Book V, 54.

87. *Sun*, June 9, 1909, 1.

88. *Weekly*, February 15, 1910.

89. J. W. Barney, "How Elon Looked to a Student Fifty Years Ago," *Elon College Alumni Magazine*, 1956, 10.

90. *Annual*, 1913, SCC, 1912, 17.

91. *Gleaner*, June 21, 1906.

92. *Sun*, June 14, 1911, 2.

93. *Alumni Directory*, 1931, 42, 1948, 24, 31.

94. *Gleaner*, April 3, 1941.

VI. THE SPREADING BRANCHES

1. *Sun*, June 1, 1899, 2; Proceedings, Book II, 113.

2. *Sun*, August 17, 1899, 2, November 21, 1899, 3, January 11, 1900, 2, May 13, 1903, 4; *Weekly*, September 23, 1899.

3. *Sun*, June 10, 1903, 4.

4. *Annual*, 1913, SCC, 1912, 17.

5. Ibid.

6. *Gleaner*, February 1, 1912.

7. *Weekly*, September 20, 1911.

8. *Weekly*, August 23, 1912; *Catalogue*, 1911–1912, 36.

9. *Weekly*, June 14, 1912. Kemp B. Johnson, of Fuquay Springs, N.C., served as a trustee and was a booster of the college.

10. *Weekly*, August 23, 1912.

11. Secretary's Records of the Board of Trustees of Elon College, North Carolina, Book I, 32, on file in the library, hereafter cited as Secretary's Records. The pages are not consecutively numbered in all parts of Book I. See also *Gleaner*, September 12, 1912.

12. *Annual*, 1915, SCC, 1914, 14; *Weekly*, August 23, 1912.

13. *Gleaner*, September 19, 1912; Secretary's Records, Book I, 31.

14. *Alumni Directory*, 1931, 12.

15. *Bulletin*, August 1913, 45; *Annual*, 1915, SCC, 1914, 14.

16. *Weekly*, August 23, September 20, 1912; Carl Brown Riddle, ed., *College Men Without Money* (New York: Thomas Y. Crowell Company, 1914), 167.

17. *Weekly*, August 23, 1912.

18. *Bulletin*, August 1913, 45; *Annual*, 1915, SCC, 1914, 10; Secretary's Records, Book I, December 13, 1913, 4.

19. *Bulletin*, January 1914, 46.

20. *Gleaner*, September 19, 1912, January 20, 1913; *Bulletin*, August 1914, 43.

21. *Bulletin*, August 1913, 46.

22. *Bulletin*, August 1914, 42; *Bulletin*, August 1913, 47.

23. *Bulletin*, August 1915, 56.

24. Secretary's Records, Book I, 34–35. When reference was made to the "gym," the term Alumni Building was used, but the residents called it North Dormitory.

25. *Annual*, 1915, SCC, 1914, 11.

26. Ibid., 14.

27. *Bulletin*, August 1914, 43.

28. *Bulletin*, August 1913, 47.

29. Secretary's Records, Book I, 15, 22.

30. Elon College Town Minutes, Book B, 8, on file in the town hall.

31. *Bulletin*, August 1913, 47; *Sun*, June 3, 1914, 6.

32. *Catalogue*, 1913–1914, 101; *Catalogue*, 1914–1915, 111; *Bulletin*, August 1914, 43.

33. *Bulletin*, January 1914, 7.

34. *Catalogue*, 1910–1911, 80.

35. *Bulletin*, January 1914, 30–31; *Annual*, 1913, SCC, 1912, 17; *Catalogue*, 1915–1916, 161.

36. Proceedings, Book VI, 101; *Catalogue*, 1915–1916, 161; *Bulletin*, August 1914, 37.

37. *Bulletin*, August 1914, 37; Secretary's Records, Book I, May 24, 1915, 16.

38. *Bulletin*, August 1914, 40, June 1919, 25; Secretary's Records, Book I, May 25, 1920, 5.

39. *Bulletin*, August 1914, 42.

40. *Bulletin*, April 1915, 15.

41. Secretary's Records, Book I, May 24, 1915, 7.

42. *Annual*, 1917, SCC, 1916, 17.

43. Secretary's Records, Book I, 34, June 1, 1914, 18; Proceedings, Book VI, 152.

44. *Catalogue*, 1914–1915, 44–51; *Sun*, November 17, 1909, 4, December 7, 1910, 11.

45. Proceedings, Book VI, 221, 245, Book VII, 111.

46. Proceedings, Book VI, 221, 223–224.

47. *Annual*, 1915, SCC, 1914, 13.

48. *Annual*, 1919, SCC, 1918, 12.

49. *Bulletin*, August 1915, 26.

50. Ibid., 27.

51. *Sun*, July 13, 1922, 6.

52. Proceedings, Book VI, 253.

53. *Catalogue*, 1914–1915, 134.

54. *Bulletin*, August 1914, 44.

55. Proceedings, Book VI, 247.

56. *Weekly*, October 26, 1910.

57. Ibid.

58. *Catalogue*, 1914–1915, 40.

59. *Weekly*, October 4, November 22, 1912.

60. *Sun*, January 28, 1914, 3.

61. Proceedings, Book IV, 192, Book VI, 199.

62. *Gleaner*, May 8, 1913.

63. *Gleaner*, August 11, 1898.

64. *Weekly*, October 4, 18, 1912, January 10, 1913; *Sun*, May 22, 1912, 2; *Gleaner*, October 4, 1912.

65. *Bulletin*, August 1913, 47.

66. *Sun*, April 21, 1915, 3; Don Metcalf, "'Modern Progress' Review Shows County in 1915," Burlington (N.C.) *Daily Times-News*, May 9, 1949.

67. *Sun*, March 31, 1915, 3.

68. *Weekly*, January 10, 1913; *Sun*, November 5, 1913, 3; *Maroon and Gold*, April 19, 1956.

69. *Weekly*, October 4, 1912; *Sun*, October 3, 1961, 2, October 10, 1961, 1, 4.

70. *Catalogue*, 1912–1913, 83.

71. *Sun*, October 3, 1961, 2.

72. *Catalogue*, 1911–1912, 65.

73. Proceedings, Book VI, 131.

74. Ibid., 47.

75. Ibid., 152.

76. Proceedings, Book VII, 98; Secretary's Records, Book I, 9, April 23, 1913.

77. *Sun*, September 6, 1894, 2; Proceedings, Book IV, 143, Book V, 114, 134; *Bulletin*, May 1911, unnumbered pages.

78. *Catalogue*, 1912–1913, 22.

79. *Gleaner*, March 22, 1900; *Bulletin*, August 1914, 43.

80. *Weekly*, November 15, 1912; *Times-News*, October 17, 1973.

81. *Weekly*, November 29, 1912.

82. *Weekly*, November 29, 1912.

83. Hook, Interviews.

84. *Catalogue*, 1913–1914, 58.

85. *Catalogue*, 1910–1911, 12.

86. Proceedings, Book VII, 129.

87. Proceedings, Book VI, 200–201; Hook, Interviews.

88. Proceedings, Book VI, 90–95; *Alumni Directory*, 1931, 24, 39, 88, 90. For President Harper's condemnation of hazing, see *Bulletin*, August 1913, 20–21.

89. Proceedings, Book VII, 5.

90. *Catalogue*, 1915–1916, 23–24; *Gleaner*, October 16, 1913.

91. Proceedings, Book VII, 131–132, 147.

92. Ibid., 6.

93. Proceedings, Book VI, 71; Book VII, 134.

94. *Sports Record Book*, D-1; *Bulletin*, August 1914, 39; *Times-News*, April 26, 1973; Records of the Elon College Athletic Association.

95. Proceedings, Book VII, 50.

96. *Catalogue*, 1915–1916, 59.

97. *Catalogue*, 1915–1916, 12.

98. *Catalogue*, 1915–1916, 59–60.

99. *Gleaner*, October 31, 1912.

100. *Sun*, October 22, 1913, 15.

101. *Gleaner*, May 8, 1913.

102. *Sun*, May 22, 1912, 15; December 11, 1912, 3.

103. *Gleaner*, May 8, 1913; Hook, Interviews; *Alumni Directory*, 1931, 89; Elon Town Minutes, B 30; *Sun*, March 5, 1957, 5, February 10, 1959, 8, February 24, 1959, 3.

104. *Private Laws of North Carolina*, 1909, Chapter 139, 348; Secretary's Records, Book I, January 21, 1913, 8.

105. Charter of Elon College, on file in the library.

106. *Bulletin*, August 1913, 44.

107. Secretary's Records, Book I, May 24, 1915, 7.

108. *Annual*, 1915, SCC, 1914, 15.

109. ACRD, Deeds of Trust Book 70, 394, Book 35, 479.

VII. THE STALWART TREE

1. *Phipsicli*, 1920, unnumbered front page; *Catalogue*, 1917–1918, 194, 200.

2. *Annual*, 1919, SCC, 1918, 11.

3. Proceedings, Book VII, 155.

4. *Annual*, 1919, SCC, 1918, 11; *Alumni Directory*, 1931, 15, 20–21, 24, 29, 31.

5. *Annual*, 1919, SCC, 1918, 11.

6. *Phipsicli*, 1920, unnumbered front page; *Bulletin*, November 1921, 46; Secretary's Records, Book I, May 20, 1919, 21.

7. *Phipsicli*, 1920, unnumbered front page.

8. Secretary's Records, Book I, May 27, 1918, 17.

9. *Bulletin*, December 1918, 38–39.

10. *Bulletin*, June 1918, 5.

11. Ibid., 38–39.

12. Ibid., 39.

13. Ibid., 40.

14. Ibid., 4.

15. Secretary's Records, Book I, May 27, 1918, 21.

16. Hook, Interviews.

17. *Bulletin*, December 1918, 5–6.

18. Ibid., 5, 18–23, 41.

19. Ibid., 6–7.

20. *Bulletin*, June 1919, 22–23.

21. Worth Bacon, "World War I Days at Elon College," *Maroon and Gold*, March 25, 1953.

22. Interview, Mrs. L. D. Martin, 1978.

23. *Sun*, October 16, 1918, 5, October 23, 1918, 15; Martin, Interview; Correspondence by author with Earle E. Sechriest (Elon '20), brother of Clarence A. Sechriest, and with Roby E. Taylor, November 1979, on file in the Elon College library.

24. *Bulletin*, December 1918, 6; Martin, Interview.

25. Bacon, "World War I."

26. Ibid.

27. *Bulletin*, December 1918, 5.

28. Ibid., 40.

29. Mackintosh, Interviews.

30. *Bulletin*, December 1918, 12–15.

31. Ibid., 16.

32. Ibid., 17.

33. Secretary's Records, Book I, May 20, 1919, 2.

34. Ibid.; *Bulletin*, December 1918, 41.

35. *Sun*, December 25, 1918, 3.

36. *Catalogue*, 1919–1920, 26.

37. Ibid., 29.

38. Ibid., 30.

39. *Catalogue*, 1920–1921, 23.

40. Ibid.

41. *Catalogue*, 1920–1921, 24–26.

42. *Phipsicli*, 1920, unnumbered pages; *Alumni Directory*, 1931, 36; *Gleaner*, December 11, 1913. Toshio Sato was a graduate of the Girl's School of the Christian Church, in Otsunomiya, Japan. She was educated at Elon by the financial generosity of J. Beale Johnson and the Reverend J. Lee Johnson, of Cardenas, North Carolina. After graduating, she returned to Japan as a teacher.

43. *Sun*, June 8, 1921, 7.

44. Proceedings, Book VII, letter inserted between pages 188 and 189.

45. Interview, R. S. Rainey, 1925, while the author was one of his students at Burlington High School.

46. Proceedings, Book VII, 188–189.

47. Secretary's Records, Book I, June 1912, 38.

48. Proceedings, Book VII, letter inserted between pages 192 and 193.

49. Proceedings, Book VII, 192–193.

50. Secretary's Records, Book I, May 20, 1919, 19.

51. A. L. Hook, ed., *The Red Book*, 1926–1927, 34–35, 39. Dr. Hook pos-

sesses several issues of *The Red Book,* the first issue of which was published in 1922 and the last in 1932.

52. *Catalogue,* 1918–1919, 42–43, 1923–1924, 41.

53. *Phipsicli,* 1920, 136, 151; Proceedings, Book VII, 194.

54. *Catalogue,* 1920–1921, 66–67.

55. *Catalogue,* 1921–1922, 66, 1923–1924, 34; Proceedings, Book VII, 90.

56. Proceedings, Book VII, 202–205.

57. *Catalogue,* 1922–1923, 42.

58. Ibid., 43.

59. *Sun,* June 20, 1917, 3; *Catalogue,* 1923–1924, 46; Hook, Interviews.

60. Proceedings, Book VII, 179.

61. *Catalogue,* 1923–1924, 46; *Maroon and Gold,* March 18, 1939, May 2, 1951.

62. *Catalogue,* 1923–1924, 35; Hook, Interviews.

63. Proceedings, Book VII, 180.

64. Hook, Interviews; *Maroon and Gold,* October 21, 1921.

65. *Gleaner,* January 6, 1921.

66. Proceedings, Book VII, 203.

67. *Bulletin,* 1915, frontispiece; *Maroon and Gold,* September 30, 1921.

68. *The Red Book,* 1926–1927, 46; Interview, Markwood Z. Rhodes, 1925, while the author was one of his students at Burlington High School.

69. *Bulletin,* June 1919, 25.

70. *Catalogue,* 1920–1921, 34.

71. Hook, Interviews; *Bulletin,* August 1913. The latter, between pages 16 and 17, contains a photograph that includes "Uncle" Pinkie Comer.

72. *Times-News,* April 26, 1973; Theodore E. Perkins, "The History of the Elon College Library" (M.A. diss., University of North Carolina, 1962).

73. *Sports Record Book,* A-41.

74. *Sports Record Book,* A-41; *Maroon and Gold,* November 11, 1921, October 27, November 10, 17, 1922; *Times-News,* October 14, 1972, September 11, 1974; Records of the Elon College Athletic Association, on file in the library.

75. *Maroon and Gold,* November 17, 1922.

76. *Maroon and Gold,* November 11, 1921, October 27, November 10, 17, 1922.

77. *Times-News,* October 14, 1972.

78. *Gleaner,* July 7, 1921.

79. *Gleaner,* January 24, 1918.

80. *Greensboro Daily News,* April 23, 1920.

81. Elon College Town Records, Book B, 69, 77, 83, 137.

82. *Gleaner,* June 30, 1921.

83. *Annual*, 1921, SCC, 1920, 39.

84. *Gleaner*, January 6, 20, 1921.

85. Secretary's Records, Book I, May 25, 1920, 7–9, 17, 20.

86. *Gleaner*, June 9, 1921.

87. Proceedings, Book VII, 202, 213.

88. Secretary's Records, Book I, May 29, 1922, 7; *Annual*, 1913, SCC, 1912, 18; Secretary's Records, Book I, 1912, 39, 1913, 7, 1915, 9, 1916, 4, 1917, 19, 1919, 4, 1921, 8, 1922, 6. See also Milo T. Morrill, *A History of the Christian Denomination in America* (Dayton, Ohio: Christian Publishing Association, 1912), 356–357. The trust had been established "for the advancement and support of home missions and educational institutions; to assist evangelical churches, missions, schools and associations; to assist Christian ministers and workers; to help needy persons desiring to become Christian ministers, teachers or workers to acquire a suitable training and education, and to establish in colleges and schools Bible teachers and lectures; and to acquire, to hold, and to dispose of such personal and real property as the said purposes of the corporation shall require."

89. *Annual*, 1921, SCC, 1920, 39.

90. Ibid., 40.

91. *Catalogue*, 1923–1924, 50; *Sun*, May 15, 1924, 4; *Alumni Directory*, 1931, 15; Elon College Registration Book I, 68, 72, on file in the library. Many years after this gift, Mrs. Parrott, then a widow, married J. Adolphus Long (Elon '05), who was then a widower, and the couple lived in Graham.

92. *Catalogue*, 1923–1924, 50–51.

93. *Catalogue*, 1923–1924, 51; *Annual*, 1913, SCC, 1912, 18; Secretary's Records, Book I, 1912, 39, 1913, 7, 1915, 9, 1916, 4, 1917, 19, 1919, 4, 1921, 8, 1922, 6; *Catalogue*, 1921–1922 through 1932–1933. The college records, which are incomplete because of the 1923 fire, show that from 1908 to 1922 the Francis Asbury Palmer Fund had given Elon College $27,500 in periodic payments, in addition to financing practically all the expenses of the annual lectures of Professors Child and Summerbell.

94. *Sun*, June 13, 1912, 7, June 11, 1913, 5, June 10, 1914, 2, May 26, 1915, 2, May 28, 1919, 4, June 1, 1921, 9, May 31, 1922, 10; Secretary's Records, Book I, 29.

95. *Sun*, November 2, 1922.

96. *Sun*, November 16, 1922.

97. The student from Japan was not Toshio Sato (Elon '20) but Chiyo Ito (Elon '25), also a graduate of the Girl's School of the Christian Church in Japan. She was the second Japanese to graduate from Elon College, after which she returned to her native land as a teacher.

VIII. THE TREE AND THE TEMPEST

1. Melvin Shreves, "Bill Terrell Sounded Alarm," *Times-News*, January 17, 1974; Terrell, Interviews.

2. Mackintosh, Interviews; Shreves, "Alarm."

3. Shreves, "Alarm"; Interview, R. S. Rainey, 1923, while the author was one of his students at Burlington High School. See also *Phipsicli*, 1923, 200, for cartoons of Rainey fighting the fire and other humorous incidents connected with the excitement.

4. *Gleaner*, January 18, 1923; *Sun*, July 5, 1923, 8–10.

5. *Maroon and Gold*, January 20, 1923.

6. Hook, Interviews; *Maroon and Gold*, January 20, 1923.

7. *Sun*, February 1, 1923, 6.

8. *Maroon and Gold*, March 16, 1923. See also *Burlington Daily News*, January 19, 1923.

9. Proceedings, Book VII, 232–233.

10. *Maroon and Gold*, January 20, 1923; Mackintosh, Interviews.

11. Proceedings, Book VII, 233.

12. Ibid.

13. Reprinted in *Sun*, February 1, 1923, 6.

14. Reprinted in *Sun*, February 1, 1923, 6–7.

15. Reprinted in *Sun*, February 1, 1923, 7.

16. *Burlington Daily News*, February 5, 1923.

17. *Sun*, February 1, 1923, 3.

18. Ibid.

19. Ibid.

20. Ibid.

21. *Gleaner*, February 1, 1923; *Sun*, February 1, 1923, 6.

22. *Sun*, February 1, 1923, 6.

23. *Gleaner*, June 26, 1923; *Sun*, July 5, 1923, 1; *Burlington* (N.C.) *Journal*, March 14, 1923; *Phipsicli*, 1923, frontispiece.

24. *Sun*, February 1, 1923, 6; Secretary's Records, Book I, May 23, 1916, 4.

25. *Annual*, 1924, SCC, 28.

26. *Sun*, February 14, 1929, 6; *Sun*, July 5, 1923, 1.

27. *Sun*, October 14, 1926, 8–9.

28. *Gleaner*, May 29, June 5, 1924.

29. *Sun*, June 7, 1923, 4.

30. Ibid.

31. Ibid.

32. Hook, Interviews; *Maroon and Gold*, February 2, 1923; *Sun*, May 7, 1925, 6.

33. *Sun*, February 14, 1929, 6; Hook, Interviews.

34. *Annual*, 1924, SCC, 28.

35. Ibid.

36. *Annual*, 1924, SCC, 29.

37. ACRD, Deeds of Trust Book 70, 394; 94, 309–320; 97, 315–321, 336–341; Secretary's Records, Book I, May 24, 1926, 34, August 17, 1926, 5–10.

38. *Annual*, 1924, SCC, 29. Bethlehem later became Southern Union College. Dr. J. E. Danieley, of Elon, served on its board of trustees. See Stokes and Scott, *Christian Church*, 251–252.

39. *Annual*, 1926, SCC, 14.

40. Ibid.

41. *Annual*, 1928, SCC, 42.

42. Ibid., 42–43.

43. Ibid., 42.

44. Ibid., 43.

45. *Sun*, October 14, 1926, 8–9.

46. *Sun*, February 14, 1929, 7.

47. *Sun*, May 5, 1927, 6.

48. *Phipsicli*, 1928, unnumbered front page.

49. *Sun*, April 20, 1925, 3.

50. Quoted in Perkins, "Elon Library," 47.

51. Perkins, "Elon Library," 48; Proceedings, Book VIII, 99.

52. *Maroon and Gold*, January 26, 1920; *Catalogue*, 1916–1917, 45.

53. *Catalogue*, 1922–1923, 47.

54. *Maroon and Gold*, September 23, 1921.

55. *Maroon and Gold*, September 29, 1922.

56. *Gleaner*, February 23, 1923.

57. *Sun*, September 10, 1924, 6.

58. *Maroon and Gold*, September 10, 1924; *Sun*, September 10, 1924, 6.

59. *Times-News*, September 30, 1958; *Elon College Alumni News*, April 1974, 4.

60. *Alumni Directory*, 1931, 59; *Maroon and Gold*, December 9, 1925.

61. The term "Chautauqua" originated at summer schools conducted at Chautauqua, New York, and came into popular usage at this time to represent a series of meetings that combined educational and recreational features.

62. *Maroon and Gold*, September 8, 1922; Stokes and Scott, *Christian Church*, 250–251.

63. *Annual*, 1926, SCC, 32; *Gleaner*, October 17, 1929.

64. The urn was later found, but because it had been damaged during its removal from the monument, it was replaced by the metal cross.

65. *Annual*, 1928, SCC, 43.

66. *The Elon Alumni Voice*, Vol. I (February 1928), No. 1, 14.

67. *Alumni Voice*, February 1928, 5–15, 41, May 1928, 19–24, August 1928, 33–38.

68. Hook, Interviews.

69. *Sports Record Book*, A-42, B-18, D-42.

70. *Times-News*, October 14, 1972; *Alumni Directory*, 1931, 68.

71. *Alumni Voice*, August 1928, 33–37.

72. Ibid., 38.

73. *Sports Record Book*, A-29, 35; D-3, 36; B-11.

74. *Gleaner*, June 28, July 19, 1923; *Burlington Journal*, November 21, 1923.

75. *Gleaner*, January 19, February 16, April 19, May 3, June 21, 1928; *Times-News*, January 13, 1928.

76. *Alumni Voice*, February 1930. The complete list of Harper's books up to this date included *The Making of Men* (Antioch Press), *The New Layman for the New Time* (Revell), *The New Church for the New Time* (Revell), *Reconstructing the Church* (Revell), *The Church in the Present Crisis* (Revell), *An Integrated Program of Religious Education* (Macmillan), *Youth and Truth* (Century), and *Character Building in Colleges* (Abingdon Press). See also *Maroon and Gold*, September 23, 1921.

77. *Gleaner*, September 8, 1932; *Sun*, June 24, 1926, 6–7.

78. *Catalogue*, 1931, 43–44.

79. Secretary's Records, Book I, May 28, 1923, 9, May 26, 1924, 37, May 24, 1927, 1, May 29, 1928, 3; *Sun*, June 3, 1926, 8.

80. *Sun*, June 3, 1926, 8, May 30, 1929, 2, June 12, 1930, 6; Secretary's Records, Book I, May 29, 1928, 3.

81. *Sun*, November 2, 1922, 8.

82. *Sun*, November 3, 1927, 11, June 25, 1931, 3, September 10, 1933, 3.

83. Secretary's Records, Book I, February 19, 1929, 1–4; *Catalogue*, 1934–1935, 16.

84. *Annual*, 1931, SCC, 8.

85. *Annual*, 1928, SCC, 43; *Annual*, 1930, 41.

86. *Annual*, 1930, SCC, 42.

87. Ibid. The college charter was amended to add twelve additional trustees so that the Congregational Churches could be represented.

88. Secretary's Records, Book I, May 26, 1931, 7.

89. *Maroon and Gold*, April 16, 1931.

90. Secretary's Records, Book I, May 26, 1931, 7.

91. *Sun*, May 28, 1931, 6.

92. *Alumni News*, August 1959, 3; *Gleaner*, May 14, 1942; *Times-News*, April 12, 1942. Harper was buried beside his son at the Stony Creek Pres-

byterian Church Cemetery, in the section of Alamance County where Mrs. Harper's family lived.

IX. THE SURVIVAL OF THE TREE

1. Proceedings, Book VIII, 101.

2. *Sun*, October 8, 1931, 1.

3. *Maroon and Gold*, November 28, 1930; *Catalogue*, 1930–1931, un-numbered front page. After eight years with Burlington Mills, West again served Elon College as business manager for several years.

4. *Annual*, 1931, SCC, 3–9.

5. Ibid., 10–11.

6. *Annual*, 1932, SCC, 24.

7. *Times-News*, October 21, 1931; *Gleaner*, November 26, 1931; *Sun*, October 21, 1931, 4.

8. *Times-News*, November 6, 1931; Secretary's Records, Book I, November 13, 1931, 3; Hook, Interviews.

9. Secretary's Records, Book I, November 13, 1931, 2–3; Smith to Shuping, February 13, 1933, Shuping Folder, Smith Files, in the Elon College library.

10. Based on the personal recollections of the author.

11. Secretary's Records, Book I, December 30, 1931, insert, William Moseley Brown to Trustees.

12. Executive Board of Trustees Folder, Smith Files.

13. *Gleaner*, September 3, December 17, 1931.

14. Shuping to Smith, November 11, 1933, Smith to Shuping, November 13, November 21, 1933, Shuping Folder and L. G. Bryngelsson Folder, Smith Files.

15. O. W. Johnson Folder, Smith Files.

16. Smith-Granville T. Prior correspondence, Miscellaneous Folder P, Smith Files.

17. W. D. Hooper to Smith, December 9, 1931, February 18, 1932, April 9, 1932, Southern Association Folder, Smith Files.

18. Proceedings, Book VIII, 121–122.

19. Executive Board of Trustees Folder, Smith Files; Secretary's Records, Book I, February 21, 1933, 11.

20. Hook, Interviews.

21. Hook, Interviews; Secretary's Records, Book I, September 17, 1932, 1–11.

22. Smith to W. D. Hooper, February 19, 1932, Southern Association Folder, Smith Files.

23. Secretary's Records, Book I, February 23, 1932, 2.

24. *Annual*, 1932, SCC, 35.

25. Ibid., 25–26.

26. Secretary's Records, Book I, May 1932, 18.

27. Proceedings, Book VIII, 112.

28. W. A. Harper Folder, Smith Files.

29. J. M. Darden Folder, Smith Files.

30. Proceedings, Book VIII, 20, 133; Secretary's Records, Book I, May 25, 1932, 10; *Catalogue*, 1932–1933, 111.

31. *Maroon and Gold*, January 26, 1923.

32. Secretary's Records, Book I, May 25, 1932, 10.

33. Mary G. L. Mackintosh (Mrs. T. H.), *Historical Sketch, Elon Community Church, 1891–1966* (Elon College, N.C.: Community Church, n.d.), unnumbered pages.

34. *Annual*, 1932, SCC, 24.

35. *Sun*, June 4, 1957, 12, reprinted from an article by Moses Crutchfield (Elon '41) in the *Greensboro Daily News*.

36. *Sports Record Book*, A-43, B-19-21, D-43-44.

37. Interview, W. E. Butler, Jr., business manager of Elon College, 1978. The coach was authorized to recruit players who could attend the college by paying them $100 provided they made and played on the institution's teams. At a later date, the same conditions were extended to a talented female drum majorette to assist in leading the band. See also *Sports Record Book*, A-43-44.

38. Interview, William H. Maness, 1977.

39. *Times-News*, October 14, 1972.

40. *Sports Record Book*, A-24, B-11, 13-14, D-30.

41. Ibid., A-44-45, B-21-22, D-44-45; Hook, Interviews; *Alumni News*, March 1942.

42. *Sports Record Book*, A-29-30, 33, 35, B-11, 13.

43. *Maroon and Gold*, January 14, 1939, January 13, 1954; Interview, J. Earl Danieley, 1978; Maness, Interview.

44. *Maroon and Gold*, January 13, 1954.

45. Hook, Interviews; Maness, Interview.

46. *Phipsicli*, 1931, 90.

47. Elon Singers Folder, Smith Files; *Maroon and Gold*, December 11, 1957.

48. Proceedings, Book VII, 209; Radio Addresses Folder, Smith Files.

49. Smith to W. C. Wicker, September 30, 1933, Southern Association Folder, Smith Files.

50. The records of the Secretary of State, Raleigh, N.C., contain the original charter.

51. Stanley C. Harrell to J. Allen Hunter, J. Allen Hunter Folder, Smith Files; *Alumni Directory*, 1931, 67; *Catalogue*, 1931–1932, front pages; *Maroon and Gold*, September 20, 1929.

52. Southern Association Folder, Smith Files.

53. *The Magazine of Elon*, Spring 1978, 1.

54. *Maroon and Gold*, April 8, 1953; Maness, Interview.

55. Secretary's Records, Book I, February 19, 1936, 19–22.

56. Proceedings, Book VIII, 209; *Catalogue*, 1934–1935, 16.

57. Proceedings, Book VIII, 216; College Audits, 1939, 18. Smith purchased the moving-picture machine for $331.84 with his own funds. In 1939 he was repaid from the profits.

58. Proceedings, Book VIII, 232.

59. Maness, Interview; Proceedings, Book VIII, 233.

60. Maness, Interview.

61. Maness, Interview.

62. Proceedings, Book VIII, 72; James Waggoner, "Of Plays and Playmaking at Elon," *Maroon and Gold*, November 10, 22, 1954; *Alumni News*, October 1946.

63. *Elon Colonnades*, Vol. I (May 1937), No. 1, 25.

64. *Elon College Alumni Directory*, 1948, 101; Secretary's Records, Book I, May 30, 1934, 3, May 29, 1935, 8; *Elon Alumni News*, January 1965, 20.

65. *Alumni Directory*, 1948, 101; Secretary's Records, Book I, May 31, 1938, 2, February 13, 1940, 1, May 29, 1941, 3, February 10, 1942, 1, May 18, 1943, 3.

66. Secretary's Records, Book I, May 1, 1934, 2.

67. Floyd Hurst Folder, Smith Files; Virginia Trust Company Folder, Smith Files.

68. Secretary's Records, Book I, April 15, 1935. A number of Smith's contemporaries who are still living heard the president relate many of his personal experiences and passed them on to the author. They are hereafter cited as Smith, Reminiscences.

69. Secretary's Records, Book I, April 15, 1935.

70. Proceedings, Book VIII, 186.

71. Shuping Folder, Smith Files.

72. Williams Company Folder, Smith Files; Secretary's Records, Book I, February 18, 1936.

73. *Annual*, 1936, SCC, 12.

74. Ibid., 13.

75. Piedmont College Folder, Smith Files; Stokes and Scott, *Christian Church*, 252.

76. *Annual*, 1940, SCC, 18–19; *Sun*, September 21, 1939, 7. During the previous decade, December 20 had been listed on the college calendars as

Founders Day, but no commemoration had been held in honor of the event.

77. *Annual*, 1942, SCC, 18.

78. *Dr. Leon Edgar Smith* (Elon College, N.C.: Elon College, 1957), unnumbered pages.

79. Secretary's Records, Book I, February 9, 1943. The letter was made a part of the minutes of the meeting of the trustees.

X. THE PRUNED TREE

1. *Times-News*, January 17, 1942; *Sun*, January 22, 1942, 2.

2. Interview, Mrs. June Murphy Looney, 1979; *Maroon and Gold*, October 16, 1951.

3. *Maroon and Gold*, October 16, 1951.

4. Secretary's Records, Book I, May 18, 1942; College Audits, 1942, 25. The annual audits are filed in the college Business Office.

5. Looney, Interview.

6. Interview, J. Earl Danieley, 1979; College Audits, 1952, 10. Insurance paid $31,455.63 for this fire loss.

7. *Maroon and Gold*, October 16, 1951.

8. For application and correspondence between Smith and Hinckley, see Civilian Pilot Training Folder, Smith Files; Hook, Interviews; *Sun*, August 2, 1945, 7; and *Alumni News*, February 1955. Both C. A. Hughes and his brother, Leroy, won high military honors as aviators in World War II, and the former became a pilot for Piedmont Air Lines after the conflict ended.

9. *Catalogue*, 1939–1940, 84; Proceedings, Book VIII, 253, 261; Interview, Forrest C. Hall (Elon '46), 1979. Hall was one of the students.

10. *Sun*, April 24, 1962, 7; Hook, Interviews; *Alumni News*, November 1941, October 1946.

11. *Alumni News*, October 1946.

12. Smith to Senator Robert R. Reynolds, November 14, 1942, in Senator Robert R. Reynolds Folder, Smith Files.

13. Ibid.; Proceedings, Book VIII, 301.

14. *Times-News*, March 4, April 22, 1943; Army Air Forces Folder, Smith Files.

15. *Times-News*, March 10, 1943; Hook, Interviews.

16. *Times-News*, March 4, 1943.

17. *Times-News*, September 23, 1943.

18. Report of the President to the Board of Trustees, May 24, 1943, 3. Copies of Smith's periodic reports from 1932 through 1957, not always included in their entirety in the Secretary's Records, are bound in five folders in the Smith Files. These periodic reports, as well as those of subsequent presi-

dents, are hereafter cited as P. R. Both the Secretary's Records and the Smith Files are in the Elon College library. See also *Times-News*, September 23, 1942.

19. *Times-News*, September 23, 1942.

20. Smith to unnamed correspondent, July 15, 1943, Army Air Forces Folder, Smith Files; Hook, Interviews.

21. *Alumni News*, October 1943; *Maroon and Gold*, February 13, 1943.

22. Major Howard E. Cox to Smith, June 23, 1943, Army Air Forces Folder, Smith Files; P. R., February 13, 1945, 9–10.

23. Hook, Interviews; *Alumni Directory*, 1979, 188.

24. Proceedings, Book VIII, 310.

25. *Alumni News*, October 1946; College Audits, 1943, 18, 1944, 21–22, 1945, 8, 18; P. R., May 24, 1943, 2.

26. *Maroon and Gold*, January 10, 1942.

27. *Maroon and Gold*, March 7, 1942.

28. *Maroon and Gold*, March 28, 1942.

29. *Maroon and Gold*, October 31, 1942.

30. Secretary's Records, Book II, May 18, 1942.

31. *Alumni News*, March 1942.

32. Ibid.

33. Proceedings, Book VIII, 301.

34. *Alumni News*, October 1943.

35. P. R., May 22, 1944, 5.

36. P. R., May 27, 1946, 2.

37. *Alumni News*, January 1943.

38. Sigma Phi Beta News Letter, June 14, 1943. Dr. D. J. Bowden sent this letter quarterly to members of the fraternity in service. The extant copies of the newsletter and the voluminous correspondence of Bowden with the soldiers are in the Elon College archives and are hereafter cited as Bowden Papers.

39. *Maroon and Gold*, October 28, 1944; Smith to Phillips, October 14, 1944, Miscellaneous P Folder, 1944, Smith Files. See also Proceedings, Book VIII, 316.

40. Bowden Papers; *Maroon and Gold*, October 4, 1947.

41. *Maroon and Gold*, Memorial Issue, undated. This issue contains photographs and biographical sketches of the casualties. See also *Maroon and Gold*, January 16, 1943.

42. *Annual*, 1944, SCC, 1944, 22.

43. *Annual*, 1938, SCC, 23.

44. *Annual*, 1944, SCC, 1944, 22–23.

45. Secretary's Records, Book II, February 11, 1947, insert in back of book.

46. P. R., May 27, 1946, 1.

47. Secretary's Records, Book II, February 12, 1946.

48. Secretary's Records, Book II, February 11, 1947.

49. *Catalogue*, 1946–1947, 17.

50. Interview, W. E. Butler, Jr., Elon College business manager, 1979.

51. P. R., May 29, 1946, February 14, 1950.

52. College Audits, 1947, 5, 1948, 6, 1949, 5.

53. Secretary's Records, Book II, February 10, 1942.

54. *Alumni News*, April, May, 1943; *Maroon and Gold*, April 20, 1935.

55. *Catalogue*, 1942–1943, 27.

56. Secretary's Records, Book II, February 12, 1946, insert at back of book.

57. *Catalogue Supplement*, 1943, 18; College Audits, 1947, 16, 1948, 14. Tuition from the aeronautics course amounted to $1,804.11 in 1947 and $643.09 in 1948. The course was not listed in the *Catalogue* after the latter year. See also *Maroon and Gold*, March 8, 1941.

58. Secretary's Records, Book II, May 18, 1942, February 12, 1946, insert at back of book.

59. Bowden Papers; Sigma Phi Beta News Letter, June 14, 1943, May 20, 1946.

60. P. R., February 10, 1948, 7.

61. Secretary's Records, Book II, Report to Trustees of Dean A. L. Hook for Spring Quarter, 1946, insert at back of book.

62. Secretary's Records, Book III, February 17, 1953. The period from 10:00 to 10:20 A.M. on Monday was for student activities chapel, and religious chapel was held on Wednesday and Friday.

63. P. R., May 25, 1953, 9, January 18, 1955.

64. P. R., May 31, 1938, 5, February 14, 1939, 4.

65. ACRD, Book of Deeds 128, 501; 130, 338–339.

66. Secretary's Records, Book I, May 28, 1940, 12.

67. P. R., February 12, 1946, 11; ACRD, Book of Deeds 134, 202.

68. ACRD, Book of Deeds 133, 317–318; Secretary's Records, Book I, May 27, 1941, 6.

69. P. R., February 11, 1941, 4.

70. P. R., May 27, 1941, 8.

71. P. R., February 11, 1941, 4.

72. P. R., February 10, 1942.

73. Interview, Zebulon H. Lynch, 1979.

74. P. R., February 8, 1944, 10, May 22, 1944, 9–10.

75. P. R., February 13, 1945, 8, May 28, 1945, 8.

76. Secretary's Records, Book II, February 11, 1947.

77. College Audits, 1952, 6.

78. P. R., January 19, 1954, 8–9.

79. P. R., May 18, 1942, 6; Smith-Monroe correspondence, Miscellaneous P Folder, 1942, Smith Files.

80. P. R., February 12, 1946, 8, May 27, 1946, 5; *Times-News*, May 24, 1951; Interviews, Professors Voigt F. Morgan and Paul S. Reddish, 1979.

81. The lake was drained so that the land could be used for a planned housing development, which never materialized for various reasons.

82. Secretary's Records, Book II, February 10, 1942.

83. P. R., May 28, 1940, 7, May 24, 1943, 9, February 8, 1944, 12–13; Danieley, Interview.

84. Secretary's Records, Book II, February 11, 1947, 6.

85. P. R., May 30, 1955, January 17, 1956.

86. *Catalogue*, 1945–1946, 24.

87. Interview, the Reverend W. Millard Stevens, a former director of the foundation, 1979.

88. *Sun*, September 11, 1941, September 23, 1944; *Alumni News*, September 1940, September 1941.

89. Mackintosh, *Community Church*.

90. Secretary's Records, Book II, February 9, 1943, May 22, 1944, February 13, May 28, 1945.

91. *Alumni News*, October 1943, 4; Telephone interview, Crutchfield, 1979; *Magazine of Elon*, November 1976, 2.

92. Crutchfield, Telephone interview.

93. Danieley, Interview; *Alumni News*, May 1951, 3.

XI. THE NEW GROWTH

1. *Sports Record Book*, football, baseball, and basketball sections.

2. Secretary's Records, Book II, May 24, 1948; P. R., February 8, 1949, 3; *Alumni News*, January 1950, 3.

3. P. R., February 13, 1945, 10.

4. P. R., February 13, 1951, 8.

5. *Alumni News*, January 1950, 3; P. R., February 10, 1948, 9, February 8, 1949, 7.

6. P. R., May 29, 1950, 5.

7. *Alumni News*, January 1950, 2; *Sports Record Book*, M-24.

8. *Alumni News*, January 1950, 2.

9. Ibid.

10. *Alumni News*, November 1950, 2.

11. *Sports Record Book*, B-24.

12. *Alumni News*, May 1951, 1.

13. P. R., February 26, 1957.

14. P. R., February 13, 1943, 13; January 19, 1954.

15. *Alumni News*, January 1943; *Sun*, July 2, 1940; *Gleaner*, September 7, 1939, October 4, 1945, June 6, 1946.

16. *Catalogue*, 1945–1946, 26–27.

17. Proceedings, Book VIII, 276.

18. P. R., February 8, 1944, 5.

19. P. R., May 22, 1944, 3, February 19, 1945, 2.

20. P. R., February 19, 1945, 2.

21. *Maroon and Gold*, September 28, 1949; Secretary's Records, Book IV, October 4, 1949.

22. P. R., February 10, 1948.

23. *Times-News*, December 14, 1946; *Alumni News*, January 1947, 1; Secretary's Records, Book V, March 21, 1949.

24. Proceedings, Book V, May 10, 1949.

25. Proceedings, Book V, October 4, November 4, 1948, September 3, 1954.

26. *The Student Handbook*, 1953–1954, 8–9. This handbook was published annually and given to all freshmen.

27. *Handbook*, 1953–1954, 9–22.

28. Ibid., 22–25.

29. *Handbook*, 1958–1959, 28; Proceedings, Book V, May 2, 1949.

30. Proceedings, Book VI, April 8, 1957.

31. Proceedings, Book V, November 21, 1948.

32. *Times-News*, April 24, 1951, April 21, 1952. Because of publication of *up ego!* (New York: Payton, Paul Publishing Co., 1951), West was nominated for honorary membership in the International Mark Twain Society. He served on the Elon faculty from 1949 to 1958.

33. Proceedings, October 6, 1956.

34. Proceedings, March 16, 1946.

35. Proceedings, December 1, 1956.

36. P. R., October 1, 1951, 1–2; January 15, 1952, 7.

37. P. R., February 13, 1951, 7.

38. P. R., May 28, 1951, 2.

39. *Alumni Directory*, 1948, 101; Secretary's Records, Book II, May 24, 1948, February 8, 1949, Book III, February 14, 1950, January 15, 1952, February 17, 1953; *Maroon and Gold*, May 16, 1951, May 25, 1954, May 24, 1955, May 22, 1957.

40. The T. B. Dawson Memorial Bible Fund was established in memory of the Reverend T. B. Dawson, a retired Christian minister who resided in the town of Elon College, where he died in 1951. His family, which made the

gift to the college, were daughters Laura (Mrs. M. A. Van Billiard), Fannie P. (Mrs. Frank S. Castor), Martha A. (Mrs. Raymond O. McDonald), Jessie (Mrs. A. L. Hook), and a son, Robert D., and their children.

41. *Times-News*, September 1, 1953.

42. P. R., January 19, 1954, 2, May 30, 1955, May 17, 1956.

43. P. R., January 17, 1956.

44. Founders Day Folder, Smith Files; *Sun*, September 15, 1955, 6.

45. *Catalogue*, 1945–1946, 39, 1942–1943, 44; P. R., May 22, 1944, 8, February 12, 1946, 8.

46. P. R., May 29, 1950, 2, May 28, 1951, 7, May 24, 1943, 8, February 12, 1946, 8; *Maroon and Gold*, January 13, 1954.

47. P. R., February 17, 1953, 2.

48. P. R., January 19, 1954, 6, May 30, 1955, 1–3, February 26, 1957, 2.

49. *Times-News*, March 11, 1949.

50. P. R., May 25, 1953, 4.

51. P. R., January 17, 1956.

52. P. R., January 17, 1956, February 26, 1957.

53. P. R., May 27, 1957.

54. *Sun*, April 12, 1956, 7; Secretary's Records, Book IV, July 3, 19, 1956, May 26, 1957, 8–9. The principal loss to the college was the dormitory space because the insurance carriers offered $27,639.00 for the building and $5,620.10 for its contents in settlement of the claim. This total of $33,259.10 was close to the $36,000 that the trustees considered the amount of their loss.

55. P. R., February 26, 1957; *Alumni Directory*, 1948, 37.

56. Secretary's Records, Book III, March 24, 1956; ACRD, Book of Corporation Charters 8, 204.

57. ACRD, Book of Corporation Charters 9, 571.

58. Secretary's Records, Book IV, February 26, 1957, 2.

59. P. R., March 12, 1957.

60. *Annual*, 1934, SCC, 13, 22; *Annual*, 1936, SCC, 32. See also Stokes and Scott, *Christian Church*, 283–285.

61. *Annual*, 1952, SCC, 40–41.

62. Stokes and Scott, *Christian Church*, 184.

63. Secretary's Records, Book IV, February 26, 1957, 2; Records of the Elon College Garden Club; *Catalogue*, 1969–1970, 28.

64. *Catalogue*, 1969–1970, 28.

65. *The Magazine of Elon*, December 1975, 13.

66. Secretary's Records, Book III, May 27, 1957.

XII. THE EXPANDING SHADE

1. *Alumni News*, October 1957, 6, May 1958, 2.

2. *Times-News*, March 21, 1958, reprinted in *Alumni News*, October 1958, 1.

3. *Alumni News*, May 1958, 2.

4. P. R., July 31, 1957.

5. *Sun*, July 16, 1957, back cover.

6. *Catalogue*, 1957–1958.

7. *Alumni News*, October 1958, 8.

8. Proceedings, September 2, 1957.

9. Ibid.

10. *Catalogue*, 1957–1958.

11. P. R., 1961.

12. *Times-News*, December 13, 1960, March 29, 1961. At the age of thirty-nine, Benson became president of the College of the Albemarle, a community college in Elizabeth City, N.C.

13. *Catalogue*, 1960–1961.

14. P. R., July 31, 1957.

15. *Catalogue*, 1958–1959, 51.

16. *Handbook*, 1958–1959, 11.

17. Proceedings, December 14, 1957.

18. *Handbook*, 1958–1959, 10, 1972–1973, 11–12. Professor John S. Graves established a spirit of camaraderie with the freshmen by often wearing a "beanie" himself while on the campus during the period.

19. P. R., September 30, 1957.

20. *Catalogue*, 1959–1960, 53, 1961–1962, 48.

21. *Catalogue*, 1956–1957, 58.

22. *Maroon and Gold*, February 26, 1958.

23. P. R., March 4, 1959.

24. Secretary's Records, October 8, 1958, 1.

25. *Catalogue*, 1960–1961, 1961–1962, 1962–1963.

26. *Magazine of Elon*, Winter 1979, 18–19. Declining health forced Graves to retire in 1977, and he died two years later.

27. Secretary's Records, May 26, 1958, 1.

28. Secretary's Records, October 7, 1959.

29. P. R., 1962, October 14, 1964.

30. *Catalogue*, 1960–1961.

31. *Catalogue*, 1964–1965; Secretary's Records, October 8, 1958, 2; P. R., March 9, 1960.

32. *Maroon and Gold*, December 18, 1958, January 14, 1959; P. R., March 9, 1960.

33. ACRD, Book of Corporations 15, 400. The Vikon Chemical Company provided services as analytical and consulting chemists. Headed by Dr. Luther B. Arnold, Jr., the enterprise began in an office rented from the college in the Duke Science Building. When this was outgrown, the company moved to the old Bank Building. Secretary's Records, February 18, 1958, 2; P. R., October 8, 1958.

34. Secretary's Records, May 26, 1958; *Alumni News*, March 1959; Secretary's Records, October 5, 1960.

35. P. R., March 1961, 4, July 15, 1961.

36. P. R., March 2, 1960. Later, the Home Economics facility was moved to the third floor of the Alamance Building and has remained there.

37. P. R., September 6, 1962; Secretary's Records, October 5, 1960, 1.

38. Secretary's Records, October 5, 1950, 1, 4; *Times-News*, December 13, 1961.

39. Secretary's Records, May 25, 1958, 1, October 5, 1960, 1, 4.

40. *Alumni News*, November 1959, 8, October 1962, 16.

41. Secretary's Records, February 13, 1951, February 1, 1963; P. R., March 6, 1963.

42. P. R., March 9, 1960, October 4, 1961.

43. P. R., March, October 4, 1961. Danieley slipped when he introduced his guest to the Burlington Rotary Club as "Gutz Metz."

44. P. R., August 31, 1957, March 9, 1960, October 10, 1962, December 6, 1963.

45. P. R., July 15, 1961.

46. Program, "Dedication of the College Organ," April 8, 1962, on file in the library.

47. Ibid.; *Alumni News*, May 1962, 2.

48. *Alumni News*, May 1958, 14.

49. *Alumni News*, June 1959.

50. *Catalogue*, 1969–1970, 40.

51. P. R., September 6, 1962.

52. *Maroon and Gold*, May 17, 1968.

53. *Maroon and Gold*, October 2, 1964.

54. 1966 Elon College Liberal Arts Forum Brochure and Program, on file in the library; *Phipsicli*, 1959.

55. 1968 Elon College Liberal Arts Forum Brochure and Program.

56. *Times-News*, March 26, 1960; *Greensboro Daily News*, March 26, 1965; *Alumni News*, September 1964, 12.

57. *Alumni News*, June 1962, 12; Interview, J. Wesley Alexander, 1979.

58. *Alumni News*, September 1964, 16; February 1968, 15.

59. *Alumni News*, September 1964, 16.

60. P. R., October 13, 1965, 2.

61. *Maroon and Gold*, May 4, 1966, 2.

62. P. R., October 13, 1965, 2.

63. *Times-News*, March 1, 1963; *Alumni News*, March 1963, 16.

64. *Catalogue*, 1963–1964, 71.

65. *Maroon and Gold*, May 20, 1957, March 2, 16, 1962; *Sun*, June 3, 1958, 12, June 9, 1959, 10, June 7, 1960, 12, June 13, 1961, 8, December 13, 1963.

66. Secretary's Records, February 18, 1958, 2.

67. Secretary's Records, April 6, 1960, 2.

68. The *Sports Records Book* lists the names of all these players and their achievements, along with many others, and the records of the teams.

69. P. R., 1962.

70. ACRD, Book of Corporations 15, 327; Stokes and Scott, *Christian Church*, 302–307.

71. Proceedings, September 2, 1957.

72. Secretary's Records, October 7, 1959, 3.

73. Records of the Town of Elon College, on file in the town hall.

74. *Maroon and Gold*, December 14, 1961; Danieley, Interview.

75. *Alumni News*, March 1963, 16.

76. *Catalogue*, 1959–1960, 25.

77. Margaret E. Gant, *The Episcopal Church in Burlington, 1879–1979* (n.p., 1979), 27; *Veritas*, January 31, 1969.

78. *Alumni News*, January 1964.

79. Secretary's Records, May 30, 1966, 1. This was the formal conclusion of the financial negotiations because the grant had been authorized and construction actually begun in 1965.

80. P. R., October 12, 1966.

81. Secretary's Records, May 30, 1966, 11.

82. Program, Founders Day, November 5, 1966, on file in the Elon College library.

83. *Alumni News*, January 1967, 1–4, 21, 26.

XIII. THE MATURE TREE

1. Secretary's Records, May 30, 1966, 1.

2. Secretary's Records, February 2, 1963; personal recollections of the author and his wife, who were both members of the history class that deMontaigne attended.

3. Records of the Registrar, Elon College.

4. Marvin Morgan, a black man who was then a student and is today a minister in the United Church of Christ, spoke in approval of the new

books, which he had examined, and was influential in settling the matter amicably.

5. Secretary's Records, October 7, 1959, 3.

6. Hugh T. Lefler and Albert R. Newsome, *North Carolina: The Story of a Southern State*, 3d ed. (Chapel Hill: University of North Carolina Press, 1973), 699–701.

7. *The Campus Crier* (Elon College, N.C.: Student Government Association, 1962–1968), Vol. V, No. 4 (undated), front cover, on file in the library.

8. *Crier*, Vol. I, No. 4.

9. *Crier*, April 15, 1966.

10. *Crier*, Vol. V, No. 4.

11. *Crier*, April 15, 1966.

12. P. R., November 17, 1965, 1.

13. *Crier*, April 15, 1966.

14. P. R., November 17, 1965, 1.

15. Ibid., 2.

16. P. R., March 6, 1966, 4. The sum mentioned in the report to the trustees was $7,588, but, according to Danieley, Interview, this was only the cost of preparing the room before furnishings and equipment were added, which brought the total to a figure in excess of $20,000. Because the gift was made by an individual, the college has no record of the final cost of the room. Despite his preference to remain anonymous, it soon became general knowledge that the donor was Robert Model (Elon '67), of Greenwich, Connecticut.

17. P. R., October 11, 1967. The principal reason the matter was not contested was because of its unusual "success." Friends of the college heard about the lunches and requested permission to patronize the buffet. To refuse them would have been embarrassing, but the purpose of the occasion was for faculty-staff association and not for institutional publicity. Under these circumstances, the sensible thing seemed to be abandoning the idea, which was the decision of the administration.

18. P. R., October 16, 1968, 10, October 14, 1970, 4.

19. *Times-News*, July 5, 1966.

20. Personal recollections of the author, whose office at the time was in South Building.

21. P. R., October 12, 1966, 3.

22. P. R., March 8, 1967, 4; *Maroon and Gold*, November 10, 1967.

23. *Maroon and Gold*, October 4, 1968.

24. *Alumni News*, October 1968, 8–9.

25. Ibid., 9.

26. Ibid.

27. J. E. Danieley to the Long Range Planning Committee, March 22,

1967, Elon College Long Range Planning Committee Folder, J. E. Danieley Files, in the Elon College library, hereafter cited as Planning Committee Folder.

28. Partly based on the personal recollections of the author, who was a member of the committee.

29. Report of the Long Range Planning Committee, 1. Planning Committee Folder, hereafter cited as Planning Report.

30. Planning Report, 1–3, 6.

31. Ibid., 9.

32. Ibid., 2.

33. *Richmond Times-Dispatch*, May 26, 1968.

34. P. R., March 21, 1968, 1–2, October 16, 1968, 1.

35. P. R., July 1, 1972, 2.

36. Secretary's Record, March 6, 1968, 10.

37. P. R., October 16, 1968, 4.

38. Planning Report, 4.

39. *Veritas*, February 15, 1969.

40. *Maroon and Gold*, October 16, 1969.

41. Ibid.

42. *Maroon and Gold*, February 26, 1970.

43. P. R., March 5, 1969, 2–3.

44. Ibid., 3.

45. *Veritas*, October 15, 1968.

46. Ibid.

47. P. R., March 5, 1969, 3.

48. *Veritas*, April 25, 1969.

49. Ibid.

50. *Maroon and Gold*, October 9, 1969.

51. *Veritas*, October 22, 1969.

52. *Maroon and Gold*, October 23, 1969.

53. Ibid.

54. Ibid.

55. *Veritas*, October 22, 1969.

56. Ibid.

57. Secretary's Records, November 7, 1969, 1–2.

58. P. R., October 20, 1971, 4.

59. P. R., April 15, 1970, 4.

60. Ibid., 5.

61. *Maroon and Gold*, December 9, 1969 (special typescript one-page edition).

XIV. THE MAJESTIC TREE

1. Interview, Dr. Robert C. Baxter, Jr., the college's Director of Development, 1967.

2. P. R., October 16, 1968, 11.

3. *Maroon and Gold*, October 11, 18, November 8, 1968.

4. Secretary's Records, October 16, 1968, 3; *Alumni News*, September 1969, 14.

5. Secretary's Records, October 14, 1970.

6. Secretary's Records, November 10, 1970, October 14, 1970.

7. Secretary's Records, March 3, 1971.

8. P. R., July 1, 1972, 2.

9. P. R., October 14, 1970, 2, October 20, 1971, 3.

10. P. R., October 20, 1971, 3.

11. Ibid.

12. P. R., January 16, 1973, 1.

13. Recommendations from the Report of the Visiting Committee to Elon College, September 26–29, 1971; Communication to the Faculty from the Office of the President, May 27, 1971, 2. Both these documents are on file in the Elon College library.

14. Recommendations.

15. Elon College Faculty By-Laws of 1970.

16. Ibid.

17. Ibid.

18. P. R., October 20, 1970, 4.

19. P. R., October 14, 1970, 3, October 20, 1971, 4.

20. P. R., October 29, 1971, 4.

21. "Book Reviews," *The North Carolina Historical Review*, Vol. LII (October 1975), No. 4, 404–405.

22. In 1979 fifty-four students were enrolled in the Brass Clinic under eight instructors.

23. P. R., October 14, 1970, 3.

24. P. R., October 14, 1970, 5.

25. P. R., October 20, 1971, 5, March 8, 1972, 4, January 29, 1973, 1.

26. P. R., March 7, 1973, 2.

27. Secretary's Records, October 15, 1969, 1.

28. Secretary's Records, April 15, 1970.

29. P. R., March 8, 1972, 3.

30. P. R., March 8, 1972, 3.

31. Secretary's Records, December 21, 1966, 1. Some other business was transacted at the meeting in addition to hiring the new coach.

32. *Maroon and Gold*, January 13, 1967. White replaced Dr. Jack Sanford as chairman of the department.

33. *Maroon and Gold*, January 27, 1967.

34. *Sports Record Book*, D-55-62, F-1.

35. Ibid., H-1-2, K-1-2.

36. Ibid., A-35, B-5, D-36.

37. Ibid., I-1, J-1.

38. Ibid., C-3.

39. P. R., March 7, 1973, 2.

40. *Alumni News*, January 1970, 6.

41. Ibid.

42. J. E. Danieley to Professor Luther Byrd, et al., September 25, 1972, Danieley Files.

43. *Times-News*, October 14, 1972.

44. *Times-News*, March 21, 1963, March 11, 1964, March 5, 1969, March 26, 1971.

45. *Bulletin*, April 1973; *Durham* (N.C.) *Herald*, March 28, 1973. Captain Denton's address was printed in pamphlet form and distributed to the public by the college.

46. *Alumni News*, June 1962, 5, June 1964, 3, July 1966, 2, July 1967, 2, May 1968, 24, October 1968, 25, April 1969, 8, September 1969, 8, July 1970, 2, June 1971, front page, June 1972, 2.

47. *Times-News*, March 29, 30, 31, 1973.

48. P. R., October 20, 1971, January 16, March 7, 1973.

49. P. R., October 18, 1972, 2; *Times-News*, October 18, 1972.

50. P. R., March 7, 1973, 1.

XV. THE FRUIT OF THE TREE

1. *Bulletin*, July–August 1973.

2. Fred Young, "Collective Negotiations for North Carolina Teachers?" *Popular Government*, Vol. 34 (March 1968), No. 5, 1–8.

3. *Bulletin*, July–August 1973.

4. Records of the Registrar, Elon College.

5. Dr. Young flew from Richmond to the Greensboro-High Point Airport, where the two faculty members met him and drove him to the meeting in Salisbury, then to the Charlotte Airport for his return to Virginia in the evening. Personal recollections of the author.

6. *Alumni News*, November 1973, 1.

7. *Magazine of Elon*, November 1976, 10.

8. *Magazine of Elon*, April 1974, unnumbered front page.

9. *Magazine of Elon*, December 1974, 7.

10. James A. Moncure, "Student Life Undergoing Changes," *Magazine of Elon*, July 1974, 5.

11. Ibid.

12. Article II, "By-Laws of the Elon College Presidential Board of Advisers," attached to Secretary's Records, October 23, 1974.

13. *Magazine of Elon*, March 1975, 8.

14. *Magazine of Elon*, July 1975, 7, September 1975, 5.

15. Secretary's Records, June 5, 1967; *The Pendulum*, February 18, September 10, 1975; *Magazine of Elon*, September 1975, 1–2.

16. *Pendulum*, March 4, October 9, 1975; *Magazine of Elon*, July 1976, 10.

17. *City-County Newspaper* (Burlington, N.C.), February 18, March 14, 1978; *Catalogue*, 1978, 16–17.

18. *Pendulum*, October 14, 1974.

19. *Magazine of Elon*, December 1974, 6.

20. *Pendulum*, May 8, September 25, 1975; *Magazine of Elon*, March 1975, 8.

21. Interviews, student Barry Simmons and Professor Thomas Keller, of the college's English Department, 1979.

22. *Pendulum*, February 18, 1975.

23. *Alumni News*, November 1973.

24. *Pendulum*, April 7, November 17, 1977.

25. *Pendulum*, October 14, 1974. See also *Magazine of Elon*, April 1974, 2. On March 6, 1974, the new building adjacent to the Alumni Memorial Gymnasium was officially named the B. Everett Jordan Gymnasium.

26. *Pendulum*, December 12, 1974, September 10, 1975.

27. *Pendulum*, September 10, November 20, December 11, 1975.

28. *Pendulum*, September 9, November 4, 1976.

29. Elon College Town Minutes, January 8, 22, 1974.

30. Presidential Report, January 22, 1975; *Magazine of Elon*, December 1974, 2–3, September 1975, 4.

31. *Magazine of Elon*, April 1975, 2–3, September 1975, 2.

32. *Magazine of Elon*, April 1975, 2.

33. *Times-News*, June 29, 1975; Interview, Richard T. Apperson, 1979.

34. *Magazine of Elon*, July 1976, 8.

35. Secretary's Records, June 27, 1974; Periodic Reports, December 1, 1976.

36. Secretary's Records, October 22, 1975.

37. *Magazine of Elon*, November 1976, 2.

38. Copy of the report supplied to the author by McCauley from his files.

39. Secretary's Records, March 6, 1974.

40. Secretary's Records, May 5, 1976.

41. *Pendulum*, September 23, 1976.
42. P. R., April 9, 1976, 2.
43. Elon College Town Minutes, April 13, 1976.
44. *Alamance* (N.C.) *News*, July 21, 1977; *City-County Newspaper*, July 23, 1977.
45. P. R., July 7, 1977.
46. *Pendulum*, September 4, 1977.
47. Ibid.
48. *Pendulum*, September 22, 1977.
49. *Pendulum*, September 15, 1977.
50. Secretary's Records, September 29, 1977; *Pendulum*, September 15, 29, 1977.
51. *Pendulum*, December 7, 1978; *Times-News*, April 6, 1979.
52. Elon College Town Minutes, April 24, May 20, 1975.
53. *Times-News*, December 23, 1975, January 15, 1976, July 11, 1979.
54. *Pendulum*, December 7, 1978.
55. *Pendulum*, November 18, 1976, March 2, 1978; *Magazine of Elon*, February 1977, 7.
56. *Magazine of Elon*, February 1976, 1.
57. *Magazine of Elon*, July 1976, 4.
58. *Times-News*, September 22, 1977.
59. *Magazine of Elon*, April 1977, 8.
60. P. R., April 8, May 11, 1976.
61. Secretary's Records, Executive Committee meeting, August 30, 1976; *Magazine of Elon*, November 1970, 3.
62. *Magazine of Elon*, April 1977, 8.
63. *Magazine of Elon*, April 1977, 8.
64. *Magazine of Elon*, Spring 1978, 8.
65. *Pendulum*, September 7, 1978.
66. *Pendulum*, November 15, 1975; Alumni Office Records.
67. *Magazine of Elon*, Spring 1978, 1.
68. *Magazine of Elon*, Spring 1979, 4.
69. *Magazine of Elon*, April 1977, 10.
70. *City-County Newspaper*, May 12, 1979.
71. *Pendulum*, September 28, 1978.
72. *Magazine of Elon*, December 1975, 6.
73. Ibid.
74. *Magazine of Elon*, July 1977, 4.
75. Ibid.
76. *Pendulum*, September 4, 1977.
77. Ibid.; *Magazine of Elon*, August 1978, 14.
78. *Alamance News*, August 16, 1979.

79. *Pendulum*, September 4, 1978.

80. *Magazine of Elon*, July 1976, 11, February 1977, 9.

81. *Alumni News*, February 1974, 1.

82. Ibid.

83. *Sports Record Book*, A-51.

84. *City-County Newspaper*, July 2, 1977.

85. *City-County Newspaper*, September 22, 1979.

86. *Magazine of Elon*, July 1977, 7.

87. *Magazine of Elon*, April 1977, 11.

88. *Times-News*, December 16, 1978.

89. *Greensboro News*, September 5, 1979; *Times-News*, September 5, 1979.

90. *Magazine of Elon*, November 1973, 1, Fall 1977, 6.

91. *Pendulum*, September 15, 1977.

92. *Pendulum*, September 22, 1977.

93. *Alumni News*, June 1973, 3; *Magazine of Elon*, July 1976, 3, August 1978, 6, Spring 1979, 8, August 1979, 2.

94. *Times-News*, June 3, 1979.

95. ACRD, Book of Corporations 25, 305; Secretary's Records, February 1978.

XVI. THE ENDURING TREE

1. *Maroon and Gold*, April 15, 1960. The speaker was Dr. Theodore A. Distler, executive director of the American Association of Colleges.

223–24, 240, 298, 320, 357, 358, 367, 370, 373–75, 395

Carnegie Foundation, 225

Carolina Biological Supply Company, 265, 454

Carolina Dormitory, 450

Carolina Hall, 313, 316

Carr, Bernard B., 447

Carr, Julian S., 109, 127

Carroll, Charles, 233

Carroll, W. H., 74

Cars. *See* Automobiles

Carson, Clarence, 347

Cartography. *See* Maps and mapping

Caswell County, N.C., 302

Catawba College, 301, 349, 353, 396, 409, 410, 422, 463

Catholics. *See* Roman Catholics and Roman Catholic churches

Cauble, David, 451

Causey, Garland, 300

Causey, Jake, 297

Cedar Lodge, 315, 339

Centre College, 399

Chamblee, Helen, 262

Chance, N.C., 129

Chandler, Mrs. William S., 357

Chandler, Wallace L., 452

Chapel and chapel attendance, 49, 60, 61, 62, 68, 114, 146, 180, 182, 203, 206, 247, 267, 287, 291, 334, 366, 385, 388

Chapel Hill, N.C., 71, 116, 119, 197, 324, 350, 366, 420

Chaplains: college, 334, 345, 466; military, 285

Chase, Carole, 459

Chatham County, N.C., 9, 15, 183

Chautauquas, 231, 469

Cheek, Paul H., 376

Chemistry, 8, 13, 52, 96, 132–34, 137, 140, 147, 233, 324, 332, 338, 347, 372, 406, 419, 428

Cheshire, James M., 318

Chicago Theological Seminary, 413

Chicoine, Victor B., 270

Child, Frank S., and Child lectures, 87, 113, 114, 143, 195, 198

Children's Home. *See* Christian Orphanage; Elon Home for Children

Choral music. *See* Music and musicians

Christian Annual, 19–20

Christian Church: founding, growth and history of, 3–45 passim, 52, 55, 56, 69, 74, 76, 78, 79, 81, 90, 109–10, 111, 113, 114, 123, 128, 145, 146, 151, 156,

161, 187–88, 193, 199, 200, 213–14, 231, 235, 236, 241, 245, 256, 271, 313, 320–22, 334, 345, 403–4, 428, 469. *See also* Elon College (college): and Christian Church; *and specific topics and individuals*

Christian Education Building. *See* Mooney Building

Christian Endeavor Society, 147, 185, 214

Christian Orphanage (later Elon Home for Children, q.v.), 101, 123, 126, 135, 185, 215, 216, 234, 236, 313, 374, 469

Christian Publishing Company, 165

Christian Publishing House, 149–50, 469

Christian Sun (The), 10, 11, 12, 13, 35, 36, 37, 38, 42, 45, 54, 56, 70, 73–74, 85, 95, 98, 105, 110, 127, 128, 148–51, 152, 208, 215, 222, 236, 269

Christian Workers Conference Fund, 313

Christians, Christianity, and Christian education, 3, 13, 16, 17, 30, 41, 52, 56, 62, 79, 85, 108, 146, 155, 165, 170, 172, 178, 181, 185, 193, 197, 206, 209, 231, 232, 241, 285, 299, 309, 311, 312, 323, 345, 346, 354, 360, 364, 390, 404, 425, 461, 464, 469. *See also specific topics, sects, denominations, churches, and clergymen*

Church History Room, 320-22, 372

Church-related colleges, 82, 145, 182, 319–20, 331, 349, 378, 410, 430

Church Relations, Director of, 338, 358

Cincinnati Conservatory, 52

Civil War, 5, 17, 18, 19

Clapp, Richard H., 269

Clark, Francis E., 214

Clark, Henry J. B., 18

Clarke, J. A., 236, 313–14

Clarke, Lee, 366

Classics, 22, 51, 52

Classroom-Office Building. *See* Powell Building

Clegg, William L., 311

Clem, Kenneth, 439

Clements, Ethel, 126

Clements, Irene, 63, 64, 85

Clemson College, 343

Clendenin, J. N. H., 22, 23

Clendenin, Kate, 54

Clendenin, Mrs. J. N. H., 22, 23

Climate and weather, 42, 153, 154, 155, 201, 208, 214, 290

Clinchy, Russell J., 269